Clarke County Virginia

Marriages

1836-1886

Patricia B. Duncan

HERITAGE BOOKS
2008

HERITAGE BOOKS
AN IMPRINT OF HERITAGE BOOKS, INC.

Books, CDs, and more—Worldwide

For our listing of thousands of titles see our website
at
www.HeritageBooks.com

Published 2008 by
HERITAGE BOOKS, INC.
Publishing Division
100 Railroad Ave. #104
Westminster, Maryland 21157

Copyright © 2008 Patricia B. Duncan

All rights reserved. No part of this book may be reproduced or transmitted in any form or by any means, electronic or mechanical, including photocopying, recording or by any information storage and retrieval system without written permission from the author, except for the inclusion of brief quotations in a review.

International Standard Book Numbers
Paperbound: 978-0-7884-4596-5
Clothbound: 978-0-7884-7177-3

INTRODUCTION

This book contains a transcription of microfilms containing marriage records of Clarke County, Virginia for the period 1836-1886. The following Interlibrary Loan microfilms were obtained from the Library of Virginia.

Clarke Co. Reel 13:
Marriage Bonds, 1836 - 1850 Unpaged
Index to Licenses, Certificates, etc., 1836 - 1865
Marriage Register 1 covering 8 Aug 1865 – 19 Aug 1879
Marriage Register 2 covering 23 Aug 1879 – 6 Feb 1890
Marriage Register 3 covering 20 Feb 1890 – 1 Jul 1933

Clarke Co. Reel 42:
Marriage Registers 3, 4, and 5 covering 1890 - 1969

Clarke Co. Reel 43:
Marriage Records, 1836-1861
Index to Marriage Records, 1836-1861

The first section of this book contains 1836-1850 marriage bond entries as well as 1836-1861 licenses, certificates, consents, and other individual documents. Two bonds were entered on each page of the bond recordings, denoted in this book by p. number. The other documents were individually numbered on the microfilm, as denoted by mf#.

The second section of this book contains a transcription of the Marriage Registers for 1865-1886. Marriage register information is arranged in this book as follows: groom's surname, given name; name of parents; age; status (single, widowed, or divorced); occupation; place of birth; place of residence; date and place of marriage; bride's surname, given name; name of parents; age; status (single, widowed, or divorced); place of birth; place of residence; date of license; comments; page number on register.

Abbreviations used in this book:

AlbmVA - Albemarle County, Virginia
(appl) – application for marriage license
AugVA – Augusta County, Virginia

b. – born
BerkVA/BerkWVA – Berkeley County Virginia/West Virginia
ClrkVA – Clarke County, Virginia
(cnst) – consent for marriage
(col) – colored
CulpVA – Culpeper County, Virginia
d/o – daughter
div – divorced
FqrVA – Fauquier County, Virginia
FredVA – Frederick County, Virginia
JeffVA/JeffWVA – Jefferson County Virginia/West Virginia
LdnVA – Loudoun County, Virginia
(lic) – license
m. – marriage
mf# - number assigned on microfilm to individual document
(MinRet) – Minister's return
MontMD – Montgomery County, Maryland
(oath) – oath as to age and/or residence
p. – page on the register where the entry appears
PageVA – Page County, Virginia
prop. m. – proposed marriage
RappVA – Rappahannock County, Virginia
RckbrVA - Rockbridge County, Virginia
RckhmVA - Rockingham County, Virginia
res. – resides
sgl – single
ShenVA - Shenandoah County, Virginia
s/o – son of
WashDC – Washington DC
wid – widowed
WrnVA – Warren County, Virginia
[ ] – indicates an author remark

As with any transcription of records, it is advisable to obtain a copy of the original document when possible to verify the accuracy. Handwriting is often difficult to read, and although every effort is made to transcribe accurately, mistakes are inevitable.

A special thanks to the Albuquerque Public Library, the Library of Virginia, certified genealogist Ms. Marty Hiatt, and Hon. Helen Butts, Clerk of the Clarke County, Virginia Circuit Court.

CERTIFICATE TO OBTAIN A MARRIAGE LICENSE.

Having applied to the Clerk of the _County_ Court of _Clarke_ for a Marriage License, and being requested, I make the following Certificate, as required by the Act of the General Assembly, passed April 7th, 1858.

Date of Marriage, _on fairre 16 October 1858_
Place of Marriage, _Clarke county_
Full Names of Parties married, _Andrew J. Sloyd & Sarah Jane Stikley_
Age of Husband, _22 years_
Age of Wife, _21 years_
Condition of Husband (widowed or single), _Single_
Condition of Wife (widowed or single), _Single_
Place of Husband's Birth, _Clarke County Virg"_
Place of Wife's Birth, _Do_
Place of Husband's Residence, _Do_
Place of Wife's Residence, _Do_
Names of Husband's Parents, _H ry ann Sarah Sloyd_
Names of Wife's Parents, _Samuel & Anselin Stikley_
Occupation of Husband, _Farmer_

Given under my hand this _16_ day of _October_ 18_58_

Andrew J. Lloyd

☞ Within two months after the Marriage shall have taken place, the Minister solemnizing the same, must certify the fact to the Clerk of the Court.

Application

License

I here by certify that my daughter mary Elizabeth
O Conner is of age & that I am hyhyly willing
that she Mary Elith of the court in black
shall Grant her when the counsh licence to
marry her given under my hand this 11th
day of September 1839
                                Elizabeth O Conner
   her
John   X Kayes
   mark
Brother Bell

Consent

Oath

To the Clerk of the County Court of Clarke County in the State of Virginia.

I HEREBY CERTIFY, That the following is a correct Statement of a Marriage solemnized by me in the County aforesaid:

Date of Marriage, Sixth September 1855
Place of Marriage, "Clifton", Clarke County
Full Names of Parties married, Josiah R. White & Frances Virg.ᵃ Taylor
Age of Husband, 35 years
Age of Wife, 22
Condition of Husband, (widowed or single,) Single
Condition of Wife, (widowed or single,) Single
Place of Husband's Birth, Loudon County, Va
Place of Wife's Birth, Clarke County, Va
Names of Husband's Parents, Josiah & Sarah White
Names of Wife's Parents, John B. & Susan Taylor
Occupation of Husband, Merchant

Given under my hand as a Minister of the Protestant Episcopal (legally authorized to solemnize Marriages,) this eighth day of September A. D. 1855.

Francis M. Whittle

☞ The Clerks of the County Courts will furnish Ministers and others with these Blanks when they may need them.

☞ This Certificate must be returned to the Clerk's Office, by the person performing the marriage ceremony, within two months after the marriage.

Minister's return

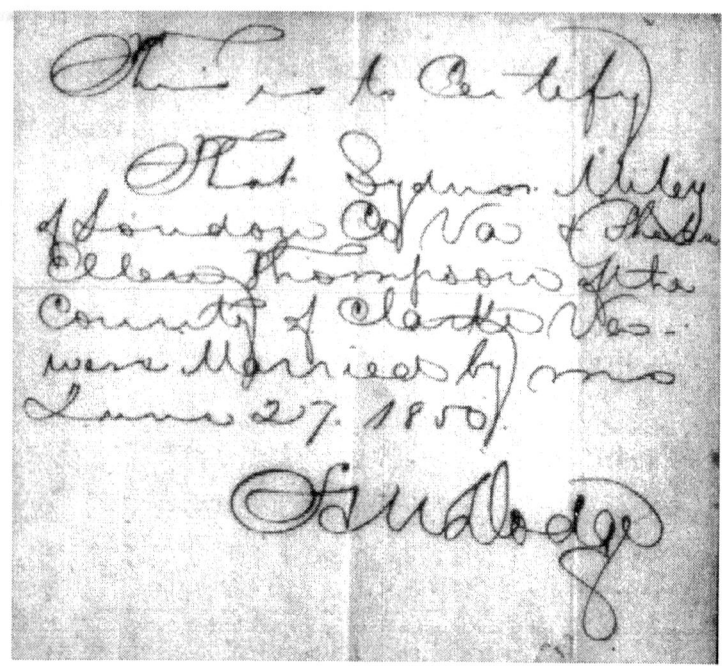

Minister's return

1836-1861
Applications, Bonds, Consents, Licenses, Minister's returns, Oaths

[not given]; and BRABHAM, Margaret, over 21y; (oath) 17 Oct 1859 by Wm. A. CASTLEMAN who is acquainted with Margaret; mf# 103

ALBIN, Andrew of ClrkVA and SWARTZ, Rachael Ann of ClrkVA; (bond) 9 May 1840 by Andrew ALBIN and Conrad SWARTZ both of ClrkVA; p. 51

ALEXANDER, Joel of ClrkVA and WILLINGHAM, Catharine of ClrkVA; (bond) 21 Dec 1844 by Joel ALEXANDER and Hathaway ALEXANDER of ClrkVA; p. 107

ALEXANDER, William C. of ClrkVA and MORGAN, Eliza A. of ClrkVA; (bond) 13 Mar 1838 by William C. ALEXANDER and Benjamin MORGAN both of ClrkVA; p. 20

ALEXANDER, William C. of ClrkVA; and MORGAN, Eliza A., 21y; (oath) 15 Mar 1838 by Benj. MORGAN. Teste Jno. HAYS; mf# 65

ALEXANDER, William of LdnVA and RAMEY, Margaret, over 21y, of ClrkVA; (oath) 4 May 1844 by Isaac RAMEY of ClrkVA; mf# 113

ALEXANDER, William R. of LdnVA and RAMEY, Margaret of ClrkVA; (bond) 4 May 1844 by William R. ALEXANDER and John BEMERSDAFFER both of LdnVA; p. 102

ANDERS, Frederick of LdnVA and WILEY, Sarah of ClrkVA; (bond) 20 Sep 1836 by Frederick ANDERS of LdnVA and Jesse MERCER of ClrkVA; p. 5

ANDERS, Frederick of LdnVA m. 29 [or 24] Sep 1836 to WILEY, Sarah of LdnVA; (MinRet) 6 Jun 1837 by Joseph H. JONES in Rockville, Md; mf# 42

ANDERSON, David of ClrkVA and HANEY, Maheluh of ClrkVA; (bond) 25 Mar 1839 by David ANDERSON and Joseph FLEMING both of ClrkVA; p. 33

ANDERSON, Evan P. of ClrkVA and ALEXANDER, Eliza of ClrkVA; (bond) 5 Jul 1837 by Evan P. ANDERSON and Jonas TRENARY of ClrkVA; p. 14

ANDERSON, Evan P. and ALEXANDER, Eliza, over 21y, of ClrkVA; (oath) 5 Jul 1837 by Jonas TRENARY; mf# 105

ANDERSON, John Eli of ClrkVA and STILLIONS, Ann Maria of
ClrkVA; (bond) 10 Aug 1841 by John Eli ANDERSON and
William STILLIONS both of ClrkVA; p. 65
ANDERSON, John Eli and STILLIONS, Ann Maria d/o William
STILLIONS of ClrkVA; (cnst) 10 Aug 1841 by Jane
ANDERSON, mother, of ClrkVA. Teste Joseph FLEMING,
Isaac RAMY; mf# 29
ANDERSON, John m. 23 Mar 1846 to LLOYD, Sarah Eliz'h;
(undated MinRet) Rich'd. H. WILMER, Minister of Prot.
Episcopal Church in the Diocese of Virginia; mf# 320
ANDERSON, John of ClrkVA and LLOYD, Sarah Elizabeth of
ClrkVA; (bond) 23 Mar 1846 by John ANDERSON and James
LLOYD both of ClrkVA; p. 128
ANDERSON, Mr., of age by statement of parents; and [not
given] of age by statement of parents; (oath) 5 Jul 1857 by
Thos. KENNERLY; mf# 71
ANDERSON, Thomas J. of ClrkVA and ASHBY, Mary of ClrkVA;
(bond) 6 Aug 1840 by Thomas J. ANDERSON and Martin
ASHBY both of ClrkVA; p. 54
ANDERSON, Washington m. 4 Oct 1842 to ROYSTON, Ann M.;
(undated MinRet) Jos. BAKER; mf# 303
ANDERSON, Washington of ClrkVA and ROYSTON, Ann Maria
of ClrkVA; (bond) 26 Sep 1842 by Washington ANDERSON
of ClrkVA and Peter ROYSTON of ClrkVA; p. 78
ANDERSON, William F. of Richland District, South Carolina and
KNIGHT, Sidney A. of ClrkVA; (bond) 15 Jan 1839 by William
F. ANDERSON of Richland District, South Carolina and
George KNIGHT of ClrkVA; p. 27
ANDERSON, William F. of Richland District, South Carolina and
KNIGHT, Sidney A.; (cnst) 15 Jan 1839 by George KNIGHT
of ClrkVA, father; mf# 109
ARMSTRONG, David T. m. 29 Dec 1842 to ANDERSON,
Henrietta K.; (undated MinRet) Jos. BAKER; mf# 305
ARMSTRONG, David T., 39y, widowed, carpenter, b. Preston
Co. Va, resides ClrkVA, s/o Andrew & Rachael
ARMSTRONG; prop. m. 8 Feb [1859] to PULLER, Mary
Catharine, abt. 20y, sgl, b. & res. ClrkVA, d/o McFarland &
Mary PULLER; (appl) 1 Feb 1859 by D. T. ARMSTRONG;
mf# 117
ARMSTRONG, David T., 39y, widowed, carpenter, b. Preston
Co. Va, resides ClrkVA, s/o Andrew & Rachel ARMSTRONG;
m. 8 Feb 1859 at Paris, FqrVA to PULLER, Mary Catherine,

20y, sgl, b. & res. ClrkVA, d/o McPharland & Mary PULLER; (MinRet) 12 Feb 1859 of J. Hoffman WAUGH of the Baltimore Annual Conference; mf# 252

ARMSTRONG, David Thomas and ANDERSON, Henrietta K., over 21y, of ClrkVA; (oath) 26 Dec 1842 by Washington ANDERSON; mf# 158

ARMSTRONG, David Thomas of ClrkVA and ANDERSON, Henrietta K. of ClrkVA; (bond) 26 Dec 1842 by David Thomas ARMSTRONG and Washington ANDERSON both of ClrkVA; p. 84

ASH, James of ClrkVA and PARKER, Mary of ClrkVA; (bond) 25 May 1842 by James ASH and Peter ROYSTON of ClrkVA; p. 74

ASHBY, Austin C. of ClrkVA and FOWLER, Mary of ClrkVA; (bond) 18 Dec 1848 by Austin C. ASHBY and William FOWLER Jr. both of ClrkVA; p. 161

ASHBY, Geo. B. m. 30 Dec 1841 to CHAMBLIN, M.; (undated MinRet) Alexander SHIRAS; mf# 34

ASHBY, George B. of ClrkVA and CHAMBLIN, Mildred of ClrkVA; (bond) 29 Dec 1841 by George B. ASHBY and Aaron CHAMBLIN both of ClrkVA; p. 70

ASHBY, Jeremiah of ClrkVA and SHAVER, Catharine of ClrkVA; (bond) 8 Apr 1848 by Jeremiah ASHBY and John SHAVER both of ClrkVA; p. 152

ASHBY, Jeremiah of ClrkVA and SMALLWOOD, Charlotte of ClrkVA; (bond) 27 Aug 1849 by Jeremiah ASHBY and Province McCORMICK & John ASHBY; p. 166

ASHBY, John W. and LONGERBEAM, Mary Frances; (bond) 30 Nov 1848 by John W. ASHBY and William LONGERBEAM and Franklin TUMBLIN of ClrkVA; p. 159

ASHBY, John W. m. 20 Jan 1842 to TOMLIN, Cath.; (undated MinRet) Alexander SHIRAS; mf# 35

ASHBY, John W. of ClrkVA and TOMLIN, Catharine of ClrkVA; (bond) 19 Jan 1842 by John W. ASHBY and Thomas CORNELL both of ClrkVA; p. 71

ASHBY, Martin and BILLMYERS, Elizabeth; (undated cnst) [18 Sep 1841 written in later] by Andrew BILLMYER, father. Witnesses P. D. SHEPHERD, Robt. ASHBY; mf# 203

ASHBY, Martin of ClrkVA and BILLMYERS, Elizabeth of ClrkVA; (bond) 2 Sep 1839 by Martin ASHBY and Robert ASHBY both of ClrkVA.; p. 38

ASHBY, Nimrod of LdnVA m. 17 Sep 1840 to SMALLWOOD, Mary A. of LdnVA; (undated MinRet) Rev. S. SHIRAS; mf# 294

ASHBY, Robert of ClrkVA and SHAFER, Sarah of ClrkVA; (bond) 21 Aug 1839 by Robert ASHBY of ClrkVA and John SHAFER of the same county; p. 37

ATHY, James T. of JeffVA and WOODWARD, Matilda of ClrkVA; (bond) 9 Oct 1848 by James T. ATHY of JeffVA and Thos. E. WOODWARD of ClrkVA; p. 158

ATHY, James T. of JeffVA and WOODWARD, Matilda of ClrkVA; (lic) 9 Oct 1848; mf# 173

BAKER, Alexander of FqrVA and HITE, Caroline Matilda of ClrkVA; (bond) 26 Aug 1839 by Alexander BAKER of FqrVA and William BAKER of ClrkVA; p. 37

BARNETT, Neill of Winchester Va. and LAKE, Elizabeth K. of ClrkVA; (bond) 9 Oct 1839 by Neill BARNETT of Winchester Va and John W. LUKE of Missouri; p. 39

BARTLETT, Thomas D. m. 27 Aug 1840 to KNIGHT, Lucy Jane; (undated MinRet) Thos. BUCK Jr.; mf# 223

BARTLETT, Thomas D. of Fred'k. Co. and KNIGHT, Lucy Jane of ClrkVA; (bond) 24 Aug 1840 by Thomas D. BARTLETT of Fred'k. Co. and George KNIGHT of ClrkVA; p. 55

BARTLETT, Thomas D. of FredVA and TIMBERLAKE, Mary D. of ClrkVA; (bond) 16 May 1846 by Thomas D. BARTLETT of FredVA and Alfred PRESCOTT of ClrkVA; p. 132

BARTON, Joseph Marx, 22y, sgl, farmer, b. Richmond Va, s/o Richard W. BARTON & Caroline MARX; m. 17 Feb 1857 in ClrkVA to NEILL, Mary, 25y, sgl, b. ClrkVA, d/o Lewis NEILL & Ann STRIBLING; (MinRet) 18 Feb 1857 by Francis M. WHITTLE, Minister of the Prot. Epis. Church; mf# 165

BASYE/BAYSYE, Joseph of RappVA and TAYLOR, Nancy Jane of ClrkVA; (bond) 14 Sep 1837 by Joseph BASYE and William KEYES both of RappVA; p. 15

BELL, James m. __ Jan 1853 to JENKINS, Rachel; (MinRet) 4 Jan 1853 by Rev. W. D. HANSON; mf# 264

BELL, James of ClrkVA and LONGERBEAM, Sarah of ClrkVA; (bond) 13 Oct 1842 by James BELL and Solomon R. JACKSON both of ClrkVA; p. 79

BELL, Joseph, 22y, sgl, b. & res. ClrkVA, farmer, s/o James BELL & Nancy HOFF; prop. m. 9 Feb 1860 in ClrkVA to WRITT, Mary C., 21y, sgl, b. LdnVA, resides ClrkVA, d/o

Thompson WRITT & Elizabeth FURR; (appl) dated 6 Feb
1860 by Joseph BELL; mf# 11
BELLMYER, William of ClrkVA and SIMMERS [SUMMERS?],
Catharine of ClrkVA; (bond) 3 Jan 1839 by William
BELLMYER and Horace P. SMITH of ClrkVA; p. 26
BENNET, Peter m. 10 Feb 1846 to McCORMICK, Mary Eliz.;
(undated MinRet) Richard H. WILMER, Minister of the P. E.
Church in the Diocese of Virginia; mf# 289
BENNET, Peter of ClrkVA and McCORMICK, Mary Elizabeth of
ClrkVA; (bond) 9 Feb 1846 by Peter BENNET and Samuel
McCORMICK both of ClrkVA; p. 126
BENNETT, Lewis H. of ClrkVA and ROYSTON, Sarah Catharine
of ClrkVA; (bond) 9 Sep 1842 by Lewis H. BENNETT and
Peter ROYSTON both of ClrkVA; p. 77
BENNETT, Richard of Washington City and FUNSTEN,
Margaret of ClrkVA; (bond) 9 Sep 1840 by Richard BENNETT
of Washington City and William G. H. JONES of ClrkVA; p. 56
BENNETT, Rich'd. and FUNSTON, Margaret [does not
specifically state she is the bride]; (cnst) 8 Sep 1840 by
Margaret FUNSTON. Teste W. G. H. JONES; mf# 134
BERKELEY, Peyton R. of Prince Edward Co. Va and LITTLE,
Frances of ClrkVA; (bond) 20 Mar 1837 by Peyton R.
BERKELEY of Prince Edward Co. Va and John MORGAN of
ClrkVA; p. 10
BERKLEY, Peyton R. (Dr.) and SETTLE, Frances; (oath) 20 Mar
1837 by A. H. SETTLE, father. Teste John MORGAN; mf# 82
BERLIN, James of ClrkVA and PEAKE, Susan D. of ClrkVA;
(bond) 26 Jul 1847 by James BERLIN and Strother H.
BOWEN both of ClrkVA; p. 142
BERLIN, Lewis of ClrkVA and FORSTER [FOSTER?], Jane
Elizabeth of ClrkVA; (bond) 26 Jan 1848 by Lewis BERLIN
and Wm. BERLIN both of ClrkVA; p. 149
BERLIN, Samuel and O'CONNER, Elizabeth, over 21y, of
ClrkVA; (oath) 28 Dec 1840 by Stephen D. CASTLEMAN;
mf# 123
BERLIN, Samuel of ClrkVA and O'CONNER, Elizabeth of
ClrkVA; (bond) 28 Dec 1840 by Samuel BERLIN and Stephen
D. CASTLEMAN both of ClrkVA; p. 59
BERLIN, William of ClrkVA and ALLEN, Margaret Ann of ClrkVA;
(bond) 12 Feb 1839 by William BERLIN and William ALLEN
of ClrkVA; p. 29

BILLMIER, Richard of ClrkVA and COTHEN, Margaret of ClrkVA; (bond) 19 Jan 1848 by Richard BILLMIER and Solomon R. JACKSON and John ASHBY all of ClrkVA; p. 148

BILLMIRE, Andrew J. m. 20 Mar 1845 to SHAVER, Martha A. Mahala; (undated MinRet) Richard H. WILMER, Minister of the P. E. Church in the Diocese of Virginia; mf# 279

BILLMIRE, Andrew of ClrkVA and SHAVER, Martha Ann Mahala of ClrkVA; (bond) 20 Mar 1845 by John SHAVER and Andrew J. BILLMIRE both of ClrkVA; p. 111

BILLMIRE, James F., 24y, sgl, cooper, b. and res. ClrkVA, s/o Andrew BILLMIRE & D. M. WILLIAMS; prop. m. 28 [Feb 1860?] in ClrkVA to SHIPE, Elizabeth, 19y, sgl, b. & res. ClrkVA, d/o Joseph SHIPE & Debora RINNEL; (appl) 28 Feb 1860 by James F. BILLMIRE; mf# 147

BILLMIRE, Rich'd. m. 25 Jan 1848 to COTHEN, Margaret; (undated MinRet) Rich'd. H. WILMER, Minister of Prot. Episcopal Church in the Diocese of Virginia; mf# 335

BIRD, Henry B. and WILLIAMS, Hannah M.; (lic) 30 Jan 1855; mf# 209

BITZER, Conrad R., 21y, sgl, b. & res. LdnVA, clerk, s/o Wm. & Sarah BITZER; prop. m. 24 Mar 1859 in ClrkVA to REED, Sarah K., 21y, sgl, b. & res. ClrkVA, d/o John & Laura Ellen REED; (appl) 23 March 1859 by Conrad R. BITZER; mf# 9

BITZER, Conrad R., 21y, sgl, clerk, b. & res. LdnVA, s/o Wm. & Sarah BITZER; m. 24 Mar 1859 at Springfield to REED, Sarah K., 21y, sgl, b. & res. ClrkVA, d/o Jos. & Louisa E. REED; (MinRet) 29 Mar 1859 by H. W. DODGE, Minister of the Gospel; mf# 210

BLUE, Joseph G., 24y, sgl, b. ClrkVA, resides Jefferson Co., s/o John BLUE & Margaret SHURFSTALL?; prop. m. 2 May 1860 in ClrkVA to JONES, Margaret R., 22y, sgl, b. & res. ClrkVA, d/o Matthew JONES & ___ WILLIAMS; (appl) 1 May 1860 by Jos. G. BLUE; mf# 8

BOARD, William and TURNER, Emily J., 40y widow of Wilson TURNER who died in Tennessee in 1848, has resided in ClrkVA for near 3 years; (oath) 13 Oct 1853 by Emily J. TURNER. Witness Chas. B. RUST; mf# 132

BOLEN, George W. of ClrkVA and COOPER, Elsey Jane of ClrkVA; (bond) 9 Apr 1845 by George W. BOLEN and John COOPER both of ClrkVA; p. 112

BOLER, George W. of ClrkVA m. 10 Apr 1845 to COOPER, Elsey Jane of ClrkVA; (undated MinRet) H. W. DODGE, Pastor 2 Bap. Ch., Up'rville, VA; mf# 234
BOLEY, Benjamin F. m. 15 Feb 1853 to ANDERSON, Maria S.; (undated MinRet) F. ISRAEL; mf# 46
BOLLON/BOLON, Thomas of ClrkVA and GOURLEY, Matilda of ClrkVA; (bond) 13 Feb 1843 by Thomas BOLLON and William GOURLEY both of ClrkVA; p. 87
BONHAM, George S. and RIELY, Harriet C.; (lic) 6 Jun 1860; mf# 241
BOWEN, Andrew J. and KERFOOT, Jane A.; (cnst) 7 Sep 1857 by Lucy J. KERFOOT, mother. Teste Edwin BOWEN; mf# 100
BOWEN, Edwin and [not given]; (cnst) 31 Mar 1836 by James BOWEN, father. Teste John M. ELLIOTT, Thos. F. BRYARLY, David TIMBERLAKE; mf# 106
BOWEN, Edwin of Fauquier Co. and BRYARLY, Mary S. of ClrkVA; (bond) 31 Mar 1836 by Edwin BOWEN & John M. ELLIOTT as security for $150; mf# 99
BOWEN, Henry M. and LINDSEY, Sarah Margaret, over 21y, of ClrkVA; (oath) 24 Mar 1851 by John T. LINDSEY, father; mf# 95
BOWEN, Henry M. m. 25 Mar 1851 to LINDSLEY, Sarah Margaret; (undated MinRet) H. W. DODGE; mf# 172
BOWEN, John A. and ISLER, Mattie C.; (cnst) 11 May 1859 by Wm. H. CARTER who states consent given by Mrs. Martha L. ISLER, mother; mf# 20
BOWEN, John A. and ISLER, Mattie C.; (lic) 11 May 1859; mf# 217
BOWEN, John A., 23y, sgl, b. Albemarle, resides Front Royal, merchant, s/o R. & N. BOWEN; prop. m. 18 May 1859 in ClrkVA to ISLER, M. C., 19y, sgl, b. & res. Clarke Co, d/o Jacob & M. L. ISLER; (appl) 16 May 1859 by Jno. A. BOWEN; mf# 43
BOWEN, Thomas C. of AlbmVA and TIMBERLAKE, Margaret B. of ClrkVA; (bond) 23 Jul 1839 by Thomas C. BOWEN of AlbmVA and Stephen D. TIMBERLAKE of ClrkVA; p. 36
BOWEN, Ths. C. and TIMBERLAKE, Margaret B.; (cnst) 23 Jul 1839 at Mount Airy by David TIMBERLAKE, father. Teste Addison TIMBERLAKE, S. D. TIMBERLAKE; mf# 154

BOWIN, Edwin of WrnVA and BRYARLY, Mary S. of ClrkVA; (cnst) 30 Mar 1836 by Saml. BRYARLY, father. Teste John M. ELLIOTT, Thos. F. BRYARLY; mf# 89

BRADFIELD, Francis M. of Snickersville, LdnVA and KEIM, Elizabeth of ClrkVA; (bond) 6 Jan 1851 by Francis M. BRADFIELD of Snickersville, LdnVA and Moses G. MILEY of ClrkVA; p. 4

BRADFORD, William Albert of Winchester Va and SMITH, Louisa Christine of ClrkVA; (bond) 12 Jun 1848 by William Albert BRADFORD of Winchester Va and Edw'd. Jaquelin SMITH of Winchester Va.; p. 155

BRAGG, Thomas J. of JeffVA and HOOE, Mary D. of ClrkVA; (bond) 23 Jul 1849 by Thomas G. BRAGG of JeffVA and James Henry HOOE of ClrkVA; p. 166

BRANDT, David and MAY, Virginia; (cnst) 21 Apr 1852 by Jacob MAY, father; mf# 159

BRENT, Charles J. of Frederick Co. and BALL, Emily Amanda, over 21y, of ClrkVA; (oath) 4 Jan 1843 by William C. KERFOOT; mf# 112

BRENT, Charles J. of FredVA and BALL, Emily Amanda of ClrkVA; (bond) 4 Jan 1843 by Charles J. BRENT of FredVA and William C. KERFOOT of ClrkVA; p. 85

BRIGGS, Thomas William of ClrkVA and CASTLEMAN, Lucinda of ClrkVA; (bond) 29 Mar 1839 by Thomas William BRIGGS and John CASTLEMAN Senr. both of ClrkVA; p. 33

BRILLHART, Jesse of FredVA and PAGET, Mary of ClrkVA; (bond) 2 Sep 1842 by Jesse BRILLHART of FredVA and John PAGET/PADGET of ClrkVA; p. 76

BRILLHEART, Jesse m. 8 Sep 1842 to PAGIT, Mary; (undated MinRet) Jos. BAKER; mf# 302

BRISON, John R. of FredVA and DEAN, Sarah A. of ClrkVA; (bond) 18 Dec 1844 by John R. BRISON of FredVA and James A. STEELE of ClrkVA; p. 107

BROMLEY/BRUMLEY, L. Smith of ClrkVA and VINCENT, Lucy Ann of ClrkVA; (bond) 1 Feb 1847 by L. Smith BRUMLEY and John VINCENT both of ClrkVA; p. 138

BROWN, Columbus, 31y, sgl, school teacher, b. Gray? Co, Ohio, res. JeffVA, s/o Turner C. & Prudence; m. 3 Dec 1858 in ClrkVA to McCORMICK, Ann B., 23y, sgl, b. & res. ClrkVA, d/o Providence & Margaret Ann; (MinRet) 3 Dec 1858 by J. H. M. LEMON; mf# 188

BROWN, James Conway and McCORMICK, Annie R.; (lic) 7 Jun 1859; mf# 242

BROWN, James W. of ClrkVA and EVERHART, Susan of ClrkVA; (bond) 14 May 1841 by James W. BROWN of ClrkVA and William G. EVERHART of ClrkVA; p. 63

BRYARLY, Richard of ClrkVA and McCORMICK, Harriet T. of ClrkVA; (bond) 24 Jan 1848 by Richard BRYARLY and Lewis F. GLASSCOCK of ClrkVA; p. 149

BRYARLY, Rich'd. m. 25 Jan 1848 to McCORMICK, Harriet; (undated MinRet) Rich'd. H. WILMER, Minister of Prot. Episcopal Church in the Diocese of Virginia; mf# 334

BUCK, Thomas C. of WrnVA and GATEWOOD, Sarah C. of ClrkVA; (bond) 17 Dec 1849 by Thomas C. BUCK of WrnVA and James MITCHELL of ClrkVA; p. 170

BURCH, Hilary m. 10 May 1853 to SOWERS, Matilda E.; (undated MinRet) B. GRIMSLEY; mf# 180

BURCHELL, John F. of ClrkVA and SOWERS, Martha Ann of ClrkVA; (bond) 18 Oct 1849 by John F. BURCHELL and William SOWERS both of ClrkVA; p. 168

BURCHELL, John of ClrkVA and BARNETT, Mildred N. of ClrkVA; (bond) 10 Jun 1848 by John BURCHELL and Neil BARNETT both of ClrkVA; p. 154

BURNS, John S. of BerkVA and EARLE, Mary L. of ClrkVA; (bond) 15 Oct 1842 by John S. BURNS of BerkVA and Alex'r. M. EARLE of ClrkVA; p. 79

BURNS, John W. m. 28 Dec 1843 to TAYLOR, Mary Ann; (undated MinRet) Jos. BAKER; mf# 301

BURNS, John Wm. of George Town DC and TAYLOR, Mary Ann of ClrkVA; (bond) 28 Dec 1843 by John Wm. BURNS, of George Town DC, Jesse TAYLOR and Jas. C. KENNON both of ClrkVA; p. 96

BURWELL, Nathaniel Jr. and PAGE, D. W.; (cnst) 6 Dec 1842 by R. P. PAGE, father, witnessed by brother Jno. E. PAGE; mf# 41

BURWELL, Nath'l. Junr. of ClrkVA and PAGE, D. W. of ClrkVA; (bond) 7 Dec 1842 by Nath'l. BURWELL Junr. and John E. PAGE both of ClrkVA; p. 83

BUSH, John S. m. 2 Oct 1845 to SMITH, Elizabeth B.; (undated MinRet) Richard H. WILMER, Minister of the P. E. Church in the Diocese of Virginia; mf# 285

BUSH, John S. of Kenton Co., Kentucky and SMITH, Elizabeth B. of ClrkVA; (bond) 30 Sep 1845 by John S. BUSH of

Kenton Co., Kentucky and Edward J. SMITH Esqr. of ClrkVA;
p. 119

BYRNE, Thomas W. of ClrkVA and THOMAS, Catharine A. of
ClrkVA; (bond) 21 Feb 1844 by Thomas W. BYRNE and
George SMIDLEY both of ClrkVA; p. 99

CAL[MESE] (ink blotch), Fielding H. and MOORE, Margaret E.;
(cnst) 16 Nov 1857 by Ann MOORE, mother; mf# 68

CAMPBELL, Hugh m. 17 Apr 1845 to JOHNSON, Catherine;
(undated MinRet) Richard H. WILMER, Minister of the P. E.
Church in the Diocese of Virginia; mf# 283

CAMPBELL, Samuel A. of ClrkVA and JOHNSTON, Catharine of
ClrkVA; (bond) 1 Aug 1848 by Samuel A. CAMPBELL and
James W. JOHNSTON both of ClrkVA; p. 157

CAMPBELL, Uriah of ClrkVA and JOHNSON, Catharine of
ClrkVA; (bond) 17 Apr 1845 by Uriah CAMPBELL and John
WILLINGHAM both of ClrkVA; p. 113

CAMPBELL, Uriah of ClrkVA and JOHNSON, Catharine, over
21y; (oath) 17 Apr 1845 by Catharine JOHNSON; mf# 25

CANEFORD, Franklin O. m. 28 Apr 1852 to TURNER, Sarah C.;
(MinRet) 14 Dec 1852 in Berryville by F. ISRAEL; mf# 230

CARLISLE, Albert 25y, b. & res. LdnVA, farmer, s/o Robert
CARLISLE & Frankie CARLISLE; prop. m. 13 Dec 1860 in
Clarke to KNIGHT, Cornelia, 18y, b. & res. ClrkVA, d/o Geo.
KNIGHT & Mary A. KNIGHT; (appl) 3 Dec 1860 by Albert
CARLISLE; mf# 23

CARPENTER, James N. and JOHNSON, Mary F. (Mrs.); (lic) 4
Oct 1852; mf# 164

CARR, John m. 20 Apr 1837 in ClrkVA to KERFOOT, Emily S.;
(MinRet) 30 Nov 1837 by W. F. BROADDUS; mf# 267

CARR, John m. 20 Apr 1837 to KERFOOT, Emily S.; (MinRet)
4/20/37 by Wm. F. BROADDUS [additional information
unreadable on microfilm]; mf# 175

CARR, John of FqrVA and KERFOOT, Emily S. of ClrkVA;
(bond) 14 Apr 1837 by John CARR of FqrVA and John
KERFOOT of ClrkVA; p. 11

CARRELL, John, 35y, sgl, cooper, b. & res. ClrkVA, s/o John
CARRELL; m. 24 May 1857 in ClrkVA to KELLY, Cornelia,
22y, sgl, b. & res. ClrkVA, d/o George KELLY & Hannah
KELLY; (MinRet) 24 May 1857 by Andrew ROBEY, Minister
of the Gospel; mf# 273

CARRIGAN, John P. of ClrkVA and STEWART, Elizabeth Jane of ClrkVA; (bond) 28 Jan 1846 by John P. CARRIGAN and William P. STEWART both of ClrkVA; p. 125
CARROLL, Daniel of ClrkVA and TINSMAN, Mary Jane of ClrkVA; (bond) 8 Aug 1846 by Daniel CARROLL and William TINSMAN both of ClrkVA; p. 135
CARROLL, Lewis of ClrkVA and HUMMER, Mary Ann of ClrkVA; (bond) 15 Aug 1846 by Lewis CARROLL and William HUMMER of ClrkVA; p. 135
CARTER, George W. of WrnVA and CASTLEMAN, Margaret Virginia of ClrkVA; (bond) 11 Sep 1849 by George W. CARTER of WrnVA and Benj. MORGAN of ClrkVA; p. 167
CARTER, Jacqueline W. and HARDESTY, Sarah E. B.; (cnst) 23 Feb 1852 by Sarah A. HARDESTY, mother. Teste Charles W. HARDESTY; mf# 12
CARTER, John W., age 29, of ClrkVA, farmer, son of James CARTER; m. 17th inst. [no other date on paper] to KNIGHT, Diconda, 23y, formerly of Frederick Co., d/o Thomas and Elizabeth KNIGHT the former deceased; (undated MinRet) Rev. H. G. BOWENS; mf# 6
CARTER, William G. of ClrkVA and BOYSTEON, Emily S. of ClrkVA; (bond) 26 Apr 1845 by William G. CARTER and Greenberry THOMPSON of ClrkVA; p. 114
CARTER, William K. of ClrkVA and HARDESTY, Catharine Ellenor of ClrkVA; (bond) 4 Feb 1846 by William K. CARTER and John PIERCE both of ClrkVA; p. 125
CASTLEMAN, Charles D. m. 14 Jan 1851 to ISLER, Maria J.; (MinRet) 13 Aug 1851 in Berryville by Joshua PETERKIN, Rector of Wickliffe Parish, ClrkVA; mf# 176
CASTLEMAN, Thomas T. of Brunswick Co. Va and LITTLE, Laura C. of ClrkVA; (bond) 24 Sep 1838 by Thomas T. CASTLEMAN of Brunswick Co. Va and Francis H. WHITING of ClrkVA; p. 25
CASTLEMAN, William A. and SHEPHERD, Margaret Ann; (cnst) 22 May 1857 by Jos. SHEPHERD; mf# 32
CASTLEMAN, William A. of ClrkVA and ISLER, Ann R. of ClrkVA; (bond) 27 Apr 1844 by William A. CASTLEMAN and John M. NUNN of ClrkVA; p. 101
CASTLEMAN, William A. of ClrkVA and SHEPHERD, Margaret Ann of ClrkVA; (bond) 22 May 1837 by William A. CASTLEMAN & Champ SHEPHERD of ClrkVA; p. 12

CAUTHORN, A. W. of Essex Co. Va and SHEPHERD, Caroline
A. of ClrkVA; (bond) 12 Nov 1850 by A. W. CAUTHORN and
P. D. SHEPHERD; p. 1
CAWTHON, Stephen of ClrkVA and DOWNING, Ann of ClrkVA;
(bond) 7 Mar 1839 by Stephen CAWTHON and Robert
ASHBY of ClrkVA; p. 31
CAWTHORN, Edwin of ClrkVA and HURT, Martha Ann of
ClrkVA; (bond) 23 Mar 1846 by Edwin CAWTHORN and
William BERRY both of ClrkVA; p. 128
CAWTHORN, Stephen of ClrkVA and DOWNING, Ann, 21y, of
ClrkVA; (oath) 7 Mar 1839 by Robert ASHBY; mf# 80
CAWTHORNE, Edwin m. 23 Mar 1846 to HURT, Martha Ann;
(undated MinRet) Rich'd. H. WILMER, Minister of Prot.
Episcopal Church in the Diocese of Virginia; mf# 319
CHAMBERLIN, Osmin of ClrkVA and JENKINS, Harriet of
ClrkVA; (bond) 25 Jan 1837 by Osmin CHAMBERLIN and
William SOWERS of ClrkVA; p. 9
CHAMBLIN, Ellzey/Ellzy of ClrkVA and CHAMBLIN, Maria of
ClrkVA; (bond) 21 May 1840 by Ellzy CHAMBLIN and Aaron
CHAMBLIN both of ClrkVA; p. 52
CHISHOLM, James of BerkVA and PAGE, Jane Byrd of ClrkVA;
(bond) 24 Jul 1847 by James CHISHOLM of BerkVA and
Richard H. WILMER of Berryville; p. 142
COLEMAN, Daniel m. 28 Sep 1843 to WARE, Harriet E.;
(undated MinRet) Jos. BAKER; mf# 299
COLEMAN/COALMAN, Daniel of ClrkVA and WARE, Harriett
Elizabeth of ClrkVA; (bond) 28 Sep 1843 by Daniel
COLEMAN and James W. WARE both of ClrkVA; p. 92
COLSTON, William of ClrkVA and GANT, Mary Ann of ClrkVA;
(bond) 7 Jan 1837 by William COLSTON and John GANT of
ClrkVA; p. 8
COOKE, Philip P. of FredVA and BURWELL, Ann C. of ClrkVA;
(bond) 11 Apr 1837 by Philip P. COOKE of FredVA and Robt.
M. PAGE of same county; p. 11
COOPER, George D., 35y, sgl, cooper, b. LdnVA, resides
ClrkVA, s/o John and Susan COOPER; m. 29 Dec 1853 at
Thompson's Hotel, Berryville to FOWLER, Susan, 30y, sgl, b.
& res. ClrkVA, d/o William & Susan FOWLER; (undated
MinRet) Chas. WHITE; mf# 182
COOPER, George Wm. of ClrkVA and RIELY, Edny Ann of
ClrkVA; (bond) 14 Jul 1845 by George Wm. COOPER and
Lester RIELY of ClrkVA; p. 116

COOPER, William Albert of ClrkVA and FOWLER, Martha Ellen of ClrkVA; (bond) 25 Sep 1843 by William Albert COOPER and William FOWLER both of ClrkVA; p. 92

CORDER, Parkerson of ClrkVA and BROWN, Emaline of ClrkVA; (bond) 6 Mar 1838 by Parkerson CORDER of ClrkVA and Elisha ROMINE of ClrkVA; p. 20

CORNWELL, Addison of ClrkVA and TRUSSELL, Tabitha Ann of ClrkVA; (bond) 22 Apr 1839 by Addison CORNWELL and Joseph FLEMING both of ClrkVA; p. 34

CORNWELL, Addison of ClrkVA and TRUSSELL, Tabitha Ann of ClrkVA; (cnst) 22 Apr 1839 by Joseph FLEMING, Guardian of girl. Teste Jno. HAYS; mf# 63

COSTLOW, Thomas of ClrkVA and STICKLE, Martha of ClrkVA; (bond) 23 Feb 1846 by Thomas COSTLOW and Henry STICKLE both of ClrkVA; p. 127

COX, William, 27y, sgl, farmer, b. FredVA, s/o William COX & Nancy McDANIEL; m. 6 Nov 1856 in ClrkVA to HOLTSCLAW, Frances Ann, 28y, sgl, b. FredVA, d/o William HOLTSCLAW & Sarah COX; (MinRet) 6 Nov 1856 by Theo. M. CARLON?, Minister of the Gospel; mf# 196

CRAIG, Parkerson of ClrkVA and GOLD, Isabella Ann of ClrkVA; (bond) 1 Nov 1837 by Parkerson CRAIG and Thomas E. GOLD of ClrkVA; p. 16

CRAWFORD, Ambrose of ClrkVA and FRANKS, Malissa of ClrkVA; (bond) 11 Oct 1842 by Ambrose CRAWFORD and Benjamin FRANKS both of ClrkVA; p. 78

CRIM, Wm. B. and ELEYET, Mary A.; (cnst) 26 Sep 1859 by John ELEYET, father; mf# 70

DANLEY, Arthur N. of Fred'k. Co. and AMBROUSE, Catharine Ann of ClrkVA; (bond) 16 Aug 1842 by Arthur N. DANLEY of Fred'k. Co. and John B. AMBROUSE of ClrkVA; p. 76

DANLEY, James T. of FredVA and GRANT, Ellen F. of ClrkVA; (bond) 5 Jul 1843 by James T. DANLEY of FredVA and Thos. W. RAYNOLDS of ClrkVA; p. 91

DARNLEY, James T. m. 5 Jul 1843 to GRANT, Ellen J.; (undated MinRet) Jos. BAKER; mf# 297

DAVIDSON, James H. of Montgomery Co; and BRADLEY, Sarah S. of Montgomery; (lic) 11 Oct 1859 by James G. HENING clerk for Montgomery Co. to the Rev. Mr. Henderson SUTER; mf# 224

DAVIS, Thomas m. 29 Nov 1836 to JENKINS, Jane; (MinRet) 22 Feb 1837 by William MONROE; mf# 306

DAVIS, Thomas of LdnVA and JENKINS, Jane of ClrkVA; (bond) 21 Nov 1836 by Thomas DAVIS of LdnVA and Augustina ATHEY of ClrkVA [letter dated 1 Nov 1836 (on page 25) from Elizabeth ATHEY mother of Jane JENKINS giving her permission.]; p. 6

DEW, Thomas R. of William & Mary College, Va and HAY, Natilia B. of ClrkVA; (bond) 16 Jun 1846 by Thomas R. DEW of William & Mary College, Va and Bennett T. NORRIS of ClrkVA; p. 133

DIEFFENDERFER, George W. of ClrkVA and EVERHART, Ann Rebecca of ClrkVA; (bond) 22 Jul 1843 by Geo. W. DIEFFENDERFER and William P. WIGGENTON of ClrkVA; p. 91

DIFFENDE[R]FER, George W. m. 25 Jul 1843 to EVERHART, Ann R.; (undated MinRet) Jos. BAKER; mf# 298

DORSEY, H. (Dr.) m. 25 Mar 1845 to CASTLEMAN, Amanda; (undated MinRet) Richard H. WILMER, Minister of the P. E. Church in the Diocese of Virginia; mf# 280

DORSEY, Hanson of WrnVA and CASTLEMAN, Amanda of ClrkVA; (bond) 24 Mar 1845 by Hanson DORSEY of WrnVA and James CASTLEMAN of ClrkVA; p. 112

DORSEY, Hanson of WrnVA and CASTLEMAN, Amanda, over 21y, of ClrkVA; (oath) 24 Mar 1845 by James CASTLEMAN; mf# 130

DOWNING, James of ClrkVA and LEE, Eliza Ann of ClrkVA; (bond) 21 May 1840 by James DOWNING and Richard ALEXANDER both of ClrkVA; p. 52

DUBBLE, Aaron m. 20 Jan 1848 to GRIM, Jane Eliza; (undated MinRet) Rich'd. H. WILMER, Minister of Prot. Episcopal Church in the Diocese of Virginia; mf# 333

DUBBLE, Aaron of ClrkVA and GRIM, Jane Eliza of ClrkVA; (bond) 19 Jan 1848 by Aaron DUBBLE and Abraham GRIM both of ClrkVA; p. 148

DUGLASS/DOUGLASS, Hugh T. m. 16 Jun 1853 to BRIGGS, Marion J.; (lic) on back of license: Francis M. WHITTLE, Minister of Prot. Epis. Church of Vir'a states he married them on 16 Jun 1853; mf# 38

DUKE, Thomas H. Jr. of ClrkVA and JOHNSON, Margaret of ClrkVA; (bond) 21 Sep 1850 by Thomas H. DUKE Jr. and Thomas H. DUKE Senr. both of ClrkVA; p. 178

DUKE, Thomas H. m. 22 Sep 1850 to JOHNSON, Margaret; (undated MinRet) John C. DICE; mf# 219

DUNBAR, John R. W. of Baltimore, Maryland and DEW, Natilia
B. (Mrs.) of ClrkVA; (bond) 16 Oct 1848 by Jno. R. W.
DUNBAR of Baltimore, Maryland and Robt. C. RANDOLPH of
ClrkVA; p. 159

DUNBARR, Herrod H. and TRIPLIT, Ann E.; (cnst) 18 Aug 1861
by Frances A. TRIPLIT, father. Teste French THOMPSON;
mf# 19

DUNN, George of ClrkVA and BRADY, Rebecca of ClrkVA;
(bond) 4 Jan 1839 by George DUNN of ClrkVA and George
TAYLOR of FredVA; p. 27

EDDY, Thomas M. and ELGIN, Rebecca J. (Mrs.); (lic) 28 Nov
1859; mf# 168

EDDY, Thomas M., 24y, sgl, farmer, b. & res. Frederick Co., s/o
Wm. & Mary EDDY; prop. m. 29 Nov 1859 in ClrkVA to
ELGIN, Rebecca J., unknown age, widowed, b. & res.
ClrkVA, d/o John & Sarah COPENHAVER; (appl) dated 28
Nov 1859 by Thos. M. EDDY; mf# 214

EDWARDS, Joseph W. and MARLOW, Sarah Ann; (lic) 16 Apr
1856; mf# 141

EICHELBERGER, Lewis of Winchester, Va and HAY, Penelope
L. of ClrkVA; (bond) 14 Mar 1839 by Lewis
EICHE[L]BERGER and John S. MILLER both of town of
Winchester, Va; p. 32

ELGIN, Nimrod T. m. 3 Jun 1849 to COPENHAVER, Rebecca
Jane; (MinRet) 6 Oct 1849 by Geo. W. HARRIS; mf# 197

ELGIN, Nimrod T. of ClrkVA and COPENHAVER, Rebecca Jane
of ClrkVA; (bond) 28 May 1849 by Nimrod T. ELGIN and
John ELEYET of ClrkVA; p. 164

ELLIOTT, Andrew Jackson of ClrkVA and CARROLL, Caroline
Matilda of ClrkVA; (bond) 10 Dec 1849 by Andrew Jackson
ELLIOTT and John CARROLL. Senr. both of ClrkVA; p. 170

ELLIOTT, Andrew Jackson of ClrkVA m. 13 Dec 1849
CARROLL, Caroline Matilda of ClrkVA; (undated MinRet) H.
W. DODGE, Pastor of 2 Bapt. Ch, Upperville; mf# 212

EVANS, Hiram P. of ClrkVA and EARLE, Sarah Jane of ClrkVA;
(bond) 16 Nov 1839 by Hiram P. EVANS of ClrkVA and Seth
MASON Junr. of ClrkVA; p. 41

FARR, Jonas Junr. of Ohio and CHATTIN, Teresa Jane of
ClrkVA; (bond) 3 Oct 1836 by Jonas FARR Junr. of Ohio and
John P. CHAMBERLIN of ClrkVA; p. 5

FELLERS, Joshua G. of ClrkVA and ELLIOTT, Susan Margaret of ClrkVA; (bond) 16 Jan 1849 by Joshua G. FELLERS and Edward JACKSON both of ClrkVA; p. 162

FELTNER, John DISKEN of ClrkVA and TALLEY, Jane Ellen of ClrkVA; (bond) 11 Jan 1843 by John Disken FELTNER and John TALLEY both of ClrkVA; p. 86

FERGUSON, Abner prop. m. 18th of present month to MARSHALL, Mary E.; (cnst) 14 Dec 1860 by John MARSHALL, father. Wit: J. Pede MARSHALL; mf# 1

FERGUSON, Abner, 22y, sgl, farmer, b. & res. FqrVA, s/o James FERGUSON & Eliza FERGUSON; prop. m. 18 Dec 1860 in ClrkVA to MARSHALL, Mary E., 20y, sgl, b. & res. ClrkVA, d/o John MARSHALL & Elizabeth MARSHALL; (appl) 15 Dec 1860 by Abner FERGUSON; mf# 91

FERGUSON, Josiah [Jr.] of ClrkVA and PEYTON, Susan Catharine of ClrkVA; (bond) 1 Nov 1845 by Josiah Ferguson Jr. and Joseph E. PEYTON both of ClrkVA; p. 120

FLEMING, Joseph of ClrkVA and ANDERSON, Sarah Ann Virginia of ClrkVA; (bond) 18 Jan 1842 by Joseph FLEMING and Solomon R. JACKSON both of ClrkVA; p. 71

FLEMING, Joseph of ClrkVA and ANDERSON, Sarah Ann Virginia, over 21y, of ClrkVA; (oath) 18 Jan 1842 by John Eli ANDERSON of ClrkVA; mf# 87

FLEMING, William of FqrVA and FLEMING, Louisa of ClrkVA; (bond) 10 Oct 1839 by William FLEMING of FqrVA and Joseph FLEMING of ClrkVA; p. 39

FLEMING, William of FqrVA; and FLEMING, Louisa, over 21y, of ClrkVA; (oath) 10 Oct 1839 by Joseph FLEMING, brother; mf# 157

FLETCHER, John G. m. 26 Jan 1846 to REYNOLDS, Sarah Jane; (undated MinRet) Richard H. WILMER, Minister of the P. E. Church in the Diocese of Virginia; mf# 287

FLETCHER, John G. of ClrkVA and RAYNOLDS, Sarah Jane of ClrkVA; (bond) 24 Jan 1846 by John G. FLETCHER and Thomas W. RAYNOLDS both of ClrkVA; p. 124

FORD, John Henry of FredVA and COPENHAVER, Alcinda Margaret of ClrkVA; (bond) 12 Jan 1850 by John Henry FORD of FredVA and John COPENHAVER of ClrkVA; p. 172

FORD, John Henry of FredVA m. 15 Jan 1850 to COPENHAVER, Alcinda Margaret of ClrkVA; (MinRet) 14 Feb 1850 by Nimrod T. ELGIN; mf# 45

FOWLER, Thomas m. 27 Mar 1845 to MERCER, Phebe; (undated MinRet) Richard H. WILMER, Minister of the P. E. Church in the Diocese of Virginia; mf# 281

FOWLER, Thomas of ClrkVA and MERCER, Pheby of ClrkVA; (bond) 24 Mar 1845 by Thomas FOWLER and William FOWLER both of ClrkVA; p. 111

FOWLER, William and LONGERBEAM, Ann; (lic) 22 Aug 1854; mf# 260

FRASHIER, John Stone of FredVA and O'CONNER, Martha Ann of ClrkVA; (bond) 5 Sep 1837 by John Stone FRASHIER of FredVA and John LOUTHAN of ClrkVA; p. 14

FRAZIER, John S. and O'CONNER, Martha Ann; (cnst) 5 Sep 1837 by Elizabeth O'CONNER, mother. Teste John LOUTHAN; mf# 3

FRIER, Matthew of JeffVA and SMITH, Susan Catharine of ClrkVA; (bond) 20 Jul 1847 by Matthew FRIER of JeffVA and Joseph SMITH of ClrkVA; p. 141

FUNSTEN, David of WrnVA and MEADE, Susan of ClrkVA; (bond) 20 Nov 1844 by David FUNSTEN of WrnVA and Walker G. PAGE of ClrkVA; p. 106

FUNSTEN, Oliver R. of ClrkVA and MEADE, Mary C. of ClrkVA; (bond) 28 Apr 1840 by Oliver R. FUNSTEN and Francis B. MEADE both of ClrkVA; p. 50

FURR, Benj'n. F., 33y, sgl, farmer, b. LdnVA, s/o Minor FURR & Phebe FURR m. Thursday, 3 Jul 1856 at residence of Mr. James McCLAUGHRY to McCLAUGHRY, Hannah, 28y, sgl, b. LdnVA, d/o James McCLAUGHRY & Rebecca McCLAUGHRY; (MinRet) 1 Aug 1856 by H. W. DODGE, Pastor Baptist Ch., Berryville; mf# 258

FURR, Daniel of ClrkVA and McKINNEY, Ellen of ClrkVA; (bond) 30 Sep 1848 by Daniel FURR and John ASHBY and Saml. MORGAN all of ClrkVA; p. 157

FURR, Enoch of ClrkVA and ANDERSON, Nancy (Mrs.) of ClrkVA; (bond) 7 Nov 1850 by Enoch FURR and Abraham H. BEAVERS both of ClrkVA; p. 179

FURR, Enoch m. 7 Nov 1850 to ANDERSON, Nancy; (undated MinRet) John C. DICE; mf# 219

FURR, James of ClrkVA and GLASSCOCK, Emily of ClrkVA; (bond) 13 Sep 1838 by James FURR and Martin ASHBY of ClrkVA; p. 24

FURR, James of ClrkVA and GLASSCOCK, Emily of ClrkVA; (cnst) 13 Sep 1838 by Stephen GLASSCOCK, father. Teste Jno. HAYS; mf# 75

FURR, John of ClrkVA and RILEY, Nancy of ClrkVA; (bond) 20 Jan 1840 by John FURR and Elisha ROMINE both of ClrkVA; p. 44

GALLOWAY, James W. of ClrkVA and WYNDHAM, Eliz'th. A. of ClrkVA; (bond) 21 Dec 1850 by Jas. W. GALLOWAY and Wm. G. EVERHART both of ClrkVA; p. 2

GATES, Jacob of ClrkVA and REED, Eliza of ClrkVA; (bond) 23 May 1838 by Jacob GATES & Henry STIPE of ClrkVA; p. 22

GIBSON, Jno. M., 24y, sgl, farmer, b. & res. LdnVA, s/o Alph[e]us & Harriet A. GIBSON; prop. m. 10 Nov 1858 in Berryville to SMITH, Lydia K., 22y, b. & res. Berryville, d/o Horace & Susan T. SMITH; (appl) 5 Nov 1858 by Jno. M. GIBSON; mf# 64

GLASS, Lewis F. of ClrkVA and McCORMICK, Mary of ClrkVA; (bond) 30 Oct 1843 by Lewis F. GLASS and Albert McCORMICK both of ClrkVA; p. 93

GOLD, John C. of St. Louis, Missouri and O'CONNER, Catharine of ClrkVA; (bond) 19 Oct 1843 by John C. GOLD of St. Louis, Missouri and Alexander WOOD of ClrkVA; p. 93

GOLD, Thomas E. of ClrkVA and ALLEN, Lucy Mildred of ClrkVA; (bond) 21 Jan 1840 by Thomas E. GOLD and William ALLEN both of ClrkVA; p. 45

GORDON, John James of ClrkVA and HUYETT, Louisa Margaret of ClrkVA; (bond) 16 Dec 1848 by John James GORDON and Henry HUYETT both of ClrkVA; p. 160

GORDON, John S. of ClrkVA and AMBROUSE, Mary Ann of ClrkVA; (bond) 12 Jan 1846 by John S. GORDON and Levi HIETT both of ClrkVA; p. 123

GORDON, John S. and AMBROUSE, Mary Ann, over 21y, of ClrkVA; (oath) 12 Jan 1846 by Levi HIETT; mf# 59

GOURLEY, William of ClrkVA and TRENARY, Catharine of ClrkVA; (bond) 2 Oct 1845 by William GOURLEY and William GRUBBS both of ClrkVA; p. 119

GRADY, Edward and SOWERS, Lucy Ellen, b. 5 Apr 1839, d/o Daniel W. & Mary Eliza SOWERS; (cnst) 8 Sep 1856 by Daniel W. SOWERS, father; mf# 150

GRANT, John L. of ClrkVA and GROVE, Catharine Amelia of ClrkVA; (bond) 31 Mar 1842 by John L. GRANT of ClrkVA and William H. HEIST of Winchester, Va; p. 73

GREEN, Charles H. and CASTLEMAN, Eloisa M.; (lic) 2 Jun 1856; mf# 204

GREEN, George W. of ClrkVA and MARSHALL, Nancy of ClrkVA; (bond) 6 Feb 1840 by George W. GREEN and John MARSHALL both of ClrkVA; p. 45

GREEN, Israel (2nd Lieutenant in U. S. Marine Corp) and TAYLOR, Edmonia Smith; (cnst) 7 Jul 1851 by Chas. Sinclair TAYLOR, brother; mf# 119

GREEN, James W. of FqrVA and MITCHELL, Ann Maria of ClrkVA; (bond) 1 May 1843 by James W. GREEN of FqrVA and John W. SOWERS of ClrkVA; p. 89

GREEN, Richard N. and FERGUSON, Mary Ann, over 21y, of ClrkVA; (oath) 18 Sep 1841 by John D. FERGUSON Jr.; mf# 202

GREEN, Richard N. and FERGUSON, Mary Ann; (cnst) 16 Sep 1841 by John D. FERGUSON; mf# 77

GREEN, Richard N. of ClrkVA and FERGUSON, Mary Ann of ClrkVA; (bond) 18 Sep 1841 by Richard N. GREEN and John D. FERGUSON Junr. both of ClrkVA; p. 66

GREENLEE, John of ClrkVA and LUKE, Emily W. of ClrkVA; (bond) 20 Mar 1839 by John GREENLEE and Jacob LUKE both of ClrkVA; p. 32

GREENWALT, Adam m. 4 Apr 1846 to POP, Barbara; (undated MinRet) Rich'd. H. WILMER, Minister of Prot. Episcopal Church in the Diocese of Virginia; mf# 322

GREENWALT, John m. 30 Jan 1848 to KERBY, Eliz'th; (undated MinRet) Rich'd. H. WILMER, Minister of Prot. Episcopal Church in the Diocese of Virginia; mf# 336

GREENWALT, John of ClrkVA and KERBY, Susan Elizabeth of ClrkVA; (bond) 28 Jan 1848 by John GREENWALT & Geo. Wm. DIEFFENDERFER both of ClrkVA; p. 150

GREENWORLD, Adam of ClrkVA and POP, Barbara of ClrkVA; (bond) 3 Apr 1846 by Adam GREENWORLD and Michael POP both of ClrkVA; p. 130

GRIFFITH, Thomas W. and EDWARDS, Martha Ann; (lic) 4 Feb 1856; mf# 4

GRIFFITH, Thos. Wm., 24y, sgl, farmer, b. LdnVA, s/o Chas. James & Margaret GRIFFITH; m. 7 Feb 1856 at residence of Henry EDWARDS to EDWARDS, Martha Ann, 19y, sgl, b. FredVA, d/o Henry & Mary Ann EDWARDS; (MinRet) 9 Feb 1856 by [cut off], Minister of Prot. Epis. Church; mf# 195

GRIFTE? [GRIFFIN?], Francis of ClrkVA and BROWN, Maria of ClrkVA; (bond) 21 Dec 1839 by Francis GRIFTE? [GRIFFIN?] of ClrkVA and Calvin PULLER of WrnVA; p. 43
GRIGGS, Thomas of JeffVA and STEPHENS, Mary Ann of ClrkVA; (bond) 18 Jan 1841 by Thomas GRIGGS of JeffVA and Lewis William STEPHENS of ClrkVA; p. 60
GRIGSBY, Henry N. of ClrkVA and McCORMICK, Frances F. of ClrkVA; (bond) 18 May 1841 by Henry N. GRIGSBY and Isaac McCORMICK of ClrkVA; p. 64
GRIGSBY, J. R. and ALEXANDER, Elizabeth M.; (cnst) 11 Oct 1858 by Benj. MORGAN, Guardian for E. M. ALEXANDER, his niece; mf# 10
GRIMES, Kemp of ClrkVA and BAXTER, Jane of ClrkVA; (bond) 26 Feb 1846 by Kemp GRIMES and Henry BAXTER Jr. both of ClrkVA; p. 127
GROBER, Samuel and ANDERSON, Marig An [Mariah Ann?]; (cnst) 31 Jan 1853 by Jacob ANDERSON. Teste W. T. SIMMONS, G. F. ANDERSON, J. W. ANDERSON; mf# 161
GROVE, James W. and PULLER, Frances Virginia; (cnst) 25 Nov 1857 by Calvin PULLER, father; mf# 72
GROVE, James W., age not given, sgl, blacksmith, b. not given, resides ClrkVA, s/o not given; m. 25 Nov 1857 at Berryville to PULLER, Frances Virginia, age not given, sgl, b. & res. ClrkVA, d/o Calvin PULLER; (MinRet) 1 Feb 1858 by J. A. HAYNES; mf# 239
GROVES, Andrew C. m. 14 Mar 1844 to CORBAN, Elizabeth C.; (undated MinRet) Jos. BAKER; mf# 246
GROVES, Andrew C. of ClrkVA and CORBIN, Elizabeth Catharine of ClrkVA; (bond) 11 Mar 1844 by Andrew C. GROVES and James N. CORBIN both of ClrkVA; p. 99
GRUBBS, William B. of WrnVA and TRENARY, Lucinda of ClrkVA; (bond) 25 Aug 1841 by William B. GRUBBS of WrnVA and William GRUBBS of WrnVA; p. 65
GRUBER, John Jr. of JeffVA and LOCK, Maria Jane of ClrkVA; (bond) 19 Nov 1845 by John GRUBER Jr. of JeffVA and John LOCK Senr. of ClrkVA; p. 121
GRUBER, John of Jefferson Co. and RIELY, Elizabeth Chloe (Mrs.), over 21y, of ClrkVA; (oath) 15 Dec 1847 by Province McCORMICK Jr.; mf# 121
GRUBER, John of JeffVA and RIELY, Elizabeth Calor (Mrs.); (bond) 15 Dec 1847 by John GRUBER of JeffVA and Province McCORMICK of ClrkVA; p. 147

GRUBER, Samuel of JeffVA; and ANDERSON, Maria Ann, d/o Jacob ANDERSON of ClrkVA; (cnst) 2 Feb 1853 by John CHAPMAN, Guardian of GRUBER. Teste George F. ANDERSON; mf# 148

GUARD, Thomas W. and HICKS, Margaret W.; (lic) 16 Nov 1861; mf# 240

HAFFLAND, William of FqrVA and SMALLWOOD, Sarah the daughter of Sarah SMALLWOOD of ClrkVA; (bond) 1 Jun 1837 by William HAFFLAND of FqrVA and John SHAFER of ClrkVA; p. 12

HAFFLAND, William of FqrVA; and SMALLWOOD, Sarah, upwards of 21y, of ClrkVA; (oath) 1 Jun 1837 by John SHAFER; mf# 79

HAINES, Richard m. 18 Dec 1845 to MILTON, Selina; (undated MinRet) Richard H. WILMER, Minister of the P. E. Church in the Diocese of Virginia; mf# 286

HAINES, Richard R. of JeffVA and MILTON, Selina P. of ClrkVA; (bond) 15 Dec 1845 by Richard R. HAINES of JeffVA and Elijah MILTON of ClrkVA; p. 121

HALL, Edward E. m. Thursday, 21 May 1840 to SMITH, Catharine V.; (undated MinRet) Rev. A. SHIRAS; mf# 56

HALL, Edward E. of Carroll Co., Maryland and SMITH, Catharine V. of ClrkVA; (bond) 21 May 1840 by Edward E. HALL of Caroll Co., Maryland and Edward J. SMITH of ClrkVA; p. 51

HALL, Robert of ClrkVA and ASHBY, Nancy of ClrkVA; (bond) 16 Jul 1846 by Robert HALL and William TUMBLIN of ClrkVA; p. 134

HANCE, Thos. C. (Dr.) of Maryland and GARNER, Mary E. of ClrkVA; (bond) 24 Dec 1849 by Dr. Thos. C. HANCE of Maryland and Joseph TULEY of ClrkVA; p. 171

HANCOCK, Charles B. and ISLER, Mattie C.; (lic) 7 Dec 1858; mf# 255

HANDLE, Edward of ClrkVA and DAWES, Mary of ClrkVA; (bond) 1 Jun 1840 by Edward HANDLE and Thomas W. BYRNE of ClrkVA; p. 53

HANSUCKER, George of ClrkVA and DEAN, Jane of ClrkVA; (bond) 10 Feb 1847 by George HANSUCKER and James A. STEELE both of ClrkVA; p. 138

HARDESTY, Adrian D. of JeffVA and PIERCE, Mary Jane of ClrkVA; (bond) 24 Feb 1845 by Adrian D. HARDESTY of JeffVA and John PIERCE Senr. of ClrkVA; p. 110

HARDESTY, Charles W. m. 19 Feb 1852 to ANDERSON, Jane
L.; (undated MinRet) Jos. BAKER; mf# 263
HARDESTY, James M. of ClrkVA and JONES, Sarah W. of
ClrkVA; (bond) 19 Jan 1846 by James M. HARDESTY and
Matthew JONES both of ClrkVA; p. 123
HARDESTY, Richard S. of ClrkVA and CARTER, Mary Eliza of
ClrkVA; (bond) 9 Dec 1839 by Richard S. HARDESTY of
ClrkVA and Watson CARTER of FredVA; p. 43
HARDESTY, William G. of ClrkVA and CLEVENGER, Sarah of
ClrkVA; (bond) 20 Jan 1838 by William G. HARDESTY of
ClrkVA and Paul PIERCE of same county; p. 19
HARRIS, Gabriel C. of FredVA and TANQUARY, Sarah M. of
ClrkVA; (bond) 17 Feb 1845 by Gabriel C. HARRIS of
FredVA and James R. BROOK of ClrkVA; p. 110
HARRIS, [James R.] [see entry below] (of Miss.) and
STROTHER, Mary A.; (cnst) 21 Sep 1841 by an uncle [can
not decipher name] states her mother and legal guardian
(father died several years ago) gives consent; mf# 111
HARRIS, James R. of Copiah Co. Mississippi and STROTHER,
Mary A. of ClrkVA; (bond) 22 Sep 1841 by James R. HARRIS
of Copiah Co., Mississippi and Turner W. ASHBY of FqrVA;
p. 67
HARRIS, Joseph of ClrkVA and WHITAKER, Elizabeth of
ClrkVA; (bond) 17 Apr 1839 by Joseph HARRIS and Jonas
WHITAKER both of ClrkVA; p. 34
HARRIS, Marshall L. of Amherst Co., Va and BERKELEY, Julia
of ClrkVA; (bond) 10 Jun 1846 by Marshall L. HARRIS of
Amherst Co., Va and Wm. B. HARRIS of ClrkVA; p. 133
HARRISON, Henry of Charles City Co., Va and BURWELL,
Frances Tabb of ClrkVA; (bond) 15 Feb 1847 by Henry
HARRISON of Charles City Co., Va and John PAGE of
ClrkVA; p. 139
HARRISS, Marshall L. m. 11 Jun 1846 to BERKLEY, Julia;
(undated MinRet) Rich'd. H. WILMER, Minister of Prot.
Episcopal Church in the Diocese of Virginia; mf# 323
HEFFLEBOWER, Samuel of ClrkVA and SOWERS, Mary Eliza
of ClrkVA; (bond) 11 Mar 1840 by Samuel HEFFLEBOWER
and Fielding L. SOWERS both of ClrkVA; p. 48
HEFFLEBOWER, Samuel of JeffVA and HEFFLEBOWER,
Elizabeth of ClrkVA; (bond) 12 Jun 1837 by Samuel
HEFFLEBOWER of JeffVA and William DEAHL of ClrkVA; p.
13

HELVESTINE, Warren R. and PIERCE, Lucy C.; (cnst) 4 Nov 1857 by John PIERCE, father; mf# 101

HESS, Abraham H. and SHAFER, Catharine d/o John SHAFER of ClrkVA; (cnst) 2 May 1848 by Eli CRUPPER to Catharine his ward. Teste Daniel J. RAMEY, John ANDERSON; mf# 85

HESS, Abraham H. of ClrkVA and SHAFER, Catharine of ClrkVA; (bond) 2 May 1848 by Abraham H. HESS and John SHAFER of ClrkVA; p. 153

HESSER, James E. and BELL, Emmeline; (lic) 31 Dec 1852; mf# 236

HIBBARD, Henry A. m. 10 Jan 1853 to WEITT, Ann Jenette; (undated MinRet) John F. HOFF; mf# 183

HIBBARD, John W. m. 7 Aug 1853 to DAVIS, Mary J.; (undated MinRet) R. N. HERNDON, Minister of the Gospel; mf# 208

HICKS, Alfred of FqrVA and BENN, Cecilia Frances of ClrkVA; (bond) 4 Jan 1841 by Alfred HICKS of FqrVA and Robert P BENN of ClrkVA; p. 60

HIETT, Levi and CARTER, Elizabeth Ruth, over 21y, of ClrkVA; (oath) 22 Oct 1849 by R.? CARTER; mf# 96

HIETT, Levi of ClrkVA and CARTER, Elizabeth Ruth of ClrkVA; (bond) 22 Oct 1849 by Levi HIETT and Wm. K. CARTER both of ClrkVA; p. 168

HISKETT, Francis W. of JeffVA and HUMMER, Elizabeth of ClrkVA; (bond) 17 Apr 1844 by Francis W. HISKETT of JeffVA and Wm. HUMMER of ClrkVA; p. 100

HITE, Hugh and MEADE, Ann; (cnst) 5 Dec 1837 by William MEADE, D. D., Guardian and uncle of the children of R. K. MEADE dec'd.; mf# 24

HITE, Hugh Holmes of FredVA and MEADE, Ann Randolph of ClrkVA; (bond) 14 Dec 1837 by Hugh Holmes HITE of FredVA and William R. SEEVERS of ClrkVA; p. 18

HITE, Isaac Irvine of ClrkVA and MEADE, Susan E. of ClrkVA; (bond) 6 Aug 1838 by Isaac Irvine HITE and James M. HITE of ClrkVA; p. 23

HITE, Isaac Irvine of ClrkVA s/o James M. HITE and MEADE, Susan E. d/o Richard K. MEADE deceased; (cnst) letter dated 5 Aug 1838 by William MEAD Guardian and uncle of children of R. K. MEADE dec'd and letter dated 6 Aug 1838 by James M. HITE, father; mf# 22

HOENNER, Henry of ClrkVA and SYFRET, Isabella of ClrkVA; (bond) 23 Oct 1847 by Henry HOENER and George KNIGHT of ClrkVA; p. 146

HOFF, Joseph of ClrkVA and TOMLIN, Joanna of ClrkVA; (bond) 23 Jun 1842 by Joseph HOFF and John LONGERBEAM of ClrkVA; p. 75

HOUGH, Humphrey and DRISH, Malissa; (cnst) 23 Sep 1857 by Jno. DRISH, father; mf# 76

HUFF, Bushrod m. 4 Jun 1840 to WATKINS, Mary J.; (undated MinRet) Rev. S. SHIRAS; mf# 290

HUFF, Bushrod of ClrkVA and WATKINS, Mary Jane of ClrkVA; (bond) 1 Jun 1840 by Bushrod HUFF and Abraham H. BEAVERS both of ClrkVA; p. 53

HUFF, Jackson m. 23 Sep 1847 to TINSMAN, Eliz'th; (undated MinRet) Rich'd. H. WILMER, Minister of Prot. Episcopal Church in the Diocese of Virginia; mf# 331

HUFF, Jackson of ClrkVA and TINSMAN, Elizabeth of ClrkVA; (bond) 21 Sep 1847 by Jackson HUFF and George TINSMAN both of ClrkVA; p. 145

HUMMER, James m. 2 Sep 1847 to BELL, Sarah Jane; (undated MinRet) Rich'd. H. WILMER, Minister of Prot. Episcopal Church in the Diocese of Virginia; mf# 328

HUMMER, James Wm. of ClrkVA and BELL, Sarah Jane of ClrkVA; (bond) 31 Aug 1847 by James Wm. HUMMER and James BELL of ClrkVA; p. 144

HUMMER, Thornton of ClrkVA and GRIM, Mary of ClrkVA; (bond) 1 Jan 1849 by Thornton HUMMER and Abraham GRIM both of ClrkVA; p. 161

HUNTSBERRY, Augustine of FredVA and STIPE, Margaret of ClrkVA; (bond) 8 Jan 1838 by Augustine HUNTSBERRY of FredVA and Henry STIPE of ClrkVA; p. 18

HUNTSBERRY, Isaac N. and JOHNSON, Isabell, over 21y; (oath) 10 Dec 1853 by John S. JOHNSTON, brother; mf# 136

HUPLEY [or HAPLEY], John of Berryville and McPHILLIN, Elizabeth Ann of ClrkVA; (bond) 28 Nov 1839 by John HUPLEY [or HAPLEY] and John McPHILLIN both of Berryville; p. 42

HURLEY, Daniel of ClrkVA and GORDON, Eliza of ClrkVA; (bond) 12 Aug 1845 by Daniel HURLEY and Thomas H. CROW both of ClrkVA; p. 117

HURLY, Daniel and GORDON, Eliza, of legal age and legally competent; (oath) 12 Aug 1845 by Eliza GORDON; mf# 146

HUYETT, Samuel of ClrkVA and JONES, Sidna of ClrkVA; (bond) 28 Oct 1839 by Samuel HUYETT and Matthew JONES both of ClrkVA; p. 40

IRWIN, James William of Kentucky and BLAKEMORE, Caroline
 Augusta of ClrkVA; (bond) 28 Aug 1844 by James William
 IRWIN of Kentucky and George C. BLAKEMORE of ClrkVA;
 p. 104
IRWIN, James William of Kentucky and BLAKEMORE, Caroline
 Augusta, over 21y, of ClrkVA; (oath) 28 Aug 1844 by George
 C. BLAKEMORE; mf# 189
ISBELLE, Thomas Montague of Cumberland Co., Va and
 ALLEN, Frances T. of ClrkVA; (bond) 19 Feb 1850 by
 Thomas Montague ISBELLE of Cumberland Co., Va and
 Edgar ALLEN of ClrkVA; p. 172
JACKSON, Andrew, 28y, sgl, miller, b. LdnVA, s/o William
 JACKSON & Nancy JACKSON; m. 28 Sep 1854 at "The
 Vineyard" to THOMSON, Emily, 19y, sgl, b. "The Vineyard"
 ClrkVA, d/o Greenberry and Elizabeth THOMSON; (MinRet)
 25 Nov 1854 by John F. HOFF, Minister of the Gospel; mf#
 206
JACKSON, Ebenezer of LdnVA and BYRNE, Catharine of
 ClrkVA; (bond) 27 Jan 1845 by Ebenezer JACKSON of
 LdnVA and Enos FARNSWORTH of ClrkVA; p. 108
JACKSON, Ebenezer of Loudoun m. 30 Jan 1845 to BYRNE,
 Catherine of ClrkVA; (undated MinRet) Pastor H. W. DODGE,
 2 Bap. Ch, Upperville, Va; mf# 5
JACKSON, Samuel A. of LdnVA and BYRNE, Sarah A. of
 ClrkVA; (bond) 2 Jan 1843 by Samuel A. JACKSON of
 LdnVA and Josiah G. KEES also of LdnVA; p. 84
JACKSON, William A. of ClrkVA and MARSHALL, Sarah of
 ClrkVA; (bond) 11 Nov 1850 by William A. JACKSON and
 John MARSHALL both of ClrkVA; p. 179
JENKINS, David of LdnVA and ACRES, Caroline of ClrkVA;
 (bond) 2 Nov 1837 by David JENKINS of LdnVA and
 Ebenezar JACKSON of ClrkVA; p. 16
JENKINS, Ebin of ClrkVA and HARVEY, Mary Ann of ClrkVA;
 (bond) 16 Jan 1844 by Ebin JENKINS and Wm. P.
 WIGGINTON both of ClrkVA; p. 97
JENKINS, Thomas and McCLAUGHLY, Ann E.; (lic) 4 Jan 1861;
 mf# 272
JENKINS, William of LdnVA and CRAWFORD, Mary of ClrkVA;
 (bond) 13 Dec 1841 by William JENKINS of LdnVA and
 Joseph ANDERSON of ClrkVA; p. 69
JOHNSON, James William, 25y, sgl, farmer, b. & res. ClrkVA,
 s/o Catharine JOHNSON; m. 4 Nov 1858 in ClrkVA to

WILLINGHAM, Ann Elizabeth, 24y, sgl, b. & res. ClrkVA, d/o William & Matilda WILLINGHAM; (MinRet) 5 Nov 1858 by W. G. WILLIAMS, Minister of M. E. Church South; mf# 213

JOHNSON, Joseph of ClrkVA and BROWN, Eleanor S. of ClrkVA; (bond) 2 Mar 1848 by Joseph JOHNSON and Wm. BERRY Esqr. & John BROWN of ClrkVA; p. 151

JOHNSON, Ransel of ClrkVA and RICHARDSON, Elizabeth of ClrkVA; (bond) 15 May 1847 by Ransel JOHNSON and Joseph B. GOURLEY of ClrkVA; p. 140

JOHNSON, Washington m. 1 Oct 1840 to DOWNING, Mary J.; (undated MinRet) Rev. S. SHIRAS; mf# 295

JOHNSON, Washington of LdnVA and DOWNING, Mary Jane of ClrkVA; (bond) 1 Oct 1840 by Washington JOHNSON of LdnVA and Benjamin DOWNING of ClrkVA; p. 56

JOHNSTON, Albert of ClrkVA and HANEY, Elizabeth of ClrkVA; (bond) 21 Feb 1842 by Albert JOHNSTON and Robert HANEY of ClrkVA.; p. 72

JOHNSTON, Morgan m. 29 Oct 1840 to BROWNLEY, Ann; (MinRet) 8 Jan 1841 in Front Royal by Robert S. BELL; mf# 237

JOHNSTON, Morgan of WrnVA and BROWNLEY, Ann of ClrkVA; (bond) 26 Oct 1840 by Morgan JOHNSTON of WrnVA and James CASTLEMAN of ClrkVA; p. 57

JOHNSTON, Morgan of WrnVA and BROWNLEY, Ann, over 21y, of ClrkVA; (oath) 26 Oct 1840 by James CASTLEMAN; mf# 122

JONES, Thomas of ClrkVA and HUYETT, Mary Jane of ClrkVA; (bond) 2 Nov 1840 by Thomas JONES and Abraham HUYETT of ClrkVA; p. 58

KEELER, Middleton of ClrkVA and HOLLOWAY, Teresa of ClrkVA; (bond) 1 Dec 1836 by Middleton KEELER & James RYAN of ClrkVA; p. 7

KENNAN, James Henry of ClrkVA and CAMFORD, Susan Rebecca of ClrkVA; (bond) 25 Jul 1850 by James H. KENNAN and George A. BELT of ClrkVA; p. 176

KERCHEVAL, Benjamin T. of ClrkVA and CARRINGTON, Mary Virginia of ClrkVA; (bond) 13 Nov 1849 by Benjamin T. KERCHEVAL and William G. CARRINGTON both of ClrkVA; p. 169

KIMBALL, Charles E. and STRIBLING, Sigismunda B., over 21y, of ClrkVA; (oath) 12 Jun 1848 by Josiah Wm. WARE; mf# 138

KIMBALL, Charles E. of Philadelphia and STRIBLING, Sigismonda E. of ClrkVA; (bond) 12 Jun 1848 by Charles E. KIMBALL of Philadelphia and Josiah Wm. WARE Esqr. of ClrkVA; p. 156

KING, Willis F. and STEEL, Sarah Francis; (lic) 4 Jun 1856; mf# 269

KING, Willis F., 29y, sgl, b. LdnVA, shoemaker, s/o William & Susan KING; m. 4 Jun 1856 at Peter COOLIE's in ClrkVA to STEEL, Sarah Frances, 27y, sgl, b. FredVA, d/o Joseph & Harriette STEEL; (MinRet) 4 Jun 1856 by Francis M. WHITTLE, Minister of the Prot. Epis. Church; mf# 55

KIRBY, Christopher C. of Winchester, Va and RICHARDSON, Eliza L. of ClrkVA; (bond) 13 May 1839 by Christopher C. KIRBY of Winchester, Va and Thornton P. PENDLETON of ClrkVA; p. 35

KNELLER, Samuel G. of Washington City and SHIVELY, Margaret Ann of ClrkVA; (bond) 9 Jan 1838 by Samuel G. KNELLER of Washington City and John RICHARDSON of ClrkVA; p. 19

KNIGHT, Henry and DORAN, Ann T.; (cnst) 5 Nov 1862 by Matthew H. DORAN who makes oath for James DORAN, father; mf# 94

KNODE, Oliver B. of ClrkVA and BAKER, Ann C. of ClrkVA; (bond) 28 Feb 1848 by Oliver B. KNODE and Wm. BAKER of ClrkVA; p. 151

KOONES, Charles M., 26y, sgl, book keeper, b. Alexandria Va, resides WashDC, s/o not given; prop. m. 25 Sep 1860 in ClrkVA to KNELLER, Mary E., 20y, sgl, b. & res. ClrkVA, d/o Saml. G. KNELLER & Margaret Ann; (appl) 24 Sep 1860 by Chas. M. KOONES; mf# 235

KROMLING, Henry, 30y, sgl, shoe & boot maker, b. York Co. Pa, s/o Jacob & Catherine KROMLING; m. 5 Feb 1857 at residence of Mr. Henry HOOE to HOOE, Frances A., 18y, sgl, b. ClrkVA, d/o Henry D. & Mary A. HOOE; (MinRet) 22 Apr 1857 by H. W. DODGE, Minister of the Gospel; mf# 257

LANHAM, Edgar of ClrkVA and COATS, Sena Ann (Mrs.) of ClrkVA; (bond) 27 Oct 1841 by Edgar LANHAM and Joseph E. PEYTON both of ClrkVA; p. 68

LANHAM, Edwin m. 8 Jan 1845 to ASHBY, Sarah Cath'e.; (undated MinRet) Richard H. WILMER, Minister of the P. E. Church in the Diocese of Virginia; mf# 276

LANHAM, Miner of ClrkVA and ASHBY, Sarah Catharine of
ClrkVA; (bond) 8 Jan 1845 by Miner LANHAM and Robert
ASHBY both of ClrkVA; p. 108

LANHAM, Richard of ClrkVA and WILEY, Catharine of ClrkVA;
(bond) 16 Sep 1845 by Richard LANHAM and George
LANHAM both of ClrkVA; p. 118

LANNOM, James of ClrkVA and FURR, Jane of ClrkVA; (bond) 9
Mar 1840 by James LANNOM and John FURR both of
ClrkVA; p. 47

LARUE, James W. m. 29 Mar 1841 to BELL, Matilda; (undated
MinRet) Thos. BUCK Jr.; mf# 51

LARUE, James W. of ClrkVA and BELL, Matilda of ClrkVA;
(bond) 22 Mar 1841 by James W. LARUE and James BELL
both of ClrkVA; p. 62

LARUE, James W. of ClrkVA and JACKSON, Frances C.; (bond)
16 Jul 1836 by James W. LARUE and Solomon R. JACKSON
both of ClrkVA; p. 3

LEACH, Charles m. 28 Dec 1843 to BRANER, Sarah Ann;
(undated MinRet) Jos. BAKER; mf# 300

LEACH, Charles of ClrkVA and BRAWNER, Sarah Ann of
ClrkVA; (bond) 28 Dec 1843 by Charles LEACH and Jas. C.
KENNON & Jesse TAYLOR all of ClrkVA; p. 97

LEE, Charles S. of BerkVA and PAGE, Margaret H. of ClrkVA;
(bond) 16 May 1849 by Charles S. LEE of BerkVA and
George R. PAGE of ClrkVA; p. 163

LEE, Christopher m. 24 Jan 1854 to THOMPSON, Juliet A.;
(undated MinRet) H. W. DODGE, M.G.; mf# 254

LEE, George W. and CORNWELL, Malvina, over 21y; (oath) 11
Apr 1854 by Whiting HAMILTON; mf# 62

LEE, James W. and THOMPSON, Charlotte E.; (cnst) 14 Aug
1858 by Benj. THOMPSON, father. Teste D. H. McGUIRE;
mf# 58

LEE, James W. see LLOYD, James W.

LEE, James Wm., 24y, sgl, shoemaker, b. LdnVA, resides
ClrkVA, s/o Squire LEE & Al[c]inda LEE; prop. m. 19 Aug
1858 in ClrkVA to THOMPSON, Charlotte E., abt 17y, sgl, b.
& res. ClrkVA, d/o Benj. THOMPSON & Juliett A.
THOMPSON; (appl) 14 Aug 1858 by James W. LEE; mf# 69

LEE, Richard Henry and PAGE, Evelyn B., over 21y, of ClrkVA;
(oath) 12 Jun 1848 by Mann R. PAGE, Esqr., father; mf# 131

LEE, Richard Henry of JeffVA and PAGE, Everlyn B. of ClrkVA; (bond) 12 Jun 1848 by Richard Henry LEE of JeffVA and Mann R. PAGE Esqr. of ClrkVA; p. 155

LEITH, Henry W. of ClrkVA and CARTER, Louisa of ClrkVA; (bond) 9 Sep 1847 by Henry W. LEITH of ClrkVA and Francis CARTER of FqrVA; p. 144

LEVI, William H. and HART, Sarah C. V.; (lic) 14 Jan 1861; mf# 215

LEWIN, Moses of ClrkVA and MOORE, Sarah Jane of ClrkVA; (bond) 7 Sep 1850 by Moses LEWIN and Alfred P. MOORE both of ClrkVA; p. 177

LEWIS, Edward P. C. and WARE, Lucy B.; (lic) 20 Mar 1859; mf# 186

LEWIS, Edward P. C., 20y, sgl, farmer, b. & res. ClrkVA, s/o L. & G. M. LEWIS; m. 23 Mar 1859 at residence of Col. WARE to WARE, Lucy B., age not given, sgl, b. & res. ClrkVA, d/o Col. J. W. & Fanny WARE; (MinRet) 23 Mar 1859 by Henderson PATER, Minister of the Episcopal Ch.; mf# 169

LEWIS, Fisher A. of JeffVA and LANE, Elizabeth T. of ClrkVA; (bond) 15 Sep 1842 by Fisher A. LEWIS of JeffVA and Josiah Wm. WARE Esqr. of ClrkVA; p. 77

LEWIS, Thomas D. m. 24 Nov 1846 to BELL, Mary Frances; (MinRet) 24 Nov 1846 by Thos. BUCK; mf# 211

LEWIS, Thomas D. of FqrVA and BELL, Mary Frances of ClrkVA; (bond) 23 Nov 1846 by Thomas D. LEWIS of FqrVA and Strother BELL of ClrkVA; p. 136

LINDSEY, J. B., 21y, sgl, b. Pleasuresville, Ky, resides Berry's ferry, merchant, s/o S. J. and H. E. LINDSEY; m. 14 Dec 1858 in Berry's ferry, Va to McCORMICK, M. E., 18y, sgl, b. & res. ClrkVA, d/o O. & S. A. McCORMICK; (MinRet) 14 Dec 1858 by B. GRIMSLEY; mf# 50

LINDSEY, James M. of ClrkVA and SOWERS, Martha L. of ClrkVA; (bond) 17 Sep 1838 by James M. LINDSEY and Henry SHEPHERD both of ClrkVA; p. 24

LINDSEY, Jos. B., 21y, sgl, merchant, b. Pleasuresville, Kentucky, resides Berry's Ferry, s/o S. J. LINDSEY & A. J. LINDSEY; prop. m. 14 Dec 1858 at Berry's Ferry to McCORMICK, Mary E., 18y, sgl, b. ClrkVA, resides Berry's Ferry, d/o Otway & Sarah A. McCORMICK; (appl) 11 Dec 1858 by J. B. LINDSEY; mf# 57

LITTLETON, Charles G. of ClrkVA and CORBIN, Amanda Melvina of ClrkVA; (bond) 5 Dec 1842 by Charles G. LITTLETON and James N. CORBIN both of ClrkVA; p. 82

LITTLETON, William D. of ClrkVA and DOWNING, Amandy E. of ClrkVA; (bond) 19 Aug 1845 by William D. LITTLETON and Benjamin DOWNING both of ClrkVA; p. 117

LITTLETON, William m. 13 Mar 1851 to MARQUISS, Mary; (MinRet) 13 Aug 1851 in Berryville by Joshua PETERKIN, Rector of Wickliffe Parish, ClrkVA; mf# 177

LLOYD [should be LEE], James W., 23y, sgl, cordwainer, b. Loudoun, resides ClrkVA, s/o Squire LEE & Alcinda LEE; m. 18 Aug 1858 in ClrkVA to THOMPSON, Charloot [Charlott] E., unknown age, sgl, b. & res. ClrkVA, d/o Benjamin THOMPSON & mother unknown; (MinRet) 19 Aug 1858 by Andrew ROBEY; mf# 207

LLOYD, Andrew J. and STICKLES, Sarah Jane; (cnst) 13 Oct 1858 by Simon STICKLES, father. Teste D. H. McGUIRE; mf# 126

LLOYD, Andrew J., 22y, sgl, farmer, b. & res. ClrkVA, s/o Henry and Sarah LLOYD; prop. m. 14 Oct 1858 to STICKLES, Sarah Jane, 21y, sgl, b. & res. ClrkVA, d/o Simon & Amelia STICKLES; (appl) 13 Oct 1858 by Andrew J. LLOYD; mf# 90

LLOYD, Harrison and BEAVERS, Ann Eliza; (lic) 15 Jul 1854; mf# 220

LLOYD, Harrison and GLASSCOCK, Elvirah; (cnst) 5 May 1845 by Emily FURR, mother. Teste James FURR, Nimrod GLASSCOCK; mf# 110

LLOYD, Harrison of ClrkVA and GLASSCOCK, Elvirah of ClrkVA; (bond) 5 May 1845 by Harrison LLOYD and Nimrod GLASSCOCK both of ClrkVA; p. 115

LLOYD, Harrison, 31y, widower, farmer, b. ClrkVA, s/o Henry & Nelly LLOYD; m. 27 Jul 1854 in ClrkVA to BEAVERS, Ann Eliza, 33y, sgl, b. LdnVA, d/o Abram & Pleasy BEAVERS; (MinRet) 1 Aug 1854 by Francis M. WHITTLE, Minister of the Prot. Epis. Church; mf# 201

LLOYD, James and ASHBY, Sarah, over 21y, of ClrkVA; (oath) 22 Mar 1847 by Martin ASHBY; mf# 84

LLOYD, James Lawrence m. 26 Aug 1852 to LEE, Elizabeth; (MinRet) 16 Sep 1852 by J. F. HOFF, Millwood; mf# 140

LLOYD, James of ClrkVA and ASHBY, Sarah of ClrkVA; (bond) 22 Mar 1847 by James LLOYD and Martin ASHBY both of ClrkVA; p. 139

LOCK, Benjamin of ClrkVA and VANCLEAVE, Rahamy of ClrkVA; (bond) 18 Dec 1845 by Benjamin LOCK and John VANCLEAVE both of ClrkVA; p. 122

LOCK, Benjamin of ClrkVA and VANCLEAVE, Ruhamy, over 21y, of Clarke; (oath) 18 Dec 1845 by John VANCLEAVE; mf# 81

LOCK, Franklin of JeffVA and HOUT, Mary Ann of ClrkVA; (bond) 5 Dec 1837 by Franklin LOCK of JeffVA and Rudolph HOUT of ClrkVA; p. 17

LOCK, Timothy H. m. 22 Mar 1853 to CRIMM, Catharine L.; (MinRet) 29 Dec 1853 by Jos. BAKER; mf# 40

LOCK, William Junr. of FredVA and GATES, Lucinda of ClrkVA; (bond) 25 Jan 1839 by William LOCK Junr. of FredVA and Jacob GATES of ClrkVA; p. 28

LOCK, Wm. m. 7 Apr ___ to GARTER [CARTER, Luden G. on typed index], Ludend? (Miss); (MinRet) 8 Mar ___ by ___; mf# 192

LONGCOR, Anthony of ClrkVA and THOMPSON, Nancy of ClrkVA; (bond) 11 Oct 1838 by Anthony LONGCOR of Clarke and Jonathan GOURLEY of FqrVA; p. 26

LONGERBEAM, Abraham of ClrkVA and FULLER, Sarah Jane of ClrkVA; (bond) 24 Mar 1846 by Abraham LONGERBEAM and McPharland FULLER both of ClrkVA; p. 129

LONGERBEAM, Abrah'm m. 2 Apr 1846 to FULLER, Sarah Ann; (undated MinRet) Rich'd. H. WILMER, Minister of Prot. Episcopal Church in the Diocese of Virginia; mf# 321

LONGERBEAM, Benjamin of ClrkVA and JENKINS, Nancy of ClrkVA; (bond) 10 Nov 1849 by Benjamin LONGERBEAM and Herod JENKINS both of ClrkVA; p. 169

LONGERBEAM, William m. 25 Jan 1837 to DAVIS, Rebecca; (MinRet) 22 Feb 1837 by William MONROE; mf# 308

LONGERBEAM, William of ClrkVA and DAVIS, Rebecca of ClrkVA; (bond) 20 Jan 1837 by William LONGERBEAM & Nimrod ASHBY of ClrkVA; p. 8

LOUTHAN, James T., 29y, sgl, farmer, b. FredVA, s/o John & Lydia LOUTHAN m. 9 Apr 1857 at Mrs. Ury CASTLEMAN's, ClrkVA to CASTLEMAN, Emeline F., 19y, sgl, b. ClrkVA, d/o Wm. A. & ___ CASTLEMAN; (MinRet) 10 Apr 1857, by Francis M. WHITTLE, Minister of the Prot. Epis. Ch.; mf# 7

LUKE, John W. of LdnVA and BLAKEMORE, Lucy Cornelia of ClrkVA; (bond) 25 May 1846 by John W. LUKE of LdnVA and George P. BLAKEMORE of ClrkVA; p. 132

LUKE, John W. of LdnVA and BLAKEMORE, Lucy Cornelia, over 21y, of ClrkVA; (oath) 25 May 1846 by George C. BLAKEMORE; mf# 124

MACTIER, Samuel of City of Baltimore and McGUIRE, Jane M. of ClrkVA; (bond) 11 Dec 1837 by Samuel MACTIER of City of Baltimore and John E. PAGE of ClrkVA; p. 17

MARK, Abraham of ClrkVA and LOCK, Rebecca Ann (Mrs.) of ClrkVA; (bond) 29 Dec 1845 by Abraham MARK and John S. GORDON both of ClrkVA; p. 122

MARKER, George E. of ShenVA and GOURLEY, Sarah Ann of ClrkVA; (bond) 2 May 1843 by George E. MARKER of ShenVA and Wm. GOURLEY of ClrkVA; p. 90

MARLOW, Stephen m. 5 Jan 1837 to WATKINS, Tacy; (MinRet) 22 Feb 1837 by William MONROE; mf# 307

MARLOW, Stephen of ClrkVA and WATKINS, Tacey of ClrkVA; (bond) 5 Jan 1837 by Stephen MARLOW and Abraham H. BEAVERS of ClrkVA; p. 7

MARPLE, George Franklin of PageVA and COATS, Amanda Elizabeth of ClrkVA; (bond) 30 Apr 1844 by George Franklin MARPLE of PageVA and Edgar LANHAM of ClrkVA; p. 101

MARSHALL, Edward C. Jr., 21y, sgl, merchant, b. FqrVA, s/o Edw'd. C. & Rebecca C. MARSHALL m. 16 Dec 1856 in Berryville to TAYLOR, Virg'a. E., 22y, sgl, b. ClrkVA, d/o Samuel & Eliza TAYLOR; (MinRet) 17 Dec 1856 by Francis M. WHITTLE, Minister of the Prot. Epis. Church; mf# 181

MARTENEY, William of Randolph Co. Va; and EARLE, Nancy, over 21y, of ClrkVA; (oath) 18 Nov 1842 by John B. EARLE; mf# 191

MARTENEY, William of Randolph Co., Va and EARLE, Nancy of ClrkVA; (bond) 18 Nov 1842 by William MARTENEY of Randolph Co., Va and John B. EARLE of ClrkVA; p. 81

MARTIN, John of Berryville and WYNDHAM, Jane N. of ClrkVA; (bond) 18 Jun 1846 by John MARTIN of Berryville and Sydnor B. WYNDHAM of ClrkVA; p. 134

MARTS, Jackson and WILEY, Sarah A.; (lic) 11 Apr 1859; mf# 216

MARTS, Samuel T. and FURR, Ann Maria; (lic) 25 Jul 1854; mf# 251

MARTS, William of ClrkVA and MERCER, Kissia of ClrkVA; (bond) 12 Feb 1840 by William MARTS and Abraham A. BEAVERS both of ClrkVA; p. 46

MASON, Henry and FOWLER, Margaret; (lic) 27 Apr 1859; mf# 200

MASON, Thompson B. and TAYLOR, Sarah C.; (lic) 23 Oct 1855; mf# 185

MASON, William H. of CulpVA and SOWERS, Emily Ann of ClrkVA; (bond) 15 Nov 1842 by Wm. H. MASON and Edw'd. M. SPILMAN both of CulpVA; p. 81

MASSEY, Edmund W. of RappVA and KENNERLY, Sarah W. of ClrkVA; (bond) 17 May 1843 by Edmund W. MASSEY of RappVA and Alexander H. EVANS of Berryville; p. 90

MASSIE, N. H. and NELSON, Eliza K.; (lic) 8 Apr 1856; mf# 190

MAYES, James Taylor of Staunton, Va and CARTER, Sarah Brawner of ClrkVA; (bond) 11 May 1846 by James Taylor MAYES of Staunton, Va and James CARTER of ClrkVA; p. 131

MAYES, James Taylor of Staunton, Va m. 14 May 1866 CARTER, Sarah Brawner of ClrkVA; (undated MinRet) H. W. DODGE, Pastor of 2nd Bap. Ch, Upperville; mf# 49

McCORMICK, John and O'CONNER, Mary Elizabeth, of age; (cnst) 11 Sep 1837 by Elizabeth O'CONNER, mother. Teste. John LOUTHAN, Strother BELL; mf# 73

McCORMICK, John of Cabell Co., Va and O'CONNER, Mary Elizabeth of ClrkVA; (bond) 12 Sep 1837 by John McCORMICK of Cabell Co., Va and Strother BELL of ClrkVA; p. 15

McCORMICK, Thomas and NEILL, Ann R.; (lic) 16 Oct 1852; mf# 271

McCORMICK, Thomas of ClrkVA and McCORMICK, Eliza of ClrkVA; (bond) 9 Dec 1839 by Thomas McCORMICK of ClrkVA and Province McCORMICK of Winchester, Va; p. 42

McCORMICK, William A. (Dr.) of Winchester, Va and PARKER, Charlotte F. of ClrkVA; (bond) 22 May 1849 by Dr. William A. McCORMICK of Winchester Va and P. McCORMICK of ClrkVA; p. 164

McCOY, Jas. Wm., 26y, sgl, millwright, b. Washington Co. Md, s/o Wm. & Elizabeth McCOY m. 23 Jan 1856 in ClrkVA to HANDLE, Sarah Ann Virginia, 24y, sgl, b. ClrkVA, d/o Nicholas & Sidney Ann HANDLE; (MinRet) 23 Jan 1856 by Thos. J. WYSONG, Minister of the Meth. E. Church; mf# 226

McCURDY, John m. 29 Apr 1841 to HEFFLEBOWER, Mary; (undated MinRet) Rev. Alexander SHIRAS; mf# 16

McCURDY, John of JeffVA and HEFFLEBOWER, Mary of ClrkVA; (bond) 28 Feb 1841 by John McCURDY of JeffVA and George HEFFLEBOWER of ClrkVA; p. 63

McDANIEL, Sebastian of JeffVA and SPOTTS, Martha Ellen of ClrkVA; (bond) 20 Jan 1846 by Sebastian McDANIEL of JeffVA and Henry HUYETT of ClrkVA; p. 124

McDONALD, John and HOLTZ[CL]AW, Jane; (cnst) 9 Dec 1843 by William HOLTSCLAW, father. Teste Joel ALEXANDER, Fantleroy HOLTSCLAW; mf# 98

McDONALD, John of WrnVA and HOLTZCLAW, Jane of ClrkVA; (bond) 11 Dec 1843 by John McDONALD of WrnVA and Joel ALEXANDER of ClrkVA; p. 95

McGUIRE, William D. of ClrkVA and MOSS, Nancy Boyd of ClrkVA; (bond) 13 Feb 1841 by William D. McGUIRE and Province McCORMICK both of ClrkVA; p. 61

McGUIRE, Wm. D. (Dr.) m. 16 Feb 1841 to MOSS, Nancy B.; (undated MinRet) Rev. Alexander SHIRAS; mf# 15

McINTYRE, C. C. of LdnVA and SHIVELY, Harriett E. of ClrkVA; (bond) 2 Jan 1850 by C. C. McINTYRE of LdnVA and S. G. KNELLER of ClrkVA; p. 171

McKENZIE, Alexander L. of Fairfax Co., Va and SYDNOR, Ann R. of ClrkVA; (bond) 5 Feb 1846 by Alexander L. McKENZIE and Francis E. JOHNSTON both of Fairfax Co., Va; p. 126

McKENZIE, Alexander S. m. 5 Feb 1846 to SYDNOR, Ann R.; (undated MinRet) Richard H. WILMER, Minister of the P. E. Church in the Diocese of Virginia; mf# 288

McMURRAY, Jno. P., 23y, sgl, b. Frederick Co., resides ClrkVA, farmer, s/o Peter & Catharine McMURRAY; prop. m. 3 Nov 1859 to DEARMONT, Sarah Jane, 21y, sgl, b. & res. ClrkVA, d/o Michael & Lucy DEARMONT; (appl) dated 31 [3?] Nov 1859 by John P. McMURRAY; mf# 17

McMURRAY, John P. and DEARMONT, Sarah Jane, over 21y; (oath) 31 Oct 1859 by Peter DEARMONT; mf# 107

McPHILLIN, Jno. James and BERLIN, Sarah Ann, over 21y, of ClrkVA; (oath) 5 Nov 1845 by Wm. BERLIN; mf# 156

McPHILLIN, John James of ClrkVA and BERLIN, Sarah Ann of ClrkVA; (bond) 5 Nov 1845 by John James McPHILLIN and Wm. BERLIN both of ClrkVA; p. 120

MERCER, Jesse P. and SHORES, Joannah; (lic) 7 Sep 1853; mf# 270

MERSER, Jesse Purnell, widower, 59y, cooper, parents not living, of ClrkVA m. 9 Sep 1853 in Berryville to SHORES,

Joannah, widow, d/o John & Nancy MARTS, 49y, also of
ClrkVA; (MinRet) Francis M. WHITTLE, Minister of Prot. Epis.
Ch. of Va; mf# 44

MILEY, Moses of LdnVA and KEEAN, Aira (Mrs.) of ClrkVA;
(bond) 3 Jun 1844 by Moses G. [MILEY] of LdnVA and
James W. BEEK of ClrkVA; p. 103

MILEY, Sydnor of LdnVA and THOMPSON, Phebe Ellen of
ClrkVA; (bond) 22 Jun 1850 by Sydnor MILEY of LdnVA and
Benjamin THOMPSON of ClrkVA; p. 175

MILEY, Sydnor of LdnVA m. 27 Jun 1850 to THOMPSON,
Phebe Ellen of ClrkVA; (undated MinRet) H. W. DODGE; mf#
245

MILLSON, John S. m. 28 Oct 1841 to PARKER, M. S.; (undated
MinRet) Alexander SHIRAS; mf# 33

MILLSON, John S. of Norfolk Borough, Va and PARKER, Mary
S. of ClrkVA; (bond) 27 Oct 1841 by John S. MILLSON of
Norfolk Borough, Va and John H. PARKER of ClrkVA; p. 68

MOORE, Armistead M. m. 14 Nov 1841 to LUKE, Susan G.;
(MinRet) 27 Oct 1842 in Richmond Co. by R. N. HERNDON;
mf# 250

MOORE, Armistead Mason of LdnVA and LUKE, Susan G. of
ClrkVA; (bond) 10 Nov 1841 by Armistead Mason MOORE of
LdnVA and John W. LUKE of ClrkVA; p. 69

MOORE, Samuel J. C., 31y, widower, attorney-at-law, b.
Charlestown, JeffVA, res. Berryville, s/o Thomas A. & Jane C.
MOORE, said Jane C. being a d/o Samuel J. CRAMER; m.
16 Feb 1858 at Dr. KOWNSLAR's in Berryville to
KOWNSLAR, Ellen, 20y, sgl, b. Middleway, JeffVA, res.
Berryville, d/o Randolph & Mary KOWNSLAR; (MinRet) 9 Mar
1858 by J. F. HOFF, Minister of the Episcopal Church; mf#
166

MOORE, Sylvanus and FRIDLEY, Abigail; (cnst) 5 Jan 1843 by
Abigail FRIDLEY. Teste W. H. SEEVER, Jas. C. KINNAN.;
mf# 27

MOORE, Sylvanus of ClrkVA and FRIDLEY, Abigail of ClrkVA;
(bond) 5 Jan 1843 by Sylvanus MOORE and Robt. G.
ASHBY both of ClrkVA; p. 85

MOORE, Wm. H., 47y, widowed, farmer, b. & res. JeffVA, s/o
John & E. MOORE; m. 12 Jun 1860 in Berryville to BEARD,
Amelia H., 34y, widow, b. & res. JeffVA, d/o Dr. STRAIGHT;
(MinRet) 12 Jun 1860 by Chas. WHITE, Minister of the
Gospel; mf# 243

MORELAND, Jeremiah of LdnVA and MERCER, Elizabeth of
ClrkVA; (bond) 10 Sep 1849 by Jeremiah MORELAND of
LdnVA and Jesse P. MERCER of ClrkVA; p. 167
MORGAN, Richard H. m. 30 Jul 1840 to HEATWELL, S. A.;
(undated MinRet) Rev. S. SHIRAS; mf# 292
MORGAN, Richard H. of ClrkVA and HEATWALL, Susan Ann of
ClrkVA; (bond) 28 Jul 1840 by Richard H. MORGAN and
William LOCK both of ClrkVA; p. 54
MURPHEY, Josiah and HOFF, Permelia; (cnst) 7 Sep 1838 by
Juli HUMMER, mother of bride. Teste Jesse MERCER,
William HUMMER; mf# 78
MURPHY, Josiah of ClrkVA and HOFF, Pamelia of ClrkVA;
(bond) 8 Sep 1838 by Josiah MURPHY and Jesse MERCER
both of ClrkVA; p. 23
MYERS, George of JeffVA and HUYETT, Sarah Elizabeth of
ClrkVA; (bond) 2 Nov 1840 by George MYERS of JeffVA and
John HUYETT of ClrkVA; p. 57
NALLS, John T. and THOMPSON, Lucy Catharine, over 21y;
(oath) 21 Dec 1858 by John THOMPSON; mf# 102
NEILL, Lewis of JeffVA and TAYLOR, Mary Louisa of ClrkVA;
(bond) 24 May 1845 by Lewis NEILL of JeffVA and John B.
TAYLOR of ClrkVA; p. 115
NEVILLE, Alexander V. and WOOD, Lucy E.; (cnst) 19 Jan 1859
by Alexander WOOD, father; mf# 108
NEVIN, Saml. W. of Pennsylvania and BALCH, Harriett M. of
ClrkVA; (bond) 27 Nov 1850 by Saml. W. NEVIN and Geo. N.
PAGE of Clarke; p. 1
NEVITT, James, 28y, manager of a farm, sgl, s/o Wm. & Nancy
NEVITT; m. 25 Aug 1853 to DUKE, Emily, 19y, sgl, d/o
Thomas H. & Sidney DUKE; (undated MinRet) F. ISRAEL;
mf# 47
NUGENT, James, 40y, sgl, laborer, b. Ireland, resides JeffVA,
s/o not known; m. 27 May 1860 near Providence Chapel to
KELLY, Eliza, 16y, sgl, b. & res. ClrkVA, d/o Hanah KELLY;
(MinRet) 27 May 1860 by Jesse PORTER; mf# 53
NUGENT, James, over 21y, sgl, b. Ireland, res. Jefferson,
laborer, s/o James NUGENT & Janey TRACY; prop. m. 27
May [1860] to KELLY, Eliza, not 21y, b. FqrVA, res. ClrkVA,
d/o George KELLY & Hannah HARDEN; (appl) 25 May 1860
by James NUGENT; mf# 26

NUN/NUNN, John M. of ClrkVA and CASTLEMAN, Elizabeth U.
of ClrkVA; (bond) 2 Sep 1843 by John M. NUN and Benj.
MORGAN both of ClrkVA; p. 92
NUNN, John R. of King & Queen Co. Va m. 11 Mar 1850 to
NUNN, Elizabeth W. (Mrs.) of ClrkVA; (undated MinRet) H.
W. DODGE; mf# 54
NUNN, John R. of King & Queen Co., Va and NUNN, Elizabeth
W. (Mrs.) of ClrkVA; (bond) 11 Mar 1850 by John R. NUNN of
King & Queen Co., Va and William A. CASTLEMAN of
ClrkVA; p. 173
ORR, William of FredVA and GOURLEY, Mahala of ClrkVA;
(bond) 25 Mar 1841 by William ORR of FredVA and William
GOURLEY of ClrkVA; p. 62
OSBORN, George H. of ClrkVA and GRANT, Eliza B. of ClrkVA;
(bond) 24 Mar 1846 by George H. OSBORN and John
GRANT both of ClrkVA; p. 129
PAGE, John Jr. Esqr. and BURWELL, Lucy M.; (cnst) 18 Dec
1843 by Geo. H. BURWELL, father; mf# 143
PAGE, John Jr. of ClrkVA and BURWELL, Lucy M. of ClrkVA;
(bond) 18 Dec 1843 by John PAGE Junr. and T. Alex'r.
TODD both of ClrkVA; p. 95
PAGE, Thomas of Powhatan Co., Va and PAGE, Sally of
ClrkVA; (bond) 31 Oct 1839 by Thomas PAGE of Powhatan
Co., Va and John PAGE Junr. of ClrkVA; p. 41
PARKER, Richard of Harpers Ferry, JeffVA and MOSS, Evelina
T. of ClrkVA; (bond) 3 Sep 1844 by Richard PARKER of
Harpers Ferry, JeffVA and Province McCORMICK of ClrkVA;
p. 105
PARRILL, James Wm. of Hampshire Co., Va and SMITH, Mary
Ann of ClrkVA; (bond) 14 Mar 1837 by James Wm. PARRILL
or Hampshire Co., Va and John M. BLAKEMORE of
Berryville; p. 10
PAUL, Isaac of Winchester, Va and CASTLEMAN, Mary Jane of
ClrkVA; (bond) 7 May 1838 by Isaac PAUL of Winchester, Va
and William CASTLEMAN of ClrkVA; p. 21
PAYNE, Henry of Frederick Co. and GROVE, Ann Rebecca,
over 21y, of ClrkVA; (oath) 1 Feb 1841, John H. FRASHER;
mf# 92
PAYNE, Henry of FredVA and GROVE, Ann Rebecca of ClrkVA;
(bond) 1 Feb 1841 by Henry PAYNE and John A. FRASHER
both of FredVA; p. 61

PAYNE, John W. and RICE, Susan A. D. of ClrkVA; (bond) 4 Nov 1836 by John W. PAYNE of FqrVA and Albert S. HIRST of ClrkVA; p. 6

PENDLETON, Gurdon H. and PAGE, Jane Byrd; (lic) 9 May 1854; mf# 228

PENDLETON, William Henry of FqrVA and RANDOLPH, Henrietta E. of ClrkVA; (bond) 8 May 1850 by William Henry PENDLETON of FqrVA and Robt. C. RANDOLPH of ClrkVA; p. 175

PETERS, Henry of ClrkVA and CRUM, Elizabeth of ClrkVA; (bond) 9 Mar 1840 by Henry PETERS and Peter CRUM both of ClrkVA; p. 48

PICKETT, John of FqrVA and KERFOOT, Sarah Ann of ClrkVA; (bond) 29 Mar 1850 by John PICKETT of FqrVA and Danl. W. SOWERS of ClrkVA; p. 174

PIERCE, John Junr. of ClrkVA and HARDESTY, Mary Ann of ClrkVA; (bond) 27 Feb 1837 by John PIERCE Junr. of ClrkVA and John PIERCE Senr. of same county; p. 9

PIERCE, Peter McMurray of ClrkVA and KNIGHT, Margaret R. of ClrkVA; (bond) 23 May 1844 by Peter McMurray PIERCE and George KNIGHT both of ClrkVA; p. 102

POP, Conrad of ClrkVA and SWARTZ, Mary Margaret of ClrkVA; (bond) 7 Jan 1843 by Conrad POP and Wm. R. SEEVERS both of ClrkVA; p. 87

POPP, William m. 12 Jun 1852 to BUNT, Christina; (MinRet) 18 Jun 1852 in Berryville by Joshua PETERKIN; mf# 256

POWERS, Philip H. and SMITH, Roberta M.; (lic) 27 Dec 1852; mf# 52

PULLER, Calvin of ClrkVA and BROWN, Patsey Ann of ClrkVA; (bond) 20 Jan 1840 by Calvin PULLER of WrnVA and Matthew W. ROYSTON of ClrkVA; p. 44

PULLIAM, Matthew m. 1 Feb 1848 to BERLIN, Eliza Virginia Newton; (undated MinRet) H. W. DODGE, Pastor, 2nd Bap. Ch., Upperville Va; mf# 229

PULLIAM, Matthew of ClrkVA and BERLIN, Eliza Virginia Newton of ClrkVA; (bond) 31 Jan 1848 by Matthew PULLIAM and Philip BERLIN both of ClrkVA; p. 150

PULSE, Charles of RckhmVA and WOODWARD, Mary Elizabeth of ClrkVA; (bond) 12 May 1846 by Charles PULSE of RckhmVA and George J. BOLTZ of BerkVA; p. 131

PULSE, Charles of RckhmVA m. 12 May 1846 to WOODWARD,
Elizabeth of ClrkVA; (undated MinRet) by H. W. DODGE, 2
Bap. Ch., Up'rville, Va; mf# 275
PULTZ, George of ClrkVA and FISHER, Catharine Ann of
ClrkVA; (bond) 30 Jul 1842 by George PULTZ and Francis H.
WHITING of ClrkVA; p. 75
RANDOLPH, Beverly of U.S. Navy and RANDOLPH, Mary C. of
ClrkVA; (bond) 14 Aug 1847 by Beverly RANDOLPH of U.S.
Navy and Nath'l. Burwell WHITING of ClrkVA; p. 143
RANDOLPH, Wm. Eston, 40y, widowed, farmer, b. Cumberland
Co. Va, res. Henry Co. Va, s/o Wm. F. & Jane C.
RANDOLPH; prop. m. 1 May 1860 in ClrkVA to RANDOLPH,
Susan W., 24y, sgl, b. & res. ClrkVA, d/o Robt. C. & Lucy N.
RANDOLPH; (appl) 30 Apr 1860 by W. E. RANDOLPH; mf#
149
REED, Stephen of ClrkVA and JENKINS, Sarah of ClrkVA;
(bond) 14 Sep 1844 by Stephen REED and Russell
BRACKETT both of ClrkVA; p. 105
REID, Alfred J. of FqrVA and SOWERS, Sarah Catharine of
ClrkVA; (bond) 21 Dec 1846 by Alfred J. REID of FqrVA and
William SOWERS of ClrkVA; p. 136
REID, Stephen and JENKINS, Sarah, over 21y, of ClrkVA; (oath)
14 Sep 1844 by Russell BRACKETT; mf# 153
REINEMAN, Conrad of ClrkVA and BOWLING, Elizabeth of
ClrkVA; (bond) 27 Dec 1843 by Conrad REINEMAN and
George GRUBER of ClrkVA; p. 96
RHODERICK, John m. 1 Sep 1840 to STONESTREET, Ailsey
A.; (undated MinRet) Rev. S. SHIRAS; mf# 293
RHODERICK, John of JeffVA and STONESTREET, Ailsey Ann
of ClrkVA and; (bond) 31 Aug 1840 by John RHODERICK of
JeffVA and Thomas L. BLAKEMORE of Battle Town ClrkVA;
p. 55
RICHARDSON, John D. of Buchanan Co., Missouri and
RICHARDSON, Mary Cornelia of ClrkVA; (bond) 11 May
1846 by John D. RICHARDSON of Buchanan Co., Missouri
and Thornton P. PENDLETON of ClrkVA; p. 130
RIELY, John J. and TAYLOR, Lucy O.; (lic) 22 Nov 1856; mf#
184
RILEY, William, age not known exactly, sgl, farmer, b. WrnVA,
res. ClrkVA, s/o George & Susannah RILEY; m. 26 Oct 1858
in ClrkVA to ANDERSON, Julia, age not known exactly, sgl,
b. LdnVA, res. ClrkVA, d/o John & Nancy ANDERSON;

(MinRet) 27 Oct 1858 by W. G. WILLIAMS, Minister of the M.
E. Church South; mf# 167

RIPPEN, John J. and HOUGH, Malissi Jane; (cnst) 14 Dec 1853 by Cornelius HOFF, father; mf# 163

RITTER [also written as RITECOR], John of FredVA and BRUMLEY, Mary of ClrkVA; (bond) 25 Mar 1848 by John RITTER of FredVA and Saml. BRUMLEY of ClrkVA; p. 152

RITTER, George Wm., 27y, sgl, laborer, b. FredVA, res. ClrkVA, s/o John RITTER & Susan HOOVER; prop. m. 17 Apr 1860 in ClrkVA to LIMERICK, Mary C., 22y, sgl, b. FredVA, res. ClrkVA, d/o Wm. LIMERICK & Eliza LIMERICK; (appl) 16 Apr 1860 by George W. RITTER; mf# 74

ROBERTS, James L. of BerkVA and RIDGWAY, Eliza Ann of ClrkVA; (bond) 2 Mar 1839 by James L. ROBERTS of BerkVA and Richard RIDGEWAY of ClrkVA; p. 30

ROBERTS, James L. of BerkVA and RIDGWAY, Eliza Ann; (cnst) 2 Mar 1839 by Richard RIDGWAY, father. Witness Jno. HAYS; mf# 205

ROBERTS, James m. ___ to RIDGEWAY, Sarah (Mrs.); (MinRet) 8 Mar ___ by ___; mf# 193

ROBINSON, R. Sidney of ClrkVA and BOWEN, Margaret A. of ClrkVA; (bond) 9 Jul 1849 by R. Sidney ROBINSON and Strother H. BOWEN both of ClrkVA; p. 165

ROBINSON, William Harrid?, 24y, sgl, b. FqrVA, res. ClrkVA, farmer, s/o John & Agnes ROBINSON; m. 19 Oct 1858 in ClrkVA to OREAR, Mary Bettie, 22y, b. & res. ClrkVA, d/o George & Catharine OREAR; (MinRet) 19 Oct 1858 by W. G. WILLIAMS; mf# 37

RODERICK, William m. 7 Oct 1841 to CHISM, Maria; (MinRet) 27 Oct 1842 in Richmond Co. by R. N. HERNDON; mf# 249

RODERICK, William of JeffVA and CHISM, Maria of ClrkVA; (bond) 6 Oct 1841 by William RODERICK of JeffVA and James C. KENNON of Berryville; p. 67

RODRICK, William of Jefferson Co. and CHISM, Maria; (cnst) 6 Oct 1841 by Maria CHISM [ink blotch]. Teste John RICK, William WISE; mf# 128

ROGERS, Theodore Esqr. of New York and BAKER, Harriet (Miss, of New York now a member of my family); (cnst) 23 May 1836, by Geo. H. BURWELL; mf# 13

ROGERS, Theodore of New York and BAKER, Harriet now of ClrkVA; (bond) 7 Jun 1836 by Theodore ROGERS of New York state and Geo. H. BURWELL of ClrkVA; p. 3

ROSE, William A. of ClrkVA and ANDERSON, Joannah Green of ClrkVA; (bond) 21 Dec 1841 by William A. ROSE and Harrison CRAWFORD both of ClrkVA; p. 70
ROSS, Charles and DAVIS, Margaret; (lic): 22 Aug 1855; mf# 268
ROSS, Simon M. and BUTLER, Sarah Ann; (lic) 18 Dec 1859; mf# 232
RUSSELL, Jessee and GRUBB, Mary A.; (undated cnst) James W. TANQUARY for his ward Mary; mf# 155
RUSSELL, Theodrick m. 21 Apr 1853 to CHAMBLINE, Martha E.; (undated MinRet) F. ISRAEL; mf# 46B
RYAN, Joseph F. and McCORMICK, Ann J.; (cnst) 11 Dec 1858 by Otway McCORMICK, father; mf# 162
RYAN, Joseph F., 33y, sgl, Sheriff of ClrkVA, b. JeffVA, res. Berryville, s/o James and Ann RYAN; prop. m. 14 Dec 1858 at Berry's Ferry to McCORMICK, Ann J., 23y, single b. ClrkVA, resides Berry's Ferry, d/o Otway McCORMICK & Sarah A. McCORMICK; (appl) dated 13 Dec 1858 by Jos. F. RYAN; mf# 145
SAUNDERS, Alexander and BRAWNER, Eliza, over 21y, of ClrkVA; (oath) 4 Jun 1847 by Eliza BRAWNER. Teste Jas. C. KENNAN, Mary KENNAN; mf# 118
SAUNDERS, Alexander of ClrkVA and BRAWNER, Eliza of ClrkVA; (bond) 5 Jun 1847 by Alexander SAUNDERS and Jas. C. KENNON both of ClrkVA; p. 141
SAUNDERS, Alex'r. m. 9 Jun 1847 to BRAWNER, Eliza; (undated MinRet) Rich'd. H. WILMER, Minister of Prot. Episcopal Church in the Diocese of Virginia; mf# 327
SCHULTZ, George W. of ClrkVA and STONER, Judith Ann of Clarke; (bond) 21 Aug 1850 by George W. SCHULTZ and Joseph F. RYAN both of ClrkVA; p. 176
SEEVERS, William R. of ClrkVA and HUMPHREYS, Emily E. of ClrkVA; (bond) 24 Nov 1840 by William R. SEEVERS and Treadwell SMITH both of ClrkVA; p. 58
SEEVERS, Wm. R. of ClrkVA m. 24 Nov 1840 to HUMPHREYS, Emily E. of ClrkVA; (MinRet) 4 Jan 1841 by W. M. ATKINSON, Pastor of the Presbyterian Church of Winchester; mf# 48
SHACKLEFORD, James H. of Richmond Co., Va and SYDNOR, Mary L. of ClrkVA; (bond) 22 Apr 1839 by James H. SHACKLEFORD of Richmond Co., Va and Saml. B. REDMAN of ClrkVA; p. 35

SHAFFER, John and LLOYD, Mary Frances; (cnst) 23 Jul 1855 by John LLOYD, father. Teste A. J. BRADFIELD; mf# 93

SHAULL, David of JeffVA and HUYETT, Mary Ann of ClrkVA; (bond) 31 Oct 1842 by David SHAULL of JeffVA and John HUYETT of ClrkVA; p. 80

SHEARRER, Jas. M., 23y, sgl, wagon maker, b. ShenVA, res. ClrkVA, s/o H. T. & Elizabeth SHEARRER; m. 15 Feb [1859] at Millwood to NEVILLE, Martha S., 20y, sgl, b. & res. ClrkVA, d/o J. H. & Mary A. NEVILLE; (MinRet) 15 Feb 1859 by Jno. W. HART; mf# 274

SHELL, Craven, 23y, sgl, b. LdnVA, res. ClrkVA, farmer, s/o John W. & Margaret SHELL; prop. m. 27 Dec 1860 in ClrkVA to BELL, Lucinda, 22y, sgl, b. & res. ClrkVA, d/o James & Nancy BELL; (appl) dated 25 Dec 1860 by Craven SHELL; mf# 18

SHEPHERD, Carter m. 17 Jan 1847 to SOWERS, Lucy; (undated MinRet) Rich'd. H. WILMER, Minister of Prot. Episcopal Church in the Diocese of Virginia; mf# 325

SHEPHERD, Carter of ClrkVA and SOWERS, Lucy Virginia of ClrkVA; (bond) 13 Jan 1847 by Carter SHEPHERD and William SOWERS both of ClrkVA; p. 137

SHEPHERD, Champ of ClrkVA and RICHARDSON, Susan O. of ClrkVA; (bond) 13 Jan 1849 by Champ SHEPHERD and Thornton P. PENDLETON both of ClrkVA; p. 162

SHEPHERD, Champ of ClrkVA and ISLER, Sarah Ann of ClrkVA; (bond) 30 Oct 1839 by Champ SHEPHERD and Jacob ISLER of ClrkVA; p. 40

SHEPHERD, Chump [Champ]; and RICHARDSON, Susan O., over 21y, of ClrkVA; (cnst) 13 Jan 1849 by Thornton P. PENDLETON who made oath as to consent of John RICHARDSON, the father of bride; mf# 97

SHIMP, George W. of FredVA and CRIM, Juliana of ClrkVA; (bond) 10 Sep 1850 by George W. SHIMP of FredVA and Jacob CRIM of ClrkVA; p. 177

SHIPE, Benjamin H. and BILLMYRE, Han[n]ah Frances; (cnst) 14 Sep 1852 by Matilda BILLMYRE, mother. Test. Jas. W. JOHNSTON; mf# 137

SHIPE, Benjamin H. m. 16 Sep 1852 to BILLMYRE, Hannah Frances; (MinRet) 16 Sep 1852 by J. F. HOFF, Millwood; mf# 140

SLUSHER, Hezekiah of ClrkVA and RYAN, Mary Ann of ClrkVA; (bond) 27 Feb 1843 by Hezekiah SLUSHER of ClrkVA and Jas. RIAN/RYAN of ClrkVA; p. 88

SMALLWOOD, Burr of ClrkVA and TUMBLIN, Louisa of ClrkVA; (bond) 14 Feb 1839 by Burr SMALLWOOD and William MORGAN of ClrkVA; p. 30

SMALLWOOD, Elisha m. 2 Feb [1851] to PARKER, Elizabeth; (MinRet) 11 Mar 1851 [or 1861, page creased on microfilm but typed index states 1851] by R ???? [too dark to read], Minister of the Gospel; mf# 21

SMALLWOOD, Thomas O., over 21y and KURL, Martha E. of ClrkVA; (oath) 19 Jun 1848 by John Westley SMALLWOOD, father; mf# 104

SMALLWOOD, Thomas Otway of LdnVA and CARROLL, Martha Ellen of ClrkVA; (bond) 21 Jun 1848 by Thomas Otway SMALLWOOD of LdnVA and John CARROLL of ClrkVA; p. 156

SMITH, James W. of ClrkVA and HIETT, Hannah of ClrkVA; (bond) 17 Feb 1842 by James W. SMITH and James E. RUSSELL both of ClrkVA; p. 72

SMITH, John m. 19 Nov 1844 to GANT, Kizzah J.; (undated MinRet) Jos. BAKER; mf# 247

SMITH, John of JeffVA and GANT, Kesiah G. of ClrkVA; (bond) 15 Nov 1844 by John SMITH of JeffVA and John GANT of ClrkVA; p. 106

SMITH, John S. of LdnVA and JACKSON, Martha E. T. of ClrkVA; (bond) 3 May 1848 by John S. SMITH of LdnVA and Ebin T. HANCOCK of ClrkVA; p. 153

SMITH, Jonathan m. 22 Sep 1845 to ISLER, Rebecca; (undated MinRet) Richard H. WILMER, Minister of the P. E. Church in the Diocese of Virginia; mf# 284

SMITH, Jonathan S. N. of ClrkVA and ISLER, Rebecca Ann of ClrkVA; (bond) 20 Sep 1845 by Jonathan S. N. SMITH and Jacob ISLER Esqr. both of ClrkVA; p. 118

SMITH, Joseph m. 24 Nov 1842 to GANT, Harriet N.; (undated MinRet) Jos. BAKER; mf# 304

SMITH, Joseph of Jefferson Co. and GANT, Harriet Newton, over 21y, of ClrkVA; (oath) 22 Nov 1842 by Martin GANT; mf# 88

SMITH, Joseph of JeffVA and GANT, Harriett Newton of ClrkVA; (bond) 22 Nov 1842 by Joseph SMITH of JeffVA and Martin GANT of ClrkVA; p. 82

SMITH, Stephen F., 42y, sgl, printer, b. Frederick Co., res. Clarksburg Va, s/o Wm. & Margaret SMITH; prop. m. 22 Nov 1859 in ClrkVA to TIMBERLAKE, Isabella, 28y, sgl, b. Frederick Co., res. ClrkVA, d/o Richard & Sarah TIMBERLAKE; (appl) 19 Nov 18[5]9 by S. F. SMITH; mf# 66

SMITH, Treadwell Jr. and McGUIRE, Lucy E. H.; (lic) 5 Nov 1859; mf# 225

SNYDER, John O. m. 25 Nov. 1852 to LOUTHAN, Lucy C.; (undated MinRet) H. W. DODGE, Pastor; mf# 187

SOWERS, Jas. W. and KERFOOT, Mary Smith; (cnst) 2 Dec 1854 in Greenville by Geo. L. KERFOOT, father; mf# 142

SOWERS, Wm. B. C. of ClrkVA and BONHAM, Lucy C. of ClrkVA; (bond) 16 Sep 1850 by Wm. B. SOWERS and Danl. S. BONHAM both of ClrkVA; p. 178

STARKIE, Benjamin m. 22 Dec 1840 to FURR, Jane W.; (undated MinRet) Rev. Alexander SHIRAS; mf# 14

STARKIE/STARKEY, Benjamin of ClrkVA and FURR, Jane Wilda of ClrkVA; (bond) 17 Dec 1840 by Benjamin STARKIE and Moses FURR both of ClrkVA; p. 59

STARTZMAN, Nath'l. of JeffVA and MARTIN, Ellen F. of ClrkVA; (bond) 16 Apr 1849 by Nath'l. STARTZMAN of JeffVA and Archibald BOWEN of ClrkVA; p. 163

STEPHENSON, James Wm. of FredVA and MOSS, Gertrude of ClrkVA; (bond) 20 May 1848 by James Wm. STEPHENSON of FredVA and John HAY of ClrkVA; p. 154

STEPTOE, Robt. C. of Bedford Co., Va and SCOTT, Elmina? L. of ClrkVA; (bond) 31 Oct 1842 by Robt. C. STEPTOE of Bedford Co., Va and John A. THOMSON of ClrkVA; p. 80

STEWART, Bushrod of JeffVA and HART, Mary of ClrkVA; (bond) 17 Aug 1844 by Bushrod STEWART of JeffVA and Edwin HART of ClrkVA; p. 103

STEWART, Joseph of ClrkVA and STEWART, Harriet Amanda of ClrkVA; (bond) 21 Aug 1844 by Joseph STEWART of ClrkVA and John SAPPINGTON of ClrkVA; p. 104

STEWART, Joseph of ClrkVA and STEWART, Harriet Amanda, over 21y, of ClrkVA; (oath) 21 Aug 1844 by John SAPPINGTON; mf# 152

STICKLE, Henry, 21y, sgl, farmer, b. & res. ClrkVA, s/o. Simon STICKLES & Amelia STICKLES; prop. m. 16 Dec 1860 in ClrkVA to WRITT, Susan E., 25y, sgl, b. FqrVA, res. ClrkVA, d/o Thompson WRITT & Elizabeth WRITT; (appl) 13 Dec 1860 by Henry STICKLES; mf# 67

STICKLE, Joseph of LdnVA and ASHBY, Harriet of ClrkVA; (bond) 26 Jun 1841 by Joseph STICKLE of LdnVA and Martin ASHBY of ClrkVA; p. 64

STICKLE, Joseph of LdnVA and ASHBY, Harriet, over 21y, of ClrkVA; (oath) 26 Jun 1841 by Martin ASHBY; mf# 86

STIPE, George E. of FredVA and ANDERSON, Harriet C. of ClrkVA; (bond) 2 Mar 1840 by George E. STIPE and Joseph ANDERSON; p. 47

STONESTREET, Benjamin m. 13 Feb 1845 to FOWLER, Roxanna; (undated MinRet) Richard H. WILMER, Minister of the P. E. Church in the Diocese of Virginia; mf# 278

STONESTREET, Benjamin of ClrkVA and FOWLER, Roxann of ClrkVA; (bond) 13 Feb 1845 by Benjamin STONESTREET and William A. COOPER; p. 109

STONESTREET, Benjamin, over 21y, of ClrkVA and FOWLER, Roxann; (oath) 13 Feb 1845 by Roxann FOWLER. Wit: Jas. C. KENNAN, William A. COOPER; mf# 115

STONESTREET, Edward of ClrkVA and KING, Matilda of ClrkVA; (bond) 1 Nov 1843 by Edw'd. STONESTREET of ClrkVA and Mason OREM of LdnVA; p. 94

SWAIN, James Harrison of ClrkVA and HISKETT, Louisa June of ClrkVA; (bond) 5 Oct 1848 by James Harrison SWAIN and William HISKETT of ClrkVA; p. 158

SWARTS, Charles and McCORMICK, Isabella; (undated cnst) Samuel McCORMICK, father. Teste A. J. BRADFIELD.; mf# 151

SWARTZ, Christian H. and KENT, Sarah Ann; (lic) 30 Dec 1858; mf# 227

SWARTZ, Christian H., 25y, sgl, res. Sniggersville; m. 2 Jan 1859 at Mr. DIFFENDAFER's to KENT, Sarah Ann, age not given, sgl, res. Mr. DIFFENDAFFER's, ClrkVA; (MinRet) 2 Jan 1859 by Henderson PATER, Minister of the Episcopal Church, Rector of Epic. Ch., Berryville; mf# 171

SWARTZ, David of ClrkVA and GORDON, Nancy of ClrkVA; (bond) 6 May 1840 by David SWARTZ and John GORDON both of ClrkVA; p. 50

SWARTZ, Franklin m. 3 Nov 1851 to BRUMLEY [or BRUMBLEY], Rebecca; (undated MinRet) Jos. BAKER; mf# 262

SYDNOR, Richard M. of Winchester and JACKSON, Matilda Jane of ClrkVA; (bond) 10 Mar 1842 by Richard M. SYDNOR of Winchester and Wm. P. WIGGENTON of ClrkVA; p. 73

SYDNOR, Richard M. of Winchester and JACKSON, Matilda Jane; (cnst) 4 Mar 1842 by Solomon R. JACKSON, father. Teste Thomas W. RAYNOLDS, W. P. WIGGINTON; mf# 125

TAPP, Lewis m. 9 Sep 1847 to ALBIN, Rachel; (undated MinRet) Rich'd. H. WILMER, Minister of Prot. Episcopal Church in the Diocese of Virginia; mf# 329

TAPSCOTT, Rob. m. 4 Apr 1843 to WOOD, Lucy F.; (undated MinRet) Jos. BAKER; mf# 296

TAPSCOTT, Robert of ClrkVA and WOOD, Lucy F. of ClrkVA; (bond) 4 Apr 1843 by Robert TAPSCOTT and Jas. T. WOOD of ClrkVA; p. 89

TAPSCOTT, Robert of FqrVA and WOOD, Lucy F. of ClrkVA, over 21y, of ClrkVA; (oath) 4 Apr 1843 by James T. WOOD; mf# 28

TAYLOR, John Henry of ClrkVA and THOMPSON, Maria (Mrs.), of age, of ClrkVA; (oath) 13 D[ec? - torn] 1851 by John ANDERSON; mf# 114

TEMPLEMAN, William S. m. 1 Apr 1851 to IDEN, Mary Catharine; (MinRet) 2 Sep ___ in Paris, Va by Thaddeus HERNDON; mf# 265

THATCHER, Thomas m. 16 Jan 1853 to ELLIOT, Catherine E.; (MinRet) 17 Jan 1853 by Rev. Wm. D. HANSON; mf# 261

THOMAS, Joseph T. of Philadelphia and MITCHELL, Belinda J. of ClrkVA; (bond) 10 Jun 1845 by Joseph T. THOMAS of Philadelphia and Joseph T. STROTHER of ClrkVA; p. 116

THOMPSON, Adam F. of ClrkVA and YOWELL, Mary E. of ClrkVA; (bond) 2 Dec 1848 by Adam F. THOMPSON and Simon YOWELL of ClrkVA; p. 160

THOMPSON, Balys/Baylis of LdnVA and COUTER, Margaret Ann of ClrkVA; (bond) 21 Aug 1847 by Balys THOMPSON of LdnVA and Edgar M. LANHAM of ClrkVA; p. 143

THOMPSON, George W. and STEWART, Mary Elenor; (cnst) 22 Dec 1852 by John STEWART, father; mf# 127

THOMPSON, William, 21y, sgl, farmer, res. ClrkVA, s/o Harrison & Maria m. Sat. 11 Feb 1854 to COOPER, Angelina, 18y, sgl, res. ClrkVA, d/o John & Eliz'h COOPER; (MinRet) 13 Feb 1854 in Berryville by F. ISRAEL, Minister; mf# 198

TIMBERLAKE, Richard; m. 25 Apr 1838 to LARUE, Frances C.; (undated MinRet) Tho. BUCK Jr.; mf# 244

TIMBERLAKE, Richard of Berkeley Co.; and LARUE, Francis C.; (cnst) 23 Apr 1838 by Samuel LARUE of ClrkVA, father. Teste Jno. HAY; mf# 61

TIMBERLAKE, Richard of BerkVA and LARAUE [LARUE], Frances C. of ClrkVA; (bond) 23 Apr 1838 by Richard TIMBERLAKE of BerkVA and Samuel LARUE; p. 21

TINSMAN, Andrew J. m. 7 Aug 1851 to CHAMBLIN, Eveline; (MinRet) 13 Aug 1851 in Berryville by Joshua PETERKIN, Rector of Wickliffe Parish, ClrkVA; mf# 179

TINSMAN, Andrew Jackson and CHAMBLIN, Eveline, over 21y, of ClrkVA; (oath) 5 Aug 1851 by Hemburn T. CHAMBLIN; mf# 129

TINSMAN, Andrew Jackson and CHAMBLIN, Evoline; (cnst) 5 Aug 1851 by Aaron CHAMBLIN, father; mf# 133

TINSMAN, George and MORELAND, Mary; (bond) 24 Feb 1840 by George TINSMAN and Abram H. BEAVERS; p. 46

TINSMAN, John Montreville and DUNCAN, Susan E.; (cnst) 18 Dec 1842 by Elizabeth LANHAM, grandmother. Witness Edgar LANHAM, Nimrod GLASSCOCK; mf# 120

TINSMAN, John Montreville of LdnVA and DUNCAN, Susan E. of ClrkVA; (bond) 19 Dec 1842 by John Montreville TINSMAN of LdnVA and Edgar LANHAM of ClrkVA; p. 83

TINSMAN, Saml. of LdnVA and LANHAM, Frances of ClrkVA; (bond) 30 Oct 1843 by Saml. TINSMAN and John M. TINSMAN of LdnVA; p. 94

TINSMAN, Thomas W. of ClrkVA and DOWNING, Acinia of ClrkVA; (bond) 7 Feb 1843 by Thomas W. TINSMAN and Benjamin DOWNING both of ClrkVA; p. 88

[TRIPLETT, Enoch] [see bond below] and ASHBY, Araannah; (cnst) 7 Sep 1843 by John ASHBY. Teste Martin ASHBY, Henery LLOYD; mf# 60

TRIPLETT, Enoch of ClrkVA and ASHBY, Araunnah of ClrkVA; (bond) 7 Sep 1843 by Enoch TRIPLETT and Martin ASHBY both of ClrkVA; p. 92

TRUSSELL, Ebin of LdnVA and FLEMING, Sivannah of ClrkVA; (bond) 21 Jan 1839 by Ebin TRUSSELL of LdnVA and Joseph FLEMING of ClrkVA; p. 28

TUCKER, Alfred B. and TAYLOR, Eliza; (lic) 19 Aug 1856; mf# 2

TUMBLIN, Snowden m. 17 Apr 1845 to WILEY, Mary Jane; (undated MinRet) Richard H. WILMER, Minister of the P. E. Church in the Diocese of Virginia; mf# 282

TUMBLIN, Snowden of ClrkVA and WILEY, Mary Jane of ClrkVA; (bond) 17 Apr 1845 by Snowden TUMBLIN, James WILEY and John LONGERBEAM all of ClrkVA; p. 113

TURNER, John m. 7 Apr 1853 to CORNWELL, Rose Anna; (undated MinRet) H. W. DODGE; mf# 221

TURNER, Thos, 27y, sgl, b. WashDC, res. ClrkVA, physician, s/o Thos. & Ellen TURNER; m. 12 Jun 1860 in ClrkVA to JANNEY, R. Belle, 19y, sgl, b. LdnVA, res. ClrkVA, d/o J. J. & O. A. JANNEY; (MinRet) 12 Jun 1860 by Chas. WHITE, Minister of the Gospel; mf# 36

TYSON, Isaac 3rd and THORNTON, Frances H.; (lic) 3 Oct 1854; mf# 199

TYSON, Isaac 3rd, 21y, sgl, merchant, b. Baltimore, Md, s/o Isaac Jr. & Hannah Ann TYSON; m. 4 Oct 1854 at Howard F. THORNTON's to THORNTON, Frances Hawes, 19y, sgl, b. RappVA, d/o Edward F. & Charlotte A. THORNTON; (MinRet) 10 Oct 1854 by Francis M. WHITTLE, Min. of Prot. Episcopal Ch.; mf# 266

VA[N]METER, William E. of Madison Co., Ohio and SHIP, Lucy L. of ClrkVA; (bond) 2 Oct 1838 by William E. VANMETER of Madison Co., Ohio and John SHIP of ClrkVA; p. 25

VANDEVENTER, Cornelius and MORGAN, Mary C.; (lic) 19 Nov 1860; mf# 238

VANDEVENTER, Cornelius, 31y, sgl, b. & res. LdnVA, farmer, s/o Isaac & Mary VANDEVENTER; prop. m. 21 Nov 1860 in ClrkVA to MORGAN, Mary C., 23y, sgl, b. & res. ClrkVA, d/o Benj. & Martha MORGAN; (appl) 19 Nov 1860 by C. VANDEVENTER; mf# 31

VASSE, Joseph Ambrose of Frederick Co. and JACKSON, Mary E. of ClrkVA; (bond) 23 Jun 1838 by Joseph Ambrose VASSE of FredVA and Arthur W. CARTER also of FredVA; p. 22

VAUGHAN, William F. of LdnVA and REED, Theresa of ClrkVA; (bond) 6 Feb 1839 by William T. VAUGHAN of LdnVA and William BALL of said county; p. 29

WAINWRIGHT, Jonathan M. of U.S. Navy and PAGE, Maria of ClrkVA; (bond) 5 Feb 1844 by Jonathan M. WAINWRIGHT of U.S. Navy and Robert P. PAGE of ClrkVA; p. 98

WALKER, James W. and BROWNLEY, Fanny; (cnst) 21 Nov 1854 at Brindon Meadow, ClrkVA by Fanny BROWNLEY; mf# 144

WARD, Geo. W. of CulpVA and FUNSTON, Julia Ann, over 21y, of ClrkVA; (oath) 9 Apr 1844 by Oliver R. FUNSTON, brother; mf# 116

WARD, George W. of CulpVA and FUNSTEN, Julia Ann of ClrkVA; (bond) 9 Apr 1844 by George W. WARD of CulpVA and Oliver R. FUNSTEN of ClrkVA; p. 100

WARE, Josiah Wm. m. 30 Jan 1845 to SMITH, Edmonia J.; (undated MinRet) Richard H. WILMER, Minister of the P. E. Church in the Diocese of Virginia; mf# 277

WARE, Josiah Wm. of ClrkVA and SMITH, Edmonia J. of ClrkVA; (bond) 29 Jan 1845 by Josiah W. WARE and John HAY both of ClrkVA; p. 109

WATSON, David H. of ClrkVA and WATSON, Susan of ClrkVA; (bond) 2 Apr 1850 by David H. WATSON and John WATSON both of ClrkVA; p. 174

WATSON, Josiah of JeffVA and LOCK, Ann Rebecca of ClrkVA; (bond) 29 Dec 1847 by Josiah WATSON and Ephraim WATSON both of JeffVA; p. 147

WELSH, Daniel, 21y, sgl, b. JeffVA, res. ClrkVA, farmer, s/o Jacob WELSH & Sally WELSH; prop. m. 9 Aug 1859 in ClrkVA to WINPIEGLER, Mary Ann Rebecca, 20y, sgl, b. FredVA, res. ClrkVA, d/o Jos. & Mary WINPIEGLER; (appl) 6 Aug 1859 by Daniel WELSH; mf# 30

WEST, Thomas m. 1 Apr 1847 to McCORMICK, Eliz'th; (undated MinRet) Rich'd. H. WILMER, Minister of Prot. Episcopal Church in the Diocese of Virginia; mf# 326

WEST, Thomas of JeffVA and McCORMICK, Ann Elizabeth of ClrkVA; (bond) 30 Mar 1847 by Thomas WEST of JeffVA and William WILLIS of ClrkVA; p. 140

WHARTON, William T. m. 9 Nov 1852 to MOSS, Elizabeth D.; (undated MinRet) J. F. HOFF, Millwood; mf# 222

WHITE, Joseph A., 27y, sgl, laborer, b. Hampshire Co. Va, res. ClrkVA, s/o James WHITE & Mary WHITE; prop. m. 15 Jan 1861 in ClrkVA to SWARTZ, Mary F., age not given, sgl, b. & res. ClrkVA, d/o Phoebe SWARTZ; (appl) 15 Jan 1861 by Joseph A. WHITE; mf# 231

WHITE, Josiah R. and TAYLOR, Frances Virginia; (lic) 3 Sep 1855; mf# 233

WHITE, Josiah R., 35y, sgl, merchant, b. LdnVA, s/o Josiah & Sarah WHITE; m. 6 Sep 1855 at "Clifton" ClrkVA to TAYLOR, Frances Virg'a., 22y, sgl, b. ClrkVA, d/o John B. & Susan TAYLOR; (MinRet) 8 Sep 1855 by Francis M. WHITTLE, Minister of the Protestant Episcopal; mf# 253

WHITING, Francis H. of ClrkVA and HUYETT, Rebecca of ClrkVA; (bond) 18 Mar 1840 by Francis H. WHITING and Abraham HUYETT both of ClrkVA; p. 49

WHITING, William W. of Fairfax Co. Va and WHITING, Lucy Elizabeth of ClrkVA; (bond) 9 Mar 1839 by William W. WHITING of Fairfax Co. Va and Robt. H. LITTLE of ClrkVA; p. 31

WHITTINGTON, Albert C. of FredVA and BRUMLEY, Nancy of ClrkVA; (bond) 4 May 1842 by Albert C. WHITTINGTON of FredVA and Lewis BRUMLEY of ClrkVA; p. 74

WILEY, George W. of ClrkVA and CARROLL, Mary of ClrkVA; (bond) 2 Dec 1850 by George W. WILEY and John CARROLL both of ClrkVA; p. 2

WILEY, James m. 4 Nov 1847 to LONGERBEAM, Rebecca; (undated MinRet) Rich'd. H. WILMER, Minister of Prot. Episcopal Church in the Diocese of Virginia; mf# 332

WILEY, James of ClrkVA and LONGERBEAM, Rebecca of ClrkVA; (bond) 4 Nov 1847 by James WILEY and Richard F. BEAVERS both of ClrkVA; p. 146

WILEY, John and LONGERBEAM, Sibby, of age; (cnst) 19 Mar 1851 by Georg[e] LONGERBEAM, father. Teste John L. LITTLETON?, Richard SWIFT; mf# 83

WILEY, John and LONGERBEAM, Sibby, over 21y, of ClrkVA; (oath) 20 Mar 1851 by Anne LONGERBEAM, sister; mf# 160

WILEY, John m. 20 Mar 1851 to LONGERBEAM, Sibby; (MinRet) 13 Aug 1851 in Berryville by Joshua PETERKIN, Rector of Wickliffe Parish, ClrkVA; mf# 178

WILEY, Samuel m. 4 Jun 1840 to MARTS, Elizabeth; (undated MinRet) Rev. S. SHIRAS; mf# 291

WILEY, Samuel of ClrkVA and MARTS, Elizabeth of ClrkVA; (bond) 17 Mar 1840 by Samuel WILEY and John MARTS both of ClrkVA; p. 49

WILKINSON, William of ClrkVA and STONESTREET, Matilda (Mrs.) of ClrkVA; (bond) 23 Sep 1847 by William WILKINSON and William DEAHL of ClrkVA; p. 145

WILKINSON, Wm. m. 23 Sep 1847 to STONESTREET, Matilda; (undated MinRet) Rich'd. H. WILMER, Minister of Prot. Episcopal Church in the Diocese of Virginia; mf# 330

WILLCOX, David H. of ClrkVA and LOCK, Mary (Mrs.) of ClrkVA; (bond) 22 Apr 1845 by David H. WILLCOX of ClrkVA and Joseph HOUT of JeffVA; p. 114

Clarke County, Virginia Marriages
1836-1861
51

WILLCOX, David H. of ClrkVA and LOCK, Mary (Mrs.), over 21y, of ClrkVA; (oath) 22 Apr 1845 by Joseph HOUT; mf# 135

WILLIAMS, Erasmus P. and SMITH, Rebecca A.; (lic) 10 Jan 1861; mf# 248

WILLIAMSON, Samuel D. of FqrVA and BROOKE, Sarah W. of ClrkVA; (bond) 25 Jun 1839 by Samuel D. WILLIAMSON of FqrVA and Thomas H. CROW of Berryville; p. 36

WILLINGHAM, John Thomas, 26y, sgl, farmer, b. & res. ClrkVA, s/o William & Matilda WILLINGHAM; m. 29 Jul 1858 in ClrkVA to HORSEMAN, Amanda Ellen, 21y, sgl, b. LdnVA, res. ClrkVA, d/o William & Sarah HORSEMAN; (MinRet) 29 July 1858 by W. G. WILLIAMS, Minister of the M. E. Church South; mf# 170

WILLNGHAM, John T. of ClrkVA and HORSEMAN, Amanda E.; (cnst) 26 Jul 1858 by Wm. HORSEMAN, father?. Teste Wm. T. MILTON; mf# 194

WILSON, Jeremiah of ClrkVA and BILLMYER, Sarah Margaret of ClrkVA; (bond) 16 Jul 1849 by Jeremiah WILSON, Richard BILLMYER and Andrew BILLMYER all of ClrkVA; p. 165

WILY, George W. of ClrkVA m. 5 Dec 1850 to CARROLL, Mary of ClrkVA; (undated MinRet) H. W. DODGE; mf# 259

WOLFE, William of ClrkVA and WILSON, Sarah Jane of ClrkVA; (bond) 2 Mar 1850 by William WOLFE and Tholemiah Rhodes WILSON both of ClrkVA; p. 173

WOOD, George B., 33y? [torn], widower, physician, b. Syracuse, N. Y., s/o Hiram & Lydia WOOD; m. 13 Aug 1857 at Rockland, ClrkVA to BONHAM, Annie, age [torn], sgl, b. ClrkVA, d/o Amos A. & A. Eliza BONHAM; (MinRet) 13 Aug 1857 by Chas. WHITE, Minister of the Gospel; mf# 174

WOOD, James T. of ClrkVA and SHIPE, Melinda of ClrkVA; (bond) 31 Aug 1841 by James T. WOOD & James M. PINE both of ClrkVA; p. 66

WOODWARD, Thomas E. of ClrkVA and SMITH, Mary Ann of ClrkVA; (bond) 17 Jan 1844 by Thomas E. WOODWARD and Joseph SMITH both of ClrkVA; p. 98

WYMAN, Samuel G. of City of Balto., Maryland and BYRD, Mary Armistead of ClrkVA; (bond) 27 Jun 1837 by Samuel G. WYMAN of City of Balto., Maryland and William Byrd PAGE of ClrkVA; p. 13

WYNDHAM, Sidnor Bayley of ClrkVA and RUSSELL, Catharine of ClrkVA; (bond) 7 Oct 1839 by Sidnor Baley WYNDHAM and Thomas W. RUSSELL of ClrkVA; p. 38

YOUNG, William H. of ClrkVA and CARRINGTON, Lucy C. of
ClrkVA; (bond) 24 Dec 1846 by William H. YOUNG and Jno.
C. BONHAM both of ClrkVA; p. 137
YOUNG, William m. 24 Dec 1846 to CARRINGTON, Lucy;
(undated MinRet) Rich'd. H. WILMER, Minister of Prot.
Episcopal Church in the Diocese of Virginia; mf# 324

MARRIAGE REGISTER
1865-1886

ADAMS, Edward (col); s/o Edward & Arabella ADAMS; 22y; sgl; farm hand; b. & res. ClrkVA; m. 26 Nov 1885 at ClrkVA to LONG, Eliza (col); d/o Joseph & Catharine LONG; 22y; sgl; b. & res. ClrkVA; (lic) 25 Nov 1885; p. 129

ADAMS, Frederick (col); s/o Edmund & Ella ADAMS; 26y; sgl; farm hand; b. & res. ClrkVA; m. 6 Jan 1881 at bride's residence to WALKER, Emma (col); d/o Paul & Judy WALKER; 21y; sgl; b. Nelson Co. Va; res. ClrkVA; (lic) 6 Jan 1881; p. 33

ADAMS, R. S.; s/o Geo. T. & Jane L. ADAMS; 27y; wid; merchant; b. FqrVA; res. ClrkVA; m. 6 Feb 1866 at Aspin Hill, ClrkVA to KERFOOT, L. W.; d/o Wm. C. & Eliza A. KERFOOT; 23y; sgl; b. & res. ClrkVA; (lic) 2 Feb 1866; p. 7

ADDISON, Andrew (mulatto); s/o Andrew & Emily ADDISON (col); 23y; sgl; coachman; b. JeffVA; res. Pennsylvania; m. 28 May 1873 at ClrkVA to THROCKMORTON, Fannie (mulatto); d/o James & Virginia THROCKMORTON (col); 19y; sgl; b. & res. ClrkVA; (lic) 26 May 1783; p. 146

ADDISON, Elijah (col); s/o Andrew & Charlotte ADDISON; 33y; sgl; farm hand; b. JeffWVA; res. ClrkVA; m. 28 Sep 1878 at ClrkVA to HARRIS, Arrena (col); d/o not known; 29y; wid; b. WrnVA; res. ClrkVA; (lic) 28 Sep 1878; p. 240

AFFLICK, Philip J.; s/o A. G. & Ann E. AFFLICK; 29y; wid; blacksmith; b. FredVA; res. Berryville; m. 4 Oct 1866 at Berryville to DEAHL, Marcella; d/o Wm. & Ann DEAHL; 23y; sgl; b. ClrkVA; res. Berryville; (lic) 3 Oct 1866; p. 19

ALBIN, James S.; s/o James & Elizabeth ALBIN; 25y; sgl; farmer; b. Hardy Co. Va; res. ClrkVA; m. 18 Nov 1869 at residence of bride's father ClrkVA to EDWARDS, Emma; d/o Henry & Mary Ann EDWARDS; 17y; sgl; b. & res. ClrkVA; (lic) 18 Nov 1869; in presence of bride's father & with his consent; p. 88

ALEXANDER, Benjamin F.; s/o Joel & Catharine ALEXANDER; 22y; sgl; farmer; b. & res. ClrkVA; m. 17 Oct 1872 at ClrkVA to WILLINGHAM, Eliza; d/o Wm. & ___ WILLINGHAM; 23y; sgl; b. & res. ClrkVA; (lic) 16 Oct 1872; p. 134

ALEXANDER, Carter (col); s/o Harry & Winney ALEXANDER; 28y; sgl; farm hand; b. AlbmVA; res. ClrkVA; m. 25 Dec 1867

at ClrkVA to BARBER, Fannie (col); d/o Peter & Fanny
BARBER; 22y; sgl; b. & res. ClrkVA; (lic) 21 Dec 1867; p. 49
ALEXANDER, George A. (col); s/o Charles & Sopha
ALEXANDER; 28y; sgl; farm hand; b. LdnVA; res. ClrkVA; m.
24 Dec 1885 at ClrkVA to JOHNSON, Mary (col); d/o John &
Matilda JOHNSON; 20y; sgl; b. & res. ClrkVA; (lic) 24 Dec
1885; consent given; p. 131
ALEXANDER, Henry M.; s/o Thos. H. & Mary E. ALEXANDER;
26y; sgl; farmer; b. & res. ClrkVA; m. 25 Nov 1885 at
Berryville to GRUBBS, Minnie L.; d/o William & Charlotte M.
GRUBBS; 18y; sgl; b. & res. ClrkVA; (lic) 25 Nov 1885; p. 129
ALEXANDER, John (col); s/o Saml. & Emily ALEXANDER (col);
24y; sgl; farm hand; b. & res. Jefferson Co.; m. 24 Dec 1868
at ClrkVA to HOLMES, Lucinda (col); d/o Bristoe & Ann
HOLMES (col); 21y; sgl; b. & res. ClrkVA; (lic) 23 Dec 1868;
p. 72
ALEXANDER, William C. (col); s/o Chas. & Avia ALEXANDER
(col); 31y; wid; farmer; b. FqrVA; res. ClrkVA; m. 31 May
1868 at ClrkVA to REED, Jinnie (col); d/o Geo. & Ellen REED
(col); 21y; sgl; b. RappVA; res. ClrkVA; (lic) 30 May 1868; p.
61
ALLDER, Robert E.; s/o S. M. and Maria ALLDER; 21y; sgl;
farmer; b. LdnVA; res. ClrkVA; m. 14 Oct 1875 at near
Castleman's Ferry to KNIGHT, Laura V.; d/o George and
Mary KNIGHT; 24y; sgl; b. LdnVA; res. ClrkVA; (lic) 13 Oct
1875; p. 188
ALLEN, Edward (col); s/o Josiah & Mary ALLEN; 32y; sgl; farm
hand; b. Amherst Co. Va; res. ClrkVA; m. 25 Mar 1885 at
Berryville to THOMPSON, Sally (col); d/o James & Laly
THOMPSON; 19y; sgl; b. & res. ClrkVA; (lic) 25 Mar 1885; p.
119
ALLEN, Henry (col); s/o Robert & Amanda ALLEN; 19y; sgl; farm
hand; b. & res. ClrkVA; m. 21 Dec 1876 at Berryville to
REED, Nancy (col); d/o unknown; 21y; sgl; b. JeffWVA; res.
ClrkVA; (lic) 21 Dec 1876; written permission by Amanda
MOSBY (her mark) for her son Henry ALLEN who was born
and raised in this county his occupation farm hand.; p. 212
ALLISON, Richard Newton; s/o John & Sarah ALLISON; 22y;
sgl; farmer; b. & res. ClrkVA; m. 6 Aug 1874 at Berryville to
FURR, Maggie; d/o Daniel & Ellen FURR; 21y; sgl; b. & res.
ClrkVA; (lic) 6 Aug 1874; p. 163

ANDERS, Thos. J.; s/o Moses & Eliza E. ANDERS; 24y; sgl; body maker; b. Woodsboro, FredMD; res. Martinsburg, BerkWVA; m. 21 Sep 1869 at bride's residence to BEEMER, E. Susan; d/o Jno. W. & Emily BEEMER; 20y; sgl; b. FredVA; res. ClrkVA; (lic) 21 Sep 1869; bride's father consent given in person before issuing; p. 85

ANDERSON, Even P.; s/o Nicholas & Annie ANDERSON; 64y; wid; glove business; b. LdnVA; res. FredVA; m. 25 Oct 1881 at Winchester Va to GARVER, Julia Ann; d/o Sariot & ___ CARPER; 39y; wid; b. FredVA; res. ClrkVA; (lic) 24 Oct 1881; p. 49

ANDERSON, Oscar F.; s/o John & Bettie ANDERSON; 27y; sgl; farmer; b. FredVA; res. Iowa; m. 7 Apr 1885 at ClrkVA to ANDERSON, Mary A.; d/o John H. & Ann N. ANDERSON; 23y; sgl; b. & res. ClrkVA; (lic) 6 Apr 1885; p. 120

ANDERSON, Robert A.; s/o Robert & Margaret ANDERSON; 29y; sgl; farmer; b. Scotland; res. ClrkVA; m. 15 Apr 1880 at ClrkVA to HUTCHINSON, Mary T.; d/o E. C. & Lucy HUTCHINSON; 30y; sgl; b. & res. ClrkVA; (lic) 15 Apr 1880; p. 19

ANNAN, Roger P.; s/o James R. & Isabella P. ANNAN; 22y; sgl; merchant; b. Cumberland, Maryland; res. ClrkVA; m. 23 Oct 1867 at bride's residence to HALL, Adelaide S.; d/o Edward & Catharine V. HALL; 18y; sgl; b. & res. ClrkVA; (lic) 22 Oct 1867; p. 44

ASHBY, Benjamin A.; s/o William & Melvina ASHBY; 27y; wid; carpenter; b. WrnVA; res. ClrkVA; m. 28 Mar 1872 at ClrkVA to UNDERWOOD, Sarah M.; d/o Joseph & Harriet UNDERWOOD; 21y; sgl; b. LdnVA; res. ClrkVA; (lic) 28 Mar 1872; p. 128

ASHBY, Benjamin Albert; s/o Wm. & Melvina ASHBY; 34y; wid; miller; b. & res. ClrkVA; m. Thursday 24 Oct 1878 at ClrkVA to KNIGHT, Maggie; d/o George & Mary KNIGHT; 26y; sgl; b. & res. ClrkVA; (lic) 19 Oct 1878; p. 242

ASHBY, Geo. H.; s/o William & Melvina ASHBY; 23y; sgl; carpenter; b. & res. ClrkVA; m. 21 Jul 1869 at bride's residence to HUGHES, Mary B.; d/o Thomas & Bettie HUGHES; 21y; sgl; b. & res. ClrkVA; (lic) 17 Jul 1869; p. 83

ASHBY, George; s/o Robert & Sarah ASHBY; 29y; sgl; farmer; b. ClrkVA; res. LdnVA; m. 5 Nov 1874 at ClrkVA to WILEY, Mary; d/o ___ & Amanda WILEY; 17y; sgl; b. & res. ClrkVA; (lic) 4 Nov 1874; p. 168

ASHBY, James R.; s/o Nimrod & May A. ASHBY; 35y; sgl; farmer; b. & res. ClrkVA; m. 28 Oct 1875 at ClrkVA to HOUGH. G. H.; d/o Samuel & Elizabeth HOUGH; 18y; sgl; b. JeffWVA; res. ClrkVA; (lic) 25 Oct 1875; p. 189
ASHBY, Jno. Robert; s/o Robert ASHBY Jr. & Sarah ASHBY; 20y; sgl; farmer; b. & res. ClrkVA; m. 11 Jul 1867 at ClrkVA to TUMLIN, Angietta; d/o ___ and Sarah TUMLIN; 22y; sgl; b. & res. ClrkVA; (lic) 10 Jul 1867; groom's father being present when this license was issued & his consent given; note stating Mrs. Sarah TUMLIN gives consent for her daughter Angietter to marry; p. 38
ATKINS, William B.; s/o Robert & Rebecca ATKINS; 21y; sgl; shoemaker; b. RappVA; res. ClrkVA; m. 8 Oct 1867 at bride's residence to LOCK, Annie Virginia; d/o Benjamine & Rohemmy LOCK; 21y; sgl; b. & res. ClrkVA; (lic) 8 Oct 1867; p. 43
BACKHOUSE [also given as BACKUS], Geo. H. C.; s/o Geo. & Catharine BACKUS; 40y; sgl; teacher; b. LdnVA; res. JeffWVA; m. 8 May 1877 at Millwood to LANGDON, Lillie E.; d/o Wm. & Almira LANGDON; 21y; sgl; b. JeffWVA; res. ClrkVA; (lic) 8 May 1877; p. 217
BAILY, Cooper (col); s/o Carter & Mary BAILY; 25y; sgl; farm hand; b. FqrVA; res. ClrkVA; m. date not given at ClrkVA to HARRIS, Kate (col); d/o ___ & Kate HARRIS; 21y; sgl; b. & res. ClrkVA; (lic) 9 Feb 1878; p. 231
BAKER, A. Goodwin; s/o A. & T. BAKER; 21y; sgl; business agent; b. Strasburg, ShenVA; res. JeffWVA; m. 24 Oct 1877 at ClrkVA to HARDESTY, Virginia Scollay; d/o Wm. G. & ___ HARDESTY; 23y; sgl; b. & res. ClrkVA; (lic) 19 Oct 1877; p. 224
BAKER, L. W.; s/o not given; 45y; wid; farmer; b. not given; res. Martinsburg, W Va; m. 18 Dec 1879 at ClrkVA to COONTZ, Emma V.; d/o Charles & Louisa COONTZ; 26y; sgl; b. FredVA; res. ClrkVA; (lic) 17 Dec 1879; p. 10
BAKER, Samuel B.; s/o Henry M. & Emma J. BAKER; 27y; sgl; manufacturer; b. & res. Winchester Va; m. 7 May 1884 at bride's residence to ROYER, Annie E.; d/o Jacob C. & Annie ROYER; 26y; sgl; b. Washington Co. Md; res. ClrkVA; (lic) 6 May 1884; p. 100
BAKER, Wm. B.; s/o Martin & Catharine BAKER; 29y; sgl; farmer; b. WrnVA; res. FredVA; m. 13 Mar 1883 at ClrkVA to

NEWCOME, Fanny C.; d/o John & Rebecca NEWCOME; 26y; sgl; b. & res. ClrkVA; (lic) 12 Mar 1883; p. 79
BALDWIN, Welby H.; s/o Joseph & Eliza H. BALDWIN; 23y; sgl; farmer; b. LdnVA; res. ClrkVA; m. 6 Mar 1884 at ClrkVA to GORDON, L. V.; d/o Geo. W. & Lydia GORDON; 23y; sgl; b. & res. ClrkVA; (lic) 8 Mar 1884; p. 96
BALDWIN, William L.; s/o Robert T. & Portia L. BALDWIN; 33y; sgl; farmer; b. & res. FredVA; m. 30 Jun 1880 at ClrkVA to KOUNSLAR, Elizabeth S.; d/o Randolph & Elizabeth KOUNSLAR; 25y; sgl; b. & res. ClrkVA; (lic) 29 Jun 1880; p. 23
BALL, Alfred (col); s/o Timothy & Maria BALL; not given; wid; farm hand; b. FredVA; res. ClrkVA; m. 2 Aug 1877 at ClrkVA to WILLIAMS, Amanda (col); d/o James & Betsy WILLIAMS; not given; sgl; b. Sussex Co. Va; res. ClrkVA; (lic) 2 Aug 1877; p. 220
BALL, Charles W.; s/o Samuel & Catharine BALL; 39y; sgl; Minister of the Gospel; b. & res. LdnVA; m. 14 May 1877 at not given to JACKSON, Rachel E.; d/o Josiah & Mary S. JACKSON; 24y; sgl; b. FredVA; res. ClrkVA; (lic) 14 May 1877; p. 218
BANISTER, James (col); s/o Thomas BANISTER & Martha; 25y; sgl; farm hand; b. & res. ClrkVA; m. 30 Jul 1885 at ClrkVA to BROWN, Eliza (col); d/o ___ & Janie BANISTER [BROWN?]; 17y; sgl; b. St. Louis; res. ClrkVA; (lic) 30 Jul 1885; consent given; p. 123
BANKS, John (col); s/o Felin and Mary BANKS; 22y; sgl; farm hand; b. & res. ClrkVA; m. 3 Feb 1881 at Millwood to MARSTON, Maria (col); d/o Parker and Nancy MARSTON; 23y; sgl; b. & res. ClrkVA; (lic) 26 Jan 1881; p. 34
BANKS, Philip (col); s/o Philip & Ella BANKS; 22y; sgl; farm hand; b. & res. ClrkVA; m. 26 Dec 1878 at ClrkVA to BROWN, Henrietta (col); d/o not known; 22y; sgl; b. & res. ClrkVA; (lic) 26 Dec 1878; p. 250
BANKS, William (col); s/o Fealin & Mary BANKS; 22y; sgl; farm hand; b. & res. ClrkVA; m. 28 Aug 1884 at ClrkVA to HUBBARD, Betsey (col); d/o Parker & Mary HUBBARD; 22y; sgl; b. & res. ClrkVA; (lic) 27 Aug [1884]; p. 104
BANNISTER, Robert (col); s/o Thomas & Martha BANNISTER; 28y; sgl; farm hand; b. & res. ClrkVA; m. 6 Jan 1875 at ClrkVA to BROWN, Jinny (col); d/o Jack _ Garey [Jack & Garey?]; 25y; sgl; b. & res. ClrkVA; (lic) 30 Dec 1874; p. 172

BARBEE, H. C.; s/o Andrew & Louisa BARBEE; 34y; sgl; merchant; b. FqrVA; res. Piedmont, FqrVA; m. 30 Sep 1868 at ClrkVA to SWANN, C. H.; d/o Philip & Ann SWANN; 27y; sgl; b. FredVA; res. ClrkVA; (lic) 21 Sep 1868; p. 66
BARBER, Charles (col); s/o Isaac & Katie BARBER (col); 52y; sgl; farmhand; b. Jefferson Co.; res. ClrkVA; m. date not given at ClrkVA to SMITH, Maria (col); d/o Charles & Charlotte SMITH (col); 25y; sgl; b. & res. ClrkVA; (lic) 12 Oct 1867; p. 43
BARBER, James; s/o William & Patty BARBER; 21y; sgl; farm hand; b. & res. ClrkVA; m. Wednesday 26 Dec 1877 at White Post to EDMONDS, Barbara A.; d/o James & Mary EDMONDS; 22y; sgl; b. & res. ClrkVA; (lic) 26 Dec 1877; p. 229
BARBER, John Abraham; s/o John S. & Rebecca J. BARBER; 23y; sgl; farmer; b. WrnVA; res. FredVA; m. Thursday 24 Oct 1878 at ClrkVA to BAKER, Sarah Elizabeth; d/o Martin R. & Catharine A. BAKER; 21y; sgl; b. WrnVA; res. ClrkVA; (lic) 19 Oct 1878; p. 242
BARBOUR, James (col); s/o Wm. & Pattie BARBOUR; 27y; sgl; farm hand; b. & res. ClrkVA; m. 16 Sep 1886 at Berryville to BURNS, Lucy (col); d/o Jackson & ___ BURNS; 40y; wid; b. LdnVA; res. ClrkVA; (lic) 16 Sep 1886; p. 142
BARBOUR, Michael (col); s/o Isaac & Katy BARBOUR (col); 40y; sgl; cook; b. & res. ClrkVA; m. 22 Oct 1870 at Clay Hill, ClrkVA to SARGENT, Ferlinda (col); d/o not given; 25y; sgl; b. & res. ClrkVA; (lic) not given; p. 101
BARNES, Walter B.; s/o Nathan & Mary BARNES; 28y; sgl; blacksmith; b. & res. JeffWVA; m. 9 Dec 1878 at Berryville to HAZSLETT, Laura W.; d/o Ferdinand F. & Jane C. HAZSLETT; 28y; sgl; b. JeffWVA; res. ClrkVA; (lic) 9 Dec 1878; p. 246
BARNETT, J. Edward; s/o Neill & Elizabeth BARNETT; 37y; sgl; farmer; b. & res. ClrkVA; m. 26 Jul 1881 at Berryville to BERLIN, Lucy V.; d/o Lewis & Elizabeth BERLIN; 31y; sgl; b. & res. ClrkVA; (lic) 25 Jul 1881; p. 44
BARR, George Wm.; s/o Adam & Catharine BARR; 25y; sgl; painter; b. & res. ClrkVA; m. 28 Apr 1884 at Berryville to KERCHEVAL, Mary M.; d/o E. & Ann KERCHEVAL; 23y; sgl; b. & res. ClrkVA; (lic) 28 Apr 1884; p. 99
BARRETT, John B.; s/o Charles & Elizabeth BARRETT; 22y; sgl; carpenter; b. & res. JeffWVA; m. 8 Sep 1885 at ClrkVA to

KENNAN, Florence; d/o Wm. B. & Emily KENNAN; 22y; sgl; b. & res. ClrkVA; (lic) 5 Sep 1885; p. 124
BARTLETT, Joseph A.; s/o Jos. C. & Ann S. BARTLETT; 29y; sgl; merchant; b. WrnVA; res. Winchester Va; m. 5 May 1868 at ClrkVA to TIMBERLAKE, Fannie G.; d/o R. M. S. TIMBERLAKE & Sarah TIMBERLAKE; 26y; sgl; b. & res. ClrkVA; (lic) 4 May 1868; p. 61
BARTLETT, Julius Karr; s/o Henry & Caroline BARTLETT; 36y; sgl; farmer; b. Missouri; res. ClrkVA; m. 12 Dec 1877 at Berryville to BERLIN, Bettie L.; d/o Lewis & Jane E. BERLIN; 22y; sgl; b. & res. ClrkVA; (lic) 11 Dec 1877; p. 227
BARTON, John W.; s/o Bailey & Sarah BARTON; 25y; sgl; farmer; b. LdnVA; res. ClrkVA; m. 6 Jun 1867 at ClrkVA to BEEVERS, Martha M.; d/o Abraham & Pleasant BEEVERS; 23y; sgl; b. & res. ClrkVA; (lic) 5 Jun 1867; p. 37
BAUGHMAN, Cyrus D.; s/o Amos & Julian BAUGHMAN; 24y; sgl; miller; b. Pennsylvania; res. ClrkVA; m. 13 Feb 1878 at Berryville to YOUNG, Mary E.; d/o Wm. H. & Lucy C. YOUNG; 21y; sgl; b. & res. ClrkVA; (lic) 13 Feb 1878; p. 232
BAUGHMAN, Milton A.; s/o Amos & Julia BAUGHMAN; 27y; sgl; miller; b. York Co. Pennsylvania; res. ClrkVA; m. 28 Aug 1884 at ClrkVA to DUBLE, Mary S.; d/o Aaron & Jane E. DUBLE; 23y; sgl; b. & res. ClrkVA; (lic) 28 Aug 1884; p. 104
BAUGHMAN, Silas F.; s/o Harry & Eliz'th BAUGHMAN; 38y; wid; merchant; b. York Co. Penn; res. ClrkVA; m. 25 Feb 1886 at bride's residence to PARSHALL, Laura V.; d/o Vincent & E. A. PARSHALL; 38y; sgl; b. Fayette Co. Penn; res. ClrkVA; (lic) 25 Feb 1886; p. 133
BAXTER, William; s/o John & Catharine BAXTER; 35y; sgl; farmer; b. Maryland; res. ClrkVA; m. 19 Aug 1879 at ClrkVA to ALEXANDER, Sarah E.; d/o James & Jane ALEXANDER; 21y; sgl; b. LdnVA; res. ClrkVA; (lic) 16 Aug 1879; p. 262
BAYLES, Chas. H.; s/o Fielding & Elizabeth BAYLES; 46y; sgl; cooper; b. Stafford Co. Va; res. ClrkVA; m. 29 Oct 1870 at ClrkVA to LONGERBEAM, Elizabeth; d/o ___ & Hannah LONGERBEAM; 43y; sgl; b. & res. ClrkVA; (lic) 27 Oct 1870; p. 102
BAYLES, Thomas; s/o Charles H. & Eliz'th BAYLES; 23y; sgl; farmer; b. & res. ClrkVA; m. 24 Feb 1881 at LdnVA to LITTLETON, Elizabeth; d/o William & Mary LITTLETON; 21y; sgl; b. & res. ClrkVA; (lic) 24 Feb 1881; p. 36

BAYLIS, William M.; s/o Harrison T. & Ann Jane BAYLIS; 29y; sgl; laborer; b. & res. FredVA; m. 21 May 1885 at ClrkVA to HARDESTY, Carrie V.; d/o Charles W. & Jane L. HARDESTY; 24y; sgl; b. & res. ClrkVA; (lic) 19 May 1885; p. 121

BAYLYS, Michael Conway; s/o Harrison & Ann BAYLYS; 28y; sgl; farming; b. & res. FredVA; m. 17 Oct 1878 at ClrkVA to HARDESTY, Julia A.; d/o Charles W. & Jane L. HARDESTY; 24y; sgl; b. & res. ClrkVA; (lic) 14 Oct 1878; p. 241

BEALL, Frank B.; s/o Frank & Martha BEALL; 23y; sgl; plasterer; b. JeffWVA; res. ClrkVA; m. 9 Jan 1884 at ClrkVA to STEEL, Laura J.; d/o John & Mary STEEL; 26y; sgl; b. JeffWVA; res. ClrkVA; (lic) 8 Jan 1884; p. 92

BEALL, Horace; s/o Richard & Susan BEALL; 30y; sgl; hardwar[e] business; b. Frostburg, Allegany Co. Md; res. JeffWVA; m. 8 Sep 1881 at Berryville to RICHARDSON, Cornelia A.; d/o John D. & Mary Cornelia RICHARDSON; not given; sgl; b. & res. ClrkVA; (lic) 5 Sep 1881; p. 46

BEAVERS, Richarard [Richard] F.; s/o A. H. & Pleasant BEAVERS; 46y; wid; farmer; b. LdnVA; res. ClrkVA; m. 13 Nov 1870 at ClrkVA to CARTER, Martha A.; d/o Geo. & Mary CARTER; 22y; sgl; b. FqrVA; res. ClrkVA; (lic) 9 Nov 1870; p. 103

BECKWITH, Frank; s/o Geo. H. & Annie Lloyd BECKWITH; 38y; sgl; lawyer; b. & res. JeffWVA; m. 4 Aug 1886 at Berryville to McDONALD, Annie Leacy; d/o Angus & Elizabeth M. McDONALD; 27y; sgl; b. Hampshire Co. W Va; res. ClrkVA; (lic) 4 Aug 1886; p. 141

BELL, Francis A.; s/o Geo. H. & Emily BELL; 24y; sgl; carpenter; b. & res. ClrkVA; m. 12 Aug 1879 at ClrkVA to COLLIER, Mary L.; d/o John N. & Mary COLLIER; 23y; sgl; b. & res. ClrkVA; (lic) 11 Aug 1879; p. 261

BELL, James A.; s/o Geo. & Emily BELL; 24y; sgl; farmer; b. & res. ClrkVA; m. 18 Jun 1876 at ClrkVA to EATON, Ellen N. E.; d/o Philip & Frances EATON; 17y; sgl; b. ShenVA; res. ClrkVA; (lic) 13 Jun 1876; p. 202

BELL, William L.; s/o William & ___ BELL; 23y; sgl; labourer; b. Alexandria Va; res. ClrkVA; m. 21 Mar 1880 at LdnVA to STICKLES, Girtrude; d/o Henry & Susan STICKLES; 18y; sgl; b. & res. ClrkVA; (lic) 20 Mar 1880; bride's parents consent given through Henry EDWARDS; p. 18

BENNETT, James W.; s/o Peter & Phebe BENNETT; 22y; sgl; farmer; b. & res. ClrkVA; m. 27 Apr 1882 at ClrkVA to POPE, Ella E.; d/o Michael & Lizzie POPE; 21y; sgl; b. & res. ClrkVA; (lic) 27 Apr 1882; p. 59

BENNETT, Lewis H.; s/o Lewis H. & Sarah C. BENNETT; 22y; sgl; plumber; b. & res. Baltimore Md; m. 18 Oct 1871 at ClrkVA to ROYSTON, Hattie; d/o Matthew W. & Minerva C. ROYSTON; 19y; sgl; b. & res. ClrkVA; (lic) 18 Oct 1871; bride's brother present; p. 117

BENNETT, Loren W.; s/o Stephen & Emily BENNETT; 26y; sgl; farmer; b. & res. Plainfield, Wyndham Co. Conn.; m. 18 Nov 1875 at White Post to HUGHES, Annie S.; d/o John & Emily HUGHES; 25y; sgl; b. ClrkVA; res. White Post; (lic) 16 Nov 1875; p. 192

BENNETT, Walter T.; s/o Webb & Mary BENNETT; 27y; sgl; clerk; b. city of New York; res. ClrkVA; m. 3 Jul 1866 at residence of bride's mother in ClrkVA to OSBURN, Hannah Elizabeth; d/o Rolin & Charlotte OSBURN; 24y; sgl; b. LdnVA; res. ClrkVA; (lic) 30 Jun 1866; p. 14

BENSON, Johnson (col); s/o ___ & Mildred BENSON; 29y; sgl; farm hand; b. RappVA; res. ClrkVA; m. 20 May 1785 at ClrkVA to THOMAS, Summerville (col); d/o not known; 23y; sgl; b. PageVA; res. ClrkVA; (lic) 20 May 1875; p. 179

BENTON, W. H. Jr.; s/o Jas. M. & Margt. A. BENTON; 24y; sgl; farmer; b. Fairfax Co. Va; res. LdnVA; m. 5 Dec 1882 at bride's residence to GORDON, Annie B.; d/o Geo. W. & Lydia Ann GORDON; 22y; sgl; b. & res. ClrkVA; (lic) 2 Dec 1882; p. 69

BERLIN, James J.; s/o Lewis & Jane Eliz'th BERLIN; 31y; sgl; farmer; b. & res. ClrkVA; m. 13 Nov 1884 at Berryville to HARDESTY, Cora H.; d/o James M. & Cordelia C. HARDESTY; 20y; sgl; b. & res. ClrkVA; (lic) 12 Nov 1884; p. 110

BERLIN, Lewis; s/o Isaac & Rosanna BERLIN; 58y; wid; blacksmith; b. & res. ClrkVA; m. 28 Nov 1883 at bride's residence to COOPER, Elizabeth M.; d/o Harrison & ___ COOPER; 40y; sgl; b. & res. ClrkVA; (lic) 27 Nov 1883; p. 89

BERRY, Jerry (col); s/o John & Peggy BERRY; 22y; sgl; farm hand; b. FqrVA; res. LdnVA; m. 18 Jun 1874 at bride's residence to TRAVIS, Maria (col); d/o Stephen & Sophia TRAVIS; 24y; sgl; b. & res. ClrkVA; (lic) 17 Jun 1874; p. 162

BERRY, Joseph (col); s/o not given; 21y; sgl; farmhand; b. not given; res. ClrkVA; m. 23 Dec [1865] at Miss Marg't.
BURCHELL's to SMITH, Eveline (col); d/o not given; not given; sgl; b. not given; res. ClrkVA; (lic) 22 Dec 1865; p. 5
BEVAN, Archibald B.; s/o George J. & Rachel BEVAN; 25y; sgl; farmer; b. England; res. ClrkVA; m. 7 Jun 1883 at ClrkVA to HARRISON, Mary C. R.; d/o Benjamin & Matilda C. HARRISON; 21y; sgl; b. & res. ClrkVA; (lic) 5 Jun 1883; p. 82
BIGGERS, A. F.; s/o A. F. BIGGERS & M. L. BIGGERS; 29y; sgl; lawyer; b. & res. Lynchburg Va; m. 14 Jul 1868 at bride's residence to SOWERS, Sallie C.; d/o Danl. W. & Mary SOWERS; 24y; sgl; b. & res. ClrkVA; (lic) 10 Jul 1868; p. 63
BIGGS, Joseph; s/o William & Mary Elizabeth BIGGS; 38y; wid; carpenter; b. RappVA; res. ClrkVA; m. 6 Nov 187 at ClrkVA to PURKS, Catherine; d/o Richard B. & ___ BIGGS [PURKS]; 23y; sgl; b. not known; res. ClrkVA; (lic) 6 Nov 1877; p. 227
BILLMIRE, James Andrew; s/o Andrew J. & Martha Ann BILLMIRE; 25y; sgl; blacksmithing; b. & res. ClrkVA; m. Thursday 16 Jan 1879 at ClrkVA to KENNON, Sallie Bettie; d/o Henry & Susan KENNON; 21y; sgl; b. & res. ClrkVA; (lic) 16 Jan 1879; p. 251
BILMIRE, John; s/o Lewis & Mahahula [Mahala?] E. BILMYRE; 23y; sgl; farmer; b. & res. ClrkVA; m. 28 Dec 1871 at ClrkVA to SHAFFER, Caroline M.; d/o J. J. & Miranda E. SHAFFER; 21y; sgl; b. & res. ClrkVA; (lic) 26 Dec 1871; p. 122
BIRD, B. O. (col); s/o Jas. & Annie E. BIRD; 27y; sgl; teacher; b. LdnVA; res. Baltimore Maryland; m. 29 Sep 1880 at Berryville to LOVETT, Portia E. (col); d/o Wilson & Martha LOVETT; 22y; sgl; b. & res. ClrkVA; (lic) 28 Sep 1880; p. 25
BLACKBURN, Bushrod (col); s/o Benj. & Kitty BLACKBURN (col); 23y; sgl; farm hand; b. & res. ClrkVA; m. 13 Apr 1871 at Berryville to STROTHER, Milley A. (col); d/o Jackson & Mary STROTHER (col); 17y; sgl; b. PageVA; res. ClrkVA; (lic) 13 Apr 1871; written permission from Jackson & Mary STROTHER for dau. age 16y ?m 10d; p. 111
BLACKBURN, Isaac N. (col); s/o Benj. & Amanda BLACKBURN; 23y; sgl; farm hand`; b. & res. ClrkVA; m. 13 Apr 1882 at ClrkVA to ALLEN, Maggie (col); d/o Merly? & Amanda ALLEN; 21y; sgl; b. & res. ClrkVA; (lic) 13 Apr 1882; p. 58
BLACKBURN, Manuel (col); s/o Benj. & Catharine BLACKBURN; 27y; sgl; farmhand; b. & res. ClrkVA; m. 12 Dec 1867 at John W. LUKE's to CARTER, Mary (col); d/o

Robert and ___ CARTER (col); 25y; wid; b. & res. ClrkVA; (lic) 12 Dec 1867; p. 47

BLACKBURN, Thomas N. (col); s/o Benjamine & Catharine BLACKBURNE (col); 26y; sgl; merchant; b. & res. ClrkVA; m. 17 Oct [1867] at Berryville to WASHINGTON, Laura (col); d/o Joshua & ___ THOMAS (col); 21y; sgl; b. PageVA; res. ClrkVA; (lic) 12 Oct 1867; p. 44

BLAIR, George (col); s/o not given; 75y; wid; not given; b. ???? ??? City [written over]; res. ClrkVA; m. date not given at Poor House to BLAIR, Frances (col); d/o not given; 25y; wid; b. & res. ClrkVA; (lic) 15 Sep 1866; p. 19

BLAIR, John (col); s/o Geo. & Hannah BLAIR; 23y; sgl; farm hand; b. ClrkVA; res. Chambersburg Penn; m. 23 Jun 1881 at Berryville to LACEY, Sallie Parker (col); d/o Geo. & Fanny LACEY; 21y; sgl; b. & res. ClrkVA; (lic) 23 Jun 1881; p. 43

BLAKE, Charles H.; s/o Charles & Rebecca BLAKE; 28y; sgl; machinist; b. JeffVA; res. ClrkVA; m. 22 Dec 1880 at Millwood to WOOD, Mary E.; d/o Alex'r. & ___ WOOD; 35y; sgl; b. & res. ClrkVA; (lic) 22 Dec 1880; p. 31

BLUM, Ernest; s/o Louis & Celestine BLUM; 31y; sgl; Professor of Languages; b. Nancy in France; res. Richmond Va; m. 24 Mar 1869 at Fairfield, ClrkVA to RICHARDSON, Mollie; d/o John D. & Mary C. RICHARDSON; 21y; sgl; b. & res. ClrkVA; (lic) 23 Mar 1869; p. 79

BOOKER, Judson H. (M.D.); s/o Erasmus & Olivia; 30y; sgl; physician; b. Richmond Co. Va; res. Northumberland Co. Va; m. 2 Dec 1885 at ClrkVA to THOMAS, Grace A.; d/o Geo. C. & Eliza THOMAS; 18y; sgl; b. & res. ClrkVA; (lic) 2 Dec 1885; p. 129

BOOTH, Edwin G. Jr.; s/o Edwin G. & Sallie T. BOOTH; 31y; sgl; physician; b. & res. Nottoway; m. Wednesday 12 Oct 1870 at Berryville to THOMSON, Clara H.; d/o Jno. A. & ___ THOMSON; 21y; sgl; b. & res. Jefferson; (lic) 8 Oct 1870; p. 101

BOSS, Alfred (col); s/o James & Caroline BOSS; 21y; sgl; laborer; b. LdnVA; res. ClrkVA; m. 20 Jun 1876 at Millwood to MITCHELL, Mary (col); d/o James & Maria MITCHELL; 18y; sgl; b. FqrVA; res. ClrkVA; (lic) 20 Jun 1876; p. 202

BOUGHNER, Homer D.; s/o D. & E. P BOUGHNER; 31y; sgl; merchant; b. Greensboro, Greene Co. Penn.; res. Clarksburg West Va; m. 28 Jan 1880 at bride's residence to KERFOOT,

Cora L.; d/o Jas. F. & ___ KERFOOT; 22y; sgl; b. & res.
ClrkVA; (lic) 27 Jan 1880; p. 14
BOWEN, James P.; s/o Edwin & Eliza F. BOWEN; 29y; sgl;
clerk; b. WrnVA; res. Galveston Texas; m. 2 Sep 1783 at
Millwood to EVANS, Mary E.; d/o Hiram P. & Sarah J.
EVANS; 30y; sgl; b. & res. ClrkVA; (lic) 28 Aug 1873; p. 148
BOWEN, William B.; s/o Edwin & Eliza F. BOWEN; 35y; sgl;
physician; b. WrnVA; res. ClrkVA; m. 13 Sep 1881 at White
Post to SOMMERVILLE, Emma L.; d/o Dr. Wm. & M. L.
SOMMERVILLE; 24y; sgl; b. Hampshire Co. W Va; res.
ClrkVA; (lic) 9 Sep 1881; p. 47
BOWERS, Jno. L.; s/o Peter & Harriet BOWERS; 20y; sgl;
farmer; b. & res. JeffVA; m. 25 Jan 1870 at bride's residence
to HUYETT, Alice C.; d/o Henry & Sally HUYETT; 20y; sgl; b.
& res. ClrkVA; (lic) not given; p. 92
BOWLER, Eli (col); s/o Richard & Abby BOWLER; 23y; sgl;
nursery business; b. Louisa Co. Va; res. Baltimore Co.
Maryland; m. 3 Jul 1882 at Berryville to WILLIS, Lucy (col);
d/o Jack & Margaret WILLIS; 22y; sgl; b. Louisa Co. Va; res.
ClrkVA; (lic) 3 Jul 1882; p. 61
BOWLING, Andrew; s/o Alexander & Elizabeth BOWLING; 28y;
sgl; miller; b. Front Royal, Va; res. AugVA; m. 8 Jun 1875 at
ClrkVA to CLAGETT, Louisa F.; d/o Hezekiah & Louisa D.
CLAGETT; 27y; sgl; b. Hardy Co. Va; res. ClrkVA; (lic) 7 Jun
1875; p. 180
BOWMAN, Isaac; s/o Abraham & Susan BOWMAN; 28y; sgl;
tinner; b. Shenandoah; res. ClrkVA; m. 13 Feb 1866 [68] at
Berryville to REED, Maggie M.; d/o William & Nancy REED;
25y; sgl; b. Jefferson; res. ClrkVA; (lic) 12 Feb 1868; p. 55
BOWMAN, Isaac; s/o Abraham & Susan BOWMAN; 38y; wid;
tinner; b. ShenVA; res. ClrkVA; m. 15 Oct 1878 at ClrkVA to
JONES, Ella A.; d/o Thomas & ___ JONES; 24y; sgl; b. &
res. ClrkVA; (lic) 14 Oct 1878; p. 241
BOXWELL, Wm. Frederick; s/o Chas. H. & Elevina BOXWELL;
22y; sgl; farmer; b. FredVA; res. ClrkVA; m. 26 May 1875 at
Berryville to SHACKLEFORD, Nannie Moss; d/o Erasmus &
Helen SHACKLEFORD; 19y; sgl; b. & res. ClrkVA; (lic) 25
May 1875; p. 179
BOYD, John; s/o Robert & Elizabeth BOYD; 23y; sgl; farmer; b.
& res. JeffVA; m. 21 Dec 1871 at ClrkVA to HUFF, Amelia;
d/o Jackson & Elizabeth HUFF; 21y; sgl; b. & res. ClrkVA;
(lic) 20 Dec 1871; p. 122

BOYD, Robert L.; s/o Woldard A. & Eliz'th BOYD; 22y; sgl;
farmer; b. Cecil Co. Maryland; res. FredVA; m. 25 Aug 1881
at ClrkVA to CARVER, Lucy Ellen; d/o Jos. & Frances
CARVER; 17y; sgl; b. FredVA; res. ClrkVA; (lic) 23 Aug 1881;
consent of bride's father given in writing; p. 45
BOYD, Robt. E.; s/o Robt. & Elizabeth BOYD; 23y; sgl; farmer;
b. JeffWVA; res. ClrkVA; m. 27 Aug 1876 at ClrkVA to
EDWARDS, Sarah F.; d/o Jas. W. & Sarah J. EDWARDS;
19y; sgl; b. & res. ClrkVA; (lic) 26 Aug 1876; p. 204
BRACKETT, Armistead Milton; s/o Russell & Frances Ann
BRACKETT; 23y; sgl; farmer; b. & res. ClrkVA; m. 22 Aug
1867 at Blue Ridge to MORELAND, Mary Ann; d/o Saml. &
Sarah MORELAND; 23y; sgl; b. & res. ClrkVA; (lic) 21 Aug
1867; p. 40
BRADY, G. W.; s/o J. P. & J. M. BRADY; 25y; sgl; rail roading; b.
FredVA; res. ClrkVA; m. 20 Oct 1874 at Charlestown W Va to
ROWLAND, Josephine S.; d/o John & Lydia ROWLAND; 22y;
sgl; b. & res. ClrkVA; (lic) 19 Oct 1874; p. 166
BRANDER, Henry (col); s/o William and Evelina BRANDER
(col); 26y; sgl; merchant's clerk; b. Richmond City; res.
ClrkVA; m. 6 Nov 1866 at Berryville to CLARK, Rachel (col);
d/o Joseph and Sarah McCARD (col); 25y; sgl; b. & res.
ClrkVA; (lic) 6 Nov 1866; p. 22
BRAXTON, Matthew (col); s/o Rome & Mary BRAXTON (col);
23y; sgl; farm hand; b. ClrkVA; res. not given; m. 31 Oct 1872
at ClrkVA to HOLLINGSWORTH, Frances (col); d/o ___ &
Catharine HOLLINGSWORTH (col); 24y; sgl; b. Frederick
Co.; res. not given; (lic) 30 Oct 1872; p. 135
BRAY, Alfred (col); s/o Lucy BRAY, father not known; 54y; wid;
farm hand; b. & res. ClrkVA; m. 20 Dec 1877 at ClrkVA to
BARBER, Patty (col); d/o not known; 40y; wid; b. & res.
ClrkVA; (lic) 20 Dec 1877; p. 228
BRAY, Alfred (col); s/o Samuel & Lucy BRAY (col); 27y; wid;
farm hand; b. & res. ClrkVA; m. 3 Nov 1867 at Millwood to
BUTLER, Clara (col); d/o Parker & Nancy BUTLER (col); 24y;
wid; b. & res. ClrkVA; (lic) 2 Nov 1867; p. 45
BRAY, Anthony (col); s/o Danl. & Lucy BRAY; 21y; sgl; farm
hand; b. & res. ClrkVA; m. 17 Jul 1879 at ClrkVA to TAYLOR,
Harriett (col); d/o not known; 23y; wid; b. & res. ClrkVA; (lic)
17 Jul 1879; p. 260
BRAY, Danl. (col); s/o Robert & Lucy BRAY; 23y; sgl; farm hand;
b. & res. ClrkVA; m. 12 Nov 1874 at Millwood to CYRAS,

Eliza (col); d/o Abraham & Jane CYRAS; 28y; sgl; b. PageVA; res. ClrkVA; (lic) 12 Nov 1874; p. 169
BREWER, William R.; s/o Wm. V. & Sarah J. BREWER; 28y; sgl; farmer; b. & res. WrnVA; m. 17 Apr 1884 at Winchester Va to NEWCOME, Rebecca M.; d/o John & Alcinda J. NEWCOME; 21y; sgl; b. Lewis Co. W Va; res. ClrkVA; (lic) 15 Apr 1884; p. 99
BRIGGS, Charles A.; s/o James & Louisa BRIGGS; 33y; sgl; farmer; b. & res. Stafford Co. Va; m. 30 Oct 1879 at ClrkVA to MORGAN, Virginia C.; d/o Benjamin & Martha A. MORGAN; 23y; sgl; b. & res. ClrkVA; (lic) 29 Oct 1879; p. 6
BRIGGS, Henry C.; s/o Thomas & Lucinda BRIGGS; 54y; sgl; farmer & miller; b. & res. ClrkVA; m. 19 Oct 1886 at ClrkVA to SPEICER, Sarah C.; d/o Saml. W. & Catherine S. SPEICER; 43y; sgl; b. not given; res. ClrkVA; (lic) 19 Oct 1886; p. 143
BRIGGS, Isham R.; s/o James & Louisa BRIGGS; 29y; sgl; farmer; b. Stafford Co. Va; res. ClrkVA; m. 19 Oct 1880 at ClrkVA to BOSWELL, Lucy S. H.; d/o Thomas & Salina BOSWELL; 21y; sgl; b. FredVA; res. ClrkVA; (lic) 19 Oct 1880; p. 26
BRIGGS, James M.; s/o James & Louisa BRIGGS; 26y; sgl; farmer; b. & res. Stafford Co. Va; m. 30 Oct 1879 at ClrkVA to CASTLEMAN, Martha M.; d/o Charles D. & Maria J. CASTLEMAN; 24y; sgl; b. & res. ClrkVA; (lic) 29 Oct 1879; p. 6
BRITTON, George M.; s/o James & Sarah BRITTON; 27y; sgl; farmer; b. & res. AugVA; m. 5 Feb 1867 at bride's residence to JONES, Hattie R.; d/o Thomas & Mary Jane JONES; 24y; sgl; b. & res. ClrkVA; (lic) 5 Feb 1867; p. 32
BROOKS, Jordan H. (col); s/o Spencer & Eliza BROOKS; 21y; sgl; farm hand; b. Henrico Co. Va; res. ClrkVA; m. 31 Mar 1881 at ClrkVA to GIBSON, Catie (col); d/o Nera & Melvina GIBSON; 21y; sgl; b. & res. ClrkVA; (lic) 31 Mar 1881; p. 37
BROOKS, Mat (col); s/o William BROOKS & Mary BROOKS; 22y; sgl; farm hand; b. & res. White Post; m. 25 Jul 1875 at residence of bride at White Post to STRANGE, Susan (col); d/o John STRANGE & Rachel STRANGE; 19y; sgl; b. at John ALEXANDER's near White Post; res. White Post; (lic) 24 Jul 1875; p. 183
BROTHERTON, Robert N.; s/o Thomas & Mary BROTHERTON; 26y; sgl; farmer; b. JeffVA; res. ClrkVA; m. 23 Feb 1881 at bride's residence to EVERHART, Gertrude J.; d/o Jacob W. &

Mary EVERHART; 22y; sgl; b. & res. ClrkVA; (lic) 22 Feb 1881; p. 36

BROWN, Benjamin (col); s/o Joseph and Martha BROWN; 25y; sgl; farm hand; b. & res. ClrkVA; m. 30 Aug 1883 at White Post to WASHINGTON, Lucinda (col); d/o ___ & ___ WASHINGTON; 29y; sgl; b. WrnVA; res. ClrkVA; (lic) 29 Aug 1883; p. 86

BROWN, Coy (col); s/o Thomas & Rebecca BROWN; 30y; sgl; farm hand; b. & res. ClrkVA; m. 27 Jul 1882 at ClrkVA to CHRISTIAN, Lucy (col); d/o not given; 22y; sgl; b. & res. ClrkVA; (lic) 27 Jul 1882; p. 61

BROWN, G. Fen; s/o Oliver M. & Susan C. BROWN; 29y; sgl; merchant; b. & res. FredVA; m. 17 Oct 1877 at ClrkVA to LUKE, Sarah Cornelia; d/o John W. & Annie LUKE; 21y; sgl; b. & res. ClrkVA; (lic) 10 Oct 1877; p. 223

BROWN, George R.; s/o Sidney S. & Mary J. BROWN; 24y; sgl; artist; b. Augusta Ga; res. Paris, FqrVA; m. 11 Oct 1865 at Mount Carmel Church near Berry's Ferry to LINDSEY, Sarah Margaret; d/o James M. & Martha S. LINDSEY; 23y; sgl; b. & res. ClrkVA; (lic) 10 Oct 1865; p. 3

BROWN, George W.; s/o William and Mary BROWN; 30y; sgl; farmer; b. & res. LdnVA; m. 14 Apr 1867 at Mount Carmell Church to LEE, Lucinda; d/o Squire and Alcinda LEE; 25y; sgl; b. LdnVA; res. ClrkVA; (lic) 12 Apr 1867; p. 34

BROWN, Henry Wilson (col); s/o Alexander & Caroline BROWN (col); 28y; sgl; farm hand; b. WrnVA; res. ClrkVA; m. 28 Sep 1867 at Berryville to THOMAS, Mary (col); d/o Joshua & Rachel Eliz'th THOMAS (col); 21y last; sgl; b. PageVA; res. ClrkVA; (lic) 28 Sep 1867; p. 42

BROWN, James (col); s/o Caesar & Peggy BROWN (col); 52y; wid; farm hand; b. & res. ClrkVA; m. 11 Jan 1868 at ClrkVA to RANDOLPH, Nancy (col); d/o Siplin & Virgin FAUNTLEROY (col); 30y; wid; b. & res. ClrkVA; (lic) 11 Jan 1868; p. 53

BROWN, James (col); s/o Charles & Lowina BROWN; 25y; sgl; farm hand; b. & res. ClrkVA; m. 24 Dec 1878 at Berryville to BITTLE?, Margaret (col); d/o James and ___ BITTLE?; 25y; sgl; b. & res. ClrkVA; (lic) 24 Dec 1878; p. 248

BROWN, James M.; s/o Jesse & Francis BROWN; 23y; sgl; farmer; b. WrnVA; res. not given; m. 31 Dec 1878 at ClrkVA to SHIPE, Laura; d/o Joseph & Debby SHIPE; 19y; sgl; b. ClrkVA; res. not given; (lic) 31 Dec 1878; p. 250

BROWN, John W.; s/o Thomas & Lucenda C. BROWN; 25y; sgl; farmer; b. RappVA; res. JeffWVA; m. 13 Feb 1873 at ClrkVA to FINNELL, Catharine E.; d/o John A. & Nancy FINNELL; 25y; sgl; b. RappVA; res. ClrkVA; (lic) not given; p. 142
BROWN, Judge D. (col); s/o ___ & Mary BROWN; 22y; sgl; coachman; b. & res. ClrkVA; m. 27 Oct 1886 at Berryville to LOVETT, Jane D. (col); d/o Wilson & Mary LOVETT; 22y; sgl; b. & res. ClrkVA; (lic) 26 Oct 1886; p. 145
BROWN, Richard (col); s/o Luke & Telia BROWN; 37y; sgl; farm hand; b. Bedford Co. Va; res. ClrkVA; m. 6 Oct 1881 at ClrkVA to REED, Jane (col); d/o Presley & ___REED; 25y; sgl; b. & res. ClrkVA; (lic) 6 Oct 1881; p. 47
BROWN, Samuel (col); s/o Aaron & Martha BROWN; 24y; sgl; farm hand; b. RappVA; res. ClrkVA; m. 16 Jan 1881 at White Post to LEWIS, Amelia (col); d/o ___ & Lettie LEWIS; 24y; sgl; b. & res. ClrkVA; (lic) 15 Jan 1881; p. 34
BROWN, Spotswood (col); s/o Spotswood & Matilda BROWN (col); 23y; sgl; farm hand; b. AlbmVA; res. ClrkVA; m. 1 Feb 1872 at Berryville to REED, Martha (col); d/o Gilson & Susan REED (col); 21y; sgl; b. & res. ClrkVA; (lic) not given; p. 125
BROWN, Tarlton (col); s/o Chas. & Clarissa BRUCE [BROWN] (col); 26y; sgl; barber & hair dresser; b. Charlotte Co. Va; res. ClrkVA; m. 24 Nov 1869 at Berryville to JACKSON, Matilda (col); d/o ___ & ___ JACKSON (col); 26y; sgl; b. & res. ClrkVA; (lic) 24 Nov 1869; p. 89
BROWN, Tarlton W. (col); s/o Charles & Clarecy BROWN; 31y; wid; barber; b. Charlotte Co. Va; res. ClrkVA; m. 17 Feb 1876 at Berryville to MYERS, Mary R. (col); d/o Robert & Heny JACKSON; 18y; sgl; b. & res. ClrkVA; (lic) 17 Feb 1876; p. 197
BROWN, Theodore; s/o James & Owings [Marth. (Math) written above] BROWN; 49y; wid; farmer; b. & res. Jefferson Co. Ky; m. 1 Mar 1870 at Millwood to MEADE, Susan Page; d/o P. N. & Fannie B. MEADE; 20y; sgl; b. & res. ClrkVA; (lic) 28 Feb 1870; p. 94
BROWN, William (col); s/o Abraham & Maria BROWN; 39y; wid; farm hand; b. FqrVA; res. ClrkVA; m. 23 Apr 1876 at White Post to GRANDERSON, Ann (col); d/o unknown; 25y; sgl; b. & res. ClrkVA; (lic) 21 Apr 1876; p. 199
BROWN, William (col); s/o Nathan & Virginia BROWN (col); 28y; sgl; farm hand; b. Jefferson Co.; res. ClrkVA; m. 7 Nov 1868 at ClrkVA to HENDERSON, Susan (col); d/o ___ & ___

HENDERSON (col); 21y; sgl; b. Frederick Co.; res. ClrkVA;
(lic) 4 Nov 1868; p. 69
BROWN, William H.; s/o Harrison & Evelina BROWN; 27y; sgl;
farmer; b. & res. ClrkVA; m. 24 Jan 1867 at ClrkVA to
BRANNON, Elnora; d/o Stewart J. and Mary BRANNON; 18y;
sgl; b. Frederick Co.; res. ClrkVA; (lic) 22 Jan 1867; p. 29
BROWN, William S.; s/o Thomas & Annie BROWN; 24y; sgl;
blacksmith; b. RckhmVA; res. ClrkVA; m. 30 Jan 1867 at
bride's residence to EVERHART, Fannie; d/o Jacob and Mary
EVERHART; 17y; sgl; b. & res. ClrkVA; (lic) 30 Jan 1867;
with consent of bride's father; p. 31
BROWN, Wilson (col); s/o __ and Eliza BROWN (col); 30y; sgl;
farm hand; b. AugVA; res. ClrkVA; m. 24 Nov 1867 at
Millwood to CATLETT, Mary (col); d/o __ and Rebecca
JOHNSON (col); 19y; sgl; b. & res. ClrkVA; (lic) 22 Nov 1867;
p. 46
BROWN, Wm.; s/o Thomas & Rebecca BROWN; 23y; sgl; on
farm; b. & res. ClrkVA; m. 5 Sep 1872 at Millwood to
BROWN, Frances; d/o __ & Mary BANKS; 19y; sgl; b. & res.
ClrkVA; (lic) 5 Sep 1872; p. 132
BROY, Charles L.; s/o Adison & Catharine BROY; 28y; sgl;
farmer; b. WrnVA; res. ClrkVA; m. 11 Jan 1882 at ClrkVA to
LOCK, Sallie H.; d/o Howard & Matilda LOCK; 19y; sgl; b. &
res. ClrkVA; (lic) 11 Jan 1882; p. 54
BROY, Edward C.; s/o Adison & Catharine BROY; 22y; sgl;
farmer; b. WrnVA; res. ClrkVA; m. 11 Jan 1882 at ClrkVA to
LOCK, Ida L.; d/o Howard & Matilda LOCK; 22y; sgl; b. & res.
ClrkVA; (lic) 11 Jan 1882; p. 55
BRUNTY, John H.; s/o James & Tabitha BRUNTY; 28y; sgl;
farmer; b. Wythe Co. Va; res. ClrkVA; m. 16 Mar 1871 at
ClrkVA to BENN, Eliza Ann; d/o James & __ BENN; 24y;
sgl; b. WrnVA; res. ClrkVA; (lic) not given; p. 110
BRYARLY, J. Elliott; s/o R. S. BRYARLY & Harriet T. BRYARLY;
25y; sgl; farmer; b. & res. ClrkVA; m. 2 Sep 1884 at bride's
residence to ALLEN, Mary B.; d/o Wm. T. & Mary E. ALLEN;
26y; sgl; b. & res. ClrkVA; (lic) 30 Aug 1884; p. 105
BUCKNER, J. P.; s/o V. & Sarah BUCKNER; 23y; sgl;
blacksmith; b. Nashville, Tennessee; res. ClrkVA; m. 2 Aug
1866 at near White Post to GARDNER, Levina A.; d/o
George & Parasais GARDNER; 19y; sgl; b. & res. ClrkVA;
(lic) 31 Jul 1866; p. 15

BUNDY, Jefferson (col); s/o Riban & Charlotte BUNDY; 35y; sgl; merchant; b. Richmond Va; res. ClrkVA; m. 21 Apr 1881 at ClrkVA to JEFFERSON, Charlotte (col); d/o not known; 25y; sgl; b. & res. ClrkVA; (lic) 21 Apr 1881; p. 39
BURCH, Julian W.; s/o Hilary & Elizabeth BURCH; 28y; sgl; farmer; b. Maryland; res. ClrkVA; m. 21 Jul 1886 at ClrkVA to KERFOOT, Lina L.; d/o Judson G. & Fannie A. KERFOOT; 18y; sgl; b. & res. ClrkVA; (lic) 16 Jul 1886; p. 140
BURKE, Francis W.; s/o Redmond & Mary BURKE; 25y; sgl; carpenter; b. JeffVA; res. Piedmont, W Va; m. 19 Oct 1871 at Berryville to EVERITT, Annie R.; d/o George R. & Juliett EVERITT; 19y; sgl; b. JeffVA; res. Berryville; (lic) 18 Oct 1871; p. 117
BURNS, Charles (col); s/o Charles & Fannie BURNS; 24y; sgl; farm hand; b. & res. ClrkVA; m. 26 Dec 1885 at ClrkVA to LIPKINS, Julia (col); d/o Ben & Milly LIPKINS; 17y; sgl; b. & res. ClrkVA; (lic) 23 Dec 1885; p. 131
BURNS, John (col); s/o Horace & Malinda BURNS; 24y; sgl; farm hand; b. & res. ClrkVA; m. 9 Jan 1883 at ClrkVA to WILLIAMS, Kate (col); d/o Townsind & Mahala WILLIAMS; 22y; sgl; b. & res. ClrkVA; (lic) 9 Jan 1883; p. 74
BURWELL, Daniel; s/o Manuel & Eliz'th; 22y; sgl; farm hand; b. & res. ClrkVA; m. 6 Jun 1871 at ClrkVA to REED, Jane; d/o not given; 21y; sgl; b. & res. ClrkVA; (lic) not given; p. 113
BURWELL, Geo. H.; s/o Geo. H. & Agnes BURWELL; 37y; wid; farmer; b. & res. ClrkVA; m. 10 Jun 1886 at Millwood to WHITING, Lucy Burwell; d/o Nath'l. B. & Camilla M. WHITING; 23y; sgl; b. & res. ClrkVA; (lic) 9 Jun 1886; p. 137
BURWELL, John P.; s/o Nath'l. & Dora W. BURWELL; 20y; sgl; farmer; b. & res. ClrkVA; m. 24 Sep 1872 at Millwood to WAINWRIGHT, Eliz'th. M.; d/o Jonathan M. & Maria P. WAINWRIGHT; 21y; sgl; b. Philadelphia Penn.; res. ClrkVA; (lic) 21 Sep 1872; p. 133
BURWELL, Philip (Dr.); s/o Nath'l. & Dora W. BURWELL; 25y; sgl; physician; b. ClrkVA; res. Ravenswood, Jackson Co. W Va; m. 29 Oct 1874 at Millwood to HARRISON, Maria H.; d/o Henry & Fannie HARRISON; 22y; sgl; b. not given; res. ClrkVA; (lic) 26 Oct 1874; p. 167
BURWELL, Thomas (col); s/o Thos. & Jane BURWELL (col); 21y; sgl; farm hand; b. & res. ClrkVA; m. 7 Dec 1781 at Berryville to JACKSON, Francis (col); d/o Harry & Martha

JACKSON (col); 20y; sgl; b. & res. ClrkVA; (lic) 7 Dec 1871; p. 120
BUSH, George W.; s/o Charles & Eliza BUSH; 21y; sgl; farmer; b. FredVA; res. ClrkVA; m. 17 Nov 1880 at ClrkVA to ROWLAND, Fannie A.; d/o Geo. H. & Charloote [Charlotte] T. ROWLAND; 26y; sgl; b. & res. ClrkVA; (lic) 16 Nov 1880; p. 28
BUTLER, Charles (col); s/o James & Arena BUTLER (col); 24y; sgl; farm hand; b. & res. ClrkVA; m. 9 Nov 1871 at Berryville to WILLIAMS, Sarah (col); d/o ___ & Sarah WILLIAMS (col); 21y; sgl; b. & res. ClrkVA; (lic) not given; p. 119
BUTLER, William (col); s/o Samuel & Clary BUTLER; 21y; sgl; farm hand; b. & res. ClrkVA; m. 21 Feb 1884 at ClrkVA to HERBERT, Sallie (col); d/o Benj. & Patsey HERBERT; 18y; sgl; b. & res. ClrkVA; (lic) 21 Feb 1884; p. 95
BUTZ, Benj. F.; s/o Benj. & Frances BUTZ; 40y; wid; railroading; b. Pennsylvania; res. ClrkVA; m. 2 Oct 1881 at ClrkVA to RITTER, Annie S.; d/o Carter & ___ RITTER; 22y; sgl; b. & res. ClrkVA; (lic) not given; p. 49
BYRD, James (col); s/o John and Molly BYRD (col); 29y; sgl; farm hand; b. & res. ClrkVA; m. 23 Aug 1868 at Millwood to ROBERTSON, Judah (col); d/o Simon ROBINSON & ___; 21y; sgl; b. & res. ClrkVA; (lic) 22 Aug 1868; note of permission for dau. by Simon ROBERTSON.; p. 65
CAMPBELL, Randolph; s/o Saml. & Catharine CAMPBELL; 32y; sgl; rail road hand; b. Berryville; res. ClrkVA; m. 12 May 1881 at ClrkVA to SHROUD, Annie; d/o Killian & Margaret SHROUD; 17y; sgl; b. JeffWVA; res. ClrkVA; (lic) 12 May 1881; p. 40
CARLYLE, Albert (col); s/o Jeffrey & Judah CARLYLE; 30y; wid; dining room waiter; b. JeffVA (Harpers ferry); res. ClrkVA; m. 8 Aug 1870 at ClrkVA to JACKSON, Annie (col); d/o Everett & Elanor JACKSON; 22y; sgl; b. & res. ClrkVA; (lic) 5 Aug 1870; p. 98
CARLYLE, Alexander; s/o Jno. & Betsy CARLYLE; 48y; wid; farmer; b. Hampshire Co. W Va; res. ClrkVA; m. 1 Aug 1882 at ClrkVA to WRIGHT, Nancy; d/o Wm. & Martha WRIGHT; 25y; sgl; b. WrnVA; res. ClrkVA; (lic) 29 Jul 1882; p. 61
CARMICHAEL, Otis; s/o Otis & P. A. CARMICHAEL; 26y; sgl; printer; b. & res. Middletown, Orange Co. New York; m. Wednesday 24 Dec 1879 at ClrkVA to LARUE, Annie C.; d/o

Jno. D. & Maria LARUE; 21y; sgl; b. & res. ClrkVA; (lic) 22 Dec 1879; p. 11
CARPER, George H.; s/o Alfred & Julia A. CARPER; 22y; sgl; farmer; b. FredVA; res. ClrkVA; m. 24 Mar 1870 at ClrkVA to GRUBBS, Serepta E.; d/o George & Maria GRUBBS; 22y; sgl; b. & res. ClrkVA; (lic) not given; p. 94
CARPER, Henry W.; s/o Geo. W. & Evelina LOCK [CARPER]; 23y; sgl; farmer; b. & res. FredVA; m. 22 Feb 1882 at ClrkVA to LOCK, Georgeanna A. V.; d/o Timothy W. & Lena LOCK; 18y; sgl; b. & res. FredVA; (lic) 21 Feb 1882; p. 56
CARPER, John A.; s/o Alfred and Julia A. CARPER; 21y; sgl; farmer; b. FredVA; res. ClrkVA; m. 6 Apr 1880 at Winchester Va to THOMPSON, Alice V.; d/o Geo. W. & Mary E. THOMPSON; 22y; sgl; b. & res. ClrkVA; (lic) 5 Apr 1880; p. 18
CARPER, John R.; s/o George & Eveline CARPER; 26y; sgl; farming; b. FredVA; res. ClrkVA; m. 28 Mar 1883 at ClrkVA to LEVI, Sarah C.; d/o Rice W. & Georgianna Levi; 30y; sgl; b. & res. ClrkVA; (lic) 27 Mar 1883; p. 80
CARPER, Joshua T.; s/o Wm. D. CARPER dec'd. & Mary M. CARPER; 21y 6th of Dec next; sgl; farmer; b. & res. FredVA; m. 8 Aug 1867 at not given to CARPER, Louisa M.; d/o William & Lucy CARPER; 20y; sgl; b. & res. ClrkVA; (lic) 6 Aug 1867; consent of husband's mother, his father being dead & consent of wife's father both given in writing (both witnessed by Steward CARPER); p. 39
CARRIER, Samuel N.; s/o Augustus & Mary CARRIER; 30y; sgl; farmer; b. & res. ShenVA; m. 26 Aug 1874 at ClrkVA to CHRISMAN, Minnie R.; d/o John H. & Lucinda CHRISMAN; 26y; sgl; b. & res. ClrkVA; (lic) 25 Aug 1874; p. 164
CARROL, Thomas; s/o John & Delphia CARROL; 32y; sgl; farmer; b. & res. ClrkVA; m. 7 Jan 1868 at ClrkVA to ALLEN, Elizabeth; d/o William & Nancy ALLEN; 27y; sgl; b. & res. ClrkVA; (lic) 3 Jan 1868; p. 51
CARROLL John R.; s/o John & Cornelia CARROLL; 23y; sgl; farmer; b. & res. ClrkVA; m. 29 Dec 1881 at ClrkVA to SHELL, Nancy A.; d/o John W. & Martha SHELL; 22y; sgl; b. LdnVA; res. ClrkVA; (lic) 29 Dec 1881; p. 53
CARROLL, Charles L.; s/o William & Eliza CARROL; 29y; sgl; farming; b. JeffWVA; res. ClrkVA; m. 6 Nov 1877 at ClrkVA to LITTLETON, Sarah Catherine; d/o William & Mary LITTLETON; 22y; sgl; b. & res. ClrkVA; (lic) 5 Nov 1877; G.

H. WRIGHT made oath as to age of Sarah C. LITTLETON; p. 226

CARROLL, Joshua P.; s/o Wm. & Eliza CARROLL; 21y; sgl; farm hand; b. JeffWVA; res. ClrkVA; m. 28 May 1878 at ClrkVA to WHITE, Mary A.; d/o Joseph & Mary F. WHITE; 18y; sgl; b. & res. ClrkVA; (lic) 22 May 1878; written consent of parents given; p. 234

CARROLL, William; s/o John & Delphia CARROLL; 32y; sgl; farmer; b. & res. ClrkVA; m. 27 May 1872 at ClrkVA to LEE, Maggie; d/o Squire & Alcinda LEE; 22y; sgl; b. LdnVA; res. ClrkVA; (lic) 27 May 1872; p. 129

CARTER, Albert (col); s/o Nathaniel & Milley CARTER (col); 21y; sgl; farm hand; b. & res. ClrkVA; m. 1 Feb 1872 at Berryville to TOKAS, Matilda (col); d/o George & Harriet Anna TOKAS (col); 22y; sgl; b. & res. ClrkVA; (lic) 1 Feb 1872; p. 125

CARTER, Archie (col); s/o Peter & Ellen CARTER; 45y; sgl; laborer; b. FqrVA; res. JeffWVA; m. Thursday, 4 Nov 1875 at Berryville to JACKSON, Eliza (col); d/o Jaqueline & Eveline STROTHER; 41y; wid; b. PageVA; res. ClrkVA; (lic) 3 Nov 1875; p. 190

CARTER, Arthur R.; s/o John A. & Bettie C. CARTER; 34y; sgl; farmer; b. & res. ClrkVA; m. 19 Mar 1884 at bride's residence to GRUBER, Rosa B. B.; d/o John & Maria J. GRUBER; 20y; sgl; b. & res. ClrkVA; (lic) 17 Mar 1884; bride's father present in person & gave consent; p. 97

CARTER, Charles C. H.; s/o Wm. A. & Mary Catharine CARTER; 26y 1st day of April 1870; sgl; farmer; b. FredVA; res. FredVA; m. 8 Sep 1870 at near Wadesville to CARTER, Edmonia V.; d/o Wm. K. & Catharine E. CARTER; 22y; sgl; b. & res. ClrkVA; (lic) 7 Sep 1870; p. 100

CARTER, Daniel (col); s/o Nathaniel & Milly CARTER; 25y next June; sgl; farm hand; b. & res. ClrkVA; m. 7 Apr 1866 at ClrkVA to RUNNER, Harriet (col); d/o __ & Sally RUNNER; not given; sgl; b. & res. ClrkVA; (lic) 6 Apr 1866; p. 10

CARTER, E. P. B.; s/o Geo. W. & Orra M. CARTER; 24y; sgl; doctor; b. Texas; res. Texas; m. 29 Sep 1884 at ClrkVA to MILBURN, Grace; d/o Jefferson & Mary MILBURN; 21y; sgl; b. LdnVA; res. ClrkVA; (lic) 29 Sep 1884; p. 107

CARTER, Edgar P.; s/o Jno. A. & Bettie C. CARTER; 31y; sgl; farmer; b. & res. ClrkVA; m. 26 Nov 1884 at bride's residence to ROBERTS, Julia C.; d/o Joel W. & Sarah ROBERTS; 24y; sgl; b. JeffWVA; res. ClrkVA; (lic) 25 Nov 1884; p. 111

CARTER, Edward; s/o John Brook CARTER & Hannah
CARTER; 24y; sgl; farmer; b. FqrVA; res. LdnVA; m.
Thursday 30 Sep 1875 at Colston Place, ClrkVA to
TUMBLIN, Mary Marina; d/o father dead, mother Anne
TUMBLIN; 21y; sgl; b. & res. ClrkVA; (lic) 29 Sep 1875; p.
186
CARTER, Fairfax (col); s/o Lucy CARTER; 58y; wid; laborer; b.
& res. ClrkVA; m. Thursday 30 Dec 1875 at Berryville to
BURNS, Melvina (col); d/o not given; 48y (age not known
exactly); wid; b. & res. ClrkVA; (lic) 30 Dec 1875; p. 195
CARTER, Geo. H.; s/o Wm. A. & Mary C. CARTER; 31y; sgl;
farmer; b. & res. FredVA; m. 17 Oct 1881 at Berryville to
CASTLEMAN, E. Carroll; d/o Chas. McC. & Eva E.
CASTLEMAN; 25y; sgl; b. LdnVA; res. ClrkVA; (lic) 14 Oct
1881; p. 48
CARTER, George (col); s/o Nat. & Milley CARTER (col); 29y;
sgl; farm hand; b. & res. ClrkVA; m. 1 Mar 1870 at Berryville
to GREENE, Mary (col); d/o not given; 21y; sgl; b. PageVA;
res. ClrkVA; (lic) 1 Mar 1870; p. 94
CARTER, James M. (col); s/o Nathaniel & Milley CARTER; 22y;
sgl; farm hand; b. & res. ClrkVA; m. 16 Jun 1881 at near
Berryville to COXEN, Mary (col); d/o Morgan & Ann COXEN;
20y; sgl; b. & res. ClrkVA; (lic) 16 Jun 1881; bride's father
was present & gave consent; p. 42
CARTER, Joseph M.; s/o Westford & Virginia F. CARTER; 31y;
sgl; farmer; b. FqrVA; res. WrnVA; m. 8 Apr 1880 at ClrkVA to
BROWN, Mollie E.; d/o Newton and Elizabeth BROWN; 24y;
sgl; b. WrnVA; res. ClrkVA; (lic) 7 Apr 1880; p. 19
CARTER, Lewis F. (col); s/o Phil & Amanda CARTER; 22y; sgl;
farm hand; b. FqrVA; res. ClrkVA; m. 24 Sep 1885 at ClrkVA
to COLSTON, Matilda (col); d/o ___ COLSTON & Mary
COLSTON; 22y; sgl; b. & res. ClrkVA; (lic) 24 Sep 1885; p.
125
CARTER, Nathaniel (col); s/o Nace & Jinnie CARTER; 60y; wid;
stone mason; b. & res. ClrkVA; m. 25 Dec 1884 at Millwood
to JACKSON, Nannie (col); d/o ___ & ___ LOVETT; 40y; wid;
b. & res. ClrkVA; (lic) 22 Dec 1884; p. 114
CARTER, Solimon (col); s/o Nathaniel & Milly CARTER; 27y; sgl;
farm hand; b. & res. ClrkVA; m. 17 Mar 1866 at ClrkVA to
POTTER, Milly (col); d/o Aaron & Lucy POTTER; 23y; sgl; b.
& res. ClrkVA; (lic) 17 Mar 1866; p. 8

CARTER, W. P.; s/o Thomas & Ann CARTER; 29y; sgl; farmer; b. & res. ClrkVA; m. 28 Feb 1867 at Christ Church Millwood to PAGE, Lucy R.; d/o R. P. & Susan R. PAGE; 25y; sgl; b. & res. ClrkVA; (lic) 27 Feb 1867; p. 33
CARTER, Walker (col); s/o Lewis & Ellen CARTER; 21y; sgl; farm hand; b. RappVA; res. ClrkVA; m. 22 Jul 1880 at Millwood to HUBBARD, Matilda (col); d/o ___ & Mary M. HUBBARD; 19y; sgl; b. ___ Co. Texas; res. ClrkVA; (lic) 22 Jul 1880; p. 23
CARTER, William H.; s/o John W. & Tecunda CARTER; 23y; sgl; farmer; b. & res. ClrkVA; m. 24 Feb 1880 at ClrkVA to CARPER, Lydia H.; d/o ___ & Mary F. CARPER; 17y; sgl; b. & res. ClrkVA; (lic) 23 Feb 1880; p. 15
CARVER, John; s/o Joseph CARVER & Frances CARVER; 20y; sgl; farm hand; b. & res. ClrkVA; m. 30 Oct 1877 at bride's father's house in ClrkVA to STUMP, Emma; d/o Simon R. F. STUMP & Elizabeth STUMP; 19y; sgl; b. & res. ClrkVA; (lic) 29 Oct 1877; p. 226
CARY, Bushrod (col); s/o Henry & Aleice? CARY; 50y; wid; farm hand; b. & res. ClrkVA; m. 12 Mar 1885 at ClrkVA to BARBER, Hannah (col); d/o A. & Harriet BARBER; 27y; sgl; b. & res. ClrkVA; (lic) 12 Mar 1885; p. 118
CASTLEMAN, Mann R. P.; s/o Alfred & Margaret L. CASTLEMAN; 28y last May; sgl; farmer; b. & res. ClrkVA; m. 22 Nov 1866 at Berryville to MILTON, Maria A.; d/o James F. & Sidney MILTON; 23y; sgl; b. FqrVA; res. ClrkVA; (lic) 21 Nov 1866; p. 24
CAVE, James; s/o John & Nancy CAVE; 24y; sgl; farm hand; b. PageVA; res. ClrkVA; m. 29 Oct 1877 at ClrkVA to PYLES, Maggie; d/o William & Ann PYLES; 19y; sgl; b. & res. ClrkVA; (lic) 29 Oct 1877; father of bride was present at the issuing; p. 225
CHAPIN, John D.; s/o not given; 26y; sgl; not given; b. not given; res. ClrkVA; m. 3 Nov 1886 at ClrkVA to KERFOOT, Nellie M.; d/o Judson G. and Fannie KERFOOT; 24y; sgl; b. & res. ClrkVA; (lic) 1 Nov 1886; p. 145
CHAPIN, William T.; s/o Charles & Mary A. CHAPIN; 21y; sgl; merchant; b. RckbrVA; res. ClrkVA; m. 10 Sep 1867 at ClrkVA to KERFOOT, Mattie A.; d/o George L. & Lucy J. KERFOOT; 21y; sgl; b. & res. ClrkVA; (lic) 5 Sep 1867; p. 40
CHAPMAN, Geo.; s/o Wm. & Margaret CHAPMAN; 24y; sgl; rail road hand; b. FredVA; res. JeffWVA; m. 13 Jan 1881 at

Berryville to GRAY, Mary F.; d/o Wm. & Ellen GRAY; 18y; sgl; b. RappVA; res. ClrkVA; (lic) 11 Jan 1881; grandfather Wm. MANUEL was present and consent to bride's marriage; p. 33

CHAPMAN, George M.; s/o Thomas & Deborah CHAPMAN; 27y; sgl; farmer; b. RckhmVA; res. ClrkVA; m. 26 Oct 1871 at ClrkVA to PERRY, Sallie J.; d/o John M. & Catharine PERRY; 21y; sgl; b. & res. ClrkVA; (lic) 25 Oct 1871; p. 119

CHAPMAN, James C.; s/o Strother & Mary A. CHAPMAN; 37y; wid; farm hand; b. Frederick Co.; res. ClrkVA; m. 16 Nov 1882 at FredVA to POPP, Lucy; d/o Michael & Mary E. POPP; 35y; sgl; b. & res. ClrkVA; (lic) 11 Nov 1882; p. 66

CHAPMAN, John W.; s/o John W. & Hannah C. CHAPMAN; 37y; wid; laborer; b. Winchester Va; res. FredVA; m. 9 Sep 1878 at ClrkVA to SIMMONS, Fannie; d/o Mr. CHAPMAN does not know; 35y; sgl; b. Cecil Co. Md; res. ClrkVA at Jno. B. CARTER place; (lic) 9 Sep 1878; p. 238

CHAPPEL, George W.; s/o James M. & Susan P. CHAPPELL; 32y; sgl; blacksmith; b. LdnVA; res. ClrkVA; m. 16 Oct 1877 at ClrkVA to LLOYD, Margaret D.; d/o James W. & Catharine LLOYD; 17y; sgl; b. & res. ClrkVA; (lic) 15 Oct 1877; father's consent given; p. 223

CHARRINGTON, Percy W.; s/o Edward & Georgeanne CHARRINGTON; 33y; sgl; merchant; b. Essex England; res. LdnVA; m. 26 Jun 1877 at Millwood to RANDOLPH, Mary H.; d/o Beverly & Mary C. RANDOLPH; 23y; sgl; b. & res. ClrkVA; (lic) 23 Jun 1877; p. 219

CHEW, Washington P.; s/o Washington & Mary CHEW; not given; sgl; printer; b. Baltimore Md; res. WashDC; m. 15 Feb 1877 at ClrkVA to LITTLE, Amanda J. [also given as Mary J.]; d/o Franklin & Mary J. LITTLE; not given; sgl; b. Harrison Co. W Va; res. ClrkVA; (lic) 14 Feb 1877; p. 215

CHRISMAN, Isaac A.; s/o John H. & Lucinda CHRISMAN; 29y; sgl; farmer; b. FredVA; res. ClrkVA; m. 30 Apr 1878 at near White Post to BRYARLY, Mary L.; d/o Richard S. & Harriet BRYARLY; 25y; sgl; b. & res. ClrkVA; (lic) 29 Apr 1878; p. 234

CHRISTIAN, Charles (col); s/o Lewis & Docie CHRISTIAN; 26y; sgl; farm hand; b. Bedford Co. Va; res. ClrkVA; m. 25 Nov 1886 at ClrkVA to WEBB, Mary (col); d/o John & Lucinda WEBB; 21y; sgl; b. & res. ClrkVA; (lic) 24 Nov 1886; p. 147

CLARK, Elijah (col); s/o Elijah & Nancey CLARK (col); 35y; sgl; farm hand; b. AlbmVA; res. ClrkVA; m. 9 Nov 1872 at Berryville to WEAVER, Sallie (col); d/o not known; 21y; sgl; b. Lynchburg, Va; res. ClrkVA; (lic) 9 Nov 1872; p. 136
CLARK, John H.; s/o John & Elizabeth CLARK; 33y; wid; farmer; b. & res. Prince William Co. Va; m. 25 Feb 1879 at ClrkVA to LEVI, Mary E.; d/o Rice W. & Benjamin LEVI; 34y; sgl; b. JeffWVA; res. ClrkVA; (lic) 24 Feb 1879; p. 254
CLARK, William F. Junr.; s/o Wm. F. & Ann CLARK; 32y; wid; pilot on Ohio River; b. Fredericksburg, Va; res. Ohio Co. W Va; m. 10 Sep 1865 at ClrkVA to ANDERSON, Lucretia E.; d/o John W. & Susan A. ANDERSON; 18y; sgl; b. JeffVA; res. ClrkVA; (lic) 9 Sept 1865; consent of bride's father given in person; p. 1
CLAY, Henry (col); s/o not known; 26y; sgl; farm hand; b. & res. ClrkVA; m. 4 Nov 1880 at ClrkVA to WILLIAMS, Margaret (col); d/o not known; 21y; sgl; b. & res. ClrkVA; (lic) 4 Nov 1880; p. 28
CLAYTON, Edward (col); s/o Robt. & Nancy CLAYTON; 38y; sgl; farm hand; b. & res. ClrkVA; m. 1 Jan 1874 at bride's residence to WILSON, Allie (col); d/o Danl. & ___ WILSON; 21y; sgl; b. & res. ClrkVA; (lic) 31 Dec 1873; p. 156
CLENDENING, Alvin C.; s/o James & Lydia CLENDENING; 28y; sgl; farmer; b. & res. BerkVA; m. 10 Mar 1885 at ClrkVA to PIERCE, Katie A.; d/o A. N. & Mary Eliz'th PIERCE; 23y; sgl; b. & res. ClrkVA; (lic) 7 Mar 1885; p. 118
CLENDENING, Thomas R.; s/o Wm. & Ruth CLENDENING; 25y last October; sgl; farmer; b. & res. LdnVA; m. 25 Jan 1866 at residence of Aaron DUBLE to BALTHAS, Sarah Jane; d/o Joseph & Rebecca BALTHAS; 26y; sgl; b. WrnVA; res. ClrkVA; (lic) 24 Jan 1866; p. 6
CLEVINGER, Thos. E.; s/o Thos. & Cath'e. CLEVINGER; 24y; sgl; farmer; b. JeffVA; res. FredVA; m. 16 Nov 1869 at ClrkVA to GRUBB, Mary L.; d/o W. B. & Mary Eliz'th GRUBB; 21y last June; sgl; b. FredVA; res. ClrkVA; (lic) 11 Nov 1869; p. 87
CLINGAN, James S.; s/o McLain & Virginia CLINGAN; 21y; sgl; farmer; b. & res. ClrkVA; m. 11 Nov 1886 at bride's residence to ALEXANDER, Laura Lee; d/o Thomas H. & Mary E. ALEXANDER; 21y; sgl; b. & res. ClrkVA; (lic) 6 Nov 1886; p. 146

CLINGAN, Samuel W.; s/o McLain & Julia CLINGAN; 26y; sgl; farmer; b. FqrVA; res. ClrkVA; m. 4 Jun 1878 at FredVA to BALDWIN, Georgia; d/o William & Anna BALDWIN; 22y; sgl; b. LdnVA; res. ClrkVA; (lic) 3 Jun 1878; p. 235
COCKEY, T. Deye; s/o T. D. & Harriet N. COCKEY; 36y; sgl; farmer; b. Baltimore Co. Md; res. ClrkVA; m. 28 May 1874 at ClrkVA to BAKER, Nannie H.; d/o Alex'r. & Caroline BAKER; 29y; sgl; b. & res. ClrkVA; (lic) 26 May 1874; p. 161
COLBERT, Scott (col); s/o ___ & ___ COLBERT (col); 28y; sgl; farm hand; b. & res. ClrkVA; m. 28 Sep 1867 at ClrkVA to POTTER, Patsy (col); d/o ___ and Mary POTTER (col); 22y; sgl; b. & res. ClrkVA; (lic) 27 Sep 1867; p. 42
COLE, Taylor E.; s/o Lewis & Mary COLE; 26y; sgl; carpenter; b. FredVA; res. Grafton W. Va; m. 28 Oct 1875 at near White Post to HENING, Emma V.; d/o Peter E. & Mary HENNING; 24y; sgl; b. FredVA; res. ClrkVA; (lic) 25 Oct 1875; p. 188
COLEMAN, John D.; s/o John & Lydia COLEMAN; 25y; sgl; farmer; b. JeffWVA; res. ClrkVA; m. 24 Jan 1883 at ClrkVA to LOUTHAN, Lizzie L.; d/o John R. and ___ LOUTHAN; 21y; sgl; b. & res. ClrkVA; (lic) 23 Jan 1883; p. 76
COLLIER, Charles; s/o John N. & Mary E. COLLIER; 22y; sgl; farmer; b. & res. ClrkVA; m. 22 Feb 1872 at ClrkVA to ALEXANDER, Adie; d/o James F. & Lydia Jane ALEXANDER; 17y; sgl; b. LdnVA; res. ClrkVA; (lic) not given; p. 127
COLSON, J??? J. and MILES, Mary [Letter dated 28 May 1876 by Charles MILES stating he gives J?? J. COLSON his permission for license to marry Mary his daughter. p. 91B]
COLSTON, Edward A.; s/o Robert A. & Matilda COLSTON; 22y; sgl; farmer; b. & res. ClrkVA; m. 4 Mar 1868 at ClrkVA to SHEPHERD, Mary E.; d/o Parkinson D. & Eliza SHEPHERD; 26y; sgl; b. & res. ClrkVA; (lic) 29 Feb 1868; p. 56
COLSTON, John T.; s/o Wm. H. & Mary Ann COLSTON; 24y; sgl; farmer; b. ClrkVA; res. Jefferson Co.; m. 14 Feb 1867 at ClrkVA to COLSTON, Susan R.; d/o Robert A. & Matilda S. COLSTON; 26y; sgl; b. & res. ClrkVA; (lic) 12 Feb 1867; p. 32
COLSTON, Randolph C.; s/o Robert A. & Matilda S. COLSTON; 29y; sgl; farmer; b. ClrkVA; res. JeffWVA; m. 14 Oct 1879 at ClrkVA to HANSUCKER, Mary E.; d/o Geo. W. & Jane HANSUCKER; 25y; sgl; b. & res. ClrkVA; (lic) 14 Oct 1879; p. 5

COMER, George F.; s/o Jacob & Susan COMER; 23y; sgl; farmer; b. PageVA; res. ClrkVA; m. 19 Apr 1870 at Winchester Va to WALLACE, Annie; d/o not given; 22y; sgl; b. & res. ClrkVA; (lic) 19 Apr 1870; p. 95
CONRAD, William G.; s/o James W. & Maria S. CONRAD; 28y; sgl; merchant; b. WrnVA; res. Benton, Montana Territory; m. Thursday 12 Oct 1876 at Poplar Hill to BOWEN, Fannie E.; d/o ___ & Almira G. BOWEN; 23y; sgl; b. not given; res. ClrkVA; (lic) 5 Sep 1876; p. 206
CONWAY, Giles M.; s/o Thomas & Mary CONWAY; 22y; sgl; farmer; b. & res. FredVA; m. 20 Jul 1877 at Millwood to McDONALD, Catharine V.; d/o Harry & Fannie McDONALD; 17y; sgl; b. & res. ClrkVA; (lic) 20 Jul 1877; p. 220
COOK, Geo. E. (col); s/o Edmund & Fanny COOK; 33y; sgl; carpenter; b. Richmond Va; res. ClrkVA; m. 20 Oct 1881 at bride's residence to COLSTON, Malinda (col); d/o Jacob & Ellen COLSTON; 24y; sgl; b. & res. ClrkVA; (lic) 20 Oct 1881; p. 48
COOK, John (col); s/o Edmund & Amanda COOK; 22y; sgl; farm hand; b. & res. ClrkVA; m. 28 Apr 1881 at ClrkVA to CHASE, Mary (col); d/o ___ & Gini CHASE; 25y; sgl; b. & res. ClrkVA; (lic) 27 Apr 1881; p. 40
COOKE, Frederick (col); s/o Burwell & Charlotte COOKE (col); 22y; sgl; farm hand; b. & res. ClrkVA; m. 9 Oct 1869 at ClrkVA to GARDINER, Hannah (col); d/o Isaac & Betsy GARDINER (col); 21y; sgl; b. & res. ClrkVA; (lic) 9 Oct 1869; p. 85
COOKE, John Esten; s/o John R. & Maria P. COOKE; 36y; sgl; lawyer; b. Frederick Co.; res. ClrkVA; m. 18 Sep 1867 at Millwood to PAGE, Mary Frances; d/o Dr. Robert and Susan R. PAGE; 26y; sgl; b. & res. ClrkVA; (lic) 9 Sep 1867; p. 41
COOKE, Tom (col); s/o Burwell COOKE & ___; 23y; sgl; farm hand; b. & res. ClrkVA; m. 21 Apr 1867 at Tuleyries Farm to WEBB, Lucinda (col); d/o unknown; 22y; wid; b. & res. ClrkVA; (lic) 19 Apr 1867; p. 34
COOPER, Charles (col); s/o Wm. & Mollie Cooper (col); 25y; sgl; farm hand; b. & res. ClrkVA; m. 17 Aug 1867 at ClrkVA to ROBINSON, Milley (col); d/o Samuel & Jane ROBINSON (col); 21y; sgl; b. & res. ClrkVA; (lic) 16 Aug 1867; p. 39
COOPER, Emanuel S.; s/o David & Mary E. COOPER; 22y; sgl; farmer; b. Frederick Co.; res. ClrkVA; m. 14 Dec 1869 at bride's residence to WILLINGHAM, Harriet V.; d/o William &

Matilda WILLINGHAM; 19y; sgl; b. & res. ClrkVA; (lic) 11 Dec 1869; p. 90
COOPER, Jacob E.; s/o Harrison & Alcinda COOPER; 22y; sgl; railroading; b. & res. ClrkVA; m. 10 Aug 1881 at ClrkVA to ROYSTON, Effa S.; d/o Geo. R. & Kate ROYSTON; 21y; sgl; b. & res. ClrkVA; (lic) 8 Aug 1881; p. 45
COOPER, John J. (col); s/o Robert & Sallie COOPER; 22y; sgl; farm hand; b. & res. ClrkVA; m. 10 Sep 1874 at Berryville to BROOKS, Alice (col); d/o Spencer & ___ BROOKS; 21y; sgl; b. Hanover Co. Va; res. ClrkVA; (lic) 2 Sep 1874; p. 164
COPENHAVER, Geo. W.; s/o M. B. & M. F. COPENHAVER; 21y; sgl; farmer; b. & res. ClrkVA; m. 5 Jun 1866 at Berryville to CASTLEMAN, Virginia C.; d/o James & Catharine CASTLEMAN; 18y; sgl; b. & res. ClrkVA; (lic) 4 Jun 1866; consent of bride's Guardian given [in] person; p. 12
COPENHAVER, Joseph H.; s/o John & Sarah COPENHAVER; 25y; sgl; farmer; b. & res. ClrkVA; m. 26 Aug 1874 at FredVA to HIGGINS, Nannie B.; d/o John B. & Mary C. HIGGINS; 18y; sgl; b. FredVA; res. ClrkVA; (lic) 24 Aug 1874; p. 163
CORDER, H. J.; s/o Simeon & Susan CORDER; 35y; sgl; farmer; b. WrnVA; res. ClrkVA; m. 4 Jun 1867 at Berryville to WRITT, Edney Jane; d/o Thompson and ___ WRITT; 21y; sgl; b. & res. ClrkVA; (lic) 4 Jun 1867; p. 36
CORDER, Sommerville; s/o Elias & Elizabeth CORDER; 24y; sgl; farmer; b. FqrVA; res. ClrkVA; m. 19 Jun 1881 at ClrkVA to WILLINGHAM, Bettie; d/o Jackson & Sarah WILLINGHAM; 26y; sgl; b. WrnVA; res. ClrkVA; (lic) 16 Jun 1881; p. 42
CORNELL, Asa; s/o Thos. CORNELL & Harriet CORNELL; 21y; sgl; farmer; b. LdnVA; res. ClrkVA; m. 11 Mar 1875 at Berryville to CHAPMAN, Sarah; d/o Wm. and Margaret CHAPMAN; 23y; sgl; b. JeffVA; res. ClrkVA; (lic) 11 Mar 1875; p. 177
CORNWELL, Edward; s/o Fielding & Linda CORNWELL; 48y; sgl; farmer; b. FredVA (now ClrkVA); res. FredVA; m. 31 Mar 1868 at White Post to RUST, Alcinda; d/o Matthew & ___ RUST; 38y; sgl; b. FredVA (now ClrkVA); res. ClrkVA; (lic) 24 Mar 1868; p. 58
CORNWELL, Harvey Washington; s/o Thomas & Mary CORNWELL; 21y; sgl; farmer; b. Frederick Co.; res. ClrkVA; m. 22 Sep 1868 at Winchester to BUCKLEY, Arry Minty; d/o Bushrod & Eliza BUCKLEY; 18y; sgl; b. Frederick Co.; res.

ClrkVA; (lic) 21 Sep 1868; written consent of bride's mother given; p. 66

COSBY, William G.; s/o Wm. H. & Sarah F. COSBY; 28y; sgl; rail road employee; b. AlbmVA; res. Richmond Va; m. 20 Oct 1880 at not given to BRIGGS, Mollie A. R.; d/o James M. & Louisa BRIGGS; 23y; sgl; b. Stafford Co. Va; res. ClrkVA; (lic) 20 Oct 1880; p. 27

COUSINS, Silas (col); s/o Jordan & Sallie COUSINS (col); 35y; wid; stone mason; b. Fluvannah Co. Va; res. ClrkVA; m. 2 Oct 1869 at ClrkVA to DIAH, Betsey (col); d/o Davy & Lucy DIAH (col); 22y; sgl; b. AugVA; res. ClrkVA; (lic) 2 Oct 1869; p. 85

COX, Samuel; s/o Samuel & Catharine COX; 24y; sgl; farmer; b. LdnVA; res. LdnVA; m. 12 Feb 1867 at ClrkVA to HESSOR, Mary D.; d/o Andrew and Mary HESSOR; 21y; sgl; b. Taylor Co. W. Va; res. ClrkVA; (lic) 2 Feb 1867; p. 31

COXIN, Howard (col); s/o Morgan and Ann COXIN; 21y; sgl; farm hand; b. & res. ClrkVA; m. 24 May 1881 at Berryville to FIELDS, Rebecca (col); d/o Adam & Sallie FIELDS; 21y; sgl; b. & res. ClrkVA; (lic) 24 May 1881; p. 41

COXIN, Jacob (col); s/o Morgan & Ann COXIN; 23y; wid; farm hand; b. & res. ClrkVA; m. 7 Apr 1881 at Berryville to BURNS [or BARNS], America (col); d/o not known; 24y; sgl; b. & res. ClrkVA; (lic) 7 Apr 1881; p. 38

COXSON, Jacob (col); s/o Morgan & Ann COXSON; 22y; sgl; farm hand; b. & res. ClrkVA; m. Tuesday 30 May 1876 at Berryville to MYRES, Elizabeth (col); d/o father not known, mother Palia MYRES; 20y; sgl; b. & res. ClrkVA; (lic) 29 May 1876; p. 201

CRIM, Wm. H.; s/o Wm. & Elizabeth CRIM; 25y; sgl; farmer; b. ShenVA; res. ClrkVA; m. 14 Jun 1866 at Charlestown to ROWLAND, Rebecca J.; d/o John & Lydia ROWLAND; 21y; sgl; b. Jefferson Co.; res. ClrkVA; (lic) 11 Jun 1866; p. 14

CRISP, William B.; s/o Grafton & ___ CRISP; 27y; sgl; atty of law; b. Maryland; res. Baltimore Md.; m. 29 Jul 1886 at Berryville to VANDEVANTER, Mary N.; d/o Cornelius & ___ VANDEVANTER; 19y; sgl; b. & res. ClrkVA; (lic) 28 Jul 1886; p. 140

CROW, Michael; s/o Isaac & Nancy CROW; 46y; wid; farmer; b. Fayette Co. Pennsylvania; res. ClrkVA; m. 25 Oct 1877 at ClrkVA to BUSHONG, Susan F.; d/o not given; 36y; wid; b. ShenVA; res. ClrkVA; (lic) 22 Oct 1877; p. 224

CROWN, Jno. O.; s/o Frederick N. & Hannah S. CROWN; 35y; sgl; editor; b. Smithburg, Washington Co. Md; res. ClrkVA; m. 14 Oct 1873 at Grace Church Berryville to SMITH, Sarah Jane; d/o Jonathan S. & Rebecca A. SMITH; 25y; sgl; b. & res. ClrkVA; (lic) 13 Oct 1873; p. 150

CRUTCHFIELD, Mencer (col); s/o John & Matilda CRUTCHFIELD; 22y; sgl; farm hand; b. Fredericksburg Va; res. ClrkVA; m. 5 Nov 1885 at ClrkVA to WHEELER, Florinda (col); d/o James & Mary WHEELER; 19y; sgl; b. & res. ClrkVA; (lic) 5 Nov 1885; father of girl present and consent given; p. 127

CULLER, Henry (Colonel); s/o Capt. Henry & Annie CULLER; 56y; wid; farmer; b. Frederick Co. Maryland; res. Frederick City Maryland; m. 6 Oct 1874 at ClrkVA to SOWERS, H. L.; d/o ___ & ___ HOLLINGSWORTH; 40y; wid; b. FredVA; res. Clarke co.; (lic) 22 Sep 1874; p. 165

CUP, David; s/o Jacob & Elizabeth CUPS; 52y; wid; farmer; b. AugVA; res. Hampshire Co. W. Va; m. 21 Jun 1870 at ClrkVA to SMITH, Sarah A.; d/o James & Elizabeth SMITH; 26y; sgl; b. & res. ClrkVA; (lic) 20 Jun 1870; p. 97

CURTIS, Edwin R.; s/o George and Annie CURTIS; 24y; sgl; civil engineer; b. & res. BerkWVA; m. 27 Dec 1882 at ClrkVA to CARTER, Susan R.; d/o John & Bettie CARTER; 21y; sgl; b. & res. ClrkVA; (lic) 26 Dec 1882; p. 73

CYRUS, Abraham (col); s/o Isaac & Jane CYRUS; 26y; sgl; house carpenter; b. & res. ClrkVA; m. 10 Aug 1867 at John MARSHALL's to WALDON, Adelaide (col); d/o Lewis & Sylva WALDON; 22y; wid; b. & res. ClrkVA; (lic) 10 Aug 1867; p. 39

DANKS, James (col); s/o Lancaster & Sarah DANKS; 60y; wid; farm hand; b. & res. ClrkVA; m. 21 Jun 1873 at ClrkVA to WILLIAMS, Rose (col); d/o ___ & Mollie WILLIAMS; 45y; wid; b. & res. ClrkVA; (lic) 20 Jun 1873; p. 146

DANKS, Joseph (col); s/o James & Christena DANKS; 33y; wid; farm hand; b. & res. ClrkVA; m. 16 Apr 1885 at ClrkVA to BERRY, Rachel (col); d/o Joseph & Evelina BERRY; 21y; sgl; b. & res. ClrkVA; (lic) 16 Apr 1885; p. 121

DANKS, Joseph (col); s/o James & Christina DANKS; 22y; sgl; farm hand; b. & res. ClrkVA; m. 1 Jun 1882 at ClrkVA to WHEELER, Bertie (col); d/o James & Fannie WHEELER; 21y; sgl; b. & res. ClrkVA; (lic) 1 Jun 1882; p. 59

DARR, Philip A.; s/o Philip & Lucinda DARR; 24y; sgl; rail road hand; b. WrnVA; res. ClrkVA; m. 30 Aug 1881 at Stone

Bridge, ClrkVA to JACKSON, Eudora D.; d/o Jno. A. & Mary A. JACKSON; 25y; sgl; b. CulpVA; res. ClrkVA; (lic) 29 Aug 1881; p. 46

DAUGHERITY, Wm. (col); s/o George & Celia DAUGHERITY (col); 49y; wid; farm hand; b. & res. ClrkVA; m. 10 Dec 1872 at ClrkVA to RUNNER, Emily (col); d/o G. L. & Aga RUNNER (col); 55y; wid; b. & res. ClrkVA; (lic) 10 Dec 1872; p. 139

DAVIS, Joseph; s/o Howell & Sarah DAVIS; 60y; wid; farmer; b. & res. LdnVA; m. 8 Oct 1874 at ClrkVA to THOMPSON, Mary F.; d/o French & Nancy THOMPSON; 35y; sgl; b. LdnVA; res. ClrkVA; (lic) 29 Sep 1874; p. 166

DAVIS, Joshua; s/o Wm. & Nancy DAVIS; 25y; sgl; farmer; b. Hampshire Co. Va; res. ClrkVA; m. 18 Dec 1873 at bride's residence to RUSSELL, Martha E.; d/o Jas. E. & Harriet A. RUSSELL; 23y; sgl; b. & res. ClrkVA; (lic) 17 Dec 1873; p. 154

DAVIS, Lewellyn L.; s/o A. W. G. & Rachael DAVIS; 26y; sgl; farmer; b. & res. Greenbrier Co. W Va; m. 29 Oct 1873 at bride's residence to HARRIS, Octavia L.; d/o Wm. B. & Lucy M. HARRIS; 27y; sgl; b. & res. ClrkVA; (lic) 27 Oct 1873; p. 152

DAVIS, William S.; s/o John & Alcinda DAVIS; 24y; sgl; farmer; b. & res. ClrkVA; m. 22 Mar 1881 at ClrkVA to GARRETT, Florence; d/o Isaac & Mary C. GARRETT; 18y; sgl; b. Hardy Co. Va; res. ClrkVA; (lic) 21 Mar 1881; p. 37

DEAHL, Wm. P.; s/o George & Martha DEAHL; 36y; sgl; farmer; b. Hanover Co. Va; res. ClrkVA; m. 6 Sep 1866 at ClrkVA to CRIDER, Mary E.; d/o Fredrick & Sarah CRIDER; 27y; sgl; b. FredVA; res. ClrkVA; (lic) 5 Sep 1866; p. 18

DEARMONT, James Thomas; s/o Michael & Lucy DEARMONT; 20y 11m 10d; sgl; farmer; b. & res. ClrkVA; m. 10 Oct 1865 at residence of Peter DEARMONT to BELL, Mary Matilda A.; d/o Strother & ___ BELL; 20y; sgl; b. & res. ClrkVA; (lic) 7 Oct 1865; consent of Wash'n. DEARMONT husband & Guardian given in writing and consent of Peter DEARMONT Guardian of wife given in person.; p. 2

DEARMONT, Washington; s/o Michael & Lucy DEARMONT; 38y; sgl; Sheriff of ClrkVA; b. & res. ClrkVA; m. Tuesday 17 Mar 1868 at Peter DEARMONT's residence ClrkVA to BELL, Hatty H.; d/o Strother & Jane A. BELL; 21y; sgl; b. & res. ClrkVA; (lic) 12 Mar 1868; p. 57

DEARMONT, Wash'n.; s/o Michael & Lucy DEARMONT; 40y; wid; farmer; b. FredVA (now Clarke); res. ClrkVA; m. 15 Sep 1870 at residence of Franklin LITTLE ClrkVA to POAGUE, Jennie E. (Mrs., mother of George POAGUE); d/o Strother H. & Jane Ellen BOWEN; 25y; wid; b. not given; res. ClrkVA; (lic) 7 Sep 1870; p. 100

DECK, Fredrick A.; s/o Fredrick D. & Elizabeth DECK; 24y; sgl; wagon maker; b. FredVA; res. ClrkVA; m. 15 Oct 1868 at ClrkVA to CARPER, Annie V.; d/o Wm. & Mary M. CARPER; 17y; sgl; b. FredVA; res. ClrkVA; (lic) 13 Oct 1868; p. 68

DECK, John W.; s/o Geo. DECK & ___ DECK; 24y; sgl; blacksmith; b. FredVA; res. ClrkVA; m. 17 May 1877 at Winchester Va to NEWCOME, Flora A.; d/o John & Alcinda NEWCOME; 21y; sgl; b. & res. ClrkVA; (lic) 16 May 1877; p. 218

DEEVERS, Joseph; s/o Richard & Mary DEEVERS; 25y; sgl; farm hand; b. PageVA; res. ClrkVA; m. 22 May 1877 at near Stone Chapel ClrkVA to WALKER, Nancy Virginia [also given as Jinnie]; d/o Samuel & Jane WALKER; 21y; sgl; b. PageVA; res. ClrkVA; (lic) 22 May 1877; p. 219

DENNY, J. Marshall; s/o Robt. L. & Eliza DENNY; 29y; sgl; farmer; b. FredVA; res. ClrkVA; m. 20 Jan 1875 at bride's residence to CHRISMAN, Larua [Laura?] C.; d/o Jno. H. & Lucinda CHRISMAN; 27y; sgl; b. FredVA; res. ClrkVA; (lic) 14 Jan 1875; p. 174

DENNY, Robert A.; s/o Robt. L. & Eliza DENNY; 27y; sgl; jeweller; b. & res. FredVA; m. 27 Oct 1886 at ClrkVA to HENING, Florence L.; d/o Peter & May HENING; 33y; sgl; b. FredVA; res. ClrkVA; (lic) 26 Oct 1886; p. 144

DEWAR, Joshua Jefferson; s/o Thomas & Eliza DEWAR; 35y; sgl; farmer; b. FredVA; res. ClrkVA; m. Wednesday 19 Mar 1879 at ClrkVA to WILSON, Elizabeth; d/o Jerry & Margaret WILSON; 22y; sgl; b. & res. ClrkVA; (lic) 15 Mar 1879; p. 255

DICKERSON, Edward (col); s/o Charles & Amy DICKINSON (col); 23y; sgl; farm hand; b. New Orleans; res. ClrkVA; m. 16 May 1869 at Millwood to JONES, Hannah (col); d/o Jere & Polly JONES; 25y; sgl; b. & res. ClrkVA; (lic) 15 May 1869; p. 81

DIEFFENDERFER, John G.; s/o Geo. B. & Camilla DIEFFENDERFER; 36y; sgl; carpenter; b. & res. Winchester, FredVA; m. 23 Jul 1881 at Berryville to HAMPSON, Isabella;

d/o ___ & Mary HAMPSON; 35y; sgl; b. London, England; res. ClrkVA; (lic) 23 Jul 1881; p. 44

DIFFENDERFER, Bennett R.; s/o George & Ann R. DIFFENDERFER; 25y; sgl; farmer; b. & res. ClrkVA; m. 2 Mar 1871 at ClrkVA to DICKS, Landora M.; d/o Edward & Catharine DICKS; 22y; sgl; b. FredVA; res. ClrkVA; (lic) not given; p. 110

DIFFENDERFER, John W.; s/o Geo. W. & Ann R. DIFFENDERFER; 25y; sgl; farmer; b. & res. ClrkVA; m. 12 Jun 1873 at ClrkVA to GRUBBS, Ann S.; d/o George W. & Maria GRUBBS; 22y; sgl; b. & res. ClrkVA; (lic) not given; p. 146

DINGES, George A.; s/o James & Elizabeth DINGES; 28y; sgl; plasterer; b. & res. FredVA; m. 6 Nov 1879 at ClrkVA to SNYDER, Georgeanna; d/o Newton & ___ SNYDER; 24y; sgl; b. Baltimore Md; res. ClrkVA; (lic) 4 Nov 1879; p. 7

DIXON, John J. (col); s/o Jackson & Louisa DIXON; 26y; sgl; railroading; b. FqrVA; res. ClrkVA; m. 12 May 1881 at bride's residence to BURNS, Violet (col); d/o Horace & Malinda BURNS; 18y; sgl; b. & res. ClrkVA; (lic) 12 May 1881; bride's mother gave her consent in person; p. 41

DOLEMAN, George (col); s/o Jacob and Maria DOLEMAN; 22y; sgl; farm hand; b. & res. ClrkVA; m. Thursday 25 Dec 1879 at Millwood to WILLIAMS, Priscilla (col); d/o John and ___ WILLIAMS; 16y; sgl; b. & res. ClrkVA; (lic) 25 Dec 1879; George DOLEMAN sworn as to father of Priscilla having given consent to issue above license; p. 12

DOLEMAN, Humphrey (col); s/o Jacob & Maria DOLEMAN; 28y; sgl; laborer; b. & res. ClrkVA; m. Wednesday 27 Dec 1876 at ClrkVA to WILLIAMS, Alice (col); d/o Lewis & Lydia WILLIAMS; 19y; sgl; b. & res. ClrkVA; (lic) 26 Dec 1876; father present & permission given; p. 212

DOLEMAN, James (col); s/o Jacob & Gracey DOLEMAN; 30y; sgl; farm hand; b. & res. ClrkVA; m. 23 Nov 1876 at ClrkVA to STRANGE, Charlotte (col); d/o not known & Adeline STRANGE; 25y; sgl; b. not known; res. ClrkVA; (lic) 23 Nov 1876; p. 209

DONALDSON, Andrew; s/o John & Betsy S. DONALDSON; 40y; sgl; farmer; b. Scotland; res. WrnVA; m. 22 Jan 1872 at ClrkVA to DUNCAN, Mary L.; d/o Wm. C. & Eliza A. KERFOOT; 35y; wid; b. & res. ClrkVA; (lic) not given; p. 124

DORSEY, Harry C.; s/o John R. & Eveline DORSEY; 28y; sgl; farmer; b. & res. Howard Co. Md; m. 17 Nov 1885 at ClrkVA to FRANCIS, Anna Lee; d/o William & Ann Eliza FRANCIS; 24y; sgl; b. LdnVA; res. ClrkVA; (lic) 16 Nov 1885; p. 128

DORTCH, Wm. T.; s/o William & Drucilla DORTCH; 46y; wid; attorney at law; b. Nash Co. North Carolina; res. Goldsboro North Carolina; m. 3 Jan 1872 at bride's residence to WILLIAMS, Harriet; d/o Allen & Helen WILLIAMS; 26y; sgl; b. & res. ClrkVA; (lic) 2 Jan 1872; p. 123

DOVE, Albin P.; s/o Thos. J. & Adelia DOVE; 29y; sgl; farmer; b. Virginia; res. ClrkVA; m. 9 Apr 1878 at ClrkVA to RUSSELL, Sarah C.; d/o Westley W. & Harriet A. RUSSELL; 23y; sgl; b. WrnVA; res. ClrkVA; (lic) 2 Apr 1878; p. 233

DOVE, Wm. W.; s/o Jefferson & Deliah DOVE; 23y; sgl; farmer; b. & res. ClrkVA; m. 28 May 1874 at ClrkVA to RUSSELL, Virginia; d/o W. W. & Harriet RUSSELL; 18y; sgl; b. & res. ClrkVA; (lic) 25 May 1874; p. 161

DOWNER, John Walter; s/o Wm. T. & Julia F. DOWNER; 25y; sgl; Doct. of dental surgery; b. King William Co. Va; res. JeffWVA; m. 23 Apr 1879 at Berryville to GREENE, Eliza Taylor; d/o Israel & Edmonia GREENE; 26y; sgl; b. & res. ClrkVA; (lic) 23 Apr 1879; p. 257

DOXSON, Isaac; s/o Geo. W. & Emily DOXSON; 20y; sgl; farm hand; b. Maryland; res. ClrkVA; m. 12 Feb 1879 at Berryville to KENDALL, Lucy; d/o Pendleton & Sarah KENDALL; 22y; sgl; b. JeffWVA; res. ClrkVA; (lic) 11 Feb 1879; p. 252

DRAKE, Alfred W.; s/o Jas. & Sarah DRAKE; 23y; sgl; tinner; b. Frederick Co.; res. ClrkVA; m. 12 Nov 1872 at bride's residence to FRYER, Bettie W.; d/o Matthew B. & Susan FRYER; 22y; sgl; b. Cumberland Maryland; res. ClrkVA; (lic) 11 Nov 1872; p. 136

DRISH, Henry; s/o John & Margaret DRISH; 30y; sgl; working in lumber; b. & res. ClrkVA; m. 25 Jan 1877 at ClrkVA to LANHAM, Rebecca V.; d/o William & Rebecca LANHAM; 23y; sgl; b. LdnVA; res. ClrkVA; (lic) 23 Jan 1877; p. 215

DRISH, John Wm.; s/o Robert & Arrissa DRISH; 19y; sgl; farmer; b. & res. ClrkVA; m. 24 Feb 1885 at Millwood to SYMONS, Mary S.; d/o Chas. A. & Martha A. SYMONS; 20y; sgl; b. FqrVA; res. ClrkVA; (lic) 23 Feb 1885; consent of groom & bride's parents given in writing; p. 117

DUBLE, John H.; s/o Adam & Jane Cath.; 30y; sgl; farmer; b. & res. ClrkVA; m. 16 Dec 1880 at ClrkVA to SNYDER, Ella T.;

d/o Newton & ___ SNYDER; 21y; sgl; b. WrnVA; res. ClrkVA; (lic) 13 Dec 1880; p. 30

DUKE, Thomas H.; s/o Thomas DUKE & Sidney DUKE; 50y; wid; farmer; b. & res. ClrkVA; m. 11 Oct 1875 at ClrkVA to DAVOLT, Elizabeth; d/o William & Elizabeth DAVOLT; 28y; sgl; b. Washington Co. Md; res. ClrkVA; (lic) 11 Oct 1875; p. 187

DUKE, William A.; s/o Thos. & Portia S. DUKE; 23y; sgl; farmer; b. & res. ClrkVA; m. 13 Jun 1884 at Berryville to SWAINEY, Clara; d/o ___ & Mary F. SWAINEY; 21y; sgl; b. BerkWVA; res. ClrkVA; (lic) 13 Jun 1884; p. 101

DUNBAR, David (col); s/o David & Hannah DUNBAR; 33y; sgl; in a ware house; b. ClrkVA; res. Pen[n]sylvania; m. 6 Dec 1866 at Audley, ClrkVA to MITCHELL, Ann (col); d/o Cornelius & Polley MITCHELL; 20y; sgl; b. & res. ClrkVA; (lic) 5 Dec 1866; p. 25

DUNKLEE, Frank E.; s/o Charles & Mary DUNKLEE; 26y; sgl; merchant; b. Salem, Roanoke Co. Va; res. Giles Co. Va; m. 28 Apr 1881 at ClrkVA to WILLIAMS, Nannie R.; d/o E. P. & R. A. WILLIAMS; 19y; sgl; b. & res. ClrkVA; (lic) 27 Apr 1881; p. 40

DUNN, Chas. E.; s/o Wm. & Jane DUNN; 21y; sgl; farmer; b. & res. FredVA; m. 18 Nov 1869 at bride's residence to SHIMP, Eliza; d/o Geo. W. & Julia A. SHIMP; 19y; sgl; b. & res. ClrkVA; (lic) 15 Nov 1869; letter of consent from Mrs. Julia A. SHIMP; p. 88

DUNN, Robert W.; s/o John & Francis DUNN; 24y; sgl; farmer; b. Prince William Co. Va; res. Frederick Co.; m. 24 Feb 1880 at ClrkVA to NUCOME, Mary S.; d/o John & Alcinda J. NUCOME; 22y; sgl; b. & res. ClrkVA; (lic) 23 Feb 1880; p. 16

DYER, George W. (col); s/o David & Lucy DYER; 26y; sgl; farm hand; b. AugVA; res. ClrkVA; m. 13 May 1874 at ClrkVA to JORDAN, Louisa (col); d/o ___ & Fany THOMPSON; 25y; wid; b. & res. ClrkVA; (lic) 13 May 1874; p. 160

EATON, John M.; s/o Philip & Frances EATON; 24y; sgl; not given; b. ShenVA; res. ClrkVA; m. 10 May 1874 at bride's residence to HOUGH, Mollie; d/o Jackson & Elizabeth HOUGH; 21y; sgl; b. & res. ClrkVA; (lic) 6 May 1874; p. 160

EBY, Clarence D.; s/o Warren & Virginia EBY; 25y; sgl; merchant; b. & res. JeffWVA; m. 24 Apr 1883 at Berryville to HARDESTY, Rose T.; d/o James & ___ HARDESTY; 23y; sgl; b. & res. ClrkVA; (lic) 24 Apr 1883; p. 81

EDMOND, Benj.; s/o Joseph & Ellen EDMOND; 25y; sgl; mechanick; b. & res. JeffVA; m. 19 Aug 1868 at Berryville to NORRISON, Fanny; d/o Alfred E. & Elizabeth NORRISON; 21y; sgl; b. BerkVA; res. ClrkVA; (lic) 19 Aug 1868; note of permission for his daughter; p. 64

EDWARDS, Benj'n. F.; s/o Henry & Mary Ann EDWARDS; 23y (20 Jun 1866); sgl; farmer; b. & res. ClrkVA; m. 2 Aug 1866 at near Berryville to PIER, Sarah Catharine; d/o John & Mary PIER; 21y (1 May 1866); sgl; b. ShenVA; res. ClrkVA; (lic) 28 Jul 1866; p. 15

EDWARDS, Henry; s/o Joseph & Nancy EDWARDS; 62y; wid; farmer; b. St. Marys Co. Maryland; res. ClrkVA; m. 14 Dec 1871 at ClrkVA to MARLOW, Tacey; d/o Wm. & Lucretia WATKINS; 52y; wid; b. FredVA; res. ClrkVA; (lic) 13 Dec 1871; p. 120

EDWARDS, John (col); s/o Simeon & Sarah EDWARDS; 27y; sgl; livery stable; b. & res. ClrkVA; m. 17 May 1883 at ClrkVA to LIGHTFOOT, Emily (col); d/o Albert & Emily LIGHTFOOT; 21y; sgl; b. & res. ClrkVA; (lic) 17 May 1883; p. 82

EDWARDS, Joseph W.; s/o Henry & Mary A. EDWARDS; 45y; wid; farmer; b. FredVA; res. ClrkVA; m. 25 Jul 1880 at ClrkVA to LONGERBEAM, Elizabeth; d/o Charles & Mary LONGERBEAM; 21y; sgl; b. LdnVA; res. ClrkVA; (lic) 24 Jul 1880; p. 24

EDWARDS, Pum (col); s/o Simon & Sarah EDWARDS; 30y; sgl; plasterer; b. & res. ClrkVA; m. 20 Mar 1884 at bride's residence to BROWN, Bettie (col); d/o ___ & Mary BROWN; 20y; sgl; b. & res. ClrkVA; (lic) 19 Mar 1884; p. 98

EDWARDS, William F.; s/o William H. & Francis EDWARDS; 27y; sgl; railroading; b. ClrkVA; res. Sandy Hook, Maryland; m. 20 [29?, see date license issued] Oct 1884 at ClrkVA to SCHOPPERT, Mary B.; d/o Thomas & Eveline SCHOPPERT; 20y; sgl; b. BerkVA; res. ClrkVA; (lic) 29 Oct 1884; consent given by brother; p. 108

ELLIOTT, Benjamin; s/o William & ___ ELLIOTT; 38y; wid; farmer; b. West Virginia; res. ClrkVA; m. 13 Mar 1879 at ClrkVA to CARTER, Jane; d/o James IRELAND & mother not known; 38y; wid; b. & res. ClrkVA; (lic) 13 Mar 1879; p. 254

ELLIOTT, Jacob D.; s/o John & Harriet ELLIOTT; 22y; sgl; farmer; b. & res. ClrkVA; m. 28 Oct 1885 at ClrkVA to BROMLEY, Martha E.; d/o James & Roberta BROMLEY; 22y; sgl; b. & res. ClrkVA; (lic) 17 Oct 1885; p. 126

ELLYET, James W.; s/o Christopher & Mary ELLYET; 27y; sgl; farmer; b. ClrkVA; res. FredVA; m. 13 Dec 1876 at Millwood to HOLLAND, Elizabeth Garner; d/o Jno. W. & Rosa B. W. HOLLAND; 19y; sgl; b. & res. ClrkVA; (lic) 11 Dec 1876; p. 211

ELSEA, Andrew J.; s/o Albert & Lutishia ELSEA; 21y; sgl; farmer; b. & res. ClrkVA; m. 23 May 1871 at bride's residence to DEWAR, Sarah C.; d/o Thos. J. & Eliza DEWAR; 21y; sgl; b. ShenVA; res. ClrkVA; (lic) 22 May 1871; p. 112

ELSEA, James D.; s/o Albert & Lutitia ELSEA; 30y; sgl; farmer; b. & res. ClrkVA; m. 18 Jan 1883 at Berryville to ELSEA, Bettie E.; d/o Newton J. & Delitha ELSEA; 28y; sgl; b. & res. ClrkVA; (lic) 16 Jan 1883; p. 75

ELSEA, Joseph H.; s/o Albert & Lutecia ELSEA; 25y; sgl; farmer; b. & res. ClrkVA; m. 23 Nov 1876 at ClrkVA to CHAPPELL, Susan V.; d/o James & Susan CHAPPELL; 25y; sgl; b. LdnVA; res. ClrkVA; (lic) 21 Nov 1876; p. 209

ELSEA, Robert T.; s/o Albert & Lettie Lou ELSEA; 22y; sgl; farmer; b. Orange Co. Va; res. ClrkVA; m. 15 Feb 1870 at ClrkVA to OWENS, Anna Elizabeth; d/o Alexander & Mary OWENS; 17y; sgl; b. FqrVA; res. ClrkVA; (lic) 14 Feb 1870; sanction of her brother; p. 93

ELSEA, Thomas H. [also given as A.]; s/o Albert & Leititia ELSEA; 25y; sgl; farmer; b. & res. ClrkVA; m. 11 Feb 1880 at ClrkVA to ELSEA, Annie H.; d/o Newton & Delitha ELSEA; 27y; sgl; b. JeffWVA; res. ClrkVA; (lic) 9 Feb 1880; p. 15

ELWELL, John M.; s/o Aron & Mary ELWELL; 30y; sgl; farmer; b. LdnVA; res. WrnVA; m. Thursday 23 Dec 1875 at ClrkVA to SHIPE, Harriet C.; d/o Joseph & L. SHIPE; 24y; sgl; b. & res. ClrkVA; (lic) 23 Dec 1875; p. 194

EMBREY, John P.; s/o Isham and Martha EMBRY; 22y; sgl; farmer; b. FqrVA; res. ClrkVA; m. 2 Jun 1878 at ClrkVA to PEARSON, Alice S.; d/o Alexander & Francis PEARSON; 21y; sgl; b. LdnVA; res. ClrkVA; (lic) 1 Jun 1878; oath by Jno. W. LANHAM that Alice S. PEARSON is 21 years of age and her parents consent.; p. 235

ENDERS, John H.; s/o John & Susan H. ENDERS; 22y; sgl; miller; b. & res. Winchester Va; m. 25 Sep 1884 at ClrkVA to HANNUN, Cora L.; d/o Wm. E. & Anna V. HANNUN; 16y; sgl; b. & res. ClrkVA; (lic) 24 Sep 1884; consent of parents given; p. 107

ENGRAM, Jonathan E.; s/o William & Delila ENGRAM; 57y; wid; coach trimmer; b. JeffWVA; res. ClrkVA; m. 30 Nov 1879 at ClrkVA to WILSON, Mary C.; d/o Benjamin & ___ CUBBS?; 46y; wid; b. Martinsburg? W Va; res. ClrkVA; (lic) 20 Nov 1879; p. 8

ETCHISON, Henry N.; s/o Frederick and Christiana ETCHISON; 36y; wid; furniture business; b. FredMD; res. Knoxville, FredMD; m. 27 Nov 1866 at bride's residence to LOUTHAN, Mary E.; d/o John and Lydia LOUTHAN; 26y; sgl; b. & res. ClrkVA; (lic) 26 Nov 1866; p. 25

EVANS, George R.; s/o ___ & Sarah EVANS; 25y; sgl; farmer; b. & res. ClrkVA; m. 8 Dec 1881 at ClrkVA to WYNDHAM, Cornelia F.; d/o T. C. & Cornelia T. WY[N]DHAM; 19y; sgl; b. & res. ClrkVA; (lic) not given; p. 52

EVANS, William A. (col); s/o Wm. A. & Hannah EVANS; 22y; sgl; merchant; b. & res. FredVA.; m. 5 Jan 1882 at ClrkVA to LOVETT, Mary V. (col); d/o Wilson & Ma[r]tha LOVET[T]; 21y; sgl; b. & res. ClrkVA; (lic) 5 Jan 1882; p. 54

EVERHART, Harry O.; s/o Wm. G. & Mary A. EVERHART; 27y; sgl; farmer; b. FredVA; res. ClrkVA; m. 11 Feb 1886 at bride's residence to MARPLE, Lela J.; d/o Hezekiah & Mary Ann MARPLE; 19y; sgl; b. & res. ClrkVA; (lic) 11 Feb 1886; grandfather was present & gave consent for bride's marriage; p. 133

FAHNESTOCK, Samuel J.; s/o Wm. & Mary FAHNESTOCK; 30y; sgl; farmer; b. Pennsylvania; res. FredVA; m. 26 Aug 1874 at ClrkVA to CHRISMAN, Sue R.; d/o John H. and Lucinda CHRISMAN; 22y; sgl; b. FredVA; res. ClrkVA; (lic) 25 Aug 1874; p. 164

FAULDING, Stephen (col); s/o Jack & Rebecca FAULDING; 24y; not given; farm hand; b. & res. ClrkVA; m. 1 Jan 1885 at ClrkVA to MYRES, Clara (col); d/o Daniel & Betsy MYRES; 18y; not given; b. & res. ClrkVA; (lic) 1 Jan 1885; p. 115

FELLERS, Wm. H. R. B.; s/o Joshua G. & Susan M. FELLERS; 21y; sgl; farmer; b. & res. ClrkVA; m. 22 Oct 1873 at ClrkVA to THARPE, Virginia L.; d/o Jonathan & Elizabeth THARPE; 18y; sgl; b. Hardy Co. Va; res. ClrkVA; (lic) 20 Oct 1873; p. 151

FELTNER, Eben; s/o Martin & Mary FELTNER; 37y; sgl; farmer; b. & res. ClrkVA; m. 6 Jun 1886 at ClrkVA to LLOYD, Mary C.; d/o ___ & Lucinda LLOYD; 22y; sgl; b. & res. ClrkVA; (lic) 5 Jun 1886; p. 137

FELTNER, James P.; s/o Martin & Mary FELTNER; 26y; sgl; Minister of the Gospel; b. & res. ClrkVA; m. 25 Feb 1879 at ClrkVA to FLEMING, Ella; d/o William & Louise FLEMING; 33y; sgl; b. LdnVA; res. ClrkVA; (lic) 20 Feb 1879; p. 253
FERGUSON, Daniel A.; s/o John H. & Ann V. FERGUSON; 24y; sgl; farmer; b. LdnVA; res. ClrkVA; m. 15 Jan 1884 at ClrkVA to MERCHANT, Margaret E.; d/o John & Mary J. MERCHANT; 27y; sgl; b. Montgomery Co. Md; res. ClrkVA; (lic) 14 Jan 1884; p. 93
FERGUSON, John M.; s/o Josiah & Susan FERGUSON; 23y; sgl; farmer; b. & res. ClrkVA; m. 9 Nov 1875 at bride's father's ClrkVA to BELT, Lucy B.; d/o Geo. W. & Casandria BELT; 21y; sgl; b. LdnVA; res. ClrkVA; (lic) 8 Nov 1875; p. 191
FERGUSON, Thomas W.; s/o Josiah & Susan C. FERGUSON; 23y; sgl; farmer; b. & res. ClrkVA; m. 23 Sep 1873 at ClrkVA to THOMPSON, Margaret A.; d/o French & Nancy THOMPSON; 26y; sgl; b. LdnVA; res. ClrkVA; (lic) 22 Sep 1873; p. 149
FIELDS, George (col); s/o Zacharia & Judy FIELDS (col); 22y; sgl; farm hand; b. & res. ClrkVA; m. 19 May 1870 at Berryville to MILES, Louisa (col); d/o Bartley & Patty MILES (col); 18y; sgl; b. & res. ClrkVA; (lic) 18 May 1870; consent bride's parents given before issuing license; p. 96
FILMORE, Samuel B.; s/o William & Nancy FILMORE; 21y; sgl; farmer; b. AlbmVA; res. ClrkVA; m. 20 Feb 1868 at ClrkVA to SMITHEY, Martha J.; d/o Richard R. and Martha J. SMITHEY; 19y; sgl; b. FredVA; res. ClrkVA; (lic) 19 Feb 1868; p. 55
FISHER, Enoch M.; s/o William & Catharine STROTHER; 33y; sgl; farmer; b. PageVA; res. ClrkVA; m. 6 Aug 1882 at ClrkVA to STROTHER, Martha Jane; d/o Geo. W. & Ann STROTHER; 18y; sgl; b. & res. ClrkVA; (lic) 6 Aug 1882; p. 62
FITZHUGH, Wm. (col); s/o Larkin & Kitty FITZHUGH (col); 31y; sgl; farm hand; b. & res. ClrkVA; m. 6 Aug 1870 at ClrkVA to TRUNNEL, Rebecca (col); d/o ___ & Charlotte; 21y; sgl; b. & res. ClrkVA; (lic) 29 July 1870; p. 98
FLEET, Jessie (col); s/o Lee & Ann FLEET; 25y; wid; laborer; b. & res. ClrkVA; m. Thursday 19 Oct 1876 at ClrkVA to STRANGE, Bettie (col); d/o Stephen & ___ STRANGE; 23y; sgl; b. & res. ClrkVA; (lic) 18 Oct 1876; p. 207

FLEMING, Charles (col); s/o ___ & Elizabeth FLEMING; 23y; sgl; farm hand; b. ShenVA; res. ClrkVA; m. 29 Aug 1878 at not given to JOHNSON, Margaret Ann (col); d/o Spencer and Jane JOHNSON; 24y; sgl; b. & res. ClrkVA; (lic) 29 Aug 1878; p. 238

FLEMING, Robert C.; s/o Wm. & Louisa FLEMING; 223y; sgl; farmer; b. LdnVA; res. JeffWVA; m. 16 Jan 1877 at ClrkVA to CHAMBLIN, Annie L.; d/o James E. & Hannah CHAMBLIN; 20y; sgl; b. & res. ClrkVA; (lic) 13 Jan 1877; p. 214

FLEMING, Thomas W.; s/o Joseph & Sarah A. FLEMING; 32y; sgl; farmer; b. & res. ClrkVA; m. 12 Dec 1871 at ClrkVA to LLOYD, Catharine; d/o Henry & Sarah LLOYD; 21y; sgl; b. & res. ClrkVA; (lic) 11 Dec 1871; p. 120

FLETCHER, Charles V. (col); s/o Malon & Clara FLETCHER; 28y; wid; farm hand; b. FqrVA; res. ClrkVA; m. 12 Oct 1882 at Berryville to McENTREE, Maria J. (col); d/o John & Sarah McENTREE; 23y; sgl; b. & res. ClrkVA; (lic) 12 Oct 1882; p. 65

FLETCHER, Hamilton S.; s/o William & Elizabeth FLETCHER; 32y; sgl; farmer; b. & res. RappVA; m. 8 Apr 1869 at bride's residence to FUNSTEN, Mary C.; d/o Oliver R. & Mary C. FUNSTEN; 22y; sgl; b. & res. ClrkVA; (lic) 6 Apr 1869; p. 80

FLETCHER, Jno. T.; s/o William & Elizabeth FLETCHER; 34y; sgl; farmer; b. & res. RappVA; m. 30 Apr 1868 at bride's residence to FUNSTEN, Louisa N.; d/o Oliver R. & Mary C. FUNSTEN; 23y; sgl; b. & res. ClrkVA; (lic) 29 Apr 1868; p. 60

FLETCHER, Joshua Clay; s/o Joshua & Marria FLETCHER; 33y; wid; school teacher; b. FqrVA; res. ClrkVA; m. 15 Aug 1875 at father's residence (Philip EATON's) to EATON, Sarah Ophelia; d/o Philip & Francis EATON; 21y; sgl; b. ShenVA; res. ClrkVA; (lic) 14 Aug 1875; p. 184

FLETCHER, Robert E.; s/o Addison & Virginia C. FLETCHER; 21y; sgl; farmer; b. WrnVA; res. ClrkVA; m. 3 Oct 1880 at bride's residence to GRUBBS, Sarah F.; d/o Geo. W. & Ann M. GRUBBS; 23y; sgl; b. & res. ClrkVA; (lic) 2 Oct 1880; p. 26

FOLEY, Moses; s/o Wm. & Abygal FOLEY; 29y; sgl; farmer; b. LdnVA; res. RappVA; m. 22 Jun 1882 at bride's residence to RUST, Virginia W.; d/o Jas. W. & Margaret A. RUST; 22y; sgl; b. LdnVA; res. ClrkVA; (lic) 21 Jun 1882; p. 60

FOLK, John; s/o Geo. & Mary FOLK; 51y; wid; mechanic; b. Pennsylvania; res. WrnVA; m. 24 Jan 1878 at Newtown,

FredVA to CLINGAN, Virginia; d/o Geo. & ___ BOARD; 52y; wid; b. Virginia; res. ClrkVA; (lic) 22 Jan 1878; p. 230
FOLKS, Horace (col); s/o David & Martha FOLKS; 22y; sgl; farm hand; b. Prince William Co. Va; res. ClrkVA; m. 11 Dec 1884 at ClrkVA to WALKER, Nancy (col); d/o John & Ellen WALKER; 25y; sgl; b. & res. ClrkVA; (lic) 10 Dec 1884; p. 112
FORD, Charles A.; s/o Wm. & Susan A. FORD; 26y; sgl; miller; b. FredVA; res. ClrkVA; m. 9 Nov 1881 at bride's residence to SPRINT, Annie S.; d/o Jno. S. & Emma SPRINT; 19y; sgl; b. & res. ClrkVA; (lic) 7 Nov 1881; bride's brother was present & stated there was no objections to the issuing the license; p. 50
FORD, Jno. H.; s/o Benj. and Rebecca FORD; 41y; wid; miller; b. JeffVA; res. FredVA; m. 1 Feb 1870 at bride's residence to COLSTON, Mary N.; d/o Robt. A. & Matilda S. COLSTON; 32y; sgl; b. & res. ClrkVA; (lic) 29 Jan 1870; p. 92
FORD, John (col); s/o Thomas & Mary FORD; 26y; sgl; farm hand; b. FqrVA; res. ClrkVA; m. 2 Aug 1883 at Millwood to STRANGE, Frances (col); d/o Philip & Easter STRANGE; 21y; sgl; b. & res. ClrkVA; (lic) 2 Aug 1883; p. 85
FORD, John Benjamin; s/o John H. & Alcinda FORD; 28y; sgl; farmer; b. FredVA; res. ClrkVA; m. Wednesday 5 Feb 1879 at ClrkVA at bride's residence to COLSTON, Wilhelma Burgess; d/o Robert A. & Matilda S. COLSTON; 25y; sgl; b. & res. ClrkVA; (lic) 3 Feb 1879; p. 252
FORD, Joseph Wm. (col); s/o Charles & Sarah FORD (col); 21y; sgl; farm hand; b. FredVA; res. ClrkVA; m. 7 Aug 1870 at White Post to MARTIN, Mary E. (col); d/o ___ & Mary MARTIN (col); 21y; sgl; b. & res. ClrkVA; (lic) 6 Aug 1870; p. 99
FORD, William (col); s/o Thornton & Elizabeth FORD; 23y; sgl; farm hand; b. FqrVA; res. ClrkVA; m. 14 Oct 1886 at White Post to CRITTENDEN, Emma (col); d/o George & Etta CRITTENDEN; 22y; sgl; b. & res. ClrkVA; (lic) 13 Oct 1886; p. 143
FORNEY, John W.; s/o John & Harriet FORNEY; 25y; sgl; railroader; b. & res. FredVA; m. 23 Jul 1885 at bride's residence to BARR, Precious Levina; d/o Adam & Cath'e. BARR; 25y; sgl; b. & res. ClrkVA; (lic) 23 Jul 1885; p. 122
FOSTER, James A.; s/o James & James [Jane] H. FOSTER; 39y; sgl; farmer; b. & res. ClrkVA; m. 8 Jun 1869 at ClrkVA to

CARTER, Sarah E. V.; d/o Richard & Sarah HARDESTY; 34y; wid; b. & res. ClrkVA; (lic) 5 Jun 1869; p. 82
FOWLE, R. Rollins; s/o William & Ester D. FOWLE; 34y; sgl; farmer; b. Alexandria; res. Fairfax Co. Va; m. 10 Oct 1866 at Grace Church, Berryville to SAUNDERS, Barbara W.; d/o Addison H. & Ellen M. SAUNDERS; 22y; sgl; b. Prince William Co. Va; res. ClrkVA; (lic) 9 Oct 1866; p. 20
FOWLER, Robert; s/o William & Alcinda FOWLER; 22y; sgl; farmer; b. & res. ClrkVA; m. 6 Dec 1883 at ClrkVA to WILLINGHAM, Ema Ann; d/o John & Amanda WILLINGHAM; 22y; sgl; b. & res. ClrkVA; (lic) 6 Dec 1883; p. 89
FOWLER, Wm. Franklin; s/o Thos. & Phebe FOWLER; 30y; sgl; farmer; b. & res. ClrkVA; m. 23 Nov 1876 at ClrkVA to SHIPE, Sarah/Sallie M.; d/o Benjamin & Hannah SHIPE; 22y; sgl; b. & res. ClrkVA; (lic) 20 Nov 1876; p. 209
FOX, Lafayette; s/o Jacob & Margaret FOX; 28y; sgl; Minister of Gospel; b. Fairfax Co. Va; res. LdnVA; m. 19 Feb 1874 at bride's residence to O'REAR, Susan C.; d/o George & Catharine O'REAR; 32y; sgl; b. Fairfax Co. Va; res. ClrkVA; (lic) not given; p. 157
FOX, Neptune (col); s/o Alfred & Martha FOX (col); 21y; sgl; farm hand; b. & res. ClrkVA; m. 19 Oct 1871 at Berryville to BUTLER, Lucy (col); d/o ___ & Isabella BUTLER (col); 21y; sgl; b. Richmond Va; res. ClrkVA; (lic) 18 Oct 1871; p. 118
FRAME, Harry C.; s/o Thos. T. & Mariann C. FRAME; 23y; sgl; farmer; b. Davis Co. Missouri; res. ClrkVA; m. 25 Sep 1878 at White Post to MASSEY, Lulu V.; d/o Edward W. & Sarah W. MASSEY; 22y; sgl; b. & res. ClrkVA; (lic) 24 Sep 1878; p. 240
FRANK, John Strother; s/o Strother and Eliza FRANK; 43y; wid; mechanic; b. ClrkVA; res. LdnVA; m. Sunday 28 Dec 1879 at ClrkVA to BRACKETT, Sarah; d/o mother Francis BRACKETT; 36y; sgl; b. LdnVA; res. ClrkVA; (lic) 27 Dec 1879; p. 12
FRANK, John; s/o Crawder & Eliza FRANK; 30y; sgl; farmer; b. & res. ClrkVA; m. 28 Nov 1867 at Berryville to LANHAM, Classy; d/o Enos & Lucy LANHAM; 21y; sgl; b. & res. ClrkVA; (lic) 28 Nov 1867; p. 46
FRANKLIN, Alexander (col); s/o Frank FRANKLIN & Maria FRANKLIN; 26y; sgl; mill hand; b. & res. ClrkVA; m. 20 Nov 1878 at Berryville to WILLIAMS, Laura (col); d/o Elie & Kitty WILLIAMS; 21y; sgl; b. FredVA; res. ClrkVA; (lic) 19 Nov 1878; p. 245

FREEMAN, J. T.; s/o Garret & Ann FREEMAN; 34y; wid; farmer; b. Fairfax Co. Va; res. not given; m. 20 Dec 1866 at Berryville to WOOD, Lucinda; d/o Bennett & Mary WOOD; 22y; sgl; b. ClrkVA; res. not given; (lic) 20 Dec 1866; p. 26

FRENCH, Moses (col); s/o Moses & Caroline FRENCH; 26y; sgl; farm hand; b. Washington Co. Md; res. ClrkVA; m. 24 Dec 1868 at Spring Hill, ClrkVA to REED, Mary L. (col); d/o James & Ellen REED; 16y; sgl; b. & res. ClrkVA; (lic) 21 Dec 1868; bride's father present when license issued; p. 71

FRITTS, John W.; s/o Geo. W. & Amanda FRITTS; 27y; sgl; merchant; b. LdnVA; res. ClrkVA; m. 3 Jan 1867 at not given to OSBURN, Jane C.; d/o Roland & Charlotte OSBURN; 21y; sgl; b. LdnVA; res. ClrkVA; (lic) 3 Jan 1867; p. 27

FRY, Joseph D.; s/o David & Rebecca FRY; 21y; sgl; farmer; b. & res. JeffVA; m. 16 Jan 1867 at bride's residence to PIERCE, Nannie; d/o Paul & Mary PIERCE; 18y; sgl; b. & res. ClrkVA; (lic) 12 Jan 1867; bride's father being present; p. 28

FRYER, Joseph R.; s/o M. B. & Susan FRYER; 25y; sgl; carpenter; b. & res. ClrkVA; m. 21 Dec 1876 at ClrkVA to BOXWELL, Edmonia; d/o Chas. H. & Eveline BOXWELL; 20y; sgl; b. FredVA.; res. ClrkVA; (lic) 21 Dec 1876; p. 211

FULLER, Geo. W.; s/o Farland and Mary FULLER; 22y; sgl; farmer; b. & res. ClrkVA; m. 25 Jul 1867 at ClrkVA to UNDERWOOD, Mary Virginia; d/o Joseph and Harriet UNDERWOOD; 21y; sgl; b. LdnVA; res. ClrkVA; (lic) 16 Jul 1867; p. 38

FUNKHOUSER, Charles E.; s/o Joseph & Ellen FUNKHOUSER; 31y; wid; farmer; b. FredVA; res. ClrkVA; m. 20 Jan 1885 at ClrkVA to GARDINER/GARDNER, Amelia C.; d/o Geo. & ___ GARDNER; 27y; sgl; b. & res. ClrkVA; (lic) 17 Jan 1885; p. 116

GALLOWAY, James F.; s/o Jas. M. & Sarah F. GALLOWAY; 27y; sgl; blacksmith; b. LdnVA; res. ClrkVA; m. 27 Feb 1883 at bride's residence to NEVILLE, Minnie V.; d/o Alex'r. V. & Lucy Eliz'th NEVILLE; 21y; sgl; b. LdnVA; res. ClrkVA; (lic) 24 Feb 1883; p. 77

GARDNER, Alfred L.; s/o Allen & Elizabeth GARDNER; 24y; sgl; shoemaker; b. AlbmVA; res. ClrkVA; m. 12 Oct 1871 at ClrkVA to GREENWALT, Mary Ann; d/o Adam & Barbara GREENWALT; 22y; sgl; b. & res. ClrkVA; (lic) 12 Oct 1871; p. 116

GARLAND, Wm. H.; s/o Fleming & Elizabeth GARLAND; 31y; wid; farmer; b. AlbmVA; res. RckhmVA; m. 13 May 1873 at ClrkVA to FORD, Sarah R.; d/o Wm. & Maria FORD; 29y; sgl; b. JeffVA; res. ClrkVA; (lic) 13 May 1873; p. 145

GARNER, John (col); s/o Peter & Maria GARNER; 21y; sgl; farm hand; b. LdnVA; res. ClrkVA; m. 18 Jul 1878 at ClrkVA to STRANGE, Malinda (col); d/o ___ & Emily COATS; 21y; sgl; b. & res. ClrkVA; (lic) 18 Jul 1878; p. 236

GARRETT, Charles Canby; s/o Henry & Catharine A. GARRETT; 26y; sgl; iron merchant; b. & res. Wilmington Delaware; m. Wednesday 22 Dec 1875 at bride's residence ClrkVA to LEE, Belle (Miss); d/o Charles S. & Margaret A. LEE; 24y; sgl; b. BerkVA; res. ClrkVA; (lic) 21 Dec 1875; p. 194

GARRETT, John W.; s/o George L. & Elizabeth GARRETT; 24y; sgl; not given; b. LdnVA; res. JeffWVA; m. 19 May 1880 at ClrkVA to CLIPP, Virginia E.; d/o John W. & Mary CLIPP; 22y; sgl; b. JeffWVA; res. ClrkVA; (lic) 19 May 1880; p. 20

GARRETT, Millard F.; s/o Joseph & Rebecca GARRETT; 23y; sgl; farmer; b. Hardy Co. W Va; res. ClrkVA; m. 29 Oct 1883 at ClrkVA to CARLISLE, Lillie D.; d/o Alexander & Caroline CARLISLE; 16y; sgl; b. Hampshire Co. W Va; res. ClrkVA; (lic) 29 Oct 1883; consent of ladies father given in person; p. 87

GARRETT, Walter; s/o Hamilton & Millie GARRETT; 21y; sgl; farmer; b. WrnVA; res. ClrkVA; m. 11 Jan 1877 at ClrkVA to McDONALD, Fannie; d/o John & Jane McDONALD; 23y; sgl; b. not known; res. Clarke co.; (lic) 10 Jan 1877; p. 213

GARROTT, Joseph B.; s/o Joseph E. & Susan GARROTT; 27y; sgl; druggist; b. Hancock, Washington Co. Md; res. Frederick Maryland; m. 6 Jun 1871 at Milton Valley to LOUTHAN, Henriana; d/o John & Lydia LOUTHAN; 23y; sgl; b. & res. ClrkVA; (lic) 5 Jun 1871; p. 112

GARVER, Samuel; s/o Jacob & Susan GARVER; 51y; sgl; farmer; b. Lancaster Co. Pennsylvania; res. ClrkVA; m. ___ Mar 1873 at Winchester Va to SEWELL, Julian; d/o not known; 32y; wid; b. FredVA; res. ClrkVA; (lic) 26 Feb 1873; p. 143

GAUNT, John; s/o Martin & Tacy Jane GAUNT; 22y; sgl; farmer; b. & res. ClrkVA; m. 19 Nov 1874 at Baptist Church Berryville to PIERCE, Adalaide Virginia; d/o Peter Mc. & Margaret PIERCE; 22y; sgl; b. & res. ClrkVA; (lic) 17 Nov 1874; p. 169

GAVER, James W.; s/o H. A. & N. W. GAVER; 27y; sgl; merchant; b. West Virginia; res. Middleton, FredVA; m. 21 Feb 1884 at Berryville to HARDESTY, Elizabeth R.; d/o Jos. R. & M. S. HARDESTY; 25y; sgl; b. & res. ClrkVA; (lic) 18 Feb 1884; p. 94

GAY, Jack (col); s/o George & Fanny GAY; 70y; wid; gardener; b. Cumberland Co. Va; res. ClrkVA; m. 10 Mar 1868 at ClrkVA to EVANS, Maria (col); d/o unknown; 47y; wid; b. not given; res. ClrkVA; (lic) not given; p. 56

GEYNOR, James; s/o Edward & Judah GEYNER; 51y; wid; stone mason; b. Ireland; res. LdnVA; m. 26 Aug 1872 at ClrkVA to SHELL, Lucinda; d/o James & Nancy BELL; 35y; wid; b. & res. ClrkVA; (lic) 26 Aug 1872; p. 131

GIBBS, Isaac A.; s/o Aaron & Sarah GIBBS; 23y; sgl; proprietor of livery; b. York Co. Pennsylvania; res. ClrkVA; m. 18 Nov 1880 at ClrkVA to CASTLEMAN, Catharine B.; d/o Wm. A. & Ann R. CASTLEMAN; 22y; sgl; b. & res. ClrkVA; (lic) 18 Nov 1880; p. 29

GIBSON, Daniel L. (col); s/o ___ & Melvina GIBSON; 21y; sgl; farm hand; b. & res. ClrkVA; m. 1 [21] Jul 1879 at ClrkVA to BROCKENBOROUGH, Mary; d/o ___ & Ann JEFFERSON; 20y; sgl; b. & res. ClrkVA; (lic) 21 Jul 1879; p. 261

GIBSON, Daniel L. (col); s/o ___ and Melvina GIBSON; 25y; wid; labourer; b. & res. ClrkVA; m. 18 Dec 1884 at ClrkVA to MITCHELL, Agnes (col); d/o Lindon and ___ MITCHELL; 25y; sgl; b. & res. ClrkVA; (lic) 16 Dec 1884; p. 113

GIBSON, George (col); s/o Horace & Margaret GIBSON; 22y; sgl; mill hand; b. & res. Fairfax Co. Va; m. 20 Oct 1886 at White Post to CRITTENDEN, Charlotte (col.; d/o George & Etta CRITTENDEN; 21y; sgl; b. & res. ClrkVA; (lic) 20 Oct 1886; p. 144

GIBSON, Thomas (col); s/o William & Clorey GIBSON; 23y; sgl; farm hand; b. & res. ClrkVA; m. 8 Nov 1883 at ClrkVA to PAGE, Mary (col); d/o John & Nulen PAGE; 23y; sgl; b. & res. ClrkVA; (lic) 8 Nov 1883; p. 88

GIBSON, William; s/o Jno. M. & Lydia R. GIBSON; 21y; sgl; farmer; b. & res. ClrkVA; m. 8 Mar 1882 at ClrkVA to MORGAN, Fannie S.; d/o John & Fannie M. MORGAN; 14y; sgl; b. & res. ClrkVA; (lic) 6 Mar 1882; mother's consent given; p. 56

GINN, George W.; s/o James & Jane GINN; 24y; sgl; farmer; b. FredVA; res. ClrkVA; m. 11 Dec 1878 at ClrkVA to BERLIN,

Anna M.; d/o George W. & Margaretta C. BERLIN; 23y; sgl;
b. & res. ClrkVA; (lic) 10 Dec 1878; p. 247
GLASCOCK, Leroy B.; s/o Nimrod & Catharine D. GLASCOCK;
31y; sgl; farmer; b. ClrkVA; res. FqrVA; m. 15 May 1873 at
bride's residence to MADDOX, Letitia D.; d/o Lorenzo D. &
Ann C. MADDOX; 27y; sgl; b. BerkVA; res. ClrkVA; (lic) 15
May 1783; p. 145
GLASS, Isaac; s/o Lewis F. and Mary M. GLASS; 29y; sgl;
farmer; b. & res. ClrkVA; m. Tuesday 2 Oct 1877 at ClrkVA to
BONHAM, Kate; d/o A. A. and Eliza BONHAM; 29y; sgl; b. &
res. ClrkVA; (lic) 1 Oct 1877; p. 223
GLOVER, Jno. B.; s/o Lewis & Elizabeth E. GLOVER; 35y; sgl;
farmer; b. & res. ClrkVA; m. 18 Nov 1868 at Berryville to
CROW, Catharine Eugenia; d/o Thos. H. & Frances A.
CROW; 28y; sgl; b. & res. ClrkVA; (lic) 17 Nov 1868; p. 70
GLOVER, Thornton Kirkland; s/o Lewis & Elizabeth E. GLOVER;
40y; sgl; proprietor; b. & res. Berryville; m. 24 Aug 1875 at
Baptist Church Berryville to YOUNG, Lillie May; d/o Wm. H. &
Lucy C. YOUNG; 23y; sgl; b. & res. Berryville; (lic) 24 Aug
1875; p. 184
GOLD, Thos. D.; s/o Thos. K. GOLD & Lucy M. GOLD; 21y; sgl;
not given; b. & res. ClrkVA; m. 27 Feb 1866 at Berryville to
BARNETT, Sarah H.; d/o Neill BARNETT & Eliz'th K.
BARNETT; 21y; sgl; b. ClrkVA; res. ClrkVA; (lic) 22 Feb
1866; p. 7
GOODRICH, Robert; s/o ___ & Rachel GOODRICH; 24y; sgl;
railroading; b. WrnVA; res. ClrkVA; m. 16 Feb 1882 at ClrkVA
to PYLES, Maggie; d/o Wm. & Ann PYLES; 25y; div; b. & res.
ClrkVA; (lic) 16 Feb 1882; p. 56
GORDON, Benjamin; s/o Jefferson & Mary GORDON; 26y; sgl;
farmer; b. & res. WrnVA; m. 8 Feb 1883 at ClrkVA to DOVE,
Susan; d/o Jefferson & Delia DOVE; 20y; sgl; b. & res.
ClrkVA; (lic) 6 Feb 1883; p. 77
GORDON, Jas. W. (Dr.); s/o Thomas J. & Mary GORDON; 36y;
sgl; Doctor of Dentistry; b. & res. FqrVA; m. 11 Jan 1883 at
Millwood to EVANS, Lulooh B.; d/o H. P. & Sarah J. EVANS;
30y; sgl; b. & res. ClrkVA; (lic) 8 Jan 1883; p. 73
GORDON, Thomas N.; s/o John S. & ___ GORDON; 32y; sgl;
farmer; b. & res. ClrkVA; m. 9 Jan 1872 at ClrkVA to
WRIGHT, Mary E.; d/o not given; 35y; wid; b. FredVA; res.
ClrkVA; (lic) 8 Jan 1872; p. 123

GORDON, William M.; s/o James & Elizabeth GORDON; 31y; wid; blacksmith; b. Alabama; res. ClrkVA; m. 14 Sep 1865 at ClrkVA to CARPER, Lucinda; d/o William & ___ CARPER; 26y; sgl; b. & res. ClrkVA; (lic) 13 Sep 1865; p. 2

GORE, Bushrod T.; s/o Thos. A. & Mary H. GORE; 27y; sgl; farmer; b. LdnVA; res. WrnVA; m. 6 May 1875 at Stone bridge, ClrkVA to FOLK, Anne E.; d/o John & Mary J. FOLK; 22y; sgl; b. FqrVA; res. ClrkVA; (lic) 3 May 1875; p. 178

GRANDSTAFF, Isaac M.; s/o Jacob & Elizabeth GRANDSTAFF; 34y; sgl; carpenter; b. ShenVA; res. ClrkVA; m. 19 Mar 1879 at ClrkVA to GRUBER, Orra S.; d/o John & Maria J. GRUBER; 27y; sgl; b. & res. ClrkVA; (lic) 19 Mar 1879; p. 255

GRAY, Warner; s/o Absolum & Frances GRAY; 23y; sgl; farmer; b. JeffVA; res. ClrkVA; m. 20 Oct 1870 at ClrkVA to BELL, Maggie; d/o James & Sallie BELL; 25y; sgl; b. & res. ClrkVA; (lic) 20 Oct 1870; p. 101

GREEN, Henry (col); s/o George & Mary GREEN; 21y; sgl; farm hand; b. Baltimore City Md; res. ClrkVA; m. 30 Jun 1870 at Berryville to LEWIS, Eliz'th. (col); d/o Jerry & Lucinda LEWIS; 21y; sgl; b. & res. ClrkVA; (lic) 30 Jun 1870; p. 98

GREEN, Lewis (col); s/o ___ & Cela GREEN; 21y; sgl; farm hand; b. & res. ClrkVA; m. 16 Mar 1882 at ClrkVA to BANISTER, Louisa; d/o Thos. & Martha BANISTER; 25y; sgl; b. & res. ClrkVA; (lic) 13 Mar 1882; p. 57

GREEN, Richard W.; s/o Richard N. & Mary A. GREEN; 31y; sgl; farmer; b. & res. ClrkVA; m. 18 Apr 1882 at ClrkVA to JOHNSTON, Annie C.; d/o James W. & Annie E. JOHNSTON; 18y; sgl; b. & res. ClrkVA; (lic) 15 Apr 1882; father's consent given; p. 58

GREEN, William W.; s/o Chas. H. & Rebecca GREEN; 33y; sgl; farmer; b. WrnVA; res. ClrkVA; m. 16 Nov 1875 at ClrkVA to CASTLEMAN, Virginia E.; d/o Chas. D. & Maria CASTLEMAN; 18y; sgl; b. & res. ClrkVA; (lic) 15 Nov 1875; p. 191

GREEN, Wilmer; s/o Rich'd. & Mary A. GREEN; 25y; sgl; miller; b. & res. ClrkVA; m. 8 Jul 1884 at ClrkVA to FLETCHER, Ada; d/o Joshua C. & S. A. FLETCHER; 19y; sgl; b. FqrVA; res. ClrkVA; (lic) 3 Jul 1884; consent of father given in person; p. 103

GREENE, John A.; s/o John S. & Margaret A. GREENE; 21y; sgl; farmer; b. Frederick; res. ClrkVA; m. 27 Oct 1868 at Berryville to HARDESTY, Betty S.; d/o Jas. M. & Sarah W.

HARDESTY; 19y; sgl; b. Frederick; res. ClrkVA; (lic) 26 Oct 1868; bride's father present & gave consent; p. 68

GREENWALT, Geo. W.; s/o Adam & Barbara GREENWALT; 28y; sgl; slake factory hand; b. & res. ClrkVA; m. 19 Sep 1878 at Berryville to BROWN, Lucy P.; d/o John & Margaret BROWN; 24y; sgl; b. Paris, FqrVA; res. ClrkVA; (lic) 19 Sep 1878; p. 239

GREENWALT, William Lester; s/o John and Elizabeth GREENWALT; 26y; sgl; farm hand; b. & res. ClrkVA; m. Thursday 18 Sep 1879 at White Post to GARRETT, Ginnie; d/o Washington and Catherine GARRETT; 16y; sgl; b. WrnVA; res. ClrkVA; (lic) 15 Sep 1879; affidavit made by R. H. ALEXANDER half brother of Ginnie GARRETT that the consent of parents has been obtained for issuance of license; p. 2

GRIGSBY, Charles (col); s/o Jack & Margaret GRIGSBY; 26y; sgl; blacksmith; b. & res. ClrkVA; m. 25 Sep 1884 at ClrkVA to STRANGE, Evelina (col); d/o John & Cloe STRANGE; 18y; sgl; b. & res. ClrkVA; (lic) 25 Sep 1884; father's consent given; p. 106

GRIMES, Albert (col); s/o Wm. & Mary GRIMES; 27y; sgl; farm hand; b. LdnVA; res. ClrkVA; m. 11 Dec 1884 at ClrkVA to WILLIAMS, Emily (col); d/o Geo. & Lucy WILLIAMS; 17y; sgl; b. JeffWVA; res. ClrkVA; (lic) 11 Dec 1884; consent of bride's mother given in writing; p. 113

GRIMES, Geo. W.; s/o Madison & Cely GRIMES; 23y; sgl; farmer; b. FqrVA; res. ClrkVA; m. 22 Dec 1867 at Berryville to FERGUSON, Sarah; d/o Josiah & Susan FERGUSON; 22y; sgl; b. & res. ClrkVA; (lic) 21 Dec 1867; p. 49

GRIMES, John E.; s/o John and Annie GRIMES; 27y; sgl; engineer; b. Delaware; res. Baltimore Md; m. 16 Dec 1886 at Berryville to BURCHELL, Lillie F.; d/o John F. & Martha A. BURCHELL; 17y; sgl; b. & res. ClrkVA; (lic) 15 Dec 1886; consent given by father in person; p. 148

GRIMES, Uriah; s/o Turner & Jinnie GRIMES; 47y; wid; farmer; b. Caroline Co. Va; res. ClrkVA; m. 2 Jan 1873 at ClrkVA to FIDLER, Lettie; d/o Israel & Nancy FIDLER; 39y; sgl; b. & res. ClrkVA; (lic) 30 Dec 1872; p. 139

GROVE, Elsei (col); s/o Geremiah & Mary GROVE; 25y; sgl; coachman; b. & res. Delaware; m. 3 Jan 1878 at Berryville to LOVETT, Lucy (col); d/o Wilson & Mary Ellen LOVETT; 27y; sgl; b. & res. ClrkVA; (lic) 2 Jan 1878; p. 230

GROVES, James A.; s/o John W. & Jane GROVE[S]; 36y; sgl; carpenter; b. & res. Frederick Co.; m. 25 Feb 1868 at White Post to DENNY, Frances L.; d/o Robt. L. & Eliza J. DENNY; 28y; sgl; b. Frederick Co.; res. ClrkVA; (lic) not given; p. 55
GRUBB, Geo. W.; s/o Walker B. & Eliz'th GRUBB; 24y; sgl; farmer; b. & res. Frederick Co.; m. 14 Nov 1872 at Winchester to NEWCOME, Mattie; d/o John & Alcinda J. NEWCOME; 18y; sgl; b. Frederick Co.; res. ClrkVA; (lic) 11 Nov 1872; p. 136
GRUBBS, Andrew J.; s/o Charles & Elizabeth GRUBBS; 28y; sgl; farmer; b. FredVA; res. ClrkVA; m. 3 Nov 1874 at Berryville to POPPE, Mary F.; d/o Michael & Elizabeth POPPE; 21y; sgl; b. & res. ClrkVA; (lic) 3 Nov 1874; p. 168
GRUBBS, George M. D.; s/o Thornberry & Mary E. GRUBBS; 22y; sgl; farmer; b. WrnVA; res. ClrkVA; m. 27 Sep 1866 at CLEVINGER's to SWARTZ, Susan Cath'e.; d/o George & Sarah Ann SWARTZ; 22y; sgl; b. FredVA; res. ClrkVA; (lic) 27 Sep 1866; p. 19
GRUBBS, J. T.; s/o Samuel & Hannah E. GRUBBS; 34y; sgl; carpenter; b. ClrkVA; res. FqrVA; m. 27 Jun 1875 at ClrkVA to ANDERSON, Annie E.; d/o John E. & Ann M. ANDERSON; 27y; sgl; b. LdnVA; res. ClrkVA; (lic) 26 Jun 1875; letter from Thos. M. FLEMING states Annie's mother who lives in Winchester gives permission.; p. 181
GRUBBS, Madison; s/o Thornberry & Mary GRUBBS; 27y; sgl; carpenter; b. & res. ClrkVA; m. 8 Oct 1867 at Winchester, FredVA to LEE, Margaret Ann; d/o William D. & Henrietta LEE; 20y; sgl; b. & res. ClrkVA; (lic) 5 Oct 1867; license issued when the bride's father was present & with his consent; p. 42
GRUBBS, Matthew R.; s/o Saml. & Hannah GRUBBS; 29y; sgl; farmer; b. & res. ClrkVA; m. 23 Dec 1880 at ClrkVA to LANHAM, Rebecca C.; d/o James & Jane LANHAM; 24y; sgl; b. & res. ClrkVA; (lic) 22 Dec 1880; p. 32
GRUBBS, William B.; s/o Wm. & Elizabeth GRUBBS; 66y; wid; farmer; b. FredVA; res. ClrkVA; m. 30 Nov 1886 at ClrkVA to ROYSTON, Lydia E.; d/o Uriah B. & Hannah ROYSTON; 56y; sgl; b. FredVA; res. ClrkVA; (lic) 29 Nov 1886; p. 147
GWYNN, Andrew (col); s/o Isaac and Mary Ann GWYNN; 29y; wid; farm hand; b. RckbrVA; res. FredVA; m. Thursday 25 Dec 1879 at White Post to WEDLOCK, Millie (col); d/o Enock and Ann WEDLOCK; 20y; sgl; b. AlbmVA; res. ClrkVA; (lic)

22 Dec 1879; consent of Millie WEDLOCK's mother given to issuing of above license.; p. 11

HADDOX, George W.; s/o Alpheus L. & Harriet HADDOX; 23y; sgl; re[s]torant keeper; b. FredVA; res. ClrkVA; m. 26 Feb 1879 at ClrkVA to BUCKLY, Harriet J.; d/o Bushrod & Eliza J. BUCKLY; 19y; sgl; b. FredVA; res. ClrkVA; (lic) 24 Feb 1879; p. 253

HAINES, Thomas S.; s/o Simeon & Elizabeth HAINES; 27y; wid; cabinet maker; b. & res. FqrVA; m. 21 Oct 1877 at ClrkVA to CORDER, Melvina; d/o Elias & Elizabeth CORDER; 27y; sgl; b. FqrVA; res. ClrkVA; (lic) 19 Oct 1877; p. 224

HALL, Frank (col); s/o Robert & Lucy HALL; 21y; sgl; farm hand; b. & res. ClrkVA; m. 31 Dec 1873 at White Post to WALKER, Jane (col); d/o ___ & ___ WALKER; 23y; sgl; b. WrnVA; res. ClrkVA; (lic) 31 Dec 1873; p. 155

HAMILTON, Charles H.; s/o James & Mary HAMILTON; 21y; sgl; farm hand; b. & res. ClrkVA; m. 18 Nov 1886 at Berryville to CONNAR, Mollie V.; d/o A. J. & ___ CONNAR; 19y; sgl; b. BerkWVA; res. ClrkVA; (lic) 17 Nov 1886; p. 146

HAMILTON, Frank L.; s/o John R. & Sarah E. HAMILTON; 22y; sgl; manufacturer of cigars; b. FredVA; res. ClrkVA; m. 29 Jun 1886 at Berryville to HART, Jennie F.; d/o ___ & Mary HART; 21y; sgl; b. & res. ClrkVA; (lic) 28 Jun 1886; p. 139

HAMMER, John C.; s/o Charles W. & Salley A. HAMMER; 57y; wid; Minister of Gospel; b. Buckingham Co. Va; res. Saline Co. Missouri; m. 13 Feb 1872 at Berryville to SMITH, Harriet N.; d/o not given; 50y; wid; b. & res. ClrkVA; (lic) not given; p. 126

HAMMOND, Wm. S.; s/o Geo. Geo. [??] & Mary HAMMOND; 24y; sgl; lawyer; b. Alleghany Co. Va; res. Bath Co. Va; m. 5 Sep 1878 at Berryville to GRIFFITH, Susie J.; d/o Jos. T. & Jane GRIFFITH; 20y; sgl; b. Montgomery Co. Md; res. ClrkVA; (lic) 5 Sep 1878; p. 238

HANES, Thomas S.; s/o Simeon & Elizabeth HANES; 22y; sgl; carpenter; b. Paris, FqrVA; res. FqrVA; m. 19 Oct 1871 at ClrkVA to FLEMING, Margaret A.; d/o Wm. & Louisa FLEMING; 23y; sgl; b. LdnVA; res. ClrkVA; (lic) 18 Oct 1871; p. 117

HANNUM, Preston L.; s/o Joseph & Mary HANNUM; 24y; sgl; farmer; b. Hampshire Co. Va; res. ClrkVA; m. 17 Feb 1870 at bride's residence to MARPEL, Jane M.; d/o Geo. & Amanda MARPEL; 21y; sgl; b. & res. ClrkVA; (lic) 16 Feb 1870; p. 93

HANSUCKER, John W.; s/o Geo. W. & Jane HANSUCKER; 33y; sgl; farmer; b. & res. ClrkVA; m. 2 Sep 1884 at ClrkVA to SHOPLAND, Elizabeth W.; d/o James & Lena SHOPLAND; 30y; sgl; b. England; res. ClrkVA; (lic) 2 Sep 1884; p. 105

HARDESTY, Adrian D. Jr.; s/o Jas. M. & Sarah HARDESTY; 26y; sgl; farmer; b. ClrkVA; res. FredVA; m. 27 May 1880 at bride's residence to HARDESTY, Eugenia T.; d/o Richard S. & Mary E. HARDESTY; 22y; sgl; b. JeffWVA; res. ClrkVA; (lic) 21 May 1880; p. 21

HARDESTY, Mathew Jones; s/o James Monroe & Sarah H. HARDESTY; 24y; sgl; farmer; b. JeffWVA; res. ClrkVA; m. 14 Sep 1876 at ClrkVA to CARTER, Sarah Elizabeth; d/o Jaqueline W. & Sarah E. V. CARTER; 23y; sgl; b. & res. ClrkVA; (lic) 11 Sep 1876; p. 205

HARDESTY, Otho J.; s/o Richard S. and Mary E. HARDESTY; 33y; wid; farmer; b. & res. ClrkVA; m. 20 Mar 1884 at Berryville to CARTER, Hattie S.; d/o Wm. H. & Charlotte CARTER; 26y; sgl; b. & res. ClrkVA; (lic) 17 Mar 1884; p. 97

HARDESTY, Richard D.; s/o James M. & Sarah HARDESTY; 26y; sgl; merchant; b. FredVA; res. ClrkVA; m. 4 Jun 1874 at Berryville to DIX, Mollie F.; d/o ___ & ___ DIX; 28y; sgl; b. King & Queen Co. Va; res. ClrkVA`; (lic) 3 Jun 1874; p. 162

HARDESTY, Wm. M.; s/o C. W. & J. L. HARDESTY; 28y; sgl; farmer; b. & res. ClrkVA; m. 24 Nov 1886 at Berryville to CARTER, Minnie F.; d/o F. B. & Lucy CARTER; 22y; sgl; b. & res. ClrkVA; (lic) 24 Nov 1886; p. 147

HARRINGTON, John W.; s/o Daniel & Joanna HARRINGTON; 25y; sgl; farming; b. Fairfax Co. Va; res. ShenVA; m. 29 May 1876 at ClrkVA to PURCELL, Catharine; d/o Edmund & Bridget PURCELL; 23y; sgl; b. WrnVA; res. ClrkVA; (lic) 27 May 1876; p. 201

HARRIS, Albin W.; s/o Joseph & Elizabeth HARRIS; 25y; sgl; farming; b. & res. LdnVA; m. 24 Jan 1878 at ClrkVA to SMALLWOOD, Caroline; d/o Thomas & Martha SMALLWOOD; 25y; sgl; b. LdnVA; res. ClrkVA; (lic) 23 Jan 1878; p. 231

HARRIS, Benjamin (col); s/o Mowen and Julia HARRIS; 29y; sgl; stone mason; b. & res. ClrkVA; m. 19 Dec 1878 at ClrkVA to HULL, Alsey (col); d/o William and Sallie HULL; 25y; sgl; b. & res. ClrkVA; (lic) 17 Dec 1878; p. 248

HARRIS, George H. L. D. (col); s/o Waren & Hay [?] HARRIS; 21y; sgl; farm hand; b. & res. ClrkVA; m. 27 Jan 1876 at

Berryville to SMITH, Mary L. (col); d/o John & Ann SMITH; 20y; sgl; b. & res. ClrkVA; (lic) 22 Jan 1876; p. 196
HARRIS, Henry (col); s/o Martin & Bridget HARRIS (col); 39y; sgl; farm hand; b. Prince William Co. Va; res. ClrkVA; m. 17 Jun 1866 at Berryville to SHOULKES, Jennie (col); d/o Charles & Rebecca JOHNSTON; 25y; wid; b. & res. ClrkVA; (lic) 16 Jun 1866; p. 14
HARRIS, Henry (col); s/o Peter & Elizabeth HARRIS; 26y; sgl; farm hand; b. King William Co. Va; res. ClrkVA; m. 22 Sep 1882 at ClrkVA to WILLIAMS, Lillie (col); d/o Sandy and Ann WILLIAMS; 19y; sgl; b. & res. ClrkVA; (lic) 22 Sep 1882; p. 64
HARRIS, James (col); s/o Peter & Kitty HARRIS (col); 31y; sgl; farm hand; b. & res. ClrkVA; m. 23 Apr 1868 at Millwood to BROCK, Haley Ann (col); d/o Frederick & ___ BROCK (col); 21y; sgl; b. & res. ClrkVA; (lic) 23 Apr 1868; p. 60
HARRIS, James (col); s/o Wm. & Betsy HARRIS; 23y; sgl; farm hand; b. & res. ClrkVA; m. 16 Apr 1885 at ClrkVA to JACKSON, Mary (col); d/o Daniel & Caroline JACKSON; 21y; sgl; b. & res. ClrkVA; (lic) 15 Apr 1885; p. 120
HARRIS, Madison (col); s/o ___ & Catharine HARRIS (col); 21y; sgl; farm hand; b. & res. ClrkVA; m. 6 Jun 1867 at ClrkVA to SETTLES, Jane (col); d/o Grayson & Martha SETTLES (col); 21y; sgl; b. WrnVA; res. ClrkVA; (lic) 5 Jun 1867; p. 37
HARRIS, Mowin (col); s/o Charles & Judah HARRIS; 57y; sgl; stone mason; b. & res. ClrkVA; m. 4 Jan 1869 at ClrkVA to WILLIAMS, Judah (col); d/o not given; 58y; sgl; b. & res. ClrkVA; (lic) 4 Jan 1869; p. 73
HARRIS, William (col); s/o Wat & Grace HARRIS; 49y; wid; farm hand; b. & res. ClrkVA; m. 1 Jan 1880 at ClrkVA to RUST, Harriet (col); d/o Wm. & Mary RUST; 25y; sgl; b. & res. ClrkVA; (lic) 1 Jan 1880; p. 14
HARRIS, William (col); s/o William & Betsy HARRIS; 23y; sgl; farm hand; b. & res. ClrkVA; m. 17 Dec 1885 at ClrkVA to HERBLERT [HERBERT], Martha; d/o Bennett & Patty HERBERT; 22y; sgl; b. & res. ClrkVA; (lic) 16 Dec 1885; p. 130
HARRIS, Wm. (col); s/o Watt & Gracey HARRIS (col); 40y; wid; farm hand; b. & res. ClrkVA; m. 7 Mar 1872 at ClrkVA to FRACTIOUS, Lucy (col); d/o ___ & Sarah FRACTIOUS; 35y; wid; b. & res. ClrkVA; (lic) 29 Feb 1872; p. 127
HARRISON, John T.; s/o Samuel & Lucetia HARRISON; 40y; wid; taylor; b. JeffWVA; res. Martinsburg W Va; m. 20 Oct

1886 at Berryville to FLAGG, Sallie B.; d/o Thomas G. & Martha M. FLAGG; 30y; sgl; b. BerkWVA; res. ClrkVA; (lic) 19 Oct 1886; p. 143

HARRISON, Wm. H.; s/o Wm. H. & Mary E. HARRISON; 21y; sgl; farmer; b. RckbrVA; res. ClrkVA; m. date not given at bride's residence to CORNWELL, Annie; d/o Thos. C. & Harriet CORNWELL; 18y; sgl; b. LdnVA; res. ClrkVA; (lic) 30 Dec 1873; p. 155

HART, Edward; s/o Thomas & Mary HART; 22y; sgl; farmer; b. & res. ClrkVA; m. 4 Mar 1880 at ClrkVA to GALLOWAY, Lucy C.; d/o James & Bettie GALLOWAY; 20y; sgl; b. & res. ClrkVA; (lic) 3 Mar 1880; p. 17

HARTGROVE, Beverly (col); s/o Beverly & Louisa HARTGROVE (col); 27y; wid; gardiner &c; b. Nelson Co. Va; res. ClrkVA; m. 27 Dec 1870 at Berryville to REED, Cornelia (col); d/o Thomas & Amanda REED (col); 21y; sgl; b. FredVA; res. ClrkVA; (lic) 27 Dec 1870; p. 105

HARVEY, Chas.; s/o Chas. & Mary O. HARVEY; 25y; not given; publisher & printer; b. & res. Baltimore Maryland; m. 5 Nov 1873 at bride's residence to PENDLETON, Virginia M.; d/o T. P. & Emily J. PENDLETON; 20y; not given; b. & res. ClrkVA; (lic) 3 Nov 1873; bride's father present & gave consent; p. 152

HASSETT, Michael; s/o Daniel & Mary M. HASSETT; 57y; wid; labourer; b. Ireland; res. Winchester Va; m. 8 May 1884 at Berryville to RUSSELL, Kate; d/o Michael & Nancy RUSSELL; 39y; sgl; b. BerkWVA; res. ClrkVA; (lic) 8 May 1884; p. 100

HAZSLETT, William E.; s/o Jackson & Juliet HAZSLETT; 36y; wid; farmer; b. & BerkWVA; m. 10 Apr 1879 at ClrkVA to HARTMAN, Kate; d/o Peter & ___ HARTMAN; 28y; sgl; b. Hampshire Co. W. Va; res. ClrkVA; (lic) 9 Apr 1879; p. 256

HEFLIN, James W.; s/o Wm. & Sallie HEFLIN; 29y; sgl; farmer; b. & res. ClrkVA; m. 4 Dec 1874 at Berryville to LANHAM, Priscilla; d/o George & Rebecca LANHAM; 28y; sgl; b. & res. ClrkVA; (lic) not given; p. 172

HEFLIN, Stephen M.; s/o Wm. & Sarah HEFLIN; 23y; sgl; farmer; b. FqrVA; res. ClrkVA; m. 5 Aug 1874 at Berryville to LLOYD, Emily J.; d/o John & Mary LLOYD; 27y; sgl; b. & res. ClrkVA; (lic) 5 Aug 1874; p. 162

HENDERSON, Jackson (col); s/o Henry & Arrena HENDERSON; 23y; sgl; blacksmith; b. Fairfax Co. Va; res.

ClrkVA; m. 28 Oct 1880 at Millwood to STRANGE, Cornelia (col); d/o Charles & Emily STRANGE; 18y; sgl; b. & res. ClrkVA; (lic) 28 Oct 1880; Chas. JACKSON made oath that there was no objection to the issuing of this license; p. 28
HENDERSON, William H. (col); s/o Moses P. HENDERSON & Mary Ellen HENDERSON; 26y; sgl; farmer; b. LdnVA; res. ClrkVA; m. 23 Aug 1882 at ClrkVA to BROWN, Elizabeth (col); d/o John and ___ BROWN; 22y; sgl; b. & res. ClrkVA; (lic) 23 Aug 1882; p. 63
HENRY, Franklin; s/o Alfred & Caroline HENRY; 23y; sgl; blacksmith; b. WrnVA; res. Winchester, Frederick Co.; m. date not given at bride's father in ClrkVA to HENRY, Fannie; d/o Nelson & Polly HENRY; 18y; sgl; b. FqrVA; res. ClrkVA; (lic) 13 Aug 1866; bride's father was present; p. 18
HENRY, John C.; s/o James and Nancy HENRY; 36y; sgl; farmer; b. & res. ClrkVA; m. 23 Mar 1866 at ClrkVA to GREEN, Emily; d/o William and Polly GREEN; 27y; sgl; b. RappVA; res. ClrkVA; (lic) 22 Mar 1866; p. 8
HENRY, Mathis W.; s/o Mathis W. HEN[R]Y & Juliet HENRY; 37y; sgl; mining and civil engineer; b. Bowling Green Kentucky; res. Hamilton Nevada; m. Tuesday 26 Oct 1875 at Millwood to BURWELL, Susie R.; d/o N. B. BURWELL & Dora BURWELL; 27y; sgl; b. ClrkVA; res. near Millwood; (lic) 15 Oct 1875; p. 188
HERN, John H.; s/o Thos. J. & Isabella HERN; 22y; sgl; farmer; b. Greenbrier Co. Va; res. LdnVA; m. 22 Jan 1871 at ClrkVA to KEYS, Florence; d/o Wm. E. & Mary A. KEYS; 19y; sgl; b. LdnVA; res. ClrkVA; (lic) 21 Jan 1871; p. 108
HESSOR, A. M.; s/o Andrew & Mary HESSOR; 30y; sgl; farmer; b. Taylor Co. Va; res. ClrkVA; m. 3 Mar 1868 at ClrkVA to GRIGSBY, Annie M.; d/o Henry N. & Frances F. GRIGSBY; 23y; sgl; b. & res. ClrkVA; (lic) 24 Feb 1868; p. 56
HETZEL, John; s/o Samuel & Sarah HETZEL; 29y; wid; farmer; b. LdnVA; res. ClrkVA; m. 21 Sep 1865 at bride's father's residence to STARKEY, Margaret E.; d/o Benjamin & Jane STARKEY; 22y; sgl; b. LdnVA; res. ClrkVA; (lic) 13 Sep 1865; p. 2
HIBBARD, James H.; s/o Jno. W. & Mary J. HIBBARD; 25y; sgl; farmer; b. & res. ClrkVA; m. 9 Apr 1885 at Berryville to JOHNSTON, Ella D.; d/o Jno. S. & Mary Louisa JOHNSTON; 23y; sgl; b. & res. ClrkVA; (lic) 4 Apr 1885; p. 120

HICKS, Jackson Smith; s/o Jeremiah and Mary F. HICKS; 22y; sgl; farmer; b. FredVA; res. ClrkVA; m. Thursday 11 Dec 1879 at Methodist Church Berryville to ANDERSON, Virginia; d/o John H. and Ann M. ANDERSON; 27y; sgl; b. & res. ClrkVA; (lic) 10 Dec 1879; p. 9
HIGGINS, Henry; s/o Solomon & Easter HIGGINS; 26y; sgl; farm hand; b. Hampshire Co.; res. ClrkVA; m. 6 Nov 1867 at LdnVA to JACKSON, Julia A.; d/o not given; 25y; sgl; b. FqrVA; res. ClrkVA; (lic) 5 Nov 1867; p. 46
HILL, Isaac (col); s/o Aden & Maria HILL; 25y; sgl; not given; b. Amherst Co. Va; res. ClrkVA; m. 21 Jan 1875 at bride's residence to STEWART, Jinnie (col); d/o ___ & Martha STEWART; 21y; sgl; b. Staunton, AugVA; res. ClrkVA; (lic) 21 Jan 1875; p. 175
HILLARD, Oliver B.; s/o John & Eliza HILLARD; 26y; sgl; blacksmith; b. FredVA; res. JeffWVA; m. 11 Jan 1876 at bride's father's ClrkVA to FIDLER, Lucy Ann; d/o Israel & Mary FIDLER; 19y; sgl; b. & res. ClrkVA; (lic) 10 Jan 1876; p. 196
HILLIARD, Grafton B.; s/o Mathias & Sarah M. HILLIARD; 27y; sgl; farm hand; b. PageVA; res. ClrkVA; m. 19 Jul 1881 at ClrkVA to ELLIOTT, Elizabeth; d/o Chris & ___ ELLIOTT; 22y; sgl; b. & res. ClrkVA; (lic) 18 Jul 1881; p. 43
HILLIARD, Jno. W.; s/o Mathias & Sarah HILLIARD; not given; sgl; carpenter; b. Frederick Co.; res. ClrkVA; m. 7 Nov 1872 at bride's residence to ROMINE, Mary Ann; d/o Elisha & Jane ROMINE; not given; sgl; b. & res. ClrkVA; (lic) 29 Oct 1872; p. 135
HILLYARD, Jacob R.; s/o John T. & Eliza HILLYARD; 29y; wid; blacksmith; b. ClrkVA; res. FredVA; m. 19 Sep 1872 at Winchester to LEE, Frances A.; d/o Wm. D. & Henrietta LEE; 18y; sgl; b. & res. ClrkVA; (lic) 16 Sep 1872; p. 132
HISKETT, Thomas W.; s/o James & Sarah HISKETT; 30y; wid; farmer; b. & res. ClrkVA; m. 6 Jun 1867 at near Berryville on A. WILLIAMS' farm to WINSBURROW, Laura Florence; d/o John W. & Ann Susan WINSBURROW; 20y 6th of next month; sgl; b. WrnVA; res. ClrkVA; (lic) 4 Jun 1867; consent of bride's father in person; p. 36
HOFF, John F.; s/o Samuel & Elizabeth HOFF; 21y; sgl; farm hand; b. & res. ClrkVA; m. 4 Sep 1879 at ClrkVA to WARE, Annie; d/o Luther & ___ WARE; 26y; sgl; b. LdnVA; res. ClrkVA; (lic) 2 Sep 1879; p. 1

HOFF, Thomas Lee; s/o Humphrey & Malissa HOFF; 20y; sgl; farmer; b. & res. ClrkVA; m. 17 Nov 1881 at Berryville to LLOYD, Adelia D.; d/o Charles H. & Mary LLOYD; 16y; sgl; b. & res. ClrkVA; (lic) 17 Nov 1881; written permission given from groom's & bride's parents & affidavit of groom taken; p. 51

HOFF, Wm.; s/o Bushrod & Jane HOFF; 23y; sgl; farmer; b. & res. ClrkVA; m. 19 Nov 1874 at bride's residence to WILEY, Rebecca V.; d/o Hezekiah & Catharine WILEY; 19y; sgl; b. & res. ClrkVA; (lic) 14 Nov 1874; p. 169

HOLLIDAY, F. W. M.; s/o R. J. McK. & Mary C. HOLLIDAY; 39y; sgl; lawyer; b. & res. FredVA; m. 9 Jan 1868 at bride's residence to McCORMICK, Hannah T.; d/o Thomas & Eliza McCORMICK; 27y; sgl; b. & res. ClrkVA; (lic) 8 Jan 1868; p. 52

HOLMS, Alex (col); s/o John & Mary HOLMS; 22y; sgl; farm hand; b. & res. ClrkVA; m. 6 Nov 1884 at ClrkVA to ELLIOTTS, Edmonia (col); d/o Andrew & Mary ELLIOTTS; 20y; sgl; b. & res. ClrkVA; (lic) 6 Nov 1884; consent of father given; p. 109

HOLTZMAN, William M.; s/o Saml. & Bettie E. HOLTZMAN; 29y; sgl; carpenter; b. PageVA; res. ShenVA; m. 7 Jul 1885 at bride's residence to SINGHASS, Kate E.; d/o Baker S. & ___ SINGHASS; 23y; sgl; b. & res. ClrkVA; (lic) 6 Jul 1885; p. 122

HOMAR, A. M.; s/o Lewis & Mary HOMAR; 25y; sgl; carpenter; b. & res. Jefferson; m. 18 Oct 1866 at ClrkVA to WILLINGHAM, Mary Frances; d/o Obedia & Eliza WILLINGHAM; 20y; sgl; b. & res. ClrkVA; (lic) 15 Oct 1866; bride's father being present; p. 20

HOOK, Jeremiah R.; s/o Wm. & Priscilla HOOK; 21y; sgl; farmer; b. Hampshire Co. W Va; res. ClrkVA; m. 9 June 1881 at ClrkVA to HANSUCKER, Mattie H.; d/o Geo. W. & Jane HANSUCKER; 21y; sgl; b. & res. ClrkVA; (lic) 9 Jun 1881; p. 41

HOOPER, James D.; s/o John R. & Emily A. HOOPER; 21y; sgl; not given; b. WrnVA; res. ClrkVA; m. 30 Apr 1872 at ClrkVA to FINNELL, Henrietta; d/o John & Nancy FINNELL; 22y; sgl; b. & res. ClrkVA; (lic) 23 Apr 1872; p. 128

HOPPER, Melton J.; s/o Wm. H. & Lucy HOPPER; 22y; sgl; farmer; b. RappVA; res. FqrVA; m. 5 Feb 1880 at FqrVA to GREEN, Emma A.; d/o James F. & Mary GREEN; 19y; sgl; b. & res. ClrkVA; (lic) 2 Feb 1880; p. 15

HOSKINS, Henry C.; s/o John & Catharine HOSKINS; 29y; wid; farmer; b. JeffVA; res. WrnVA; m. 14 Oct 1873 at ClrkVA to CLINGAN, Mary E.; d/o McLean CLINGAN & Virginia CLINGAN; 28y; sgl; b. & res. ClrkVA; (lic) 11 Oct 1873; p. 150

HOUGH, Randolph K.; s/o A. T. M. & Harriet HOUGH; 22y; sgl; farmer; b. & res. ClrkVA; m. 24 Nov 1869 at ClrkVA to TAPSCOTT, Florinda Martin; d/o Robert & Lucy TAPSCOTT; 22y; sgl; b. & res. ClrkVA; (lic) 23 Nov 1869; p. 89

HOWARD, Ely T. (col); s/o John & Julia HOWARD; 23y; sgl; farm hand; b. FredVA; res. ClrkVA; m. 8 Mar 1883 at ClrkVA to COLSTON, Katie (col); d/o ___ & Mary COLSTON; 21y; sgl; b. & res. ClrkVA; (lic) 7 Mar 1883; p. 78

HOWARD, John W. (col); s/o John and Julia Ann HOWARD; 25y; sgl; farm hand; b. LdnVA; res. ClrkVA; m. Thursday 29 May 1879 at Berryville to TRACEY, Celia (col); d/o ___ and Viney TRACEY; 22y; sgl; b. FqrVA; res. ClrkVA; (lic) 28 May 1879; p. 258

HOWELL, James F.; s/o Samson & Anna HOWELL; 37y; sgl; wagon maker; b. LdnVA; res. ClrkVA; m. 17 Oct 1865 at Berryville to KERCHEVAL, Emma; d/o John Courntney & Elizabeth KERCHEVAL; 20y; sgl; b. JeffWVA; res. ClrkVA; (lic) 17 Oct 1865; p. 4

HUBBARD, Adam (col); s/o Charles & Betsey HUBBARD (col); 26y; sgl; farm hand; b. & res. ClrkVA; m. date not given at ClrkVA to JOHNSON, Leaneh (col); d/o Alexander & Mary JOHNSON (col); 28y; sgl; b. FqrVA; res. ClrkVA; (lic) 9 Apr 1868; p. 60

HUBBARD, John F. (col); s/o Bennett & Pattie HUBBARD; 21y; sgl; farm hand; b. & res. ClrkVA; m. 18 Jan 1883 at Millwood to FRAXTIOUS, R. P. (col); d/o Jas. & Lucy FRAXTIOUS; 21y; sgl; b. & res. ClrkVA; (lic) 18 Jan 1883; p. 76

HUFF, Herod Thomas; s/o Jackson & Eliz'th HUFF; 23y; sgl; farmer; b. & res. ClrkVA.; m. 14 Nov 1872 at bride's residence to WILSON, Mollie; d/o Jeremiah & Margaret WILSON; 19y; sgl; b. & res. ClrkVA; (lic) 12 Nov 1872; p. 137

HUGHES, Thos. S.; s/o Thos. & Elizabeth HUGHES; 24y; not given; farmer; b. & res. ClrkVA; m. 19 Mar 1874 at Milldale, WrnVA to SHIPE, Arthealice J.; d/o Joseph & Deboias SHIPE; 20y; not given; b. & res. ClrkVA; (lic) 19 Mar 1874; written permission by Deboias SHIPE (her mark) for daughter Arthealia J. SHIP to Thomas S. HUGHES, witness Josiah McDONALD; p. 159

HULL, Geo. Wm. (col); s/o Wm. & Sallie HULL (col); 22y; sgl; not given; b. & res. ClrkVA; m. 10 Jan 1872 at Berryville to ROBINSON, Charlotte (col); d/o ___ & Charity ROBINSON (col); 23y; sgl; b. & res. ClrkVA; (lic) not given; p. 123
HULVER, Hiram; s/o John & Sarah HULVER; 21y; sgl; farmer; b. Hardy Co. Va; res. ClrkVA; m. 3 [or 2, written over] Aug 1866 at Berryville to TETES, Maria; d/o Levi & Scottee TETES; 21y; sgl; b. Hardy Co. Va; res. ClrkVA; (lic) 2 Aug 1866; p. 16
HUMMER, John W.; s/o Thornton & Mary HUMMER; 22y; sgl; carpenter; b. JeffVA; res. Piedmont W Va; m. 12 Sep 1871 at ClrkVA to BEEMER, Rosanna; d/o John W. & Emma BEEMER; 20y; sgl; b. FredVA; res. ClrkVA; (lic) 11 Sep 1871; p. 115
HUMMER, Mason; s/o Wm. & Julia HUMMER; 35y; sgl; farmer; b. & res. ClrkVA; m. 4 Feb 1869 at bride's residence to REED, Frances A.; d/o Stephen & Sallie REED; 23y; sgl; b. & res. ClrkVA; (lic) 3 Feb 1869; p. 76
HUMSTON, E. A. (M.D.); s/o Dr. J. A. HUMSTON & Annie HUMSTON; 26y; sgl; physician; b. & res. Henry Co. Ky; m. 28 Nov 1882 at bride's residence to HUMSTON, Annie M.; d/o B. F. & Annie HUMSTON; 24y; sgl; b. ShenVA; res. ClrkVA; (lic) 25 Nov 1882; p. 69
HUNTON, Thos.; s/o Thomas E. & Jane C. HUNTON; 23y; sgl; farmer; b. & res. FqrVA; m. 23 Feb 1869 at ClrkVA to KERFOOT, Ellen C.; d/o Franklin J. & Harriet W. E. KERFOOT; 27y; sgl; b. & res. ClrkVA; (lic) 22 Feb 1869; p. 77
HUNTSBERRY, Henry C.; s/o Augustine & Margaret HUNTSBERRY; 26y; sgl; farmer; b. & res. FredVA; m. 12 Oct 1865 at residence of bride's father to BILMIRE, Mary M.; d/o William H. & Catherine BILMIRE (nee SEYMORE); 19y; sgl; b. ShenVA; res. ClrkVA; (lic) 9 Oct 1865; consent of bride's father given in person; p. 3
HUTCHISON, Wm. Thomas; s/o Warren W. & Mary E. HUTCHISON; 30y; sgl; merchant; b. King William Co. Va; res. ClrkVA; m. 3 Jul 1879 at Berryville to CASTLEMAN, Nannie S.; d/o Wm. A. & Ann R. CASTLEMAN; 24y; sgl; b. & res. ClrkVA; (lic) 2 Jul 1879; p. 259
HUTCHSON, Jacob (col); s/o Daniel & Elizabeth HUTCHSON (col); 23y; sgl; farmer; b. & res. ClrkVA; m. 24 Jan 1872 at ClrkVA to HALL, Sinah (col); d/o not given; 21y; wid; b. not known; res. ClrkVA; (lic) not given; p. 124

IBINS, John (col); s/o Benjamin & Elizabeth IBINS; 25y; sgl; farm hand; b. CulpVA; res. ClrkVA; m. 30 Sep 1880 at ClrkVA to ROBINSON, Sidney (col); d/o Miles & Julia ROBINSON; 21y; sgl; b. & res. ClrkVA; (lic) 30 Sep 1880; p. 25

ISELING, Henry; s/o Battasen & Laura ISELING; 22y; sgl; farming; b. Maryland; res. ClrkVA; m. 1 Jul 1884 at ClrkVA to DAVIS, Annie L.; d/o Thomas & Elizabeth DAVIS; 21y; sgl; b. JeffWVA; res. ClrkVA; (lic) 30 Jun 1884; p. 102

JACKSON, Abraham E.; s/o Josiah & Mary JACKSON; 25y; sgl; farmer; b. FredVA; res. ClrkVA; m. 18 Dec 1879 at ClrkVA to EVERHART, Ella; d/o Jacob W. & Mary EVERHART; 28y; sgl; b. & res. ClrkVA; (lic) 17 Dec 1879; p. 10

JACKSON, Archer (col); s/o William & Mary JACKSON (col); 22y; sgl; farm hand; b. St. Charles, Missouri; res. ClrkVA; m. 30 Jan 1866 [68] at Berryville to PAGE, Lizzie (col); d/o ___ and Rose PAGE; 21y; sgl; b. & res. ClrkVA; (lic) 30 Jan 1868; p. 54

JACKSON, Charles (col); s/o Fuller & Kitty JACKSON; 52y; wid; farm hand; b. WrnVA; res. ClrkVA; m. 11 Mar 1875 at ClrkVA to STROTHER, Mary (col); d/o ___ & Sallie STROTHER; 41y; wid; b. PageVA; res. ClrkVA; (lic) 10 Mar 1875; p. 176

JACKSON, Chas. (col); s/o Chas. & Nannie JACKSON (col); 23y; sgl; carriage driver; b. & res. ClrkVA; m. 7 May 1870 at Millwood to BROWN, Sarah (col); d/o Thomas & Rebecca BROWN (col); 17y; sgl; b. & res. ClrkVA; (lic) 6 May 1870; consent bride's parents given before issuing license; p. 96

JACKSON, Coldridge L. (col); s/o Wm. A. & Sarah S. JACKSON; 21y; sgl; farmer hand; b. Middleboro Massachusetts; res. ClrkVA; m. 30 Dec 1886 at bride's residence to JORDON, Mary V. (col); d/o ___ & Louisa DYER; 16y; sgl; b. & res. ClrkVA; (lic) 27 Dec 1886; p. 150

JACKSON, Daniel (col); s/o Jacob & Emily JACKSON (col); 23y; sgl; farm hand; b. & res. ClrkVA; m. 5 Dec 1872 at ClrkVA to JACKSON, Caroline (col); d/o not given; 22y; sgl; b. & res. ClrkVA; (lic) 5 Dec 1872; p. 138

JACKSON, Danl. (col); s/o Jacob & Emily JACKSON (col); 21y; sgl; farm hand; b. Amherst Co.; res. ClrkVA; m. 28 Dec 1870 at Bethel, ClrkVA to ASHBY, Martha (col); d/o Julia RUFFINS (col); 21y; sgl; b. not given; res. ClrkVA; (lic) 27 Dec 1870; p. 106

JACKSON, Edmund (col); s/o father not known, mother Melvina GIBSON [JACKSON?]; 22y; sgl; farm hand; b. & res. ClrkVA;

m. 3 May 1876 at ClrkVA to GIBSON, Louisa (col); d/o not given; 26y; sgl; b. & res. ClrkVA; (lic) 2 May 1876; p. 200
JACKSON, Everett (col); s/o Ever[e]tt & Eleanor JACKSON; 21y; sgl; waiter; b. & res. ClrkVA; m. 12 Aug 1866 at Millwood to BROWN, Eliza (col); d/o John & Jane STRANGE; 22y; wid; b. & res. ClrkVA; (lic) 10 Aug 1866; p. 17
JACKSON, George (col); s/o Washington & Martha JACKSON; 21y; sgl; farm hand; b. & res. ClrkVA; m. 17 Sep 1874 at Millwood to DEDFORTH, Susan (col); d/o Jim & Minerva BROWN; 22y; wid; b. Millwood; res. ClrkVA; (lic) 17 Sep 1874; p. 165
JACKSON, George; s/o Wm. & Anne JACKSON; 45y; wid; farmer; b. & res. FqrVA; m. 6 Oct 1868 at ClrkVA to KILE, Harriet; d/o George & ___ KILE; 45y; sgl; b. LdnVA; res. ClrkVA; (lic) 5 Oct 1868; p. 67
JACKSON, Israel (col); s/o Manuel & Lotty JACKSON (col); 29y; sgl; farm hand; b. & res. ClrkVA; m. 9 Jan 1868 at Greenville, ClrkVA to WILLIAMS, Casiah (col); d/o Simon & Rachael WILLIAMS (col); 21y; sgl; b. & res. ClrkVA; (lic) 8 Jan 1868; p. 52
JACKSON, Jerome (col); s/o Philip & Milly JACKSON; 24y; wid; farm hand; b. & res. ClrkVA; m. 12 Jul 1883 at ClrkVA to CARTER, Mollie (col); d/o ___ & Lucy CARTER; 21y; sgl; b. & res. ClrkVA; (lic) 11 Jul 1883; p. 84
JACKSON, John (col); s/o Everitt & Ellena JACKSON; 21y; sgl; farm hand; b. & res. ClrkVA; m. 15 Jan 1873 at bride's residence to JAMISON, Mary (col); d/o ___ & Winney JAMISON; 20y; sgl; b. not given; res. ClrkVA; (lic) 10 Jan 1873; p. 140
JACKSON, John (col); s/o Geo. & Martha JACKSON; 23y; sgl; farm hand; b. & res. ClrkVA; m. 23 Dec 1880 at ClrkVA to HOWARD, Martha (col); d/o ___ & Fannie HOWARD; 26y; sgl; b. & res. ClrkVA; (lic) 23 Dec 1880; p. 32
JACKSON, Marcus (col); s/o Wm. JACKSON & Jeannetta WHITE; 21y; sgl; laborer; b. & res. ClrkVA; m. 1 Jul 1875 at Berryville to JOHNSON, Sarah (col); d/o ___ JOHNSON & Harriet TOCAS; 18y; sgl; b. & res. ClrkVA; (lic) 1 Jul 1875; p. 182
JACKSON, Richard (col); s/o Richard & Easter JACKSON; 28y; sgl; waiter; b. & res. ClrkVA; m. 20 Apr 1875 at Berryville to ALVERSON, Elizabeth (col); d/o not given; 23y; sgl; b. Hampshire Co. Va; res. ClrkVA; (lic) 20 Apr 1875; p. 178

JACKSON, Robert (col); s/o Jacob & Ema JACKSON; 24y; sgl; farm hand; b. & res. ClrkVA; m. 23 Dec 1880 at ClrkVA to RANDOLPH, Isabelle (col); d/o James & Mary RANDOLPH; 23y; sgl; b. & res. ClrkVA; (lic) 23 Dec 1880; p. 32

JACKSON, William A.; s/o Richard & Mary Ann JACKSON; 32y; sgl; carpenter; b. & res. FredVA; m. 13 May 1869 at ClrkVA to DOWNING, Allie; d/o John and ___ DOWNING; 25y; sgl; b. FredVA; res. ClrkVA; (lic) 10 May 1869; p. 81

JACKSON, William; s/o Cyrus & Nancy; 30y; wid; farmer; b. & res. ClrkVA; m. 23 Jun 1869 at Berryville to MITCHELL, Mary; d/o Samuel & Jane; 29y; sgl; b. & res. ClrkVA; (lic) 23 Jun 1869; p. 83

JACOBS, Franklin P.; s/o Michael & Nellie JACOBS; 21y; sgl; farming; b. & res. ClrkVA; m. 25 Oct 1877 at ClrkVA to SMALLWOOD, Frances; d/o Thomas & Martha E. SMALLWOOD; 20y; sgl; b. & res. ClrkVA; (lic) 24 Oct 1877; consent given by Thomas SMALLWOOD father of bride; p. 225

JACOBS, Herbert C.; s/o Rozell & Susan JACOBS; 29y; wid; farmer; b. LdnVA; res. ClrkVA; m. 19 Oct 1880 at ClrkVA to JACKSON, Maria F.; d/o Jonah & Mary JACKSON; 23y; sgl; b. FredVA; res. ClrkVA; (lic) 19 Oct 1880; p. 26

JEFFERS, Addison (col); s/o ___ and ___ JEFFERS (col); 21y; sgl; farm hand; b. Henrico Co. Va; res. ClrkVA; m. 4 Apr 1868 at Berryville to PRINCE, Ann (col); d/o Charles and Lucy PRINCE (col); 23y; sgl; b. & res. ClrkVA; (lic) 3 Apr 1868; p. 59

JEFFERSON, Thos. (col); s/o Harry & Delpha JEFFERSON (col); 24y; sgl; farm hand; b. JeffVA; res. ClrkVA; m. 27 Feb 1869 at ClrkVA to WHITE, Lavina (col); d/o Thos. & Louisa WHITE (col); 22y; sgl; b. JeffVA; res. ClrkVA; (lic) 25 Feb 1869; p. 78

JENKINS, David W.; s/o John H. & Mary J. JENKINS; 27y; sgl; carpenter; b. ClrkVA; res. Winchester, FredVA; m. 26 Oct 1869 at Millwood to DOREN, Mary E.; d/o James & Mary DOREN; 23y; sgl; b. & res. ClrkVA; (lic) 23 Oct 1869; p. 86

JENKINS, Herod; s/o Herod & Matilda JENKINS; 20y; sgl; farmer; b. & res. ClrkVA; m. date not given to HOUGH, Annie; d/o Armstead & Harriet HOUGH; 21y; sgl; b. & res. ClrkVA; (lic) 9 Jun 1866; written permission dated 8 Jun 1866 from Herod & Matilda JENKINS; p. 13

JENKINS, Jesse; s/o Herod & Matilda JENKINS; 24y; sgl; farmer; b. & res. ClrkVA; m. 30 May 1867 at ClrkVA to BRABHAM, Sarah; d/o H. W. & Elizabeth BRABHAM; 22y; sgl; b. & res. ClrkVA; (lic) 28 May 1867; p. 35

JENKINS, John T.; s/o Eben & Matilda JENKINS; 28y; sgl; farmer; b. & res. ClrkVA; m. 3 Dec 1874 at ClrkVA to HOUGH, Elizabeth; d/o Alfred & Sallie JONES; 32y; wid; b. & res. ClrkVA; (lic) 3 Dec 1874; p. 171

JENKINS, Richard (col); s/o Presley & Jane JENKINS; 23y; sgl; farm hand; b. & res. ClrkVA; m. 11 Jan 1877 at near Berryville to ROBINSON, Margaret (col); d/o Saml. & Jane ROBINSON; 23y; sgl; b. & res. ClrkVA; (lic) 11 Jan 1877; p. 214

JENKINS, Thomas W.; s/o Ebin & Mary JENKINS; 25y; sgl; farmer; b. & res. ClrkVA; m. 21 Jul 1881 at LdnVA to JONES, Harriet (Mrs.); d/o Henry & Betsey STICKELS; 30y; wid; b. & res. ClrkVA; (lic) 20 Jul 1881; p. 44

JETT, Lewis (col); s/o George & Eliza JETT; 27y; sgl; farm hand; b. RappVA; res. ClrkVA; m. 26 Dec 1879 at ClrkVA to ELLIS, Lucy Ann (col); d/o Andrew ELLIS, mother's name not known; 19y; sgl; b. & res. ClrkVA; (lic) 24 Dec 1879; p. 12

JOBE, Benjamin M.; s/o ___ & ___ JOBE; 25y; sgl; farmer; b. & res. PageVA; m. 3 Mar 180 at bride's residence to SLUSHER, Bettie E.; d/o Hezekiah & Mary A. SLUSHER; 24y; sgl; b. PageVA; res. ClrkVA; (lic) 2 Mar 1880; p. 16

JOHNASTON, John A.; s/o John S. & Alberta JOHNASTON; 23y; sgl; farmer; b. & res. ClrkVA; m. 17 Dec 1884 at Berryville to WHITTINGTON, Alice C.; d/o Chas. L. & Martha C. WHITTINGTON; 21y; sgl; b. & res. ClrkVA; (lic) 16 Dec 1884; p. 113

JOHNSON, B. F.; s/o Saml. & Catharine JOHNSON; 25y; sgl; farmer; b. & res. ClrkVA; m. 14 Jun 1866 at ClrkVA to LEE, Eliza; d/o Squire & Lucinda LEE; 23y; sgl; b. & res. ClrkVA; (lic) 2 Jun 1866; p. 12

JOHNSON, Edward (col); s/o Jackson & Harriet JOHNSON; 21y; sgl; farm hand; b. & res. ClrkVA; m. Thursday 10 Jul 1879 at Millwood to ROBINSON, Lizzie (col); d/o Simon ROBINSON, mother's name not known; 21y; sgl; b. & res. ClrkVA; (lic) 10 Jul 1879; p. 260

JOHNSON, Geo. W. (col); s/o Geo. W. & Betsey JOHNSON; 32y; sgl; farmer; b. & res. JeffWVA; m. 9 Nov 1881 at

Berryville to McCARD, Rebecca; d/o Job & Sarah Ann
McCARD; 29y; sgl; b. & res. ClrkVA; (lic) 9 Nov 1881; p. 50
JOHNSON, Jackson (col); s/o Cartrell & Hannah JOHNSON;
48y; sgl; farm hand; b. Caroline Co. Va; res. ClrkVA; m. 5
Aug 1866 at the Parsonage to BANKS, Harriet (col); d/o
George & Pattie BANKS; 46y; sgl; b. & res. ClrkVA; (lic) 4
Aug 1866; p. 16
JOHNSON, Jackson (col); s/o Cato & Hannah JOHNSON; 65y;
wid; farm hand; b. & res. ClrkVA; m. 28 Jan 1883 at ClrkVA to
WORMLY, Sidney (col); d/o Philip & Amanda WORMLY; 30y;
sgl; b. & res. ClrkVA; (lic) 23 Dec 1882; p. 72
JOHNSON, James (col); s/o Isham and Ann JOHNSON; 25y;
sgl; farm hand; b. RckbrVA; res. ClrkVA; m. 19 Aug 1880 at
ClrkVA to STROTHER, Emily (col); d/o not known; 21y; sgl;
b. & res. ClrkVA; (lic) 11 Aug 1880; p. 25
JOHNSON, Jas. Walter; s/o Franklin L. & Mary Jane JOHNSON;
23y; sgl; farmer; b. & res. ClrkVA; m. 26 Feb 1885 at bride's
residence to SHROUT, Florence M.; d/o Lewis & Annie
SHROUT; 19y; sgl; b. & res. ClrkVA; (lic) 25 Feb 1885;
bride's parents gave consent through Conrad POPP in
person; p. 118
JOHNSON, John Thomas (col); s/o Albert & Matilda JOHNSON;
28y; sgl; merchandise; b. Orange Co. Va; res. ClrkVA; m. 4
Sep 1884 at ClrkVA to DYER, Betsy (col); d/o David & Lucy
DYER; 26y; sgl; b. & res. ClrkVA; (lic) 4 Sep 1884; p. 106
JOHNSON, Philip (col); s/o Spencer & Susan JOHNSON (col);
22y; sgl; farm hand; b. & res. ClrkVA; m. 4 Apr 1869 at
ClrkVA to JONES, Christianna (col); d/o ___ & ___ JONES
(col); 22y; sgl; b. Jefferson Co.; res. ClrkVA; (lic) 29 Mar
1869; p. 79
JOHNSON, Riley (col); s/o ___ & Emily JOHNSON; 22y; sgl;
farm hand; b. WrnVA; res. ClrkVA; m. 4 Mar 1886 at
Berryville to STROTHER, Charlotte (col); d/o ___ & Charlotte
STROTHER; 25y; sgl; b. & res. ClrkVA; (lic) 4 Mar 1886; p.
133
JOHNSON, Robert E.; s/o __ & ___ JOHNSON; 24y; sgl; picture
framer; b. Hampshire Co. W Va; res. FredVA; m. 6 Feb 1883
at bride's residence to STUMP, Alice Frances; d/o Simon R.
& Eliz'th STUMP; 16y; sgl; b. & res. ClrkVA; (lic) 3 Feb 1883;
license issued at the request of the bride's father; p. 76
JOHNSON, Thomas M.; s/o Jas. W. & Ann Eliz'th JOHNSON;
24y; sgl; farmer; b. & res. ClrkVA; m. 15 Dec 1885 at bride's

residence to CHAPPELL, Susie E.; d/o Jno. T. & Levenia J. CHAPPELL; 15y; sgl; b. & res. ClrkVA; (lic) 15 Dec 1885; bride's mother was present when license was issued & gave consent; p. 130
JOLLIFFE, John M.; s/o John and Lucy M. JOLLIFFE; 25y; sgl; farmer; b. & res. ClrkVA; m. 4 Aug 1868 at bride's residence to McCORMICK, Kate M.; d/o Otway & Sarah Ann McCORMICK; 22y; sgl; b. & res. ClrkVA; (lic) 3 Aug 1868; p. 64
JONES, Doras H.; s/o Thomas & Mary Jane JONES; 23y; sgl; farmer; b. & res. ClrkVA; m. 26 Mar 1873 at Berryville to BERLIN, Mary C.; d/o Lewis & Jane E. BERLIN; 24y; sgl; b. & res. ClrkVA; (lic) 26 Mar 1873; p. 144
JONES, George (col); s/o George & Martha JONES; 22y; sgl; laborer; b. & res. ClrkVA; m. Thursday 18 May 1876 at Berryville to BURNS, Kitty (col); d/o Charles & Fannie BURNS; 17y; sgl; b. & res. ClrkVA; (lic) 18 May 1876; p. 200 [p. 91b - Letter dated 18 May 1876 from J. Rice SMITH D. C. states Warner COOPER uncle of Kitty BURNS made oath that the parents of Kitty are perfectly willing that she shall marry George JONES.]
JONES, Harrison (col); s/o Garland & Eve GILMORE (col); 27y; sgl; farm hand; b. RckhmVA; res. ClrkVA; m. 17 Nov 1870 at Berryville to MYERS, Arina (col); d/o Charles & Pallas MYERS (col); 21y; sgl; b. & res. ClrkVA; (lic) not given; p. 103
JONES, Leonard; s/o Matthew & Elizabeth JONES; 49y; wid; farmer; b. BerkVA; res. ClrkVA; m. 25 Feb 1869 at Berryville to BOWSER, Mary H.; d/o Christian & Lucinda BOWSER; 37y; sgl; b. BerkVA; res. ClrkVA; (lic) not given; p. 78
JONES, Lewis C. (col); s/o Rosetta BANKS (col); 22y; sgl; farm hand; b. & res. ClrkVA; m. 29 Dec 1870 at Berryville to JACKSON, Sarah (col); d/o Charles & Sarah JACKSON (col); 21y; sgl; b. WrnVA; res. ClrkVA; (lic) 28 Dec 1870; p. 106
JONES, Lewis Cass William (col); s/o Adeline BANKS & Charles JONES; 26y; wid; school teacher (at times); b. & res. ClrkVA; m. 15 Jul 1875 at near Berryville at residence of bride to STROTHER, Emily (col); d/o Mary STROTHER & Jackson STROTHER; 24y; sgl; b. PageVA; res. ClrkVA; (lic) 14 Jul 1875; p. 182
JONES, M. W.; s/o Thomas & Mary J. JONES; 37y; sgl; deputy treasurer; b. JeffWVA; res. ClrkVA; m. 24 Jun 1886 at

Berryville to MARKS, Laura S.; d/o Jacob A. & A. E. MARKS; 20y; sgl; b. FredVA; res. ClrkVA; (lic) 24 Jun 1886; p. 139

JONES, Theodore (col); s/o James & Jane JONES; 21y; sgl; farm head; b. & res. ClrkVA; m. 14 Aug 1879 at ClrkVA to ROBINSON, Amanda (col); d/o Mires & Julia ROBINSON; 19y; sgl; b. & res. ClrkVA; (lic) 14 Aug 1879; consent of parents given; p. 262

JONES, Theodore (col); s/o James & Jane JONES; 25y; wid; farm hand; b. & res. ClrkVA; m. 7 Jul 1886 at Berryville to BUTLER, Florence (col); d/o James & Martha BUTLER; 19y; sgl; b. & res. ClrkVA; (lic) 2 Jul 1886; p. 139

JORDAN, William H. (col); s/o Washington & Louisa JORDAN; 22y; sgl; farm hand; b. Pennsylvania; res. ClrkVA; m. 13 May 1886 at ClrkVA to TATE, Ida M. (col); d/o Nathan & Martha TATE; 22y; sgl; b. Pennsylvania; res. ClrkVA; (lic) 13 May 1886; p. 136

KABLE, Levi; s/o Isaac & Julia KABLE; 25y; sgl; lumber business; b. & res. Northumberland Co. Pa; m. 19 Jan 1886 at ClrkVA to MORRIS, Mary; d/o John & Ann MORRIS; 20y; sgl; b. & res. ClrkVA; (lic) 18 Jan 1886; consent given by bride's mother; p. 132

KANE, William M.; s/o Morris & Mary KANE; 25y; sgl; farmer; b. & res. JeffWVA; m. 20 Feb 1884 at ClrkVA to FENTON, Cordelia C.; d/o Dennis & Ann FENTON; 21y; sgl; b. & res. ClrkVA; (lic) 19 Feb 1884; p. 94

KEELER, Joseph W.; s/o Middleton & Teresa KEELER; 37y; sgl; merchant; b. & res. ClrkVA; m. 13 Feb 1884 at bride's residence to SHEARER, Mattie E.; d/o Henry & Elizabeth SHEARER; 27y; sgl; b. & res. ClrkVA; (lic) 11 Feb 1884; p. 94

KELLY, Andrew J.; s/o Robert & Salelia; 22y; sgl; farmer; b. & res. LdnVA; m. 23 Oct 1884 at ClrkVA to FOWLER, Ida; d/o Wm & Alcinda FOWLER; 18y; sgl; b. & res. ClrkVA; (lic) 20 Oct 1884; consent of father in person; p. 108

KELLY, Geo. W.; s/o Geo. & Hannah KELLY; 26y; sgl; farmer; b. & res. LdnVA; m. 14 Jan 1869 at bride's residence to WILEY, Casiah; d/o Samuel & Elizabeth WILEY; 23y; sgl; b. & res. ClrkVA; (lic) 11 Jan 1869; p. 74

KENDALL, Dorsey; s/o Henry & Harriet KENDALL; 22y; sgl; farmer; b. & res. ClrkVA; m. 31 Oct 1883 at ClrkVA to HARRIS, Laura O.; d/o Wm. B. & Lucy HARRIS; 22y; sgl; b. & res. ClrkVA; (lic) 30 Oct 1883; p. 88

KERCHEVAL, John W.; s/o Edward V. & Ann KERCHEVAL; 22y; sgl; wagon maker; b. & res. Berryville; m. 22 Oct 1873 at Berryville to STOLLE, William Annie; d/o Wm. F. & Charlotte STOLLE; 21y; sgl; b. & res. Berryville; (lic) 21 Oct 1873; p. 152
KERNS, George N.; s/o Wm. & Matilda KERNS; 24y; sgl; farmer; b. & res. Smithfield, JeffWVA; m. 15 Sep 1874 at Berryville to MERCER, Annie E.; d/o John W. & Susan MERCER; 24y; sgl; b. & res. Smithfield, JeffWVA; (lic) 15 Sep 1874; p. 165
KERRICK, Walter B.; s/o Matthew N. & Lucy A. KERRICK; 22y; sgl; farmer; b. & res. FqrVA; m. 20 Feb 1873 at bride's residence to BARR, Martha C.; d/o Adam & Cath'e. BARR; 25y; sgl; b. & res. ClrkVA; (lic) 19 Feb 1873; p. 142
KIGER, Wm. J.; s/o James M. & Mary KIGER; 22y; sgl; farmer; b. & res. ClrkVA; m. 25 Feb 1869 at ClrkVA to TAYLOR, Elizabeth V.; d/o James L. & Ellen C. TAYLOR; 18y; sgl; b. FredVA; res. ClrkVA; (lic) 22 Feb 1869; present bride's father; p. 77
KIMMELL, Andrew Jackson; s/o Jno. N. & Nancy KIMMELL; 29y; sgl; carpenter; b. & res. ClrkVA; m. 13 Oct 1879 at ClrkVA to PEIRCE, Gertrude N.; d/o A. N. & Mary E. PEIRCE; 19y; sgl; b. & res. ClrkVA; (lic) 13 Oct 1879; p. 3
KING, Edward; s/o Edward and Mary KING; 24y; sgl; blacksmith; b. Troy New York; res. ClrkVA; m. 5 Jun 1882 at ClrkVA to NORMAN, Sarah; d/o ___ and Hannah NORMAN; 24y; sgl; b. Virginia; res. ClrkVA; (lic) 5 Jun 1882; p. 60
KITCHEN, John N.; s/o George & Maria L. KITCHEN; 28y; wid; farmer; b. & res. ClrkVA; m. 15 Mar 1866 at ClrkVA to McDONALD, Malinda C.; d/o James & Elizabeth McDONALD; 25y; sgl; b. Hampshire Co.; res. ClrkVA; (lic) 14 Mar 1866; p. 8
KITE, Solon T.; s/o James & Margaret KITE; 22y; sgl; farmer; b. & res. PageVA; m. 6 Mar 1873 at ClrkVA to KOONTZ, Elizabeth A.; d/o John N. & FormsSanta KOONTZ; 22y; sgl; b. PageVA; res. ClrkVA; (lic) 3 Mar 1872; p. 143
KNIGHT, Abner; s/o David & Phariba KNIGHT; 34y; sgl; school teacher; b. Wilkinson Co. Georgia; res. ClrkVA; m. 3 Dec 1867 at Berryville to BENN, Sarah Frances; d/o James and ___ BENN; 22y; sgl; b. & res. ClrkVA; (lic) 30 Nov 1867; p. 47
KNIGHT, Henry; s/o Thomas & Elizabeth KNIGHT; 36y; wid; farmer; b. & res. ClrkVA; m. 20 Dec 1870 at ClrkVA to

CARTER, Julia; d/o Wm. & Emily E. CARTER; 24y; sgl; b. & res. ClrkVA; (lic) 19 Dec 1870; p. 104
KNIGHT, Wm. H.; s/o Wesley & Mary KNIGHT; 23y; sgl; miller; b. & res. FredVA; m. 9 Aug 1882 at Berryville to GRUBB, Mary Blanche; d/o Wm. & Charlotte GRUBB; 22y; sgl; b. & res. ClrkVA; (lic) 9 Aug 1882; p. 62
KOUNSLAR, Randolph; s/o Randolph and Elizabeth S. KOUNSLAR; 23y; sgl; farmer; b. & res. ClrkVA; m. 23 Sep 1873 at Berryville to STRIBLING, Alice M.; d/o John W. & Ann STRIBLING; 19y; sgl; b. Winchester Va; res. ClrkVA; (lic) 22 Sep 1873; p. 149
LACEY, George (col); s/o Frederick & Maria LACEY; 23y; sgl; farm hand; b. PageVA; res. ClrkVA; m. 24 Dec 1878 at ClrkVA to PARKER, Fannie (col); d/o not given; 22y; sgl; b. & res. ClrkVA; (lic) 24 Dec 1878; p. 249
LAKE, Alexander J.; s/o Jurdon & Mary LAKE; 38y; sgl; farmer; b. RappVA; res. ClrkVA; m. 19 Dec 1867 at ClrkVA to GOODRIDGE, Rachael; d/o Adrian & ___ GOODRIDGE; 38y; sgl; b. WrnVA; res. ClrkVA; (lic) 19 Dec 1867; p. 49
LAKE, Henry; s/o Jordan & Mary A. LAKE; 22y; sgl; farmer; b. RappVA; res. ClrkVA; m. 23 Jan 1872 at ClrkVA to LAKE, Elizabeth; d/o Vincent & Fannie LAKE; 20y; sgl; b. RappVA; res. ClrkVA; (lic) 23 Jan 1871; p. 108
LAMKINS, Frank (col); s/o Lewis and Hannah LAMKINS; 24y; sgl; farm hand; b. FredVA; res. ClrkVA; m. 28 Nov 1883 at bride's residence to KIRK, Sally Ann; d/o Geo. Wm. & Rachel Ann KIRK; 17y; sgl; b. JeffWVA; res. ClrkVA; (lic) 28 Nov 1883; p. 89
LANCASTER, John F.; s/o John F. & Hannah LANCASTER; 26y; sgl; rail road employee; b. JeffWVA; res. ClrkVA; m. 9 Feb 1881 at Berryville to SPRINT, Mary R.; d/o John W. & ___ SPRINT; 25y; sgl; b. & res. ClrkVA; (lic) 9 Feb 1881; p. 35
LANCASTER, Milton M.; s/o Jno. F. & Hannah LANCASTER; 24y; sgl; blacksmith; b. Jefferson Co.; res. ClrkVA; m. 10 Feb 1870 at bride's residence to SNYDER, Virginia H.; d/o Daniel & Cynthia SNYDER; 24y; sgl; b. Jefferson Co.; res. ClrkVA; (lic) 10 Feb 1870; p. 93
LANGLEY, Edgar A.; s/o Philip & Margaret LANGLEY; 22y; sgl; farmer; b. & res. FredVA; m. 3 Nov 1885 at Berryville to GRUBB, Lula R.; d/o Walter B. & Elizabeth GRUBB; 20y; sgl; b. FredVA; res. ClrkVA; (lic) 3 Nov 1885; p. 127

LANHAM, Daniel; s/o James and Jane LANHAM; 32y; sgl; farmer; b. & res. ClrkVA; m. Thursday 7 Dec 1876 at Berryville to FURR, Olivia; d/o Ephren and Amanda FURR; 20y; sgl; b. & res. ClrkVA; (lic) 7 Dec 1876; letter of permission from bride's father dated 6 Dec; p. 210
LANHAM, George R.; s/o Enos & Lucinda LANHAM; 25y; sgl; blacksmith; b. & res. ClrkVA; m. 10 Apr 1879 at ClrkVA to SHIPE, Fannie M.; d/o Joseph & Debous SHIPE; 17y; sgl; b. WrnVA; res. ClrkVA; (lic) 9 Apr 1879; p. 256
LANHAM, George; s/o William & Rebecca LANHAM; 25y; sgl; farmer; b. LdnVA; res. ClrkVA; m. 31 Jan 1867 at ClrkVA to LANHAM, Margaret E.; d/o James & Jane LANHAM; 21y; sgl; b. & res. ClrkVA; (lic) 28 Jan 1867; p. 30
LANHAM, James A.; s/o James & Jane LANHAM; 25y; sgl; farmer; b. & res. ClrkVA; m. 10 Sep 1878 at Berryville to HOFF, Henrietta; d/o Humphry & Malissa HOFF; 21y; sgl; b. & res. ClrkVA; (lic) 10 Sep 1878; p. 239
LANHAM, James W.; s/o George & Sallie LANHAM; 21y; sgl; farm hand; b. & res. ClrkVA; m. 13 Jan 1875 at ClrkVA to LLOYD, Lucinda; d/o John & Polly LLOYD; 30y; sgl; b. & res. ClrkVA; (lic) 13 Jan 1875; p. 174
LANHAM, Samuel; s/o William & Rebecca LANHAM; 24y; sgl; farmer; b. LdnVA; res. ClrkVA; m. 19 Dec 1871 at ClrkVA to SMALLWOOD, Amanda; d/o Burr & Louisa SMALLWOOD; 23y; sgl; b. & res. ClrkVA; (lic) __ Dec 1871; p. 121
LANHAM, Thomas B.; s/o Enos & Lucinda LANHAM; 25y; sgl; farmer; b. Barbour Co. Va; res. ClrkVA; m. 21 Jan 1868 at ClrkVA to STICKEL, Barbary A.; d/o Joseph & Harriet STICKEL; 19y; sgl; b. FqrVA; res. ClrkVA; (lic) 14 Jan 1868; written consent by Joseph STICKEL filed; p. 53
LANHAM, Thomas B.; s/o Enos & Lucy LANHAM; 35y; wid; carpenter; b. Barbour Co. W Va; res. ClrkVA; m. 18 Sep 1877 at near Berryville to WILLINGHAM, Alice G.; d/o William & Matilda WILLINGHAM; 22y; sgl; b. & res. ClrkVA; (lic) 18 Sep 1877; p. 222
LARUE, C. C.; s/o Samuel & Juliet C. LARUE; 39y; sgl; farmer; b. & res. ClrkVA; m. 16 Jun 1868 at Popular Mead to ClrkVA to LARUE, Maria; d/o Joel & Massie OSBURN; 39y; wid; b. LdnVA; res. ClrkVA; (lic) 10 Jun 1868; p. 62
LAVENDER, Charles (col); s/o not given; 21y; sgl; farm hand; b. not given; res. ClrkVA; m. 13 Feb 1873 at ClrkVA to

WITHERS, Missouri (col); d/o not given; 21y; sgl; b. not given; res. ClrkVA; (lic) 11 Feb 1873; p. 142
LAVENDER, Giles (col); s/o Geo. & Clara LAVENDER (col); 21y; sgl; farm hand; b. & res. ClrkVA; m. 12 Sep 1869 at White Post to PEIRSON, Annie (col); d/o James & Emily PIERSON (col); 21y; sgl; b. & res. ClrkVA; (lic) 9 Sep 1869; p. 84
LAWS, Cassius D. (M.D.); s/o E. T. & Rose LAWS; 28y; sgl; physician; b. FqrVA; res. WrnVA; m. 5 Nov 1885 at ClrkVA to SOWERS, Alice M.; d/o Jno. W. & Mary SOWERS; 27y; sgl; b. & res. ClrkVA; (lic) 4 Nov 1885; p. 127
LAWS, Charles H. (col); s/o Ralph & Betsey LAWS; 21y; sgl; farm hand; b. & res. ClrkVA; m. 2 Oct 1873 at White Post to ROBINSON, Roberta V. (col); d/o Henry & Mary ROBINSON; 21y; sgl; b. & res. ClrkVA; (lic) 1 Oct 1873; p. 150
LAWS, Charles H. (col); s/o Thomas & Mary LAWS; 30y; sgl; farm hand; b. & res. ClrkVA; m. 7 [or 6, written over] Apr 1881 at Berryville to McCARD, Mary (col); d/o Job & Sarah McCARD; 21y; sgl; b. & res. ClrkVA; (lic) 5 Apr 1881; p. 38
LAWS, Christopher (col); s/o not given; 22y; sgl; carriage driver; b. & res. ClrkVA; m. 23 Oct 1879 at ClrkVA to CARTER, Maria (col); d/o Saul & Mary CARTER; 17y; sgl; b. & res. ClrkVA; (lic) 23 Oct 1879; p. 5
LAWS, James W. (col); s/o ___ & Mary LAWS (col); 36y; sgl; farm hand; b. & res. ClrkVA; m. 26 Sep 1871 at Winchester Va to STRANGE, Susan (col); d/o Stephen & ___ STRANGE (col); 21y; sgl; b. & res. ClrkVA; (lic) 26 Sep 1871; p. 116
LAWS, Joel N.; s/o E. T. & J. J. LAWS; 26y; sgl; merchant; b. FqrVA; res. ClrkVA; m. 13 Apr 1869 at bride's residence to KERFOOT, Georgie; d/o Wm. C. & Eliza A. KERFOOT; 20y; sgl; b. & res. ClrkVA; (lic) 10 Apr 1869; p. 81
LAWS, Norval W.; s/o Ebin T. & Sarah J. LAWS; 27y; sgl; merchant; b. Upperville, FqrVA; res. ClrkVA; m. 19 Sep 1872 at Millwood to EVANS, Alice W.; d/o Hiram P. & Sarah J. EVANS; 22y; sgl; b. & res. ClrkVA; (lic) 17 Sep 1872; p. 133
LAWS, Thomas (col); s/o Thomas & Mary LAWS; 25y; sgl; farm hand; b. & res. ClrkVA; m. Wednesday 16 Oct 1878 at Berryville to JENKINS, Bettie (col); d/o Presley & Jane JENKINS; 23y; sgl; b. & res. ClrkVA; (lic) 16 Oct 1878; p. 242
LAWSON, Jacob (col); s/o Thomas & Harriet LAWSON; 22y; sgl; farm hand; b. CulpVA; res. ClrkVA; m. 2 Jul 1885 at Millwood to BANKS, Mary (col); d/o ___ & Lizzie BANKS; 24y; sgl; b. & res. ClrkVA; (lic) 2 Jul 1885; p. 122

LAWSON, Marcus Jackson; s/o Jackson and Mary LAWSON; 24y; sgl; farm hand; b. WrnVA; res. ClrkVA; m. Thursday 28 Aug 1879 at ClrkVA to LEWIN, Maria Virginia; d/o Moses and Sarah LEWIN; 21y; sgl; b. & res. ClrkVA; (lic) 23 Aug 1879; p. 1

LAWSON, Zackariah (col); s/o Caleb & Margaret LAWSON; 31y; sgl; farm hand; b. & res. LdnVA; m. 1 Jan 1885 at Berryville to SANDS, Almira (col); d/o ___ & Mary SANDS; 21y; sgl; b. LdnVA; res. ClrkVA; (lic) 1 Jan 1885; p. 114

LAYTON, Benjamin (col); s/o Henry & Kate LAYTON; 22y; sgl; carpenter; b. & res. ClrkVA; m. 26 Feb 1874 at Millwood to BROWN, Betsey (col); d/o Thos. & Rebecca BROWN; 21y; sgl; b. & res. ClrkVA; (lic) 26 Feb 1874; p. 158

LAYTON, Daniel (col); s/o Henry & Katie LAYTON; 34y; sgl; farm hand; b. & res. ClrkVA; m. Wednesday 16 Apr 1879 at Millwood to JONES, Nancy (col); d/o John & Nancy JONES; 34y; sgl; b. Richmond Va; res. ClrkVA; (lic) 11 Apr 1879; p. 257

LEASURE, J. H.; s/o John & Cassea LEASURE; 25y; sgl; farmer; b. Allegany Co. Maryland; res. Maryland; m. 21 Feb 1871 at ClrkVA to PATTERSON, Mollie L.; d/o John & Harriet PATTERSON; 22y; sgl; b. & res. ClrkVA; (lic) 20 Feb 1871; p. 109

LEE, Arthur Allen; s/o Wm. LEE & Henrietta LEE; 23y; sgl; farmer; b. & res. ClrkVA; m. 26 Feb 1874 at ClrkVA to FIDLER, Fannie R.; d/o Israel & Nancy FIDLER; 21y; sgl; b. & res. ClrkVA; (lic) 25 Feb 1874; p. 158

LEE, George (col); s/o Thomas & Betsy LEE; 22y; sgl; farm hand; b. WrnVA; res. ClrkVA; m. 11 Apr 1883 at ClrkVA to CHAMP, Mary (col); d/o ___ & Matilda CHAMP; 18y; sgl; b. & res. ClrkVA; (lic) 11 Apr 1883; p. 80

LEE, James W.; s/o James W. & Elizabeth LEE; 20y; sgl; farmer; b. & res. ClrkVA; m. 27 Apr 1881 at ClrkVA to DRISH, Virginia E.; d/o Robert & Rissa DRISH; 16y; sgl; b. & res. ClrkVA; (lic) 26 Apr 1881; consent of parents given; p. 39

LEE, John D. (col); s/o Jacob & Hannah LEE; 31y; sgl; farm hand; b. Orange Co. Va; res. ClrkVA; m. 21 Apr 1881 at Berryville to CARTER, Rina (col); d/o George & Rachel CARTER; 19y; sgl; b. & res. ClrkVA; (lic) 20 Apr 1881; p. 39

LEE, John William; s/o Christopher LEE & Julia LEE; 22y; sgl; farmer; b. & res. ClrkVA; m. 17 Dec 1878 at ClrkVA to PAYNE, Margaret Virginia; d/o James S. and Margaret Ann

PAYNE; 17y; sgl; b. & res. ClrkVA; (lic) 16 Dec 1878; John F. PAYNE made oath as to the consent of parents of Margaret Ann [Virginia] PAYNE to issue license; p. 247
LEE, Lewis (col); s/o James & Nancy LEE; 36y; sgl; farm hand; b. FqrVA; res. ClrkVA; m. 8 Jul 1883 at ClrkVA to BLAND, Charlotte (col); d/o Caleb & Maria BLAND; 30y; sgl; b. FqrVA; res. ClrkVA; (lic) 7 Jul 1883; p. 83
LEE, Ludwell L.; s/o James W. & Charlotte LEE; 21y; sgl; farmer; b. & res. ClrkVA; m. 13 Jan 1881 at ClrkVA to THOMPSON, Sarah Ann; d/o Baylis E. & Amanda THOMPSON; 17y; sgl; b. & res. ClrkVA; (lic) 10 Jan 1881; father's consent given; p. 33
LEE, Rich'd. H.; s/o not given; 20y; sgl; not given; b. not given; res. ClrkVA; m. 10 Nov 1869 at Berryville to SMITH, Mary E.; d/o not known; 18y; sgl; b. not given; res. ClrkVA; (lic) 10 Nov 1869; Letter from M. S. THOMPSON states Richard Henry LEE presents himself to you to marry Mary E. SMITH who lives with me, she is of age & has no Guardian & he is all right also. I will settle with you tomorrow.; p. 86
LEE, Robert C.; s/o William & Loretta LEE; 28y; sgl; farmer; b. & res. ClrkVA; m. 17 May 1877 at Winchester Va to RITTER, Margaret E.; d/o William & Lucy CARPER; 40y; wid; b. FredVA; res. ClrkVA; (lic) 16 May 1877; p. 219
LEE, William B.; s/o Richard H. & E. B. LEE; 28y; sgl; Minister of the Gospel; b. ClrkVA; res. CulpVA; m. 25 Sep 1879 at Berryville to KOUNSLAR, S. Jane B.; d/o Randolph & Elizabeth S. KOUNSLAR; 26y; sgl; b. & res. ClrkVA; (lic) 24 Sep 1879; p. 2
LESTER, Benjamin F.; s/o John & Eliza LESTER; 33y; wid; shoemaker; b. South Carolina; res. ClrkVA; m. 11 Apr 1877 at Brucetown, FredVA to SWARTZ, Anna K.; d/o not known; not given; wid; b. Virginia; res. ClrkVA; (lic) 10 Apr 1877; p. 217
LEVI, John B.; s/o Rice W. & Georgia Ann LEVI; 26y; sgl; farmer; b. & res. ClrkVA; m. 9 Dec 1886 at ClrkVA to FOWLER, Mary Elizabeth; d/o Wm. & Alcinda FOWLER; 22y; sgl; b. & res. ClrkVA; (lic) 8 Dec 1886; p. 148
LEVI, Robert C.; s/o Rice W. & Georgianna LEVI; 26y; sgl; farmer; b. & res. ClrkVA; m. 7 Mar 1882 at near Berryville to SHEARER, Nettie B.; d/o ___ & ___ SHEARER; 22y; sgl; b. FredVA; res. ClrkVA; (lic) 6 Mar 1882; p. 57
LEWIS, Jno. W.; s/o Chas. & Mary Ann LEWIS; 24y; sgl; shoemaker; b. LdnVA; res. ClrkVA; m. 26 May 1872 at ClrkVA to STONESTREET, Margaret; d/o Jno. & Margt.

STONESTREET; 21y; sgl; b. & res. ClrkVA; (lic) 23 May 1872; p. 129
LEWIS, Lewis W.; s/o Franklin & Mary LEWIS; 23y; sgl; farmer; b. BerkVA; res. ClrkVA; m. 19 Apr 1870 at Berryville to WHITTINGTON, Anne E.; d/o David & Catharine WHITTINGTON; 21y; sgl; b. Jefferson Co.; res. ClrkVA; (lic) 18 Apr 1870; p. 95
LEWIS, Lorenzo; s/o Geo. W. & Emily C. LEWIS; 32y; sgl; farmer; b. Baltimore Md; res. ClrkVA; m. 28 Apr 1885 at bride's residence to McCORMICK, Rose E.; d/o Francis & Rosanna E. McCORMICK; 29y; sgl; b. & res. ClrkVA; (lic) 27 Apr 1885; p. 121
LEWIS, Richard (col); s/o Filbert & Elizabeth LEWIS (col); 22y; sgl; farm hand; b. Madison Co.; res. ClrkVA; m. 26 Dec 1867 at ClrkVA to ROBERSON, Mary (col); d/o Samuel & Jane ROBERSON (col); 21y; sgl; b. & res. ClrkVA; (lic) 24 Dec 1867; p. 50
LEWIS, Wm. T.; s/o Thomas D. & Mary F. LEWIS; 27y; sgl; farmer; b. Prince William Co. Va; res. ClrkVA; m. 3 Dec 1874 at White Post to DAVIS, Lucy F.; d/o Baalis & ___ DAVIS; 28y; sgl; b. & res. ClrkVA; (lic) 1 Dec 1874; p. 171
LICKLITER, John; s/o John & Sarah LICKLITER; 21y; sgl; farmer; b. PageVA; res. ClrkVA; m. 27 Dec 1877 at Millwood to GARRETT, Bertie; d/o Hamilton & Milly GARRETT; 23y; sgl; b. & res. ClrkVA; (lic) 27 Dec 1877; p. 229
LIGGONS, Charles (col); s/o John & Sarah Ann LIGGONS; 33y; sgl; laborer; b. Nelson Co. Va; res. ClrkVA; m. Sunday 16 Apr 1876 at near Berryville to DANKS, Caroline (col); d/o James & Christine DANKS; 23y; sgl; b. & res. ClrkVA; (lic) 15 Apr 1876; p. 199
LIGHTFOOT, Geo. Wm. (col); s/o Albert & Agnes LIGHTFOOT; 30y; sgl; school teacher; b. & res. ClrkVA; m. 26 Oct 1882 at bride's residence to HULL, Josephine (col); d/o ___ & Charlotte HULL; 19y; sgl; b. & res. ClrkVA; (lic) 25 Oct 1882; p. 66
LIGHTFOOT, Hunter (col); s/o Albert & Aggie LIGHTFOOT; 24y; sgl; hostler; b. & res. ClrkVA; m. 8 Jan 1885 at Berryville to WILLIAMS, Rachel Jane (col); d/o Bartlett & Mahalie WILLIAMS; 21y, sgl; b. & res. ClrkVA; (lic) 8 Jan 1885; p. 115
LINGAMFELTER, Charles Scott; s/o Walter & Margaret LINGAMFELTER; 24y; sgl; minister; b. BerkVA; res. Berryville; m. Wednesday 1 Nov 1876 at Berryville to

LUPTON, Rebecca M.; d/o John & Elizabeth LUPTON; 22y; sgl; b. ClrkVA; res. Berryville; (lic) 31 Oct 1876; p. 207
LINKENS, Harvey (col); s/o Aaron & Maria LINKENS; 21y; sgl; farm hand; b. RckbrVA; res. ClrkVA; m. 15 Sep 1870 at A. N. PIERCE's ClrkVA to GIBSON, Mary Ellen (col); d/o Madison GIBSON, mother's name unknown; 21y; sgl; b. JeffVA now W Va; res. ClrkVA; (lic) 2 Sep 1870; p. 100
LINTON, Albert (col); s/o Henry & Lucy LINTON; 28y; sgl; horse grooming; b. LdnVA; res. Washing. City; m. 3 Feb 1876 at ClrkVA to DYER, Susan (col); d/o David & Susan DYER; 22y; sgl; b. RckhmVA; res. ClrkVA; (lic) 3 Feb 1876; p. 197
LIPPITT, Chas. E.; s/o Edward R. & Mary F. LIPPITT; 40y; sgl; physician; b. LdnVA; res. ClrkVA; m. 20 Jan 1869 at bride's residence to McCORMICK, Nannie; d/o Thomas & Eliza McCORMICK; 26y; sgl; b. & res. ClrkVA; (lic) 20 Jan 1869; p. 75
LIPSCOMB, Benj. (col); s/o Judas & Julia LIPSCOMB (col); 22y; sgl; farmhand; b. Hanover Co. Va; res. ClrkVA; m. 12 Dec 1867 at John W. LUKE's to HUNTER, Millie (col); d/o Benj. & Catharine BLACKBURN (col); 21y; wid; b. & res. ClrkVA; (lic) 12 Dec 1867; p. 48
LLOYD, Benjamin F.; s/o John W. & Mary LLOYD; 24y; sgl; farmer; b. & res. ClrkVA; m. 21 Jan 1873 at ClrkVA to RILEY, Mary C.; d/o James & Rebecca RILEY; 23y; sgl; b. & res. ClrkVA; (lic) 21 Jan 1873; p. 141
LLOYD, Chas. N.; s/o John & Mary A. LLOYD; 21y; sgl; farmer; b. & res. ClrkVA; m. __ Aug 1874 at ClrkVA to DRISH, Margaret E.; d/o Geo. W. & Cassie Ann DRISH; 21y; sgl; b. & res. ClrkVA; (lic) 10 Aug 1874; p. 163
LLOYD, Geo. W.; s/o Henry & Sarah LLOYD; not given; sgl; farmer; b. & res. ClrkVA; m. 27 Nov 1873 at bride's residence to LANHAM, Rebecca; d/o William & Rebecca LANHAM; not given; sgl; b. & res. ClrkVA; (lic) 20 Nov 1873; p. 153
LLOYD, James S.; s/o James L. & Elizabeth LLOYD; 23y; sgl; farmer; b. & res. ClrkVA; m. 13 Nov 1878 at ClrkVA to SHAFER, Martha Ann; d/o John J. & M. E. SHAFER; 22y; sgl; b. & res. ClrkVA; (lic) 12 Nov 1878; p. 244
LLOYD, Nathaniel; s/o David & Jane LLOYD; 21y; sgl; cooper; b. & res. ClrkVA; m. 1 Oct 1879 at Berryville to EVERHART, Rose E.; d/o Wm. G. & Mary EVERHART; 23y; sgl; b. & res. ClrkVA; (lic) 29 Sep 1879; p. 3

LLOYD, Thomas L.; s/o Henry & Sarah LLOYD; 25y; sgl; farmer; b. & res. ClrkVA; m. 15 Feb 1877 at ClrkVA to FELTNER, Harriet A.; d/o Martin & Mary FELTNER; 31y; sgl; b. & res. ClrkVA; (lic) 12 Feb 1877; p. 215
LOCK, Josiah R.; s/o John & Rebecca LOCK; 45y; wid; farmer; b. & res. ClrkVA; m. 12 Mar 1873 at ClrkVA to CARTER, Catharine E.; d/o Richard & ___ HARDESTY; 45y; wid; b. JeffVA; res. ClrkVA; (lic) 11 Mar 1873; p. 144
LOCKE, Franklin Hawkins; s/o Jno. B. & Ann LOCKE; 39y; wid; farmer; b. JeffWVA; res. ClrkVA; m. Thursday 6 Jan 1876 at bride's residence to WILLINGHAM, Anne; d/o William & Matilda WILLINGHAM; 33y; sgl; b. & res. ClrkVA; (lic) 5 Jan 1876; p. 195
LOCKE, Jno. W.; s/o Howard & Matilda LOCKE; 23y; sgl; farmer; b. & res. ClrkVA; m. 4 Mar 1884 at ClrkVA to KEENAN, Emma S.; d/o James H. & Susan KENNAN; 18y; sgl; b. & res. ClrkVA; (lic) 3 Mar 1884; p. 96
LOCKE, Pierce J.; s/o F. H. & Eliz'th LOCKE; 22y; sgl; farmer; b. & res. ClrkVA; m. 19 Mar 1884 at bride's residence to RUTTER [RITTER], Sarah; d/o James & Rachel BELL; 27y; sgl [wid]; b. & res. ClrkVA; (lic) 19 Mar 1884; p. 98
LOCKE, Thos. F.; s/o Thos. & Estha A. LOCKE; 22y; sgl; farmer; b. & res. JeffWVA; m. 28 Aug 1872 at bride's residence to BLUE, Sarah E.; d/o John & Margaret BLUE; 21y; sgl; b. & res. ClrkVA; (lic) 24 Aug 1872; p. 131
LOCKHART, Henry A.; s/o James & Mahala LOCKHART; 23y; sgl; farmer; b. FredVA; res. LdnVA; m. 2 Apr 1885 at Berryville to HOOK, Fannie; d/o Wm. and ___ HOOK; 30y; sgl; b. Hampshire Co. Va; res. ClrkVA; (lic) 2 Apr 1885; p. 119
LONG, Charles W.; s/o Robert & Joanna LONG; 28y; sgl; farmer; b. FqrVA; res. ClrkVA; m. 6 Jun 1880 at ClrkVA to SHELL, Sarah M.; d/o Stephen D. & Emely SHELL; 18y; sgl; b. & res. ClrkVA; (lic) 4 Jun 1880; p. 21
LONG, Lewis M.; s/o Robt. & Joanna LONG; 28y; sgl; merchant; b. FqrVA; res. JeffWVA; m. 15 Apr 1880 at bride's residence to COPENHAVER, Jane O.; d/o ___ & Mary COPENHAVER; 22y; sgl; b. & res. ClrkVA; (lic) 14 Apr 1880; p. 19
LONGERBEAM, Abraham L.; s/o Abraham & Sarah Jane LONGERBEAM; 22y; sgl; farmer; b. & res. ClrkVA; m. 7 Apr 1886 at bride's residence to TINSMAN, Mdelle Zenobie; d/o Ludwell L. & Sarah TINSMAN; 18y; sgl; b. & res. ClrkVA; (lic)

7 Apr 1886; Wm. B. LONGERBEAM made oath that there
was no objections to the bride's marriage; p. 134
LONGERBEAM, Benjamin J.; s/o Benjamin & Nancy
LONGERBEAM; 22y; sgl; farmer; b. & res. ClrkVA; m. 16 Nov
1885 at ClrkVA to ROYSTON, Anna/Any M.; d/o Peter R. &
Mary ROYSTON; 20y; sgl; b. & res. ClrkVA; (lic) 11 Nov
1885; consent of father given; p. 128
LONGERBEAM, James L.; s/o Charles & Mary LONGERBEAM;
23y; sgl; farmer; b. & res. ClrkVA; m. 23 Dec 1883 at ClrkVA
to REED, Mary E.; d/o Stephen & Sallie REED; 21y; sgl; b. &
res. ClrkVA; (lic) 21 Dec 1883; p. 91
LONGERBEAM, Jno. D.; s/o Benjamin & Nancy LONGERBEAM;
28y; sgl; farmer; b. & res. ClrkVA; m. 14 Mar 1880 at ClrkVA
to LEE, Julia A.; d/o James W. & Elizabeth LEE; 18y; sgl; b. &
res. ClrkVA; (lic) 12 Mar 1880; license returned not executed;
p. 18
LONGERBEAM, Jno. H.; s/o Abraham & Sarah Jane
LONGERBEAM; 21y; sgl; cooper; b. & res. ClrkVA; m. 7 Sep
1873 at bride's residence to EATON, Permellia R.; d/o Philip
& Frances EATON; 17y; sgl; b. ShenVA; res. ClrkVA; (lic) 5
Sep 1873; bride's father present & consenting to the same; p.
148
LONGERBEAM, Jno. W.; s/o Charles & Mary LONGERBEAM;
21y; sgl; farmer; b. JeffWVA; res. ClrkVA; m. 27 Aug 1876 at
ClrkVA to MARLOW, Margaret; d/o Stephen & Lacey
MARLOW; 21y; sgl; b. & res. ClrkVA; (lic) 26 Aug 1876; p.
204
LONGERBEAM, Ulises G.; s/o John & Eliza LONGERBEAM;
21y; sgl; farm hand; b. & res. ClrkVA; m. 9 Dec 1885 at
ClrkVA to TINSMAN, Mary H.; d/o Ludwell & Sarah
TINSMAN; 19y; sgl; b. & res. ClrkVA; (lic) 8 Dec 1885;
consent given; p. 131
LONGERBEAM, William B.; s/o Abraham & Sarah Jane
LONGERBEAM; 21y; sgl; farmer; b. & res. ClrkVA; m. 2 Feb
1881 at LdnVA to TINSMAN, Louisa R.; d/o Ludwell & Sarah
TINSMAN; 20y; sgl; b. & res. ClrkVA; (lic) 29 Jan 1881; p. 35
LOTT, John; s/o John & Sarah LOTT; 22y; sgl; farmer; b.
Pennsylvania; res. Washington City; m. 5 Sep 1876 at ClrkVA
to WRIGHT, Margaret E.; d/o John & Mary WRIGHT; 22y;
sgl; b. WrnVA; res. ClrkVA; (lic) 4 Sep 1876; p. 205
LOUTHAN, John; s/o John K. and Lucy Ann LOUTHAN; 21y; sgl;
carpenter; b. & res. ClrkVA; m. 3 Mar 1880 at bride's

residence to CARTER, Katie M.; d/o Franklin B. & Lucie T.
CARTER; 22y; sgl; b. & res. ClrkVA; (lic) 2 Mar 1880; p. 16
LOUTHAN, Robert P.; s/o John & Lydia LOUTHAN; 29y; sgl;
farmer; b. & res. ClrkVA; m. 22 Dec 1880 at ClrkVA to
SLUSHER, Annie M.; d/o Hezekiah & Ann SLUSHER; 28y;
sgl; b. & res. ClrkVA; (lic) 20 Dec 1880; p. 30
LOVETT, David (col); s/o John and Jilica LOVETT; 50y; wid;
farmer; b. FredVA; res. ClrkVA; m. 2 Aug 1883 at ClrkVA to
BROOKS, Willie Ann (col); d/o not known; 43y; wid; b.
FredVA; res. ClrkVA; (lic) 2 Aug 1883; p. 84
LOVETT, Robert (col); s/o David & Catharine LOVETT; 22y; sgl;
farm hand; b. FredVA; res. ClrkVA; m. 9 Oct 1884 at ClrkVA
to BROOKS, Nannie (col); d/o Lewis & Willyann BROOKS;
20y; sgl; b. & res. ClrkVA; (lic) 9 Oct 1884; p. 108
LOWRY, Granison (col); s/o Philip & Eveline LOWRY; 23y; sgl;
farm hand; b. WrnVA; res. ClrkVA; m. 10 Jan 1873 at ClrkVA
to SMITH, Fannie (col); d/o not given; 24y; sgl; b. ___ [may
be WrnVA]; res. ClrkVA; (lic) 10 Jan 1873; p. 140
LUCAS, John (col); s/o Geo. & Lucinda LUCAS; 32y; sgl; farm
hand; b. LdnVA; res. ClrkVA; m. 20 Dec 1883 at ClrkVA to
THORNLEY, Annie (col); d/o Solomon & ___ THORNLEY;
28y; sgl; b. FqrVA; res. ClrkVA; (lic) 20 Dec 1883; p. 91
LUCAS, Townsend (col); s/o Jube & Julia LUCAS; 26y; sgl; farm
hand; b. FqrVA; res. ClrkVA; m. 24 Apr 1879 at Berryville to
JACKSON, Caroline (col); d/o not known; 23y; sgl; b.
Washington City DC; res. ClrkVA; (lic) 24 Apr 1879; p. 258
LYLES, Charles (col); s/o James & Annie LYLES (col); 26y; sgl;
labourer; b. Fredrick City Md; res. ClrkVA; m. 16 Aug 1868 at
Mr. Wm. D. SMITH's house to JACKSON, Matilda (col); d/o
Jackson & Matilda JACKSON (col); 18y; sgl; b. & res. ClrkVA;
(lic) 15 Aug 1868; p. 64
LYNN, Lewis C.; s/o Luther L. & Mary F. LYNN; 29y; sgl; farmer;
b. & res. Prince William Co. Va; m. 22 Nov 1881 at bride's
residence to BONHAM, Hannah T.; d/o A. A. & Eliza
BONHAM; 31y; sgl; b. & res. ClrkVA; (lic) 21 Nov 1881; p. 52
MAGILL, Frank; s/o George & Jane MAGILL; 25y; sgl; farm
hand; b. & res. ClrkVA; m. 28 Dec 1869 at bride's residence
to TAYLOR, Judy; d/o Davy & Martha TAYLOR; 21y; sgl; b. &
res. ClrkVA; (lic) not given; p. 91
MAJOR, Samuel; s/o not given; 35y; sgl; farmer; b. & res.
CulpVA; m. Wednesday 15 Oct 1879 at ClrkVA to BUCK,

Lillie Lizzie; d/o Thos. F. and Lizzie BUCK; 24y; sgl; b.
WrnVA; res. ClrkVA; (lic) 14 Oct 1879; p. 4

MAPHIS, J. Luther; s/o Jno. M. & Elizabeth A. MAPHIS; 26y; sgl; merchant; b. ShenVA; res. FredVA; m. 19 Nov 1884 at ClrkVA to BROMLEY, Katie E.; d/o John & Martha BROMLY; 21y; sgl; b. & res. ClrkVA; (lic) 17 Nov 1884; p. 110

MARKS, Jacob William; s/o Jacob A. & Ann E. MARKS; 28y; sgl; tinner; b. FredVA; res. ClrkVA; m. Tuesday morning 7 Jan 1879 at Berryville to DINKLE, Laura A.; d/o Charles A. & Anne E. DINKLE; 23y; sgl; b. Pennsylvania; res. ClrkVA; (lic) 6 Jan 1879; p. 250

MARLOW, Elijah; s/o Stephen & Tacy MARLOW; 28y; wid; farmer; b. & res. ClrkVA; m. 3 Feb 1876 at Berryville to BILLMIRE, Lutia; d/o Andrew J. & Mahala BILLMIRE; 16y; sgl; b. & res. ClrkVA; (lic) 2 Feb 1876; p. 196

MARLOW, Elijah; s/o Stephen & Tasen MARLOW; 23y; sgl; farmer; b. & res. ClrkVA; m. 17 Feb 1867 at Episcopal Parsonage to WOLFE, Hannah E.; d/o not given; 19y; sgl; b. Maryland; res. not given; (lic) 16 Feb 1867; Wm. G. HARRIS present; p. 32

MARPLE, Hezekiah; s/o Frederick and Sarah MARPLE; 39y; wid; farmer; b. Frederick Co.; res. ClrkVA; m. 24 Jan 1867 at ClrkVA to TALEY, Mary Ann; d/o Isaac and Fannie TALEY; 24y; sgl; b. JeffVA; res. ClrkVA; (lic) 23 Jan 1867; p. 30

MARSHALL, Alfred C.; s/o Alex'r. MARSHALL & Emily J. MARSHALL; 26y; sgl; farmer; b. & res. ClrkVA; m. 10 Oct 1866 at Berryville to PRICHARD, Mame; d/o A. G. & Ann E. AFFLICK; 24y; wid; b. FredVA; res. ClrkVA; (lic) 9 Oct 1866; p. 20

MARSHALL, Jas. W.; s/o Alex'r. & Emily MARSHALL; 21y; sgl; farmer; b. & res. ClrkVA; m. 16 Nov 1869 at Berryville to LANCASTER, Sally D.; d/o John F. & Hannah LANCASTER; 20y; sgl; b. JeffVA; res. ClrkVA; (lic) 13 Nov 1869; p. 87 [p. 91b - Letter dated 11 Nov 1869 by John F. LANCASTER stating the clerk is authorized to issue a license for marriage of James MARSHALL & his daughter Sarah.]

MARSHALL, John (col); s/o James & Maria MARSHALL; 50y; wid; occupation not given; b. FqrVA; res. ClrkVA; m. 26 Oct 1878 at ClrkVA to JACKSON, Vena (col); d/o Charles Jack [JACKSON?] and ___ JACKSON; 22y; sgl; b. & res. ClrkVA; (lic) 23 Oct 1878; p. 243

MARTENUS, James (col); s/o Primus & Rachel MARTENUS; 26y; sgl; farm hand; b. & res. ClrkVA; m. 14 Jun 1883 at Berryville to MITCHELL, Louisa (col); d/o Samuel & Ann MITCHELL; 19y; sgl; b. & res. ClrkVA; (lic) 11 Jun 1883; p. 83
MARTIN, Geo. W.; s/o John & Rebecca MARTIN; 40y; wid; farmer; b. & res. WrnVA; m. 24 Oct 1876 at ClrkVA to BROY, Fannie; d/o Elijah & Jane BROY; 30y; sgl; b. WrnVA; res. ClrkVA; (lic) 24 Oct 1876; p. 207
MARTS, Jesse F.; s/o John & Sarah Ann MARTS; 21y; sgl; farm hand; b. LdnVA; res. JeffWVA; m. 21 Jan 1880 at ClrkVA to HOFF, Mattie; d/o Bushrod & Jane HOFF; 22y; sgl; b. & res. ClrkVA; (lic) 21 Jan 1880; p. 14
MARTS, John T.; s/o Alfred & Joanna MARTS; 41y; wid; farmer; b. ClrkVA; res. LdnVA; m. 9 Apr 1876 at ClrkVA to LEWIN, Millie Frances; d/o Samuel & Annie LEWIN; 31y; sgl; b. WrnVA; res. ClrkVA; (lic) 7 Apr 1876; p. 198
MASH, James H. (col); s/o Warren & Velie? MASH; 35y; sgl; blacksmith; b. & res. ClrkVA; m. 29 Apr 1887 at Berryville to FIELDS, Malinda (col); d/o Adam & Sally FIELDS; 24y; sgl; b. & res. ClrkVA; (lic) 29 Apr 1886; p. 135
MASON, Jas. (col); s/o not given; 22y; sgl; farm hand; b. WrnVA; res. ClrkVA; m. 22 May 1870 at Millwood to BARRETT, Alice (col); d/o not given; 21y; sgl; b. AlbmVA; res. ClrkVA; (lic) 21 May 1870; p. 97
MASON, Wesley (col); s/o James & Jinnie MASON (col); 40y; wid; farm hand; b. JeffWVA; res. ClrkVA; m. 7 Nov 1872 at ClrkVA to RANDOLPH, Mary (col); d/o not given; 30y; sgl; b. & res. ClrkVA; (lic) 6 Nov 1872; p. 135
MASSEY, Samuel (col); s/o Prim & Matilda MASSEY; 24y; sgl; farm hand; b. RappVA; res. JeffWVA; m. 3 Jul 1884 at ClrkVA to WILSON, Clara (col); d/o not known; 22y; sgl; b. PageVA; res. ClrkVA; (lic) 3 Jul 1884; p. 103
McABOY, Wm. B.; s/o Francis M. & Deniza McABOY; 23y; sgl; farmer; b. Hampshire Co. Va; res. ClrkVA; m. 12 Aug 1866 at near or at Berryville to SHIPE, Elizabeth; d/o Moses & Malinda SHIPE; 21y; sgl; b. LdnVA; res. ClrkVA; (lic) 10 Aug 1866; p'd. to W. GLASS next day; p. 17
McATEE, W. A.; s/o Harrison & Jane McATEE; 34y; sgl; farmer; b. LdnVA; res. ClrkVA; m. 26 Oct 1871 at ClrkVA to SICAFOUSE, Mary E.; d/o Harrison & Elizabeth COOPER; 26y; wid; b. FredVA; res. ClrkVA; (lic) 25 Oct 1871; p. 118

McCARTY, Robt. W.; s/o Bellington & Jennie McCARTY; 24y; sgl; farmer; b. LdnVA; res. ClrkVA; m. 6 Aug 1885 at bride's residence to TUMBLIN, Sarah Cath'e.; d/o Snowden & Mary Jane TUMBLIN; 23y; sgl; b. & res. ClrkVA; (lic) 3 Aug 1885; p. 123

McCAULEY, John William; s/o John G. & Martha C. McCAULEY; 24y; sgl; farmer; b. & res. ClrkVA; m. 20 Mar 187 at ClrkVA to ATKINS, Annie; d/o Robert & Rebecca ATKINS; 27y; sgl; b. RappVA; res. ClrkVA; (lic) 18 Mar 1878; p. 233

McCLAUGHRY, John B.; s/o Jas. & Rebecca McCLAUGHRY; 26y; sgl; farmer; b. & res. ClrkVA; m. 19 Nov 1868 at bride's residence to JENKINS, Martha E.; d/o Thos. & Ellen JENKINS; 18y; sgl; b. & res. ClrkVA; (lic) 16 Nov 1868; bride's father was present when license was issued; p. 70

McCORMICK, DAWSON; s/o Edward & Ellen L. McCORMICK; 23y; sgl; farmer; b. & res. ClrkVA; m. 6 Sep 1883 at Berryville to BROWN, Margaretta Moss; d/o J. C. and Annie R. BROWN; 22y; sgl; b. & res. ClrkVA; (lic) 5 Sep 1883; p. 86

McCORMICK, John W.; s/o Otway & Sarah Ann McCORMICK; 35y; sgl; farmer; b. & res. ClrkVA; m. 6 Feb 1868 at ClrkVA to SMITH, Lucy E. H.; d/o David H. McGUIRE & Eliza McGUIRE; 29y; wid; b. & res. ClrkVA; (lic) 5 Feb 1868; p. 54

McCORMICK, P. F.; s/o Martin & Onora McCORMICK; 25y; sgl; farmer; b. Washington Co. Mo.; res. not given; m. 7 Jun 1866 at Rev'd. Chas. WHITE's to HULVEY, Susan E.; d/o John & Sarah HULVEY; 25y; sgl; b. Hardy Co. Va; res. not given; (lic) 5 Jun 1866; p. 13

McCORMICK, P. Jr.; s/o P. & Margretta McCORMICK; 25y; sgl; farmer; b. & res. ClrkVA; m. 6 Dec 1871 at Berryville to McCORMICK, Bessie T.; d/o Wm. & Sarah McCORMICK; 20y; sgl; b. Jefferson; res. ClrkVA; (lic) 5 Dec 1871; p. 119

McCORMICK, Samuel; s/o Francis & Rosanna E. McCORMICK; 33y; sgl; farmer; b. & res. ClrkVA; m. 7 Dec 1882 at Berryville to LEWIS, Esther M.; d/o George W. & Emily LEWIS; 26y; sgl; b. & res. ClrkVA; (lic) 5 Dec 1882; p. 70

McCORMICK, Thomas; s/o Thomas & Eliza McCORMICK; 23y; sgl; farmer; b. & res. ClrkVA; m. 19 Dec 1871 at Frankford, ClrkVA to McCORMICK, Nannie; d/o Frances [Francis] & Rose McCORMICK; 24y; sgl; b. & res. ClrkVA; (lic) 18 Dec 1871; p. 121

McDANIEL, John P.; s/o Josiah & Jane? E. McDANIEL; 24y; not given; farmer; b. Bedford Co. Va; res. ClrkVA; m. 27 Dec

1883 at ClrkVA to ROY, Katie S.; d/o Richard B. & Sophia ROY; 24y; not given; b. WrnVA; res. ClrkVA; (lic) 26 Dec 1883; father of bride gives consent in person; p. 92

McDONALD, David H.; s/o David & Hannah McDONALD; 24y; sgl; farmer; b. & res. BerkWVA; m. 6 Feb 1873 at ClrkVA to GRUBB, Mary V.; d/o Charles & Elizabeth GRUBB; 19y; sgl; b. FredVA; res. ClrkVA; (lic) 5 Feb 1873; bride's brother present; p. 141

McDONALD, Ernest; s/o Harry and ___ McDONALD; 24y; sgl; farm hand; b. WrnVA; res. ClrkVA; m. 25 Aug 1886 at ClrkVA to ELLIOTT, Gertrude; d/o Christopher and ___ ELLIOTT; 22y; sgl; b. & res. ClrkVA; (lic) 24 Aug 1886; license discharged, no marriage; p. 141

McDONALD, Jarrot; s/o John & Eva McDONALD; 66y; wid; farmer; b. FredVA; res. ClrkVA; m. 3 May 1870 at ClrkVA to ROYSTON, Minerva C.; d/o Matthew & Harriet CARPENTER; 49y; wid; b. LdnVA; res. ClrkVA; (lic) not given; p. 96

McDONALD, John S.; s/o John & Jane McDONALD; 22y; sgl; farmer; b. & res. ClrkVA; m. 30 Dec 1879 at ClrkVA to GARRETT, Allie W.; d/o Hamilton & Milly J. GARRETT; 18y; sgl; b. WrnVA; res. ClrkVA; (lic) 29 Dec 1879; p. 13

McDONALD, Josiah; s/o Jarrett & Elizabeth McDONALD; 29y; wid; farmer; b. WrnVA; res. ClrkVA; m. 12 Jan 1870 at bride's residence to KENNAN, Mary C.; d/o Jas. H. & Susan R. KENNAN; 18y; sgl; b. & res. ClrkVA; (lic) 11 Jan 1870; bride's father was present when license was issued; p. 92

McDONALD, Marshall; s/o Augusta & Lacey A. McDONALD; 31y; sgl; teacher; b. Romney, Va; res. Lexington, Va; m. 17 Dec 1867 at Frankford, ClrkVA to McCORMICK, Mary E.; d/o Francis & Rose McCORMICK; 27y; sgl; b. & res. ClrkVA; (lic) 17 Dec 1867; p. 48

McDONALD, Walter P.; s/o Harry & Fannie McDONALD; 25y; wid; farmer; b. ClrkVA; res. JeffWVA; m. 21 Dec 1881 at ClrkVA to JACKSON, Rissa; d/o Josiah & Mary JACKSON; 21y; sgl; b. & res. ClrkVA; (lic) 21 Dec 1881; p. 53

McDONALD, Walter P.; s/o Harry & Tamer? McDONALD; 21y; sgl; farmer; b. WrnVA; res. ClrkVA; m. 8 Aug 1877 at Berryville to SOWERS, Rose Lee; d/o Daniel W. & Mary E. SOWERS; 23y; sgl; b. & res. ClrkVA; (lic) 8 Aug 1877; (oath) Rose that she is over 21y.; p. 220

McDONOLD, Josiah; s/o Jarrett & Elizabeth McDONOLD; 25y; sgl; farmer; b. WrnVA; res. ClrkVA; m. 5 Apr 1866 at ClrkVA

to WILLINGHAM, Sarah C.; d/o Obid R. & Eliza
WILLINGHAM; 23y; sgl; b. & res. ClrkVA; (lic) 27 Mar 1866;
p. 9

McGILLE, David (col); s/o Wm. & Nelly McGILLE; 29y; sgl; farm
hand; b. ClrkVA; res. JeffWVA; m. 20 Nov 1884 at ClrkVA to
CARTER, Louisa (col); d/o Go. & Lucy CARTER; 22y; sgl; b.
& res. ClrkVA; (lic) 20 Nov 1884; p. 110

McGRUDER, Charles; s/o Wm. Lewis & Sarah Matilda
McGRUDER; 21y last August; sgl; shoemaker; b. Winchester,
FredVA; res. Frederick Co.; m. 23 Oct 1866 at Berryville to
PYLE, Ann; d/o Wm. & Ann PYLE; 22y; sgl; b. JeffVA; res.
ClrkVA; (lic) 23 Oct 1866; p. 21

McGUIRE, Andrew (col); s/o Alfred & Delphi McGUIRE (col);
23y; sgl; farm hand; b. & res. ClrkVA; m. 25 Jul 1869 at
ClrkVA to GUY, Eunis (col); d/o James & Mary GUY (col);
21y; sgl; b. & res. ClrkVA; (lic) 24 Jul 1869; p. 84

McMURRAY, Jno. P.; s/o Peter & Catharine McMURRAY; 33y;
wid; farmer; b. & res. ClrkVA; m. 3 May 1871 at ClrkVA to
CREBS, Ella G.; d/o John H. & Maria L. CREBS; 20y; sgl; b.
& res. ClrkVA; (lic) 3 May 1871; written consent from John H.
CREBS; p. 111

MEADE, C. Grimes; s/o Richard K. & Jane B. MEADE; 27y; sgl;
merchant; b. & res. ClrkVA; m. 23 Jun 1875 at White Post to
MASSEY, Mary Elizabeth; d/o E. W. & Sarah MASSEY; 24y;
sgl; b. & res. ClrkVA; (lic) 21 Jun 1875; p. 181

MEADE, Edgar S.; s/o Richard R. & Jane B. MEADE; 35y; sgl;
merchant; b. & res. ClrkVA; m. 1 Nov 1881 at ClrkVA to
GRYMES, Lucy; d/o Curtus & ___ GRYMES; 26y; sgl; b. King
George Co. Va; res. Alexandria Va; (lic) 1 Nov 1881; p. 49

MEADE, George C.; s/o Richard & Jane B. MEADE; 23y; sgl;
farmer; b. & res. ClrkVA; m. 18 Aug 1878 at ClrkVA to FORD,
Ella N.; d/o William & Sarah FORD; 19y; sgl; b. FredVA; res.
ClrkVA; (lic) 17 Aug 1878; brother present with consent of
parents of Ella N. FORD for the issuing of this license; p. 237

MEADE, Philip C.; s/o Francis B. & Mary M. MEADE; 26y; sgl;
farmer; b. & res. ClrkVA; m. 4 Nov 1874 at bride's residence
to COOKE, Alethea C.; d/o Philip & Ann B. COOKE; 25y; sgl;
b. & res. ClrkVA; (lic) 27 Oct 1874; p. 167

MENDENHALL, J. R.; s/o Jesse & Lydia A. MENDENHALL; 32y;
sgl; book keeper; b. Philadelphia Pa; res. Lewistown Pa; m. 7
Oct 1884 at Berryville to CASTLEMAN, Maggie Lee; d/o Wm.

A. & Ann R. CASTLEMAN; 22y; sgl; b. & res. ClrkVA; (lic) 4 Oct 1884; p. 107

MERCER, Jesse F.; s/o Nathaniel & Lydia MERCER; 21y; sgl; farmer; b. & res. ClrkVA; m. 23 Jun 1881 at ClrkVA to CARROLL, Eliza; d/o John & Cornelia CARROLL; 21y; sgl; b. & res. ClrkVA; (lic) 23 Jun 1881; p. 42

MERCER, Jessee; s/o Jesse & Mary MERCER; 22y; sgl; farmer; b. & res. ClrkVA; m. 17 Sep 1868 at Thos. L. HUMPHREY's residence to ASHBY, Susan; d/o Nimrod & Mary Agnes ASHBY; 17y; sgl; b. & res. ClrkVA; (lic) 15 Sep 1868; sworn to by Chas. F. WILEY as to the willingness of the bride's parents; p. 66

MERCER, John T.; s/o Jesse & Margaret MERCER; 24y; sgl; farmer; b. ClrkVA; res. LdnVA; m. 12 Jan 1869 at LdnVA to BEAVER, Virginia C.; d/o Abraham & Plassie BEAVER; 21y; sgl; b. & res. ClrkVA; (lic) 9 Jan 1869; p. 73

MERCHANT, James T.; s/o John & Jane MERCHANT; 23y; sgl; farmer; b. Montgomery Co. Maryland; res. ClrkVA; m. 14 Oct 1879 at ClrkVA to MYRES, Annie M.; d/o Abraham & Catherine MYRES; 17y; sgl; b. Frederick Co. Maryland; res. ClrkVA; (lic) 13 Oct 1879; p. 3

MERRITT, Henry C.; s/o Jacob & Barbara MERRITT; 24y; sgl; farmer; b. Cabel Co. Va; res. JeffWVA; m. 20 Dec ___ at bride's residence to BILMIRE, Lucy C.; d/o Wm. H. & Sarah C. BILMIRE; 22y; sgl; b. FredVA; res. ClrkVA; (lic) 8 Dec 1866; p. 26

MESMER, Thomas G.; s/o Jacob & Ann MESMER; 45y; sgl; carpenter; b. & res. FredVA; m. 17 Nov 1879 at ClrkVA to KIGER, Mary E.; d/o James M. & Mary E. KIGER; 26y; sgl; b. & res. ClrkVA; (lic) 16 Nov 1879; p. 7

METZ, John W.; s/o Jno. W. & Susanna METZ; 35y; sgl; farming; b. Frederick City Md; res. ClrkVA; m. 27 Feb 1879 at ClrkVA to BERLIN, Mary J.; d/o Philip & Sarah J. BERLIN; 18y; sgl; b. & res. ClrkVA; (lic) 27 Feb 1879; p. 254

MILEY, Herod T.; s/o Moses G. and Ara MILEY; 21y; sgl; farmer; b. LdnVA; res. ClrkVA; m. 1 May 1866 at Castleman's Ferry to JENKINS, Rachel T.; d/o Thomas and Ellen JENKINS; 18y; sgl; b. & res. ClrkVA; (lic) 30 Apr 1866; consent of bride's father given in person; p. 11

MILEY, Moses G.; s/o Jacob & Frances MILEY; 52y; wid; farmer; b. LdnVA; res. ClrkVA; m. 17 May 1866 at ClrkVA to

WILSON, E. Jane; d/o John & ___ WILSON; 43y; sgl; b.
FqrVA; res. ClrkVA; (lic) 10 May 1866; p. 11
MILLER, Charles W.; s/o Thomas & Susan MILLER; 26y; sgl;
farmer; b. & res. LdnVA; m. 18 Dec 1879 at ClrkVA to
BRABHAM, Amelia; d/o Charles H. & Martha BRABHAM;
19y; sgl; b. & res. ClrkVA; (lic) 15 Dec 1879; p. 10
MILLER, John; s/o Geo. & Julia MILLER; 26y; sgl; blacksmith; b.
Baltimore Co. Maryland; res. ClrkVA; m. 21 Dec 1869 at
bride's residence to BOXWELL, Martha V.; d/o Chas. H. &
Eveline BOXWELL; 19y; sgl; b. FredVA; res. ClrkVA; (lic) 21
Dec 1869; father was present when the license issued; p. 91
MILLER, Robert M.; s/o Henry & Lydia MILLER; 28y; sgl; farmer;
b. & res. Jefferson Co.; m. 5 Dec 1867 at ClrkVA to
HARRISON, Sidney E.; d/o Isaac & Mary HARRISON; 25y;
sgl; b. WrnVA; res. ClrkVA; (lic) 2 Dec 1867; p. 47
MILLS, John (col); s/o Joseph & Maria MILLS; 21y; sgl; farm
hand; b. & res. ClrkVA; m. 27 Aug 1878 at ClrkVA to
COOPER, Lettie (col); d/o Jacob & Ann COOPER; 21y; sgl;
b. JeffWVA; res. ClrkVA; (lic) 14 Aug 1878; p. 237
MILTON, James F. Jr.; s/o James F. & Sidney MILTON; 25y; sgl;
sadler; b. FqrVA; res. Berryville; m. 17 Sep 1872 at Berryville
to THOMAS, Sarah A.; d/o James W. & Mirenda THOMAS;
25y; sgl; b. ClrkVA; res. Berryville; (lic) 16 Sep 1872; p. 132
MILTON, William T.; s/o Alexander R. & Harriet MILTON; 29y;
sgl; farmer; b. JeffVA; res. ClrkVA; m. 30 Oct 1867 at
Berryville to DUNCAN, Fanny C.; d/o Stephen & Louisa P.
DUNCAN; 22y; sgl; b. Louisiana; res. ClrkVA; (lic) 28 Oct
1867; p. 45
MINOR, C. H. (col); s/o C. H. & Lucy MINOR; 31y; sgl; Minister;
b. Amherst Co. Va; res. ClrkVA; m. 20 Nov 1884 at Berryville
to WILLIS, Catharine (col); d/o Jackson & Jane WILLIS; 18y;
sgl; b. & res. ClrkVA; (lic) 20 Nov 1884; C. H. KENNEY made
affidavit that the parents of the bride do not object to the
issuance of the license; p. 111
MITCHELL, Henry (col); s/o ___ & Jinnette MITCHELL; 38y; wid;
farm hand; b. & res. ClrkVA; m. ___ Dec 1882 at ClrkVA to
LEWIS, Lucy (col); d/o ___ & Eliza LEWIS; 24y; sgl; b.
WrnVA; res. ClrkVA; (lic) 5 Dec 1882; p. 70
MITCHELL, James (col); s/o London & Eveline MITCHELL (col);
22y; sgl; farm hand; b. & res. ClrkVA; m. 16 Mar 1871 at
Berryville to FLETCHER, Emily (col); d/o unknown; 21y; sgl;
b. Staunton Va; res. ClrkVA; (lic) not given; p. 110

MITCHELL, John W.; s/o A. D. & Mary M. MITCHELL; 26y; sgl; Minister of the Gospel; b. & res. RckbrVA; m. 12 Feb 1884 at bride's residence to HOOK, Mattie C.; d/o Wm. W. & Priscilla HOOK; 23y; sgl; b. Hampshire Co. W Va; res. ClrkVA; (lic) 9 Feb 1884; p. 93

MITCHELL, Loudon (col); s/o Antney & Aggie MITCHELL (col); 58y; wid; farm hand; b. Prince William Co.; res. ClrkVA; m. 21 Sep 1869 at Berryville to LARKLEY, Evelina (col); d/o George & Nancy LEWIS (col); 48y; wid; b. & res. ClrkVA; (lic) 14 Sep 1869; p. 84

MITCHELL, Stephen (col); s/o Samuel & Ann MITCHELL; 22y; sgl; farm hand; b. & res. ClrkVA; m. 11 Nov 1886 at Berryville to BROWN, Martha (col); d/o A. & Louisa BROWN; 22y; sgl; b. JeffWVA; res. ClrkVA; (lic) not given; p. 145

MOCK, George R.; s/o Joseph A. and Frances MOCK; 21y; sgl; farmer; b. FqrVA; res. ClrkVA; m. 24 Oct 1867 at Stonebridge, ClrkVA to JACKSON, Mary C.; d/o Dempsey and Elizabeth JACKSON; 22y; sgl; b. FredVA; res. ClrkVA; (lic) 23 Oct 1867; p. 44

MOORE, Eden C.; s/o Sylvanus & ___ MOORE; 24y; sgl; carpenter; b. & res. ClrkVA; m. 24 Feb 1873 at bride's residence to SMITH, Maggie J.; d/o John & ___ SMITH; 23y; sgl; b. LdnVA; res. ClrkVA; (lic) 24 Feb 1873; p. 143

MOORE, Samuel Scollay; s/o S. J. C. MOORE & Eleanor C. MOORE; 26y; sgl; lawyer; b. JeffVA now W Va; res. ClrkVA; m. 29 Apr 1880 at Berryville Episcopal Church to McCORMICK, Elvira Jett; d/o Edward McCORMICK & Ellen L. McCORMICK; 21y; sgl; b. & res. ClrkVA; (lic) 29 Apr 1880; p. 20

MOORE, Thornton (col); s/o Edward & Martha Ann MOORE; 23y; sgl; dining room servant; b. FqrVA; res. ClrkVA; m. 30 Nov 1882 at Berryville to WILLIAMS, Sarah (col); d/o ___ and ___ WILLIAMS; 25y; sgl; b. JeffWVA; res. ClrkVA; (lic) 30 Nov 1882; p. 68

MORALES, Julian; s/o Leo MORALES & C. MORALES; 31y; sgl; carpenter; b. & res. ClrkVA; m. 14 Sep 1875 at Berryville to SHACKLEFORD, Jane T.; d/o Erasmus & Hellen SHACKLEFORD; 27y; sgl; b. & res. ClrkVA; (lic) 14 Sep 1875; p. 185

MORAN, Francis B.; s/o Charles & Arabella J. MORAN; 22y; sgl; farmer; b. New York; res. AlbmVA; m. 29 Jun 1871 at bride's residence to BLACKBURN, Jane W.; d/o Richard S. & Sara

A. BLACKBURN; 29y; sgl; b. not given; res. ClrkVA; (lic) 29
Jun 1871; p. 113
MORELAND, Saml. C.; s/o not given; 23y; sgl; farmer; b. LdnVA;
res. ClrkVA; m. 25 Feb 1875 at ClrkVA to HARRAS,
Henrietta; d/o not given; 23y; sgl; b. LdnVA; res. ClrkVA; (lic)
22 Feb 1875; p. 176
MORELAND, Townsend; s/o Jeremiah & Elizabeth MORELAND;
23y; sgl; farmer; b. LdnVA; res. ClrkVA; m. 16 Sep 1783 at
Berryville to KNIGHT, Kate; d/o George & Sarah KNIGHT;
22y; sgl; b. not given; res. ClrkVA; (lic) 15 Sep 1873; p. 148
MORGAN, John; s/o Benj'n. & Martha A. MORGAN; 28y; sgl;
farmer; b. & res. ClrkVA; m. 28 Mar 1866 at residence of
bride's brother to SOWERS, Frances M.; d/o George K. &
Frances E. SOWERS; 25y; sgl; b. & res. ClrkVA; (lic) 22 Mar
1866; p. 9
MORGAN, Robert P.; s/o John & Margaret MORGAN; 30y; sgl;
Sheriff of ClrkVA Va; b. ClrkVA; res. Berryville; m. 18 Oct
1871 at Berryville to CROW, Ida G.; d/o Thomas H. &
Frances A. CROW; age not given; sgl; b. ClrkVA; res.
Berryville; (lic) not given; p. 118
MORGAN, William N.; s/o Jno. C. & Sallie L. MORGAN; 23y; sgl;
clerk; b. Illinois; res. Roanoke Va; m. 17 Dec 1885 at
Greenway Court Va to BEALE, Nannie C.; d/o S. F. G. &
Bettie BEALL; 26y; sgl; b. FqrVA; res. ClrkVA; (lic) 16 Dec
1885; p. 130
MORGAN, Wm. C.; s/o Benjamin & Martha A. MORGAN; 31y;
sgl; attorney at law; b. & res. ClrkVA; m. 6 Jun 1867 at
ClrkVA to SHEPHERD, Sarah Amelia; d/o Champ & Sarah A.
SHEPHERD; 22y; sgl; b. & res. ClrkVA; (lic) 5 Jun 1867; p.
36
MORISON, G. Port.; s/o G. P. & Jane Eliz'th MORISON; 29y;
sgl; physician; b. & res. BerkWVA; m. 9 Apr 1884 at ClrkVA to
PIERCE, Annabel Lee; d/o A. N. & Mary Eliz'th PIERCE; 25y;
sgl; b. & res. ClrkVA; (lic) 5 Apr 1884; p. 99
MORRISON, Daniel B.; s/o Daniel B. & Jane V. MORRISON;
30y; wid; farmer; b. Berkeley Co. now W Va; res. JeffWVA;
m. 3 Oct 1872 at Berryville to HOWARD, Leila; d/o Howard &
M. F. HOWARD; 24y; sgl; b. George Town DC; res. ClrkVA;
(lic) 2 Oct 1872; p. 134
MORRISON, J. Wesley; s/o Bartholomew & Mary Jane
MORRISON; 24y; sgl; carpenter; b. JeffWVA; res. ClrkVA; m.
28 Feb 1884 at Berryville to ROUTZONG, Jennie F.; d/o Ezra

& Mary ROUTZONG; 22y; sgl; b. Frederick Co. Maryland; res. ClrkVA; (lic) 27 Feb 1884; p. 96

MORTON, James (col); s/o Winston & Louisann MORTON (col); 29y; sgl; farm hand; b. Orange Co. Va; res. ClrkVA; m. 20 Dec 1873 at White Post to RUNNELLS, Patty (col); d/o James & Henry [Henrietta?] RUNNELLS; 21y; sgl; b. & res. ClrkVA; (lic) 18 Dec 1873; p. 154

MOSEA, George (col); s/o Wm. & Sallie MOSEA; 27y; wid; farm hand; b. RckhmVA; res. ClrkVA; m. 22 Dec 1870 at White Post to WILLIAMS, Frances (col); d/o ___ & Clora WILLIAMS; 17y; sgl; b. & res. ClrkVA; (lic) 20 Dec 1870; consent of the step father John STRANGE & consent wife; p. 105

MOSS, George (col); s/o George & Tulip MOSS; 27y; sgl; farm hand; b. WrnVA; res. ClrkVA; m. 9 Sep 1886 at Berryville to GIBSON, Virginia (col); d/o not known; 22y; sgl; b. & res. ClrkVA; (lic) 9 Sep 1886; p. 142

MOULDEN, Charles E.; s/o Levi and Ann Eliza MOULDEN; 30y; sgl; blacksmith; b. Montgomery Co. Md; res. ClrkVA; m. 8 Nov 1866 at ClrkVA to ALBAN, Allie M.; d/o James and Elizabeth ALBAN; 27y; sgl; b. Hardy Co. Va; res. ClrkVA; (lic) 8 Nov 1866; p. 22

MOUNT, Charles E.; s/o James & Hannah MOUNT; 50y; sgl; farmer; b. & res. LdnVA; m. 11 Mar 1880 at ClrkVA to O'REAR, Maria L.; d/o not known; 38y; sgl; b. & res. ClrkVA; (lic) 3 Mar 1880; p. 17

MURPHY, James T.; s/o James & Sarissa [Larissa?] MURPHY; 30y; sgl; carpenter; b. & res. ClrkVA; m. 6 Sep 1866 at Berryville to BARTON, Mary V.; d/o Azekiel & Susanna BARTON; 23y; sgl; b. & res. ClrkVA; (lic) 5 Sep 1866; p. 18

MURPHY, John S. C.; s/o Geo. W. & Fannie MURPHY; 25y; sgl; railroad agent; b. ShenVA; res. Mt. Jackson Virginia; m. 16 Oct 1883 at Millwood to COONTZ, J. E.; d/o Charles W. & Lou COONTZ; 23y; sgl; b. FredVA; res. ClrkVA; (lic) 15 Oct 1883; p. 87

MURRAY, Lawrence (col); s/o Reuben & Hannah MURRAY; 32y; wid; laborer; b. Orange Co. Va; res. ClrkVA; m. 4 Sep 1879 at ClrkVA to STRANGE, Flora (col); d/o names not known; 25y; sgl; b. & res. ClrkVA; (lic) 4 Sep 1879; p. 1

MYERS, Geo. W.; s/o Jos. & Elizabeth MYERS; 22y; sgl; blacksmith; b. JeffVA; res. ClrkVA; m. 18 Feb 1869 at bride's residence to GALLOWAY, Annie E.; d/o Madison & Frances

GALLOWAY; 23y; sgl; b. LdnVA; res. ClrkVA; (lic) 16 Feb 1869; p. 77
MYERS, Henry J.; s/o Abraham & Catharine MYERS; 21y; sgl; blacksmith; b. Pennsylvania; res. ClrkVA; m. 24 Nov 1874 at ClrkVA to GALLOWAY, Josey; d/o Madison & Frances GALLOWAY; 22y; sgl; b. LdnVA; res. ClrkVA; (lic) 23 Nov 1874; p. 170
NAIL, William H.; s/o Daniel & Rhoda NAIL; 26y; sgl; blacksmith; b. WrnVA; res. ClrkVA; m. 2 Aug 1866 at ClrkVA to ATKINS, Eliza. E.; d/o Robert & Rebecca Jane ATKINS; 24y; sgl; b. RappVA; res. ClrkVA; (lic) 1 Aug 1866; p. 16
NELSON, Jacob (col); s/o Jacob & Rachael NELSON; 23y; sgl; laborer; b. & res. ClrkVA; m. 7 Nov 1878 at ClrkVA to BELL, Ellen (col); d/o Benj. & Jane BELL; 21y; sgl; b. & res. ClrkVA; (lic) 7 Nov 1878; p. 244
NELSON, Michael (col); s/o Jacob & Rachel NELSON (col); 33y; sgl; farm hand; b. & res. ClrkVA; m. 14 Jan 1871 at Berryville to PARKER, Catharine (col); d/o Rebecca PARKER (col); 32y; sgl; b. & res. ClrkVA; (lic) 14 Jan 1871; p. 107
NELSON, Samuel (col); s/o Alfred & Sallie NELSON; 23y; sgl; farm hand; b. LdnVA; res. ClrkVA; m. 19 Mar 1874 at ClrkVA to THOMLEY, Gertrude (col); d/o Charles & Alice THOMLEY; 17y; sgl; b. LdnVA; res. ClrkVA; (lic) 17 Mar 1874; p. 159
NESSMITH, James M.; s/o Thomas & Margaret A. NESSMITH; 25y; sgl; blacksmith; b. Winchester Va; res. Strasburg Va; m. 16 Jun 1875 at Berryville to SHACKELFORD, Hannah V.; d/o Erasmus & Helen SHACKELFORD; 23y; sgl; b. ClrkVA; res. Berryville; (lic) 15 Jun 1875; p. 180
NEVILLE, Joseph D.; s/o Grabiel [Gabriel?] & Elizabeth NEVILLE; 27y; sgl; farmer; b. WrnVA; res. FredVA; m. 29 Feb 1872 at ClrkVA to McCAULEY, Amanda; d/o John G. & Martha McCAULEY; 25y; sgl; b. & res. ClrkVA; (lic) 27 Feb 1872; p. 127
NICKINS, John (col); s/o John & Jane NICKINS; 26y; sgl; horse training; b. LdnVA; res. ClrkVA; m. 12 Sep 1882 at ClrkVA to WILLIAMS, Ella (col); d/o ___ & Harriet PHILIPS; 26y; sgl; b. & res. ClrkVA; (lic) 11 Sep 1882; p. 63
NORRIS, Franklin G. B.; s/o John & Susan C. NORRIS; 21y; sgl; wheelright; b. FredMD; res. JeffWVA; m. 1 Nov 1882 at Berryville to SMITH, Annie M.; d/o Thomas & Rebecca SMITH; 21y; sgl; b. Washington Md; res. ClrkVA; (lic) 1 Nov 1882; p. 66

OATES, Thomas H.; s/o Daniel & Mary OATES; 28y; sgl; not given; b. FredVA; res. Hampshire Co. Va; m. 2 Dec 1884 at Winchester Va to FULLER, Lula M.; d/o Bushrod & Mary FULLER; 21y; sgl; b. & res. ClrkVA; (lic) not given; p. 112
OLIVER, Manly Thomas; s/o J. W. & Fannie OLIVER; 26y; sgl; carpenter; b. & res. WrnVA; m. 22 Dec 1886 at ClrkVA to ROYSTON, Nannie E.; d/o George R. & Kate ROYSTON; 21y; sgl; b. & res. ClrkVA; (lic) 21 Dec 1886; p. 149
OSBURN, Armistead (col); s/o William & Sidney OSBURN (col); 21y; sgl; farm hand; b. LdnVA; res. ClrkVA; m. 19 Aug 1871 at ClrkVA to MITCHELL, Amanda (col); d/o not known; 21y; sgl; b. WrnVA; res. ClrkVA; (lic) 19 Aug 1871; p. 114
OSBURN, Lewelen P.; s/o Rowland & Charlotte OSBURN; 43y; sgl; farmer; b. LdnVA; res. ClrkVA; m. 28 Nov 1882 at ClrkVA to GRUBBS, L. Belle; d/o William & Lucinda GRUBBS; 29y; sgl; b. & res. ClrkVA; (lic) 24 Nov 1882; p. 69
OWEN, James W.; s/o Tolaiferro & Mary OWEN; 21y; sgl; blacksmith; b. Frederick Co.; res. ClrkVA; m. 9 Feb 1869 at Berryville to SCROGGINS, Bettie; d/o ___ and ___ SCROGGIN; 27y; sgl; b. WrnVA; res. ClrkVA; (lic) 8 Feb 1869; p. 76
OWEN, James William; s/o Thomas R. & Mary OWEN; 26y; sgl; farmer; b. FredVA; res. WrnVA; m. Tuesday 28 Nov 1876 at Berryville to MERCER, Ruth Helen; d/o William & Susan MERCER; 24y; sgl; b. JeffWVA; res. ClrkVA; (lic) 28 Nov 1876; p. 210
OWENS, James C.; s/o Alexander & Mary OWENS; 23y; sgl; farmer; b. Prince Wm. Co. Va; res. ClrkVA; m. 20 Sep 1877 at Berryville to SHRYOCK, Asserina C.; d/o John M. & Jane E. SHRYOCK; 21y; sgl; b. FredVA; res. ClrkVA; (lic) 18 Sep 1877; p. 222
OWENS, Wm. A.; s/o Alex'r. & Mary N. OWENS; 26y; sgl; farmer; b. LdnVA; res. JeffWVA; m. 4 Feb 1875 at Berryville to SHRYOCK, Frances Virginia; d/o John M. & Jane E. SHRYOCK; 22y; sgl; b. FredVA; res. ClrkVA; (lic) 1 Feb 1875; p. 176
PAGE, George R.; s/o Mann R. & Margaret H. PAGE; 39y; wid; farmer; b. JeffWVA; res. ClrkVA; m. 12 Dec 1865 at Hill & Dale to TIMBERLAKE, Sallie C.; d/o R. M. & Sarah TIMBERLAKE; 35y; sgl; b. & res. ClrkVA; (lic) 7 Dec 1865; p. 5

PAGE, Henry D.; s/o James J. & Virginia N. PAGE; 28y; sgl;
clergyman; b. Lewis Co. W Va; res. CulpVA; m. 27 Dec 1882
at ClrkVA to GREGG, Sarah N.; d/o Cephus & Mary M.
GREGG; 27y; sgl; b. Pittsburg; res. ClrkVA; (lic) 26 Dec 1882;
p. 72

PAGE, R. Powel; s/o Dr. R. P. & S. R. PAGE; 27y; sgl; farmer; b.
& res. ClrkVA; m. 18 Dec 1873 at Christ Church Millwood to
BURWELL, Agnes A.; d/o Geo. H. & A. A. BURWELL; 23y;
sgl; b. & res. ClrkVA; (lic) 17 Dec 1873; p. 153

PAGE, Wm. B.; s/o Mann R. & Helen M. PAGE; 32y; sgl; farmer;
b. & res. ClrkVA; m. 26 May 1873 at bride's residence to
LIPPITT, Laura A.; d/o Dr. ___ and Mary F. LIPPITT; 30y; sgl;
b. Alexandria Co. Va; res. ClrkVA; (lic) not given; p. 145

PAGENHARDT, Charles L.; s/o Chas. A. & Angeline
PAGENHARDT; 22y; sgl; gunsmith &c; b. Alleghany Co.
Maryland; res. not given; m. 8 Nov 1876 at ClrkVA to
STEWART, Minnie F.; d/o Jno. R. & Caroline C. STEWART;
22y; sgl; b. ClrkVA; res. not given; (lic) 8 Nov 1876; p. 208

PAINE, Horace (col); s/o Wm. & Nancy PAINE (col); 28y; wid;
hostler; b. Lexington Va; res. ClrkVA; m. 10 May 1868 at
ClrkVA to McCORD, Fanny (col); d/o ___ MITCHELL; 21y;
wid; b. ClrkVA; res. not given; (lic) 9 May 1868; p. 61

PARKER, Benjamin B.; s/o Charles & Maria PARKER; 24y; sgl;
coach maker; b. & res. Middleburg Va; m. 4 Jun 1884 at
ClrkVA to WYNKOOP, Mary F.; d/o Geo. W. and Susan A.
WYNKOOP; 24y; sgl; b. LdnVA; res. ClrkVA; (lic) 3 Jun 1884;
p. 100

PATTERSON, Edward C.; s/o John & Harriet PATTERSON; 21y;
sgl; miller; b. & res. ClrkVA; m. 19 Sep 1871 at ClrkVA to
GRUBBS, Alberta; d/o Jackson & Emily GRUBB; 18y; sgl; b.
FredVA; res. ClrkVA; (lic) 19 Sep 1871; p. 115

PATTERSON, Franklin W. (col); s/o Geo. & Dicey PATTERSON;
23y; sgl; farm hand; b. Lynchburg Va; res. ClrkVA; m. 11 Jan
1883 at bride's residence to STRANGE, Mary (col); d/o ___ &
Malinda STRANGE; 18y; sgl; b. & res. ClrkVA; (lic) 10 Jan
1883; p. 74

PATTERSON, James B.; s/o John & Harriet A. PATTERSON;
32y; wid; farmer; b. & res. ClrkVA; m. date not given at
ClrkVA to WHITTINGTON, Hannah E.; d/o Richard & Sarah
WHITTINGTON; 34y; sgl; b. & res. ClrkVA; (lic) 2 Mar 1867;
p. 33

PATTERSON, Robt. F.; s/o James M. & Margaret W. PATTERSON; 29y; sgl; lawyer; b. & res. Claiborne Co. Tennessee; m. 28 Jan 1867 at bride's res. to CASTLEMAN, Mary F.; d/o James & Catharine CASTLEMAN; 23y; sgl; b. & res. ClrkVA; (lic) 28 Jan 1867; p. 30
PAUL, John; s/o Peter & Maria PAUL; 35y; sgl; lawyer; b. & res. RckhmVA; m. 19 Nov 1874 at bride's residence to GREEN, Kate S.; d/o Chas. H. & Anjamima GREEN; 27y; sgl; b. WrnVA; res. ClrkVA; (lic) 18 Nov 1874; p. 170
PAYNE, Albert N. (col); s/o John & Emily PAYNE; 22y; sgl; furnace hand; b. Amherst Co. Va; res. Harrisburg Pa; m. 12 Jun 1884 at ClrkVA to ROBINSON, Harriet A. (col); d/o Scott & Dinah ROBINSON; 20y; sgl; b. & res. ClrkVA; (lic) 12 Jun 1884; consent of father given; p. 101
PAYNE, John Franklin; s/o James S. & Margaret PAYNE; 21y; sgl; farmer; b. & res. ClrkVA; m. Thursday 5 Apr 1877 at ClrkVA to TRUSSELL, Susan Ida; d/o Samuel & Joanna TRUSSELL; 18y; sgl; b. LdnVA; res. ClrkVA; (lic) 3 Apr 1877; Susan Ida TRUSSELL's parents are both dead her Guardian George CHAPPELL being present gave his consent.; p. 216
PAYNE, Thomas Fenton; s/o James S. & Margaret PAYNE; 26y; sgl; farmer; b. & res. ClrkVA; m. Tuesday 21 Dec 1875 at Methodist Church Berryville to TAPSCOTT, Maria; d/o Robert & Lucy TAPSCOTT; 26y; sgl; b. & res. ClrkVA; (lic) 20 Dec 1875; p. 193
PAYNE, William (col); s/o Thomas & Amanda PAYNE; 22y; sgl; farm hand; b. Madison Co. Va; res. ClrkVA; m. 17 May 1883 at ClrkVA to LOVETT, Sarah (col); d/o Barret & Eliza LOVETT; 23y; sgl; b. & res. ClrkVA; (lic) 16 May 1883; p. 82
PAYNTER, Joseph; s/o Robt. & Mary PAYNTER; 68y; wid; farmer; b. & res. WrnVA; m. 26 Jul 1876 at ClrkVA to COPENHAVER, Virginia L.; d/o John & Sarah COPENHAVER; 30y; sgl; b. & res. ClrkVA; (lic) 22 Jul 1876; p. 203
PAYTON, James W.; s/o Franklin & Caroline PAYTON; 21y; sgl; farmer; b. RappVA; res. ClrkVA; m. 14 Oct 1879 at ClrkVA to HIBBARD, Mary L.; d/o John W. & Mary J. HIBBARD; 21y; sgl; b. & res. ClrkVA; (lic) 14 Oct 1879; p. 4
PEER, James; s/o John and Mary PEER; 21y; sgl; blacksmith; b. ShenVA; res. ClrkVA; m. 16 Jan 1868 at ClrkVA to RUDUFF, Mary Ann; d/o ___ and Bettie RUDUFF; 21y; sgl; b. ShenVA; res. ClrkVA; (lic) 13 Jan 1868; p. 53

PEIRCE, Bige T.; s/o Jacob & Mary PEIRCE; 22y; sgl; farm hand; b. & res. ClrkVA; m. 11 Aug 1886 at ClrkVA to LLOYD, Sarah; d/o __ & Sarah LLOYD; 17y; sgl; b. & res. ClrkVA; (lic) 10 Aug 1886; consent of mother given; p. 141

PENDLETON, Henry (col); s/o Wash & Sarah PENDLETON; 22y; sgl; farm hand; b. & res. ClrkVA; m. 6 Mar 1884 at ClrkVA to BALL, Maria (col); d/o Alfred & Lucy BALL; 24y; sgl; b. & res. ClrkVA; (lic) 5 Mar 1884; p. 97

PENDLETON, Lewis (col); s/o Washington & Sarah PENDLETON; 22y; sgl; farm hand; b. JeffWVA; res. ClrkVA; m. 29 Mar 1883 at ClrkVA to COOK, Mima (col); d/o John & Sallie COOK; 21y; sgl; b. & res. ClrkVA; (lic) 28 Mar 1883; p. 80

PERKS, Benjamin F.; s/o Rich'd. B. and Ann PERKS; 23y; sgl; farmer; b. CulpVA; res. ClrkVA; m. 11 Nov 1884 at bride's residence to LLOYD, Mary Eliz'th; d/o A. J. & Mary A. LLOYD; 16y; sgl; b. JeffWVA; res. ClrkVA; (lic) 10 Nov 1884; bride's father present & gave consent; p. 109

PERKS, John Wesley; s/o R. B. & Mary Ann PERKS; 28y; sgl; thresher &c; b. CulpVA; res. ClrkVA; m. 6 Dec 1882 at bride's residence to JOHNSTON, Mary Louisa; d/o Jno. S. & Mary Louisa JOHNSTON; 23y; sgl; b. & res. ClrkVA; (lic) 2 Dec 1882; p. 70

PERRY, William; s/o ___ & ___ PERRY; 53y; wid; minister; b. & res. RckhmVA; m. 6 Nov 1866 at bride's residence to BONHAM, Emma V.; d/o Daniel S. and Ann C. BONHAM; 21y; sgl; b. & res. ClrkVA; (lic) 5 Nov 1866; p. 21

PHILLIPS, Henry (col); s/o ___ & Harriet PHILLIPS; 26y; sgl; farm hand; b. & res. ClrkVA; m. 25 Mar 1886 at Berryville to GREEN, Mary (col); d/o ___ & ___ GREEN; 23y; sgl; b. & res. ClrkVA; (lic) 25 Mar 1886; p. 134

PIER, Perry W.; s/o John & Mary PIER; 22y; sgl; farmer; b. Hampshire Co. Va; res. ClrkVA; m. 29 Jun 1783 at ClrkVA to GRIFFITH, Mary Elizabeth; d/o Thos. W. & Martha A. GRIFFITH; 17y; sgl; b. & res. ClrkVA; (lic) 26 Jun 1873; bride's father present; p. 147

PIERCE, Wm. G.; s/o John & Elizabeth PIERCE; 27y; wid; farmer`; b. & res. ClrkVA; m. 30 Jul 1868 at ClrkVA to HENNING, Sarah A.; d/o Jos. R. & Jane HENNING; 23y; sgl; b. FredVA; res. ClrkVA; (lic) 29 Jul 1868; p. 63

PINE, George W.; s/o James & Susan F. PINE; 25y; sgl; stone mason; b. & res. ClrkVA; m. 31 May 1870 at Millwood to

RUSSELL, Mary Jane; d/o Wesley RUSSELL & Harriet
RUSSEL; 26y; sgl; b. & res. ClrkVA; (lic) 30 May 1870; p. 97
PINE, John M.; s/o James M. & Susan F. PINE; 26y; sgl; farmer;
b. & res. ClrkVA; m. 2 Jun 1880 at ClrkVA to DAVIS,
Jaqueline S.; d/o John M. & Susan F. PINE [DAVIS]; 17y; sgl;
b. & res. ClrkVA; (lic) 31 May 1880; p. 21
PINE, Marshall M.; s/o James M. & Susan F. PINE; 28y; sgl;
shoe & boot maker; b. & res. ClrkVA; m. 26 Apr 1877 at
ClrkVA to THOMPSON, Amanda; d/o Baliss and Martha
THOMPSON; 26y; sgl; b. & res. ClrkVA; (lic) 25 Apr 1877; p.
217
PIPHER, Wm. M.; s/o Joseph & Eveline PIPHER; 34y; sgl;
farmer; b. FredVA; res. ClrkVA; m. 10 Oct 1871 at ClrkVA to
BELL, Caroline V.; d/o Hiram O. & Frances E. BELL; 29y; sgl;
b. & res. ClrkVA; (lic) 9 Oct 1871; p. 116
POLLARD, Stephen (col); s/o Lige & Ann POLLARD; 25y; sgl;
farm hand; b. & res. ClrkVA; m. 17 Jun 1886 at Berryville to
JACKSON, Lottie (col); d/o Wash and Martha JACKSON;
22y; sgl; b. & res. ClrkVA; (lic) 16 Jun 1886; p. 138
POPE, Benjamin F.; s/o Conrad & Mary POPE; 21y; sgl; farmer;
b. & res. ClrkVA; m. 17 Aug 1865 at Conrad POPE's
residence in ClrkVA to YATES, Susan; d/o William & ___
YATES; 22y; sgl; b. FredVA; res. ClrkVA; (lic) 16 Aug 1865;
p. 1
POPKINS, Shepherd; s/o William & Elizabeth POPKINS; 22y;
sgl; farmer; b. LdnVA; res. ClrkVA; m. 8 Aug 1878 at ClrkVA
to MORELAND, Susan; d/o Samuel & Sarah MORELAND;
26y; sgl; b. LdnVA; res. ClrkVA; (lic) 6 Aug 1878; p. 237
POPP, George H.; s/o R. & ___ POPP; 26y; sgl; farmer; b. & res.
ClrkVA; m. 13 Jan 1881 at FredVA to HANNUN, Annie V.; d/o
James & Harriet RUSSELL; 32y; wid; b. & res. ClrkVA; (lic)
12 Jan 1881; p. 34
PORTER, Edward (col); s/o Edward and Hannah PORTER; 23y;
sgl; farm hand; b. RappVA; res. Millwood; m. 28 Aug 1875 at
Milldale, WrnVA to KING, Mildred (col); d/o John and Caroline
KING; 21y; sgl; b. ClrkVA; res. Millwood; (lic) 27 Aug 1875; p.
184
POSTON, John W.; s/o Wm. & Susan POSTON; 21y; sgl;
farmer; b. & res. LdnVA; m. 18 Nov 1869 at bride's residence
to FOWLER, Catharine V.; d/o Thos. & Evy FOWLER; 19y;
sgl; b. & res. ClrkVA; (lic) 16 Nov 1869; bride's father present
when this license was issued; p. 88

POSTON, Randolph T.; s/o John & Mary POSTON; 24y; sgl; farmer; b. & res. ClrkVA; m. 3 Sep 1885 at ClrkVA to ROWLAND, Jennie; d/o James & Charlotte ROWLAND; 22y; sgl; b. & res. ClrkVA; (lic) 31 Aug 1885; p. 124

POSTON, Thomas L.; s/o ___ & Helen POSTON; 17y; sgl; farmer; b. & res. ClrkVA; m. 1 Sep 1870 at ClrkVA to SPOTTS, Sarah C.; d/o John Wiley & Mary SPOTTS; 24y; sgl; b. & res. ClrkVA; (lic) 1 Sep 1870; letter dated from Healon POSTON giving permission for her son Thomas L. POSTON; p. 99

POTTER, George (col); s/o Benjamin & Mary Jane POTTER; 25y; sgl; farm hand; b. & res. ClrkVA; m. 14 Jan 1875 at Millwood to RANDOLPH, Isabella (col); d/o Harry & Berta RANDOLPH; 22y; sgl; b. & res. ClrkVA; (lic) 14 Jan 1875; p. 174

POTTER, Richard A. (col); s/o Aaron & Hannah POTTER; 40y; sgl; barber; b. & res. ClrkVA; m. 21 Oct 1886 at ClrkVA to DYER, Susan (col); d/o David & Lucy DYER; 38y; sgl; b. AugVA; res. ClrkVA; (lic) 21 Oct 1886; p. 144

POTTER, Thomas H. (col); s/o Thomas H. POTTER & Kate; 33y; sgl; stone mason; b. LdnVA; res. ClrkVA; m. 12 May 1886 at Berryville to LIGHTFOOT, Kate (col); d/o Albert & Agnes LIGHTFOOT; 23y; sgl; b. & res. ClrkVA; (lic) 10 May 1886; p. 135

PUGH, Charles W.; s/o Elisha and Mary PUGH; 24y; sgl; farmer; b. Dunille? Co. Pennsylvania; res. FredVA; m. 16 Sep 1879 at ClrkVA to STUMP, Lara Jane; d/o Robert and Elizabeth STUMP; 19y; sgl; b. & res. ClrkVA; (lic) 16 Sep 1879; consent of parent given by order to Clerk; p. 2

PULLIAM, Philip Ransom; s/o Matthew & Eliza PULLIAM; 24y; sgl; mechanic; b. & res. ClrkVA; m. 7 Nov 1877 at Berryville to GAUNT, Elizabeth Lee; d/o Martin & Jane GAUNT; 21y; sgl; b. & res. ClrkVA; (lic) 6 Nov 1877; p. 227

PURKS, William Henry; s/o Richard B. and Ann PURKS; 23y; sgl; blacksmith; b. CulpVA; res. ClrkVA; m. Tuesday 8 Jul 1879 at ClrkVA at Henry TAPSCOTT's to HANVY, Margaret; d/o Wm. and Hannah C. HANVY; 20y; sgl; b. JeffWVA; res. ClrkVA; (lic) 5 Jul 1879; by consent of Jas. F. MURPHY uncle of Margaret HANVY; p. 260

PYLE, James R.; s/o William & Ann PYLE; 30y; sgl; carpenter; b. & res. ClrkVA; m. 20 Nov 1884 at ClrkVA to LANDON

[LANHAM], Virginia; d/o ___ & Nancy LANHAM; 18y; sgl; b. & res. ClrkVA; (lic) 20 Nov 1884; mother's consent given; p. 111

PYLE, William F.; s/o William and Annie PYLE; 23y; sgl; farmer; b. Jefferson Co.; res. ClrkVA; m. 29 Aug 1867 at bride's residence to FERGUSON, Joanah; d/o Josiah and Susan C. FERGUSON; 17y; sgl; b. & res. ClrkVA; (lic) 28 Aug 1867; bride's father was present when this license was issued.; p. 40

RAGLAN, Rich'd. (col); s/o D. RAGLAN & Rosanna RAGLAN; 58y; wid; hostler; b. & res. AlbmVA; m. date not given at ClrkVA to MUNDY, Caroline (col); d/o not given; 43y; wid; b. LdnVA; res. ClrkVA; (lic) 19 Nov 1866; p. 24

RAMEY, William T.; s/o Wm. C. & Ellen RAMEY; 23y; sgl; farmer; b. ClrkVA; res. JeffWVA; m. 27 Nov 1883 at bride's residence to THOMPSON, Ida J.; d/o A. J. & T. T. THOMPSON; 25y; sgl; b. & res. ClrkVA; (lic) 26 Nov 1883; p. 88

RANDOLPH, Archie C.; s/o Robt. C. & Lucy N. RANDOLPH; 48y; sgl; phisian; b. & res. ClrkVA; m. 29 Sep 1881 at ClrkVA to HENRY, Susie R. [written as BURWELL]; d/o Nathaniel & Dorah BURWELL; 33y; wid; b. & res. ClrkVA; (lic) 23 Sep 1881; p. 47

RANDOLPH, Frank (col); s/o Fredrerick [Frederick] & Palace RANDOLPH (col); 36y; sgl; farm hand; b. & res. ClrkVA; m. 17 Sep 1871 at Berryville to LEWIS, Harriet (col); d/o ___ & Jane LEWIS; 26y; sgl; b. & res. ClrkVA; (lic) 16 Sep 1871; p. 115

RANDOLPH, George (col); s/o Philip & ____ RANDOLPH; 33y; sgl; farm hand; b. & res. ClrkVA; m. 20 Sep 1883 at ClrkVA to BANKS, Mary (col); d/o not known; 33y; sgl; b. & res. ClrkVA; (lic) 20 Sep 1883; p. 86

RANDOLPH, Henry (col); s/o ___ & Ann Randolph (col); 23y; sgl; farmer; b. not given; res. ClrkVA; m. 10 Nov 1870 at Millwood to POTTER, Rachael (col); d/o George & Ann POTTER (col); 21y; sgl; b. not given; res. ClrkVA; (lic) not given; p. 103

RANDOLPH, Henry (col); s/o John & Hannah RANDOLPH; 60y; wid; farm hand; b. & res. ClrkVA; m. 16 Sep 1882 at Millwood to WILLIAMS, Martha (col); d/o Edward and ___ WILLIAMS; 30y; sgl; b. & res. ClrkVA; (lic) 11 Sep 1882; p. 63

RANDOLPH, Robert (col); s/o Phil & Nancy RANDOLPH; 26y; sgl; farm hand; b. & res. ClrkVA; m. 24 Jun 1886 at Millwood

to CARTER, Lucy (col); d/o Nat & Elizabeth CARTER; 23y; sgl; b. & res. ClrkVA; (lic) 21 Jun 1886; p. 138
RANDOLPH, Thos. H. R.; s/o Robt. C. and Lucy M. RANDOLPH; 26y; sgl; farmer; b. & res. ClrkVA; m. 4 Feb 1869 at Christ Church Millwood to BURWELL, Eliza Page; d/o George H. & Agnes BURWELL; 23y; sgl; b. & res. ClrkVA; (lic) 3 Feb 1869; p. 75
RANSOM, Albert (col); s/o Saml. & Catharine RANSOM (col); 21y; sgl; house servant; b. & res. ClrkVA; m. 31 Dec 1867 at ClrkVA to ROBERSON, Mary Ann (col); d/o Mortimer & Charity ROBERSON (col); 23y; wid; b. & res. ClrkVA; (lic) 30 Dec 1867; p. 50
REED, Matthew (col); s/o Tildon & Amanda REED; 22y; sgl; farm hand; b. & res. FredVA; m. 26 Dec 1872 at bride's residence to WILLIAMS, Minerva J. (col); d/o Levi & Cath'e WILLIAMS; 19y; sgl; b. & res. ClrkVA; (lic) 26 Dec 1872: bride's father present & gave his consent; p. 139
REED, Nelson Jr. (col); s/o Nelson & Gustava REED; 23y; sgl; farm hand; b. & res. ClrkVA; m. 25 Dec 1886 at ClrkVA to COLSTON, Arrena (col); d/o Jacob & Ellen COLSTON; 22y; sgl; b. & res. ClrkVA; (lic) 25 Dec 1886; p. 149
REED, Samuel Owen (col); s/o Spencer & Ann REED (col); 24y; sgl; farmhand; b. & res. ClrkVA; m. 18 Aug 1866 at ClrkVA to JACKSON, Amanda (col); d/o Dolman & Polly JACKSON (col); 21y; sgl; b. & res. ClrkVA; (lic) 11 Aug 1866; p. 17
REED, Thomas (col); s/o Nelson & Gustavia REED; 23y; sgl; farm hand; b. JeffVA; res. ClrkVA; m. 21 Oct 1880 at ClrkVA to ANDERSON, Elizabeth (col); d/o ___ & ___ ANDERSON; 22y; sgl; b. Richmond Va; res. ClrkVA; (lic) 21 Oct 1880; p. 27
REID, John R.; s/o Marcus B. & Susan A. REED; 26y; sgl; farmer; b. & res. ClrkVA; m. 22 Dec 1868 to THOMPSON, Martha A.; d/o Baylis & Margaret A. THOMPSON; 19y; sgl; b. LdnVA; res. ClrkVA; (lic) 22 Dec 1868; bride's father present when license was issued; p. 71
REID, Wm. W.; s/o M. B. REID and Susan A. ASHBY; 25y; sgl; farm hand; b. & res. ClrkVA; m. 9 Sep 1875 at near Millwood to CARTER, Fannie F.; d/o John W. CARTER and A. K. CARTER; 17y; sgl; b. & res. ClrkVA; (lic) 8 Sep 1875; p. 185
REYNOLDS, Lyman G.; s/o Peter & Rhoda REYNOLDS; 28y; sgl; farmer; b. Michigan; res. ClrkVA; m. 12 Oct 1865 at Millwood to MYERS, Mahala; d/o John & Winny SHAFFER;

35y; widow of Libel? MYERS; b. & res. ClrkVA; (lic) 11 Oct 1865; p. 4

RICAMORE, George; s/o Philip & Martha RICAMORE; 23y; sgl; carpenter; b. BerkVA; res. Berryville; m. 14 Feb 1872 at Berryville to PULLIAM, Mary V.; d/o Matthew & Eliza PULLIAM; 21y; sgl; b. ClrkVA; res. Berryville; (lic) not given; p. 126

RICHARDSON, Josiah A.; s/o N. W. & E. A. RICHARDSON; 23y; sgl; tobacconist; b. & res. FredVA; m. 30 Nov 1869 at bride's residence to BATEMAN, Annie E.; d/o M. M. & R. BATEMAN; 22y; sgl; b. Summerset Co. New Jersey; res. ClrkVA; (lic) 26 Nov 1869; p. 89

RICHARDSON, Webster; s/o Naylor W. & Ester A. RICHARDSON; 24y; sgl; druggist; b. & res. FredVA; m. 8 Oct 1868 at ClrkVA to HARDESTY, Mary Virginia; d/o James M. & Sarah W. HARDESTY; 21y; sgl; b. FredVA; res. ClrkVA; (lic) 5 Oct 1868; p. 67

RICHEY, John S.; s/o F. H. & Eliza RICHEY; 25y; sgl; merchant; b. Pennsylvania; res. RckhmVA; m. 24 Oct 1877 at father's residence ClrkVA to LOCK, Ellen M.; d/o Jno. M. & Bettie C. LOCK; 23y; sgl; b. JeffWVA; res. ClrkVA; (lic) 23 Oct 1877; p. 225

RIDDELL, A. A.; s/o Jas. & Rebecca J. RIDDELL; 37y; sgl; farmer; b. & res. ShenVA; m. 28 Jan 1871 at Middletown, FredVA to SCRUGGS, Susan C.; d/o ___ & ___ SWARTS; not given; wid; b. LdnVA; res. ClrkVA; (lic) 27 Jan 1871; p. 108

RIDENOUR, Jno.; s/o Daniel & Lucinda RIDENOUR; 26y; sgl; farmer; b. WrnVA; res. ClrkVA; m. 22 Oct 1865 at Millwood to WAMAX, Mary Jane; d/o Jessee WAMAX & Lucinda WAMAX; 18y; sgl; b. ShenVA; res. ClrkVA; (lic) 21 Oct 1865; consent of bride's stepfather, her father being dead.; p. 4

RINKER, John H.; s/o Moses RINKER and Lydia RINKER; 21y; sgl; farmer; b. ShenVA; res. ClrkVA; m. Tuesday 12 Oct 187 at ClrkVA near burnt factory to STUMP, Mary C.; d/o Rot [Ro't.?] STUMP and Betsy STUMP; 23y; sgl; b. & res. ClrkVA; (lic) 11 Oct 1875; p. 187

RINKER, Romanus; s/o Jacob and Mary RINKER; 26y; sgl; farmer; b. ShenVA; res. Frederick Co.; m. 7 Feb 1867 at bride's residence to ROGERS, Mary Jane; d/o William F. and Catharine ROGERS; 22y; sgl; b. ShenVA; res. ClrkVA; (lic) 4 Feb 1867; p. 31

RITTER [RUTTER], George W.; s/o William & Betsy RUTTER; 23y; sgl; farmer; b. LdnVA; res. ClrkVA; m. 3 Aug 1880 at ClrkVA to POLAND, Sarah E.; d/o ___ & Betsy POLAND; 25y; sgl; b. LdnVA; res. ClrkVA; (lic) 3 Aug 1880; p. 24

RITTER, Franklin; s/o Henry & Margaret RITTER; 39y; wid; miller; b. FredVA; res. Harpers ferry W Va; m. 20 Oct 1874 at bride's residence to ALEXANDER, Annie W.; d/o Thos. W. & Mary ALEXANDER; 20y; sgl; b. & res. ClrkVA; (lic) 19 Oct 1874; bride's father present & assenting; p. 166

RITTER, Leven Adams; s/o Jno. T. & Isa Eliza RITTER; 23y; sgl; farmer; b. FqrVA; res. LdnVA; m. 14 Jan 1875 at LdnVA to BELL, Sarah Ann; d/o Jas. & Rachel BELL; 18y; sgl; b. & res. ClrkVA; (lic) 13 Jan 1875; p. 173

RITTER, Matthias R.; s/o John M. & Deborah RITTER; 24y; sgl; plasterer; b. FredVA; res. not given; m. 2 Aug 1876 at ClrkVA to PERRY, Eveline; d/o Benj. F. & Eveline PERRY; 22y; sgl; b. ClrkVA; res. not given; (lic) 31 Jul 1876; p. 203

RITTER, R. Hermine; s/o Jacob & Margaret RITTER; 24y; sgl; shoemaker; b. Alexandria, Fairfax Co. Va; res. ClrkVA; m. 22 Dec 1868 at Millwood to KEELER, L. C.; d/o Middleton & Cherissa KEELER; 25y; sgl; b. & res. ClrkVA; (lic) 22 Dec 1868; p. 71

ROACH, Philip E.; s/o Jas. & Eliz. ROACH; 23y; sgl; farmer; b. Alexandria Co. Va; res. Prince George Md; m. 15 May 1867 at Berryville to THOMPSON, Mattie; d/o W. B. & Catharine THOMPSON; 21y; sgl; b. JeffVA; res. Berryville; (lic) 14 May 1867; p. 35

ROBERTS, Benjamin C.; s/o William J. & Fanny ROBERTS; 29y; sgl; carpenter; b. & res. JeffWVA; m. 14 Jan 1885 at ClrkVA to CARTER, Mary L.; d/o John A. & Betty C. CARTER; 25y; sgl; b. & res. ClrkVA; (lic) 12 Jan 1885; p. 116

ROBERTSON, Antony (col); s/o Charity ROBERTSON mother's name & Antony ROBERTSON; 28y; wid; farm hand; b. & res. ClrkVA; m. Wednesday 26 Dec 1877 at ClrkVA to GRAY, Hattie (col); d/o Elias & Maria GARY; 24y; sgl; b. WrnVA; res. ClrkVA; (lic) 24 Dec 1877; p. 229

ROBINSON, Anthony (col); s/o Anthony & Charity ROBINSON (col); 23y; sgl; farm hand; b. & res. ClrkVA; m. 31 Mar 1869 at ClrkVA to PARKER, Susan Ann (col); d/o ___ & Susan PARKER (col); 21y; sgl; b. & res. ClrkVA; (lic) 30 Mar 1869; p. 80

ROBINSON, Chas. (col); s/o John and Louisa ROBINSON (col); 21y; sgl; farm hand; b. & res. ClrkVA; m. 29 Dec 1868 at ClrkVA to JOHNSTON, Susan (col); d/o Daniel & Lucinda JOHNSTON (col); 21y; sgl; b. JeffVA; res. ClrkVA; (lic) 29 Dec 1868; p. 72

ROBINSON, Frederick (col); s/o Saml. & Jane ROBINSON; 22y; sgl; farm hand; b. & res. ClrkVA; m. 29 May 1879 at Berryville to LAWS, Martha (col); d/o Thos. & Mary LAWS; 21y; sgl; b. & res. ClrkVA; (lic) 29 May 1879; p. 259

ROBINSON, Henry (col); s/o Saml. & Louisa ROBINSON; 23y; sgl; not given; b. FqrVA; res. ClrkVA; m. 12 Jun 1879 at ClrkVA to BANISTER, Rachel (col); d/o Thos. & Martha BANISTER; 21y; sgl; b. & res. ClrkVA; (lic) 12 Jun 1879; p. 259

ROBINSON, James W.; s/o Daniel & Mary ROBINSON; 29y; wid; not given; b. & res. WrnVA; m. 26 Dec 1878 at ClrkVA. to STOKES, Sarah E.; d/o Isaac A. & Ellen STOKES; 27y; sgl; b. WrnVA; res. ClrkVA; (lic) 25 Dec 1878; p. 249

ROBINSON, Olie (col); s/o Samson & Phebe A. ROBINSON (col); 37y; wid; farm hand; b. ClrkVA; res. JeffWVA; m. 12 May 1872 at Berryville to FESTUS, Tamson (col); d/o Hamilton & Cilia JEFFERS (col); 25y; wid; b. FredVA; res. ClrkVA; (lic) 11 May 1872; p. 129

ROBINSON, Sam. (col); s/o Anthony & Charity ROBINSON; 21y; sgl; farm hand; b. & res. ClrkVA; m. 26 Nov 1865 at Sudley, ClrkVA to MYERS, Sally (col); d/o Charles & Pallas; 18y; sgl; b. & res. ClrkVA; (lic) 25 Nov 1865; p. 5

ROBINSON, Thomas (col); s/o Samuel & Jane ROBINSON; 24y; sgl; farm hand; b. & res. ClrkVA; m. 1 Jan 1879 at ClrkVA to STRANGE, Mollie (col); d/o John STRANGE, mother's name not known; 22y; sgl; b. & res. ClrkVA; (lic) 24 Dec 1878; p. 249

ROGERS, James W.; s/o Sandford P. & Susan ROGERS; 84y; sgl; farmer; b. LdnVA; res. Messori [Missouri]; m. 15 Oct 1879 at ClrkVA to COLSTON, Georgie M.; d/o Robert A. & Matilda S. COLSTON; 25y; sgl; b. & res. ClrkVA; (lic) 14 Oct 1879; p. 4

ROGERS, Winter; s/o W. W. ROGERS & Ann R. ROGERS; 20y; sgl; merchant; b. & res. Paris, FqrVA; m. 14 Dec 1875 at near Berryville to GREEN, Jennie S.; d/o Charles & Angemara? GREEN; 20y; sgl; b. WrnVA; res. ClrkVA; (lic) 13 Dec 1875; p. 193

ROLLS, Isaac N. (col); s/o Samuel & Mary ROLLS; 31y; sgl; farm hand; b. PageVA; res. ClrkVA; m. 14 Aug 1885 at ClrkVA to ROBINSON, Eliza (col); d/o dead, not known; 31y; wid; b. & res. ClrkVA; (lic) 10 Aug 1885; p. 123

ROWLAND, Clinton O.; s/o James & Charlotte ROWLAND; 24y; sgl; farming; b. & res. ClrkVA; m. 22 Nov 1882 at Berryville to CARPER, Ida B.; d/o George & Eviline CARPER; 21y; sgl; b. WrnVA; res. ClrkVA; (lic) 21 Nov 1882; p. 68

ROWLAND, John James; s/o James H. & Charlotte T. ROWLAND; 23y; sgl; farming; b. & res. ClrkVA; m. 28 Jan 1879 at Berryville to LOCKE, Lucy G.; d/o John Wm. & Orry LOCKE; 22y; sgl; b. JeffWVA; res. ClrkVA; (lic) 27 Jan 1879; p. 251

ROY, Richard B.; s/o Carter D. & Sarah ROY; 42y; wid; farmer; b. WrnVA; res. ClrkVA; m. 8 Feb 1882 at ClrkVA to HOLLAND, Emily H.; d/o John W. & Rosa HOLLAND; 22y; sgl; b. & res. ClrkVA; (lic) 8 Feb 1882; p. 55

ROYSTON, Charles L.; s/o Peter R. & Mary ROYSTON; 24y; sgl; farmer; b. & res. ClrkVA; m. 27 Apr 1878 at ClrkVA to DOVE, Martha A.; d/o Thos. J. & Adelia DOVE; 23y; sgl; b. & res. ClrkVA; (lic) 27 Apr 1878; p. 234

ROYSTON, Geo. R.; s/o Uriah B. & Hannah ROYSTON; 48y; wid; farmer; b. & res. ClrkVA; m. 17 Aug 1881 at bride's residence to COOPER, Annie V.; d/o Harrison & Alcinda COOPER; 26y; sgl; b. & res. ClrkVA; (lic) 15 Aug 1881; p. 45

ROYSTON, John F.; s/o Peter K. & Mary ROYSTON; 28y; sgl; farmer; b. & res. ClrkVA; m. 21 Feb 1884 at ClrkVA to SMALLWOOD, Julia A.; d/o Sylvester & Sarah Ann SMALLWOOD; 18y; sgl; b. & res. ClrkVA; (lic) 20 Feb 1884; father's consent given; p. 95

ROYSTON, Robert W.; s/o Mathew W. & Manerva ROYSTON; 27y; sgl; farmer; b. ClrkVA; res. not given; m. 14 Sep 1876 at not given to MORRISON, Sarah C.; d/o Thomas M. & Marenda MORRISON; 26y; sgl; b. FredVA; res. not given; (lic) 11 Sep 1876; p. 205

ROYSTON, Walter S.; s/o Peter R. & Mary ROYSTON; 25y; sgl; farmer; b. & res. ClrkVA; m. 20 Feb 1885 at ClrkVA to SMALLWOOD, Virginia E.; d/o Sylvester & Sarah SMALLWOOD; 17y; sgl; b. & res. ClrkVA; (lic) 19 Feb 1885; consent of father given; p. 117

ROYSTON, Z. V.; s/o Joseph A. & Harriet ROYSTON; 23y; sgl; shoemaker; b. & res. FqrVA; m. 22 Jan 1867 at Vineyard,

ClrkVA to LONG, Jane F.; d/o Robert and Joeanna LONG; 19y; sgl; b. FqrVA; res. ClrkVA; (lic) 10 Jan 1867; bride's Guardian being present; p. 28

RUFFINS, John (col); s/o Abraham & Martha RUFFINS; 30y; sgl; farm hand; b. & res. FredVA; m. 28 Feb 1878 at ClrkVA to JOHNSON, Martha (col); d/o ___ & Fannie JOHNSON; 24y; sgl; b. & res. ClrkVA; (lic) 28 Feb 1878; p. 232

RUNNER, Thos. (col); s/o Richard & Harriet RUNNER (col); 30y; sgl; farm hand; b. & res. ClrkVA; m. 9 Dec 1869 at bride's residence to FIELDS, Maria (col); d/o Daniel & Jane FIELDS (col); 21y; sgl; b. & res. ClrkVA; (lic) 7 Dec 1869; p. 90

RUSSELL, Bennett W.; s/o Thomas W. & Maria RUSSELL; 26y; sgl; farmer; b. FredVA; res. ClrkVA; m. 7 Jan 1875 at ClrkVA to SINGHASS, Mary R.; d/o Baker H. & Elizabeth C. SINGHASS; 20y; sgl; b. FredVA; res. ClrkVA; (lic) 6 Jan 1875; bride's father present; p. 173

RUSSELL, Frank J.; s/o Michael & Nancy RUSSELL; 24y; sgl; farmer; b. & res. ClrkVA; m. 10 Jan 1883 at Winchester Va to SLUSHER, Ida E.; d/o Hezekiah & Mary SLUSHER; 23y; sgl; b. & res. ClrkVA; (lic) 9 Jan 1883; p. 74

RUSSELL, Henry C.; s/o Wesley & Harriet RUSSELL; 28y; sgl; carpenter; b. FqrVA; res. ClrkVA; m. 20 May 1785 at ClrkVA to SHIPE, Virginia; d/o Benj. H. & Hannah SHIPE; 22y; sgl; b. & res. ClrkVA; (lic) 10 May 1875; p. 178

RUSSELL, James E.; s/o James E. & Harriet A. RUSSELL; 23y; sgl; miller; b. & res. ClrkVA; m. 10 Mar 1874 at ClrkVA to WYNDHAM, Mary V.; d/o Tho[r]nton O. & Cornilia F. WYNDHAM; 19y; sgl; b. LdnVA; res. ClrkVA; (lic) 9 Mar 1874; bride's father present & assenting; p. 159

RUSSELL, James Joel; s/o Thomas W. & Maria RUSSELL; 22y; sgl; farmer; b. ClrkVA; res. West Virginia; m. __ Dec 1878 at ClrkVA to SINGHASS, Alice Lavinia; d/o Baker S. & Elizabeth SINGHASS; 22y; sgl; b. FredVA; res. ClrkVA; (lic) 7 Dec 1878; p. 246

RUSSELL, James; s/o W. W. & Harriet RUSSELL; 21y; sgl; farmer; b. FqrVA; res. ClrkVA; m. 30 Sep 1873 at ClrkVA to McDONALD, Martha; d/o John & Jane McDONALD; 20y; sgl; b. & res. ClrkVA; (lic) 22 Sep 1873; p. 149

RUSSELL, Jefferson D.; s/o W. W. & Harriet RUSSELL; 23y; sgl; carpenter; b. & res. ClrkVA; m. 22 Oct 1885 at ClrkVA to REED, Sarah J.; d/o M. B. & Susan REED; 24y; sgl; b. & res. ClrkVA; (lic) 20 Oct 1885; p. 126

RUSSELL, John M.; s/o Wm. W. & Harriet RUSSELL; 30y; sgl; carpenter; b. & res. ClrkVA; m. 15 Feb 1883 at ClrkVA to CLINE, Virginia H.; d/o Michael & Sarah CLINE; 24y; sgl; b. FredVA; res. ClrkVA; (lic) 14 Feb 1883; p. 77
RUSSELL, Thomas A.; s/o James E. & Harriet A. RUSSELL; 25y; sgl; farming; b. & res. ClrkVA; m. 16 Jan 1879 at ClrkVA to BROWN, Sarah E.; d/o Wm. M. and Sarah J. BROWN; 18y; sgl; b. FredVA; res. ClrkVA; (lic) 13 Jan 1879; p. 251
RUSSELL, Wm. H.; s/o Thaddeus & Cath'e. RUSSELL; 30y; sgl; farmer; b. LdnVA; res. ClrkVA; m. date not given at bride's residence to KEEN, Margaret Ann; d/o ___ & Frances BRACKETT; 25y; wid; b. & res. ClrkVA; (lic) 12 Jan 1874; p. 156
RUSSELL, Wm.; s/o Michael & Annie RUSSELL; 24y; sgl; farmer; b. & res. ClrkVA; m. 9 Jan 1871 at Winchester Va to LONG, Kate M. F.; d/o not known; 21y; sgl; b. BerkVA; res. ClrkVA; (lic) 7 Jan 1871; p. 107
RUST, Ashby Madison; s/o Charles B. RUST & Mary A. RUST; 24y; sgl; farmer; b. & res. WrnVA; m. Tuesday 18 Mar 1879 at residence of Geo. K. SOWERS in ClrkVA to BURCH, Delia Elizabeth; d/o Hiliary & Elizabeth BURCH; 23y; sgl; b. Maryland; res. ClrkVA; (lic) 15 Mar 1879; p. 255
SALE, John O.; s/o R. R. & Catharine SALE; 42y; wid; clerk; b. Caroline Co. Va; res. Richmond Va; m. 5 Nov 1868 at bride's residence to LOUTHAN, Amanda; d/o John & Lydia LOUTHAN; 25y; sgl; b. & res. ClrkVA; (lic) 4 Nov 1868; p. 69
SAMPSELL, William B.; s/o Henry & Lucy SAMPSELL; 22y; sgl; farmer; b. LdnVA; res. ClrkVA; m. 15 Nov 1881 at ClrkVA to PULLER, Annie E.; d/o Bushrod & Mary E. PULLER; 22y; sgl; b. & res. ClrkVA; (lic) 14 Nov 1881; p. 51
SANDERS, Jesse (col); s/o Robt. & Annie SANDERS (col); 37y; sgl; farm hand; b. & res. JeffWVA; m. 10 Jun 1871 at Millwood to HERBERT, Bettie (col); d/o not given; 25y; sgl; b. & res. ClrkVA; (lic) not given; p. 112
SANDERS, John (col); s/o Dennis & Darky Ann SANDERS; 27y; sgl; farm hand; b. Westmoreland Co. Va; res. ClrkVA; m. 11 Dec 1870 at ClrkVA to CARTER, Mary (col); d/o Henry and Ellen REED; 21y; sgl; b. RappVA; res. ClrkVA; (lic) 10 Dec 1870; p. 104
SANDERS, Joshua (col); s/o James & Violet SANDERS; 32y; wid; farm hand; b. Franklin Co. Pennsylvania; res. ClrkVA; m. 16 Mar 1876 at ClrkVA to WILLIAMS, Letitia (col); d/o not

known & Violet WILLIAMS; 21y; sgl; b. & res. ClrkVA; (lic) 16 Mar 1876; p. 198
SCHLACK, Charles H.; s/o John F. & Mary A. SCHLACK; 27y; sgl; farmer; b. Pennsylvania; res. ClrkVA; m. 25 May 1886 at Berryville to HAUPTMAN, Annie; d/o John & Catharine HAUPTMAN; 21y; sgl; b. Pennsylvania; res. ClrkVA; (lic) 20 May 1886; p. 136
SCHOOLEY, Joseph E.; s/o Rubin E. & Rachel L. SCHOOLEY; 22y; sgl; blacksmith; b. Waterford, LdnVA; res. LdnVA; m. 19 Nov 1874 at Methodist Church Berryville to THOMAS, Mary C.; d/o Jas. W. & Maranda THOMAS; 21y; sgl; b. & res. ClrkVA; (lic) 18 Nov 1874; p. 170
SEALS, Dennis (col); s/o Peter and Patsy SEALS (col); 54y; wid; farm hand; b. Fairfax Co. Va; res. ClrkVA; m. 9 Jan 1868 at ClrkVA to JOHNSON, Betsy (col); d/o ___ & ___ SOUDER (col); 40y; wid; b. & res. ClrkVA; (lic) 8 Jan 1868; p. 52
SEBOLD, Chas. W.; s/o Danl. D. & Phebe P. SEBOLD; 23y; sgl; farmer; b. Hunterdon Co. New Jersey; res. ClrkVA; m. 26 Nov 1868 at ClrkVA to BATEMAN, Sallie M.; d/o Moses & ___ BATEMAN; 23y; sgl; b. Summersett Co. New Jersey; res. ClrkVA; (lic) 13 Nov 1868; p. 69
SHACKELFORD, John H.; s/o Erasmus & Helen SHACKELFORD; 24y; sgl; carpenter; b. & res. ClrkVA; m. 5 Feb 1874 at Berryville to LANCASTER, Mollie E.; d/o John F. & Hannah LANCASTER; 21y; sgl; b. JeffVA; res. ClrkVA; (lic) 4 Feb 1874; p. 157
SHACKLEFORD, William C.; s/o James H. & Mary L. SHACKLEFORD; 32y; sgl; coach painter; b. & res. ClrkVA; m. 17 Jun 1880 at ClrkVA to BRYAN, Rebecca C.; d/o John E. & Mary BRYAN; not given; sgl; b. RckhmVA; res. ClrkVA; (lic) 17 Jun 1880; p. 22
SHAFER, John T.; s/o Jno. J. and Miranda E. SHAFER; 26y; sgl; farmer; b. & res. ClrkVA; m. 29 Nov 1866 at bride's residence to WRITT, Darcus Jane; d/o Thomson & Elizabeth WRITT; 32y; sgl; b. FqrVA; res. ClrkVA; (lic) 29 Nov 1866; p. 25
SHELL, John J.; s/o John & Martha SHELL; 26y; sgl; railroading; b. LdnVA; res. ClrkVA; m. 23 Nov 1882 at Berryville to SHAFER, Margaret A.; d/o John & Maranda SHAFER; 25y; sgl; b. & res. ClrkVA; (lic) 22 Nov 1882; p. 68
SHENK, Erastus R.; s/o Samuel H. & Harriet SHENK; 20y; sgl; stage driver; b. PageVA; res. Winchester Va; m. 23 Jan 1872 at ClrkVA to CHRISMORE, Catharine; d/o Franklin & Ann

CHRISMORE; 18y; sgl; b. FredVA; res. ClrkVA; (lic) not given; written permission from Harriet A. SHENK dated 20 Jan 1872.; p. 124

SHEPHERD, Champ; s/o Joseph & Amelia H. SHEPHERD; 53y; wid; farmer; b. Frederick Co. (now Clarke); res. ClrkVA; m. 17 Sep 1867 at White Post to RICHARDS, Martha E.; d/o Daniel B. & Rebecca RICHARDS; 28y; sgl; b. & res. ClrkVA; (lic) 14 Sep 1867; p. 41

SHEPHERD, Geo. C.; s/o Champ & Sarah Ann SHEPHERD; 31y; sgl; farmer; b. & res. ClrkVA; m. 23 Dec 1873 at Grace Church Berryville to MORGAN, Ella C.; d/o Benj. & Martha MORGAN; 23y; sgl; b. & res. ClrkVA; (lic) 20 Dec 1873; p. 154

SHEPHERD, John R.; s/o Champ & Susan SHEPHERD; 28y; sgl; farmer; b. & res. ClrkVA; m. 4 Jul 1881 at Berryville to HEFLIN, Sarah Cath'e.; d/o ___ & Mary Cath'e. HEFLIN; 21y; sgl; b. & res. ClrkVA; (lic) 4 Jul 1881; p. 43

SHEPHERD, Jos. H.; s/o Champ & Sarah A.? SHEPHERD; 25y; sgl; flour merchant; b. & res. ClrkVA; m. 9 Jan 1866 at Hill & Dale to MORGAN, Martha E.; d/o Benjamin & Martha A. MORGAN; 26y; sgl; b. & res. ClrkVA; (lic) 1 Jan 1866; p. 6

SHIMP, Wm. M.; s/o Geo. W. & Juliet A. SHIMP; 18y; sgl; farmer; b. & res. ClrkVA; m. 26 Nov 1872 at ClrkVA to ROSBROUGH, Eliza; d/o Harrison & Mary E. ROSBROUGH; 21y; sgl; b. Hampshire Co.; res. ClrkVA; (lic) 23 Nov 1872; groom's mother written consent given; p. 137

SHIPE, James M.; s/o Benjamin & Hannah SHIPE; 22y; sgl; blacksmith; b. & res. ClrkVA; m. 10 May 1883 at ClrkVA to SELMAN, Nannie J.; d/o Benj. T. & Sarah C. SELMAN; 22y; sgl; b. & res. ClrkVA; (lic) 9 May 1883; p. 81

SHIPE, John W.; s/o Jacob & Nancy SHIPE; 23y; sgl; blacksmith; b. & res. WrnVA; m. Thursday 26 Mar 1868 at residence of bride's mother, ClrkVA to SHIPE, Mary C.; d/o Joseph SHIPE dec'd. & Debba SHIPE; 20y; sgl; b. & res. ClrkVA; (lic) 25 Mar 1868; consent of bride's mother given in writing attested by two witnesses.; p. 58

SHOEMAKER, Thomas E.; s/o David F. & Catharine SHOEMAKER; 27y; sgl; farmer; b. Cumberland Co. Del.; res. JeffWVA; m. 4 Jun 1884 at ClrkVA to KITCHEN, Lizzie E.; d/o Jno. N. & Lucy W. KITCHEN; 24y; sgl; b. & res. ClrkVA; (lic) 3 Jun 1884; p. 101

SHOPLAND, Alfred; s/o James & Elenor SHOPLAND; 27y; sgl; farmer; b. Maryland; res. ClrkVA; m. 27 Nov 1878 at ClrkVA to LOUTHAN, Georgeanna; d/o John K. & Lucy Ann LOUTHAN; 24y; sgl; b. & res. ClrkVA; (lic) 25 Nov 1878; p. 246

SHOPLAND, Harry R.; s/o James & Elenor SHOPLAND; 31y; sgl; farmer; b. England; res. ClrkVA; m. 4 Nov 1886 at ClrkVA to BERLIN, Laura L.; d/o Lewis & Bettie BERLIN; 22y; sgl; b. & res. ClrkVA; (lic) 3 Nov 1886; p. 146

SHRECK, Joseph M.; s/o Jacob & Nancy SHRECK; 27y; sgl; farm hand; b. & res. FredVA; m. 18 Jul 1867 at Bruce Town to CRIM, Maria Jane; d/o Jacob & Eliza CRIM; 25y; sgl; b. & res. ClrkVA; (lic) 17 Jul 1867; p. 38

SHROUT, Lewis; s/o Kilian & Ann SHROUT; 22y; sgl; farmer; b. & res. ClrkVA; m. 9 Jan 1866 at residence of Wm. HEDGES in ClrkVA to POPE, Ann Virginia; d/o Conrad & Mary Marg't. POPE; 19y; sgl; b. & res. ClrkVA; (lic) 8 Jan 1866; consent of bride's father in person; p. 6

SHRYOCK, Walter R.; s/o John M. & Jane E. SHRYOCK; 24y; sgl; carpenter; b. FredVA; res. ClrkVA; m. 2 Dec 1880 at Berryville to SHACKLEFORD, Margaret; d/o E. & Hellen SHACKLEFORD; 25y; sgl; b. & res. ClrkVA; (lic) 2 Dec 1880; p. 29

SHUGERT, Rezin D.; s/o Reason & Elizabeth PULLIAM [SHUGERT]; 25y; sgl; sadle & harness maker; b. JeffWVA; res. ClrkVA; m. 18 Nov 1879 at ClrkVA to PULLIAM, Rhoda E.; d/o Mathew & Eliza PULLIAM; 22y; sgl; b. & res. ClrkVA; (lic) 17 Nov 1879; p. 8

SIMS, Charles (col); s/o Hannibal & Winney; 26y; sgl; farm hand; b. LdnVA; res. ClrkVA; m. 20 May 1866 at Dr. Wm. D. McGUIRE's farm to PAGE, Lucy Ann (col); d/o __ & Lucy; 23y; sgl; b. & res. ClrkVA; (lic) 19 May 1866; p. 11

SLACK, James W.; s/o A. H. & Belinda SLACK; 27y last Feb; sgl; miller; b. LdnVA; res. FqrVA; m. 24 Sep 1868 at James M. CHAPPELL's east of Shenandoah River to CHAPPELL, Amanda M.; d/o James M. & Susan CHAPPELL; 28y; sgl; b. LdnVA; res. ClrkVA; (lic) 22 Sep 1868; p. 67

SLOW, C. Henry (col); s/o David and Penny SLOW (col); 42y; sgl; restoraunt keeper; b. Louisa Co.; res. ClrkVA; m. 15 Jan 1867 at Berryville to POTTER, Fannie (col); d/o George and Ann POTTER (col); 22y; sgl; b. & res. ClrkVA; (lic) 14 Jan 1867; p. 29

SLOW, Thomas (col); s/o David & Penny SLOW (col); 36y; sgl;
farm hand; b. Louisa Co. Va; res. ClrkVA; m. 18 Jan 1868 at
ClrkVA to FISHER, Milley (col); d/o Frederick & Alsey
FISHER (col); 33y; sgl; b. & res. ClrkVA; (lic) 15 Jan 1868; p.
54
SMALLWOOD, Bushrod; s/o Burr & Eliza SMALLWOOD; 22y;
sgl; farmer; b. & res. ClrkVA; m. 13 Sep 1877 at ClrkVA to
LLOYD, Margaret; d/o Laurence & Betty LLOYD; 22y; sgl; b.
& res. ClrkVA; (lic) 13 Sep 1877; (oath) James A. LANHAM
that Margaret is over 21 years of age.; p. 221
SMALLWOOD, George; s/o Thomas & Martha E. SMALLWOOD;
20y; sgl; farmer; b. & res. LdnVA; m. 12 Nov 1874 to
KNIGHT, Mary E.; d/o George and ___ KNIGHT; 20y; sgl; b.
& res. ClrkVA; (lic) 7 Nov 1874; p. 168
SMALLWOOD, John F.; s/o Buckner & Louisa SMALLWOOD;
22y; sgl; farmer; b. & res. ClrkVA; m. 13 Nov 1881 at ClrkVA
to LANHAM, Annie; d/o ___ & Precilla LANHAM; 21y; sgl; b.
& res. ClrkVA; (lic) 11 Nov 1881; p. 51
SMALLWOOD, Thomas W.; s/o Thomas & Martha
SMALLWOOD; 22y; sgl; farmer; b. & res. ClrkVA; m. 24 Jan
1878 at ClrkVA to HARRIS, Caroline; d/o Joseph & Elizabeth
HARRIS; 22y; sgl; b. FqrVA; res. ClrkVA; (lic) 23 Jan 1878; p.
231
SMITH, Chas. H.; s/o Treadwell & Ann C. SMITH; 33y; sgl;
farmer; b. Berryville; res. ClrkVA; m. 4 Apr 1866 at Berryville
to BLACKBURN, Eliza S.; d/o R. S. & Ellen BLACKBURN;
25y; sgl; b. Jefferson Co.; res. Berryville; (lic) 3 Apr 1866; p. 9
SMITH, Chas. W. (col); s/o James & Eliza SMITH; 27y; sgl; farm
hand; b. FredVA; res. ClrkVA; m. 10 Jul 1884 at Millwood to
GORDON, Nannie; d/o Frank & ___ GORDON; 22y; sgl; b. &
res. ClrkVA; (lic) 9 Jul 1884; p. 103
SMITH, J. Rice; s/o J. S. & Rebecca A. SMITH; 25y; sgl; clerk; b.
ClrkVA; res. Danville Illinois; m. 4 Jun 1872 at Berryville to
SHEPHERD, Sallie C.; d/o Harry & Sarah SHEPHERD; 24y;
sgl; b. & res. ClrkVA; (lic) 4 Jun 1872; p. 130
SMITH, John H. (col); s/o John & Matilda SMITH; 24y; sgl;
farmer; b. LdnVA; res. ClrkVA; m. 4 Mar 1880 at ClrkVA to
JONES, Phebe (col); d/o Nathan & Phebe JONES; 22y; sgl;
b. FredVA; res. ClrkVA; (lic) 4 Mar 1880; p. 17
SMITH, John; s/o Lewis R. & M. SMITH; 24y; sgl; miller; b. & res.
FredVA; m. 26 Mar 1876 at father's residence ClrkVA to ERB,

Mary Jane; d/o Christopher & Mary Ellen ERB; 23y; sgl; b.
Maryland; res. ClrkVA; (lic) 24 Mar 1876; p. 198

SMITH, Joseph H. (col); s/o Thomas & Pricilla SMITH; 22y; sgl;
farm hand; b. & res. ClrkVA; m. 22 Mar 1883 at ClrkVA to
HUNTER, Sarah M. (col); d/o Henry & Millie HUNTER; 21y;
sgl; b. & res. ClrkVA; (lic) 21 Mar 1883; p. 79

SMITH, Manson P.; s/o Benj. F. and Amelia SMITH; 34y; sgl;
farmer; b. Hampshire Co. Va; res. Pettiss Co. Missouri; m. 10
Jan 1871 at ClrkVA to AFFLICK, Nannie V.; d/o James &
Catharine AFFLICK; 29y; sgl; b. FredVA; res. ClrkVA; (lic) 10
Jan 1870 [71]; p. 107

SMITH, Michael; s/o James & Ann C. SMITH; 30y; sgl; on public
works; b. Ireland; res. ClrkVA; m. 21 Feb 1872 at ClrkVA to
HARPER, Jane; d/o Joshua & Lucy HARPER; 20y; sgl; b.
RappVA; res. ClrkVA; (lic) not given; p. 126

SMITH, R. Emmett; s/o Walter A. & Charlotte SMITH; 40y; wid;
farmer; b. & res. FqrVA; m. 1 Mar 1866 at Berryville to
BOWSER, Catharine V.; d/o Christian & Lucy BOWSER; 24y;
sgl; b. & res. ClrkVA; (lic) 28 Feb 1866; p. 7

SMITH, Richard (col); s/o Rich'd. & Mary SMITH (col); 22y; sgl;
farm hand; b. RappVA; res. ClrkVA; m. 20 Jun 1868 at
Berryville to LEE, Polly (col); d/o not known; 21y; wid; b.
Lynchburg; res. ClrkVA; (lic) not given; p. 62

SMITH, Zachariah (col); s/o J. W. & M. J. SMITH; not given; sgl;
farm hand; b. & res. ClrkVA; m. 20 Dec 1877 at Berryville to
COBB, Jennett (col); d/o F[r]ank & Julia COBB; not given; sgl;
b. North Carolina; res. ClrkVA; (lic) 19 Dec 1877; p. 228

SNYDER, John G.; s/o Daniel & Cynthia SNYDER; 34y; sgl;
farmer; b. Fredrick Co.; res. ClrkVA; m. 5 Nov 1867 at
Berryville to HICKS, Anna Louisa; d/o Live [Levi] & Sallie
HICKS; 30y; sgl; b. Jefferson Co.; res. ClrkVA; (lic) 30 Oct
1867; p. 45

SNYDER, Thomas M.; s/o Daniel & Scintha SNYDER; 25y; sgl;
farmer; b. JeffVA; res. ClrkVA; m. 11 Nov 1873 at bride's
residence to MARSHALL, Mary E.; d/o Alex'r. & Emily
MARSHALL; 26y; sgl; b. & res. ClrkVA; (lic) 10 Nov 1873; p.
153

SODEN, Ezekiel; s/o John & Lettie SODEN; 24y; sgl; farmer; b.
New Jersey; res. ClrkVA; m. 20 Nov 1879 at ClrkVA to
STUMP, Annie; d/o Simeon R. T. & Elizabeth STUMP; 23y;
sgl; b. & res. ClrkVA; (lic) 20 Nov 1879; p. 8

SOWERS, Augustus W.; s/o Wm. B. & Bettie A. SOWERS; 21y; sgl; farmer; b. & res. ClrkVA; m. 13 May 1886 at Berryville to BRYAN, Minnie; d/o John & ___ BRYAN; 21y; sgl; b. & res. ClrkVA; (lic) not given; p. 136

SOWERS, Ellwood J.; s/o Wm. B. & Bettie SOWERS; 23y; sgl; farmer; b. & res. ClrkVA; m. 19 Nov 1885 at ClrkVA to SHACKLEFORD, Rebecca; d/o James H. & Mary L. SHACKLEFORD; 27y; sgl; b. & res. ClrkVA; (lic) 19 Nov 1885; p. 128

SOWERS, Walter H.; s/o Wm. B. & Betsy SOWERS; 23y; sgl; farmer; b. & res. ClrkVA; m. 17 Apr 1883 at ClrkVA to HESKETT, Wiliner V.; d/o Thomas & Harriet HESKETT; 25y; sgl; b. & res. ClrkVA; (lic) 17 Apr 1883; p. 81

SOWERS, William B. C.; s/o William and Catharine SOWERS; 38y; wid; farmer; b. & res. ClrkVA; m. 6 Nov 1866 at ClrkVA to TURLEY, Catharine K.; d/o Sylvester and Catharine TURLEY; 21y; sgl; b. RckhmVA; res. ClrkVA; (lic) 6 Nov 1866; p. 23

SPAULDING, Albin H.; s/o Geo. S. & Catharine SPAULDING; 24y; sgl; farmer; b. & res. ClrkVA; m. 1 Mar 1883 at ClrkVA to THOMPSON, Louisa Jane; d/o Wm. F. & A. THOMPSON; 20y; sgl; b. & res. ClrkVA; (lic) 27 Feb 1883; p. 78

SPECK, Joseph L.; s/o Frederick & Susan SPECK; 23y; sgl; farm; b. & res. FredVA; m. 27 Oct 1875 at bride's father's ClrkVA to SHAFFER, Annie R.; d/o Hen[r]y & Eliza SHAFFER; 19y; sgl; b. Lancaster Co. Pa; res. ClrkVA; (lic) 26 Oct 1875; p. 189

SPILLMAN, Charles; s/o Jeremiah & Margaret SPILMAN; 28y; sgl; farmer; b. New Brunswick; res. ClrkVA; m. Monday 13 Feb 1871 at Winchester Va to CONWAY, Ellen; d/o James & Catharine CONWAY; 25y; sgl; b. Ireland; res. ClrkVA; (lic) 11 Feb 1871; p. 109

SPRINT, Thomas H.; s/o John W. & Emily SPRINT; 29y; sgl; merchant; b. & res. ClrkVA; m. 26 May 1886 at Berryville to HUMSTON, Mamie; d/o Benj. F. & Fannie HUMSTON; 23y; sgl; b. ShenVA; res. ClrkVA; (lic) 26 Mar 1886; p. 137

SPROUTS, James William (col); s/o ___ & Emily SPROUTS; 36y; wid; well digger; b. FredVA.; res. ClrkVA; m. 24 Nov 1881 at Berryville to HALL, Sarah Margaret (col); d/o Robert & Lucy HALL; 21y; sgl; b. & res. ClrkVA; (lic) 22 Nov 1881; p. 52

STADDEN, George; s/o John & Elizabeth STADDEN; 25y; sgl; farmer; b. Milton Pennsylvania; res. Williamsport Pennsylvania; m. 20 Mar 1872 at residence of bride's father to HAWTHORNE, Ella V.; d/o John B. & Ellen HAWTHORNE; 23y; sgl; b. Lewisburg Pennsylvania; res. ClrkVA; (lic) 19 Nov 1872; p. 128
STAPLES, Bradford (col); s/o John & Carey A. STAPLES; 24y; sgl; hotel waiter; b. AlbmVA; res. Berryville; m. 26 Nov 1874 at Berryville to JACKSON, Sarah S. (col); d/o not given; 28y; wid; b. Boston Massachusetts; res. Berryville; (lic) 26 Nov 1874; p. 171
STARKEY, Geo. W.; s/o Benj. S. & Jane W. STARKEY; 28y; sgl; farmer; b. & res. ClrkVA; m. 3 Nov 1885 at Berryville to PIERCE, Mary J.; d/o Peter Mc & Margt. E. PIERCE; 29y; sgl; b. & res. ClrkVA; (lic) 3 Nov 1885; p. 126
STEEL, James A.; s/o John & Nancy STEEL; 56y; sgl; carpenter; b. FredVA; res. ClrkVA; m. 11 Jun 1872 at ClrkVA to OSBORN, Sarah A. A.; d/o Rolla & ___ OSBURN; 22y; sgl; b. FredVA; res. ClrkVA; (lic) 7 Jun 1872; p. 130
STEELE, John S.; s/o Thomas & Mary STEELE; 24y; sgl; carriage maker; b. & res. FredVA; m. 28 Dec 1882 at ClrkVA to KROUSE, Susan E.; d/o Joseph & Mary KROUSE; 22y; sgl; b. Washington Co Md; res. ClrkVA; (lic) 25 Dec 1882; p. 72
STEPHENS, Edwin A.; s/o Edwin A. & Martha B. STEPHENS; 21y; sgl; lawyer; b. Philadelphia; res. Hoboken New Jersey; m. 28 Oct 1879 at ClrkVA to LEWIS, Emily C.; d/o G. W. & Emily C. LEWIS; 21y; sgl; b. & res. ClrkVA; (lic) 20 Oct 1879; p. 6
STEPHUS, Robert H. (col); s/o Wm. H. & Laura STEPHUS; 25y; sgl; clerk in store; b. Caroline Co. Va; res. New York; m. 22 Dec 1880 at ClrkVA to BIRD, Elizabeth (col); d/o father not known, mother Ann PARKER; 19y; sgl; b. & res. ClrkVA; (lic) 21 Dec 1880; p. 31
STEVENS, John; s/o Edwin A. & Martha B. STEVENS; 26y; sgl; real estate business; b. & res. Hoboken New Jersey; m. 25 Jun 1883 at Grace Church Berryville to McGUIRE, Mary M.; d/o David H. & Eliza McGUIRE; 29y; sgl; b. & res. ClrkVA; (lic) 23 Jun 1883; p. 83
STEVENSON, Richard (col); s/o Edgar & Violet STEVENSON; 24y; sgl; laborer; b. & res. ClrkVA; m. Thursday 23 Sep 1875 at Berryville to JONES, Mary (col); d/o father dead, mother

Harriet JONES; 22y; sgl; b. & res. ClrkVA; (lic) 23 Sep 1875; p. 186

STEWART, Bushrod; s/o Bushrod & Mary STEWART; 24y; sgl; farmer; b. & res. JeffWVA; m. 17 Jan 1878 at Berryville to SWARTS, Mary Jane; d/o Charles & Isabellia STARTS [SWARTS]; 18y; sgl; b. & res. ClrkVA; (lic) 16 Jan 1878; father present consent given; p. 230

STEWART, Frank M.; s/o John R. & Carrie STEWART; 23y; sgl; farmer; b. BerkWVA; res. ClrkVA; m. 27 Feb 1883 at ClrkVA to CHAPMAN, Lizzie G.; d/o M. P. & ___ CHAPMAN; 22y; sgl; b. BerkWVA; res. ClrkVA; (lic) 26 Feb 1883; p. 78

STEWART, James H.; s/o Jno. L. & Jane E. STEWART; 23y; sgl; farm hand; b. JeffWVA; res. FredVA; m. 12 Oct 1882 at bride's residence to CARVER, Josephine; d/o Joseph & Fannie CARVER; 21y; sgl; b. FredVA; res. ClrkVA; (lic) 12 Oct 1882; p. 64

STEWART, Wilton R.; s/o John R. & Carolina C. STEWART; 27y; sgl; physician; b. BerkWVA; res. ClrkVA; m. 8 Sep 1881 at White Post to GRYMES, Rosalie L.; d/o ___ & ___ GRYMES; 21y; sgl; b. not given; res. ClrkVA; (lic) 6 Sep 1881; p. 46

STICKEL, Simon P.; s/o Simon & Amelia STICKEL; 27y; sgl; farmer; b. & res. ClrkVA; m. 9 Apr 1868 at ClrkVA to FINNELL, Columbia J.; d/o Jessee & Adaline FINNELL; 25y; sgl; b. RappVA; res. ClrkVA; (lic) 9 Apr 1868; p. 59

STICKELS, Joseph; s/o Henry & Betsy STICKELS; 22y; sgl; farmer; b. & res. ClrkVA; m. 23 Dec 1866 at ClrkVA to EDWARDS, Maria; d/o Henry and Mary Ann EDWARDS; 19y; sgl; b. & res. ClrkVA; (lic) 22 Dec 1866; bride's father being present; p. 27

STICKLE, Joseph A.; s/o Joseph & Harriet STICKLE; 27y; sgl; farm; b. & res. LdnVA; m. 16 Nov 1882 at Berryville to HOFF, Effa S.; d/o Humphrey & Malissa HOFF; 17y; sgl; b. FqrVA; res. ClrkVA; (lic) 16 Nov 1882; p. 67

STICKLER, William F.; s/o John S. & Jane W. STICKLER; 33y; sgl; sadler; b. Lynchburg; res. ClrkVA; m. 21 Feb 1867 at Paris to BROWN, Nannie J.; d/o Barnam & ___ SMALLWOOD; 27y; sgl; b. WrnVA; res. ClrkVA; (lic) 19 Feb 1867; p. 33

STICKLES, John A.; s/o Simon & Amelia E. STICKLES; 21y; sgl; farmer; b. & res. ClrkVA; m. 2 Jan 1872 at ClrkVA to KENNAN, Virginia B.; d/o Jas. H. & Susan R. KENNAN; 18y;

sgl; b. & res. ClrkVA; (lic) 2 Jan 1872; bride's father present;
p. 122
STICKLES, Joseph; s/o George & Jane STICKLES; 57y; wid;
farmer; b. LdnVA; res. ClrkVA; m. 19 Feb 1871 at ClrkVA to
WRIGHT, Susan; d/o James & Margaret COSTLELOW; 44y;
wid; b. WrnVA; res. ClrkVA; (lic) 17 Feb 1871; p. 109
STICKLES, Michael; s/o Henry & Betsy STICKLES; 24y; sgl;
farmer; b. FqrVA; res. ClrkVA; m. 29 Dec 1870 at ClrkVA to
DAVIS, Mary; d/o Samuel & Mary DAVIS; 23y; sgl; b.
Hampshire Co.; res. ClrkVA; (lic) 27 Dec 1870; p. 105
STICKLES, Simon J.; s/o Joseph & Harriet STICKLES; 23y; sgl;
farmer; b. & res. LdnVA; m. 16 Nov 1882 at Berryville to
HOFF, Mary J.; d/o Humphrey & Malissa HOFF; 19y; sgl; b.
FqrVA; res. ClrkVA; (lic) 16 Nov 1882; p. 67
STICKLES, Thomas S.; s/o Simon S. & Elizabeth STICKLES;
22y; sgl; farmer; b. & res. ClrkVA; m. 14 Jul 1868 at Berryville
to GRUBBS, Elizabeth A.; d/o William & Lucinda GRUBBS;
22y; sgl; b. & res. ClrkVA; (lic) 14 Jul 1868; p. 63
STICKLES, Thomas W.; s/o Henry & Elizabeth STICKLES; 28y;
wid; farmer; b. LdnVA; res. ClrkVA; m. 24 Jan 1875 at ClrkVA
to HAWS, Maggie; d/o Asa & Elizabeth HAWS; 21y; sgl; b.
LdnVA; res. ClrkVA; (lic) 22 Jan 1875; written permission by
Mrs. Elizabeth HAWS for Maggie HAWS 22 years old.; p. 175
STICKLEY, Charles M.; s/o Samuel STICKLEY & Mary E.
STICKLE[Y]; 22y; sgl; farmer; b. ShenVA; res. FredVA; m. 6
Apr 1875 at bride's residence to PANGLE, Mary A.; d/o Isaac
N. & Mary PANGLE; 24y; sgl; b. FredVA; res. ClrkVA; (lic) 6
Apr 1875; p. 177
STOLLE, Lewis Vanner; s/o William F. & Charlotte STOLLE;
24y; sgl; mechanic; b. & res. Berryville; m. Thursday 11 Nov
1875 at Methodist Church Berryville to GREENWALDT,
Sarah Elizabeth; d/o Adam & Barbara GREENWALDT; 22y;
sgl; b. & res. Berryville; (lic) 11 Nov 1875; p. 191
STRANGE, James (col); s/o John & Jane STRANGE (col); 21y;
wid; farm hand; b. & res. ClrkVA; m. 5 Oct 1867 at Millwood
to SMITH, Helen (col); d/o James & Ann SMITH (col); 21y;
wid; b. & res. ClrkVA; (lic) 5 Oct 1867; p. 43
STRANGE, John (col); s/o Rubin & Betsey STRANGE; 30y; wid;
farm hand; b. & res. ClrkVA; m. 13 Jan 1867 at White Post to
WILLIAMS, Clora (col); d/o Macklin & Evaline WILLIAMS;
25y; sgl; b. & res. ClrkVA; (lic) 12 Jan 1867; p. 28

STRANGE, Reulen [Reuben?] (col); s/o John & Cloe STRANGE; 23y; sgl; farm hand; b. & res. ClrkVA; m. 14 Aug 1879 at White Post to WILLIAMS, Catharine (col); d/o Sandy & Harriet WILLIAMS; 17y; sgl; b. & res. ClrkVA; (lic) 14 Aug 1879; consent given by her father in person; p. 262

STRANGE, Stephen (col); s/o John & Jane STRANGE (col); 22y; sgl; farm hand; b. & res. ClrkVA; m. 29 Oct 1870 at ClrkVA to WILLIAMS, Millie A. (col); d/o Edward & Sallie WILLIAMS (col); 21y; sgl; b. & res. ClrkVA; (lic) 29 Oct 1870; p. 102

STRANGE, Stephen (col); s/o John & Jane STRANGE; 26y; wid; farm hand; b. & res. ClrkVA; m. 3 Mar 1874 at ClrkVA to ROBINSON, Delilah (col); d/o Henry & Louisa ROBINSON; 21y; sgl; b. & res. ClrkVA; (lic) 23 Feb 1874; p. 158

STRIBLING, Edward M.; s/o John and Ann STRIBLING; 23y; sgl; farmer; b. Staunton Va; res. ClrkVA; m. 11 Jan 1883 at Berryville to KOUNSLAR, Lydia; d/o Randolph & Elizabeth J. KOUNSLAR; 26y; sgl; b. & res. ClrkVA; (lic) 10 Jan 1883; p. 75

STROTHER, Franklin; s/o Geo. W. & Ann STROTHER; 21y; sgl; farm hand; b. LdnVA; res. ClrkVA; m. 7 Nov 1878 at Berrys ferry to BOWEN, Mary; d/o not known; 22y; sgl; b. & res. not known; (lic) 6 Nov 1878; p. 243

STROTHER, Jacob (col); s/o Jackson & Mary STROTHER; 25y; sgl; farm hand; b. PageVA; res. ClrkVA; m. 10 Jan 1884 at ClrkVA to TOLIVER, Florence M. (col); d/o Benjamin & Lucinda TOLIVER; 23y; sgl; b. RckhmVA; res. ClrkVA; (lic) 10 Jan 1884; p. 93

SULLIVAN, Jas.; s/o Owen & Mary F. SULLIVAN; 26y; sgl; labourer; b. New York; res. Winchester Va; m. 1 Apr 1875 at Winchester Va to RUSSELL, Mollie; d/o Michael & Nancy RUSSELL; 22y; sgl; b. & res. ClrkVA; (lic) 31 Mar 1875; p. 177

SWANN, Philip H.; s/o Philip & Ann SWANN; 25y; sgl; farmer; b. & res. FredVA; m. 18 Dec 1866 at Berryville to CROW, M. Ellouisa; d/o Thos. H. & Frances CROW; not given; sgl; b. ClrkVA; res. Berryville; (lic) 17 Dec 1866; p. 26

SWARTZ, Franklin; s/o Conrad & Olevia SWARTZ; 40y; wid; farmer; b. & res. FredVA; m. 26 Jan 1869 at ClrkVA to GORDON, Lucy; d/o ___ & ___ CARPER; 30y; wid; b. FredVA; res. ClrkVA; (lic) 26 Jan 1869; p. 75

SWARTZ, Franklin; s/o George & Sarah SWARTZ; 20y; sgl; farmer; b. FredVA; res. ClrkVA; m. 10 Oct 1872 at Winchester Va to LESTER, Adaline; d/o John & Eliza LESTER; 19y; sgl; b. North Carolina; res. ClrkVA; (lic) not given; mother of the groom present & brother of the bride present; p. 134

SWARTZ, Thomas N.; s/o Frank & Rebecca SWARTZ; 21y; sgl; farmer; b. & res. ClrkVA; m. 3 Apr 1879 at ClrkVA to POPP, Mary; d/o Michael & Elizabeth POPP; 21y; sgl; b. & res. ClrkVA; (lic) 2 Apr 1879; p. 256

SWIMLEY, Martin Miller; s/o Martin & Jane SWIMLEY; 31y; sgl; farmer; b. JeffWVA; res. ClrkVA; m. 20 Jan 1885 at Berryville to CARTER, Mattie B.; d/o Wm. H. & Charlotte A. CARTER; 20y; sgl; b. & res. ClrkVA; (lic) 17 Jan 1885; bride's father present & gave consent; p. 116

SWINK, M. V.; s/o Washington & Malinda SWINK; 30y; sgl; farmer; b. & res. AugVA.; m. 27 Nov 1866 at ClrkVA to GREEN, Catharine; d/o Wm. & Mary GREEN; 20y; sgl; b. FqrVA; res. ClrkVA; (lic) 26 Nov 1866; Benj. R. GREEN makes application; p. 24

SYRUS, Abraham (col); s/o Isaac & Jane SYRUS; 39y; wid; carpenter; b. PageVA; res. ClrkVA; m. 19 Dec 1884 at Millwood to JACKSON, Amanda (col); d/o ___ & Catharine JACKSON; 22y; sgl; b. RappVA; res. ClrkVA; (lic) 17 Dec 1884; p. 114

TALLY, Samuel Henry; s/o John & Barbary TALLY; 23y; sgl; farmer; b. LdnVA; res. ClrkVA; m. Thursday 10 Oct 1878 at ClrkVA at Hezekiah MARPLE's residence to CLEM, Sarah Amanda; d/o Michael & Sarah CLEM; 18y; sgl; b. FredVA; res. ClrkVA; (lic) 10 Oct 1878; Hezekiah MARPLE with whom she has been living since childhood is present with her mother's consent; p. 241

TANQUARY, Charles W.; s/o James & Lutia TANQUARY; 25y; sgl; farmer; b. & res. FredVA; m. date not given at ClrkVA to RICHARD, Mary E.; d/o Jacob & Harriet RICHARD; 26y; sgl; b. & res. FredVA; (lic) 25 Nov 1878; p. 245

TANQUARY, William W.; s/o James & Maria TANQUARY; 35y; sgl; miller; b. LdnVA; res. FredVA; m. 7 Apr 1868 at bride's residence to GRANT, Emma Frances; d/o John Lee & Catharine GRANT; 24y; sgl; b. & res. ClrkVA; (lic) 6 Apr 1868; p. 59

TAPSCOTT, Henry C.; s/o Robert and Lucy TAPSCOTT; 33y; sgl; farmer; b. & res. ClrkVA; m. 17 Nov 1880 at ClrkVA to

SOWERS, Elizabeth F.; d/o Wm. B. C. & Lucy SOWERS; 21y; sgl; b. not known; res. ClrkVA; (lic) 17 Nov 1880; p. 29
TAPSCOTT, James E.; s/o Robert & Lucy TAPSCOTT; 24y; sgl; farmer; b. & res. ClrkVA; m. 27 Apr 1882 at ClrkVA to STICKLES, Henrietta; d/o Henry & Susan STICKLES; 19y; sgl; b. & res. ClrkVA; (lic) 26 Apr 1882; consent given; p. 59
TAPSCOTT, Joseph Baker (col); s/o Robert & Lucy TAPSCOTT; 31y; sgl; farmer; b. & res. ClrkVA; m. 28 Jan 1875 at bride's residence to ALEXANDER, Amanda R. (col); d/o Jas. F. & Jane ALEXANDER; 23y; sgl; b. LdnVA; res. ClrkVA; (lic) 27 Jan 1875; p. 175
TAPSCOTT, William C. R.; s/o N. B. & E. V. TAPSCOTT; 35y; sgl; green grocing; b. Buckingham Co. Va; res. ClrkVA; m. 21 Dec 1880 at Berryville to CRAMPTON, Mattie C.; d/o ___ & ___ KIGER; 28y; wid; b. FredVA; res. ClrkVA; (lic) 21 Dec 1880; p. 31
TATE, George (col); s/o Lee & Hannah TATE; 27y; sgl; farm hand; b. & res. JeffWVA; m. 15 Jan 1874 at ClrkVA to CHAPMAN, Hettie (col); d/o not given; 26y; sgl; b. & res. ClrkVA; (lic) 13 Jan 1874; p. 156
TATE, Meade (col); s/o Nathan & Martha TATE; 23y; sgl; farm hand; b. Harrisburg, Pa; res. ClrkVA; m. 8 Oct 1885 at ClrkVA to McCARD, Rose (col); d/o Mon. & Kate McCARD; 22y; sgl; b. JeffWVA; res. ClrkVA; (lic) 8 Oct 1885; p. 125
TAVENNER, John W.; s/o Eli & Sarah TAVENNER; 32y; sgl; farmer; b. LdnVA; res. ClrkVA; m. Thursday 19 Mar 1868 at Berryville to SOWERS, Alberta A.; d/o Fielding L. & ___ SOWERS; 28y; sgl; b. & res. ClrkVA; (lic) 19 Mar 1868; p. 57
TAYLOR, Albert S.; s/o John H. & Margaret A. TAYLOR; 39y; sgl; contractor; b. FredVA; res. ClrkVA; m. 20 Jan 1885 at bride's residence to GAUNT, S. Jannett; d/o Martin & Jane GAUNT; 37y; sgl; b. & res. ClrkVA; (lic) 17 Jan 1885; p. 117
TAYLOR, Alexander (col); s/o Cha[r]les & Sylvia TAYLOR; 31y; sgl; farm hand; b. PageVA; res. ClrkVA; m. 28 Oct 1874 at ClrkVA to STRANGE, Nelly (col); d/o Henry & Jennett STRANGE; 22y; sgl; b. & res. ClrkVA; (lic) 28 Oct 1874; p. 167
TAYLOR, Belford (col); s/o Jack & Rachael TAYLOR (col); 44y; wid; farm head; b. & res. ClrkVA; m. 26 Jan 1868 at ClrkVA to WILLIAMS, Kitty (col); d/o Alexander & Patty LEWIS (col); 29y; wid; b. & res. ClrkVA; (lic) 4 Jan 1868; p. 51

TAYLOR, Belford (col); s/o John and Harriet TAYLOR; 19y; sgl; farm hand; b. & res. ClrkVA; m. 12 Dec 1878 at ClrkVA to NORRIS, Ginnie (col); d/o Harry and Lucy NORRIS; 21y; sgl; b. & res. ClrkVA; (lic) 12 Dec 1878; mother of Belford TAYLOR present & asked that the license be issued; p. 247
TAYLOR, Charles (col); s/o Charles TAYLOR & Harriett TAYLOR; 21y; sgl; farm hand; b. & res. ClrkVA; m. 29 Dec 1885 at ClrkVA to DOLEMAN, Mollie (col); d/o Jake and Maria DOLEMAN; 18y; sgl; b. & res. ClrkVA; (lic) 29 Dec 1885; consent given; p. 132
TAYLOR, David (col); s/o John and Harriet TAYLOR; 21y; sgl; farm hand; b. & res. ClrkVA; m. 9 Feb 1882 at ClrkVA to BARBER, Emily (col); d/o ___ & Pattee BARBER; 21y; sgl; b. & res. ClrkVA; (lic) 9 Feb 1882; p. 55
TAYLOR, Guy (col); s/o David & Martha TAYLOR; 23y; sgl; farm hand; b. & res. ClrkVA; m. 15 Oct 1873 at ClrkVA to GREEN, Caroline (col); d/o Lewis & ___ GREEN; 21y; sgl; b. BerkVA; res. ClrkVA; (lic) 15 Oct 1873; p. 151
TAYLOR, Jacob (col); s/o Peter & Susan TAYLOR; 52y; wid; farm hand; b. Roanoke Co. Va; res. ClrkVA; m. 19 Dec 1876 at White Post to STRANGE, Jane (col); d/o not known; 52y; wid; b. & res. ClrkVA; (lic) 19 Dec 1876; p. 211
TAYLOR, James (col); s/o Abel & Tenah TAYLOR; 30y; sgl; farm hand; b. LdnVA; res. ClrkVA; m. 11 Feb 1874 at Berryville to FAIRFAX, Lavinia (col); d/o Abraham FAIRFAX & ___; 25y; sgl; b. & res. ClrkVA; (lic) 11 Feb 1874; p. 157
TAYLOR, Robert (col); s/o Henry & Patsy TAYLOR; 23y; sgl; labourer; b. JeffWVA; res. ClrkVA; m. 19 Dec 1883 at Berryville to THOMAS, Laura (col); d/o Harry & Jane THOMAS; 22y; sgl; b. & res. ClrkVA; (lic) 19 Dec 1883; p. 90
TAYLOR, Thornton (col); s/o David & Martha TAYLOR; 23y; sgl; farm hand; b. & res. JeffWVA; m. 3 Aug 1878 at ClrkVA to PARKER, Rachel (col); d/o ___ & Susan PARKER; 21y; sgl; b. JeffWVA; res. ClrkVA; (lic) 3 Aug 1878; p. 236
TEETES, David; s/o Jacob and Barbara TEETES; 21y; sgl; farmer; b. Hardy Co.; res. ClrkVA; m. 8 Nov 1866 at Berryville to WILSON, Rachel; d/o Isaac & Eliza WILSON; 25y; sgl; b. Jefferson Co.; res. ClrkVA; (lic) 8 Nov 1866; p. 22
TEETS, Laban W.; s/o Jacob TEETS & Barbara TEETS; 23y; sgl; farmer; b. Hardy Co.; res. ClrkVA; m. 7 Jun 1866 at Rev'd. Chas. WHITE to WILSON, Virginia; d/o Isaac & Eleza

WILSON; 16y; sgl; b. Hardy Co.; res. ClrkVA; (lic) 5 June 1866; p. 13

TEMPLEMAN, James E.; s/o Nathaniel & Deihlea TEMPLEMAN; 32y; sgl; farmer; b. FqrVA; res. ClrkVA; m. 19 Dec 1871 at ClrkVA to RILEY, Sarah M.; d/o Moses & Sarah RILEY; 23y; sgl; b. WrnVA; res. ClrkVA; (lic) not given; p. 121

THARP, Benjamin F.; s/o Jas. R. & Malinda THARP; 22y; sgl; farmer; b. Hardy Co. W Va; res. ClrkVA; m. 25 Mar 1885 at Berryville to FOX, Lucy Ann; d/o Jas. Wm. & Ann Susan FOX; 18y; sgl; b. WrnVA; res. ClrkVA; (lic) 24 Mar 1885; p. 119

THARP, William H.; s/o Jonnathon and Elizabeth THARP; 22y; sgl; farmer; b. Hardy Co. W. Va; res. ClrkVA; m. 17 Nov 1875 at ClrkVA to BUSH, Martha Ellen; d/o Chas. A. & Eliza Jane BUSH; 21y; sgl; b. FredVA; res. ClrkVA; (lic) 16 Nov 1875; p. 192

THARPE, Joshua [also written as Joseph]; s/o Jonathan & Elizabeth THARPE; 21y; sgl; farmer; b. Hardy Co. W Va; res. ClrkVA; m. 30 Jul 1878 at Berryville to ROUTZONG, Lottie E.; d/o Ezra & Elizabeth ROUTZONG; 21y; sgl; b. Maryland; res. ClrkVA; (lic) 30 Jul 1878; p. 236

THOMAS, Albert C.; s/o Wm. & Nancy THOMAS; 21y; sgl; farmer; b. & res. LdnVA; m. 27 Dec 1883 at bride's residence to SHAFER, Betsy Ann; d/o Jno. T. & Dorcas Jane SHAFER; 15y; sgl; b. & res. ClrkVA; (lic) 22 Dec 1883; p. 91

THOMAS, Frank (col); s/o ___ & Viney TAYLOR; 21y; sgl; farm hand; b. Maryland; res. ClrkVA; m. 7 Jul 1886 at bride's residence to THOMAS [NEWMAN?, see parent's surname], Carrie (col); d/o ___ & ___ NEWMAN; 21y; sgl; b. LdnVA; res. ClrkVA; (lic) 6 Jul 1886; p. 140

THOMAS, Franklin (col); s/o Peter & Caroline THOMAS; 23y; sgl; farm hand; b. PageVA; res. ClrkVA; m. 14 Apr 1866 at Berryville to TAYLOR, Julia (col); d/o Charles TAYLOR & Sylvia; 25y; sgl; b. PageVA; res. ClrkVA; (lic) 13 Apr 1866; p. 10

THOMAS, James [also written as John] W.; s/o James M. & Harriet J. THOMAS; 23y; sgl; farmer; b. & res. BerkWVA; m. 18 Jan 1883 at ClrkVA to STEWART, Rosa M.; d/o John R. & C. C. STEWART; 23y; sgl; b. BerkWVA; res. ClrkVA; (lic) 18 Jan 1883; p. 75

THOMAS, Lewis (col); s/o Lewis & Polly THOMAS; 24y; sgl; farm hand; b. & res. ClrkVA; m. 17 Aug 1882 at ClrkVA to

WHEELER, Millie Ann (col); d/o James & Mary WHEELER; 18y; sgl; b. & res. ClrkVA; (lic) 17 Aug 1882; p. 62

THOMAS, Matthew (col); s/o Mack & Mary THOMAS (col); 24y; sgl; farm hand; b. & res. ClrkVA; m. 20 Jul 1871 at Berryville to WILLIAMS, Rebecca (col); d/o David & Charlotte WILLIAMS (col); 22y; sgl; b. & res. ClrkVA; (lic) 19 Jul 1871; p. 114

THOMPSON, Albert W.; s/o Albert & Nancy THOMPSON; 21y; sgl; farmer; b. & res. ClrkVA; m. 12 Jul 1883 at ClrkVA to LLOYD, Laura E.; d/o James L. & Elizabeth LLOYD; 20y; sgl; b. & res. ClrkVA; (lic) 9 Jul 1883; father's consent given in person; p. 84

THOMPSON, Caleb (col); s/o Anna THOMPSON (parents dead); 21y; sgl; farm hand; b. ShenVA; res. at David MEADE's near White Post; m. 25 Jul 1875 at White Post to WHITE, Laura Elizabeth (col); d/o Eliza WHITE (father dead); 20y; sgl; b. FqrVA; res. at David MEADE's near White Post; (lic) 23 Jul 1875; p. 183

THOMPSON, George N.; s/o Joseph & Clarissa F. THOMPSON; 23y; sgl; farmer; b. Madison Co. Va; res. ClrkVA; m. 31 May 1874 at Millwood to HILE, Nancy; d/o John & Mary HILE; 19y; sgl; b. Franklin Co. Pennsylvania; res. ClrkVA; (lic) 26 May 1874; father present & gave consent; p. 161

THOMPSON, James (col); s/o Newman & Rebecca THOMPSON (col); 24y; sgl; farm hand; b. WrnVA; res. ClrkVA; m. 6 Dec 1870 at Berryville to BELL, Lettie (col); d/o not known; 30y; wid; b. & res. ClrkVA; (lic) 6 Dec 1870; p. 104

THOMPSON, Jno. S.; s/o Isham & Emily E. THOMPSON; 23y; sgl; carpenter; b. Randolph Co. Georgia; res. ClrkVA; m. 8 Apr 1869 at LdnVA to BARTON, Tacy C.; d/o Hezekiel & Susan BARTON; 18y; sgl; b. & res. ClrkVA; (lic) 7 Apr 1869; bride's brother present when the license was issued; p. 80

THOMPSON, John H.; s/o Wm. F. & Maria Eliz'th THOMPSON; 22y; sgl; farmer; b. & res. ClrkVA; m. 17 Mar 1881 at LdnVA to BAYLES, Virginia; d/o Charles & Eliz'th BAYLES; 21y; sgl; b. & res. ClrkVA; (lic) 16 Mar 1881; p. 36

THOMPSON, John P.; s/o Baylis & Margaret THOMPSON; 24y; sgl; farmer; b. & res. ClrkVA; m. 28 Jan 1883 at ClrkVA to THOMPSON, Mary E.; d/o Baylis E. & Amanda V. THOMPSON; 19y; sgl; b. & res. ClrkVA; (lic) 22 Dec 1882; p. 71

THOMPSON, John S.; s/o John M. & Emily THOMPSON; 39y; wid; farmer; b. Randolph Co. Georgia; res. ClrkVA; m. 28 Aug 1883 at ClrkVA to HARRIS, Laura R.; d/o Joseph & Elizabeth HARRIS; 27y; sgl; b. LdnVA; res. ClrkVA; (lic) 27 Aug 1883; p. 85

THOMPSON, Philip (col); s/o Tasco & Francis THOMPSON; 27y; sgl; farm hand; b. & res. WrnVA; m. 21 Nov 1878 at Berryville to WILLIAMS, Comfort (col); d/o not known; 27y; wid; b. & res. WrnVA; (lic) 21 Nov 1878; p. 245

THOMPSON, Thomas; s/o Albert & Nancy THOMPSON; 21y; sgl; farmer; b. & res. ClrkVA; m. 6 Jan 1885 at ClrkVA to CHAPPELL, Nannie M.; d/o John & Vena CHAPPELL; 17y; sgl; b. & res. ClrkVA; (lic) 6 Jan 1885; consent of parents given in writing; p. 115

THOMPSON, Wm. T.; s/o Wm. B. & C. M. THOMPSON; 31y; wid; Presbyterian Minister; b. Frederick; res. Mars Bluff, Marion Co. S.C.; m. 11 Jun 1872 at Berryville to WHITE, Annie; d/o Jno. R. & ___ WHITE; 22y; sgl; b. LdnVA; res. ClrkVA; (lic) 10 Jun 1872; p. 130

THOMPSON, Zachariah; s/o Baylis & Margaret THOMPSON; 20y; sgl; farming; b. LdnVA; res. ClrkVA; m. 11 Aug 1880 at ClrkVA to McDONALD, Willie Lee; d/o Charles W. & Eliza McDONALD; 17y; sgl; b. WrnVA; res. ClrkVA; (lic) 10 Aug 1880; p. 24

THORNLEY, Jos. (col); s/o Joseph & Nancy; about 50y; wid; farmhand; b. & res. ClrkVA; m. 23 Dec 1865 at Paul PIERCE's in ClrkVA to BLACKBURN, Amanda (col); d/o not given; 35y; wid; b. & res. ClrkVA; (lic) 22 Dec 1865; p. 5

THORNTON, David (col); s/o ___ & Mary THORNTON; 33y; sgl; not given; b. & res. ClrkVA; m. 13 Aug 1885 at bride's residence to GRIGSBY, Susan (col); d/o Jack & Margaret GRIGSBY; 28y; sgl; b. & res. ClrkVA; (lic) 12 Aug 1885; 19 Aug 1885 this license returned by David THORNTON on account of his inability to marry; p. 124

THUSTON, Scott (col); s/o Benj. & Harriet THUSTON; 29y; sgl; labourer; b. & res. ClrkVA; m. 30 Oct 1884 at Berryville to YOUNG, Mary Elizabeth (col); d/o Moses & Sarah YOUNG; 22y; sgl; b. & res. ClrkVA; (lic) 30 Oct 1884; p. 109

TILFORD, John B.; s/o John B. & Catharine H. TILFORD; 23y; sgl; merchant; b. Lexington Ky; res. New York; m. 15 Dec 1869 at Berryville to HAMMOND, Florinda J.; d/o George W.

& Sarah A. HAMMOND; 23y; sgl; b. Winchester Va; res. Berryville; (lic) not given; p. 90

TILLETT, Thomas R.; s/o Samuel A. & Jane G. TILLETT; 36y; sgl; miller; b. LdnVA; res. ClrkVA; m. 17 Jan 1867 at bride's residence to RUSSELL, Mary Jane; d/o Thomas & Ellen G. RUSSELL; 38y; sgl; b. LdnVA; res. ClrkVA; (lic) 15 Jan 1867; p. 29

TIMBERLAKE, D. W.; s/o David & Elizabeth TIMBERLAKE; 30y; sgl; merchant; b. & res. FredVA; m. 8 Aug 1865 at Hill & Dale to TIMBERLAKE, Eliza S.; d/o M. S. & Sarah TIMBERLAKE; 31y; sgl; b. & res. ClrkVA; (lic) 7 Aug 1865; p. 1

TIMBERLAKE, William D.; s/o R. M. S. & Sarah TIMBERLAKE; 55y; wid; farmer; b. & res. ClrkVA; m. 3 Jul 1884 at ClrkVA to KERFOOT, Almira J.; d/o John & Elizabeth HOPPER; 55y; wid; b. RappVA; res. ClrkVA; (lic) 3 Jul 1884; p. 102

TINSMAN, Francis M.; s/o Henry & Nancey TINSMAN; 29y; wid; school teacher; b. & res. LdnVA; m. 24 Dec 1878 at ClrkVA to TRENARY, Sallie E.; d/o James F. & Letitia TRENARY; 25y; sgl; b. & res. LdnVA; (lic) 21 Dec 1878; p. 248

TOKAS, George (col); s/o Wm. & Abby TOKAS (col); 54y; wid; farm hand; b. FredVA; res. ClrkVA; m. 13 Mar 1869 at ClrkVA to LEWIS, Harriet (col); d/o not given; 40y; wid; b. & res. ClrkVA; (lic) 13 Mar 1869; p. 78

TOMBLIN, Jno. Thomas; s/o Snowden & Mary Jane TOMBLIN; 21y; sgl; farmer; b. & res. ClrkVA; m. 18 Mar 1869 at ClrkVA to LONGERBEAM, Eliz'th.; d/o ___ & Elizabeth LONGERBEAM; 23y; sgl; b. & res. ClrkVA; (lic) 16 Mar 1869; p. 79

TOMLIN, Wm.; s/o ___ & Sarah TOMLIN; 30y; sgl; cooper; b. & res. ClrkVA; m. 21 Oct 1873 at ClrkVA to STICKLES, Mary S.; d/o Simon & Milley STICKLES; 25y; sgl; b. & res. ClrkVA; (lic) 21 Oct 1873; p. 151

TRACEY, Ab (col); s/o Cyrus & Vina TRACY; 23y; sgl; farm hand; b. & res. ClrkVA; m. 25 May 1876 at ClrkVA to ROBINSON, Florence (col); d/o Saml. & Jane ROBINSON; 17y; sgl; b. & res. ClrkVA; (lic) 25 May 1876; p. 200

TRACY, Wm. (col); s/o ___ & Vina TRACY; 27y; sgl; farm hand; b. & res. ClrkVA; m. 9 Nov 1876 at ClrkVA to TRAVIS, Rebecca Frances (col); d/o Levi & ___ TRAVIS; 19y; sgl; b. & res. ClrkVA; (lic) 8 Nov 1876; p. 208

TRAVERSE, George W. (col); s/o John & Maria TRAVERSE; 21y; sgl; farm hand; b. FqrVA; res. ClrkVA; m. 23 Oct 1879 at

ClrkVA to ROBINSON, Isabella (col); d/o Samuel & Terisa ROBINSON; 17y; sgl; b. & res. ClrkVA; (lic) 21 Oct 1879; p. 5
TRAVERSE, Hays (col); s/o Hays & Melvina TRAVERSE; 25y; sgl; farm hand; b. FqrVA; res. ClrkVA; m. 30 Apr 1886 at ClrkVA to WILLIAMS, Alice; d/o John & Rose WILLIAMS; 25y; sgl; b. & res. ClrkVA; (lic) 21 Apr 1886; p. 135
TRAVIS, Willis (col); s/o Stephen & Susan TRAVIS; 23y; sgl; farm hand; b. WrnVA; res. FqrVA; m. 28 Dec 1886 at ClrkVA to WILLIAMS, Lila (col); d/o Geo. & Nancy WILLIAMS; 21y; sgl; b. & res. ClrkVA; (lic) 27 Dec 1886; p. 150
TRENT, Edward (col); s/o Wm. & Mary TRENT; 27y; wid; farm hand; b. AugVA; res. ClrkVA; m. 20 Aug 1884 at ClrkVA to BROWN, Indiana (col); d/o Geo. & Lucy BROWN; 21y; sgl; b. & res. ClrkVA; (lic) 15 Aug 1884; p. 104
TRIER, Lewis F.; s/o Christian & Margaret TRIER; not given; sgl; carpenter; b. Baltimore Md; res. not given; m. 24 Apr 1877 at Winchester Va to FENTON, Annie; d/o Dennis & Anni FENTON; not given; sgl; b. ClrkVA; res. not given; (lic) 10 Apr 1877; p. 216
TRUSSELL, Herbert H.; s/o Samuel & Joanna TRUSSELL; 21y; sgl; farmer; b. & res. ClrkVA; m. 8 Aug 1883 at ClrkVA to ROYSTON, Fannie M.; d/o Peter R. & Mary ROYSTON; 22y; sgl; b. & res. ClrkVA; (lic) 7 Aug 1883; p. 85
TRUSSELL, Howard; s/o Thomas & Jane TRUSSELL; 35y; sgl; farmer; b. LdnVA; res. FqrVA; m. 1 Sep 1868 at Charles TRUSSELL's to MOORE, Lucy E.; d/o Alfred P. & Lucinda MOORE; 20y; sgl; b. & res. ClrkVA; (lic) 31 Aug 1868; bride's brother was present when given; p. 65
TRUSSELL, Samuel M.; s/o Nimrod & Ann Eliza TRUSSELL; 30y the 23rd of next month; wid; farmer; b. & res. ClrkVA; m. 12 Oct 1865 (took place 13th) at residence of bride's father to MILEY, Sarah Margaret; d/o Moses G. and Airy MILEY; 19y; sgl; b. LdnVA; res. ClrkVA; (lic) 9 Oct 1865; consent of bride's father given in person; p. 3
TUCKER, George; s/o John R. & Elizabeth TUCKER; 23y; sgl; farmer; b. & res. Madison Co. Va; m. 15 Nov 1866 at Simeon YOWELL's to YOWELL, Ann Maria; d/o Simeon & Ann YOWELL; 22y; sgl; b. & res. ClrkVA; (lic) 14 Nov 1866; p. 23
TUMBLIN, Snowden F.; s/o Snowden & Mary J. TUMBLIN; 20y; sgl; farmer; b. LdnVA; res. ClrkVA; m. 16 Jan 1873 at ClrkVA to FOWLER, Sarah; d/o Wm. & Annie FOWLER; 15y; sgl; b. & res. ClrkVA; (lic) 13 Jan 1873; p. 141

TUMLIN, James W.; s/o Snowden & Mary Jane TUMLIN; 21y; sgl; farmer; b. & res. ClrkVA; m. 9 May 1867 at ClrkVA to SMALLWOOD, Rebecca Ann; d/o Burr & Louisa SMALLWOOD; 19y; sgl; b. & res. ClrkVA; (lic) 7 May 1867; by the written consent of bride's father filed; p. 34

TURNER, Anderson (col); s/o Stephen & Kitty TURNER; not given; sgl; farm hand; b. AlbmVA; res. ClrkVA; m. 14 Mar 1878 at ClrkVA to CARTER, Kitty (col); d/o Geo. & Rachel CARTER; not given; sgl; b. & res. ClrkVA; (lic) 14 Mar 1878; p. 232

TURNER, Charles D.; s/o Andrew J. & Rebecca TURNER; 21y; sgl; farm hand; b. PageVA; res. ClrkVA; m. 22 Oct 1878 at ClrkVA to HOFF, Martha E.; d/o Cornelius HOUGH; 36y; sgl; b. & res. ClrkVA; (lic) 22 Oct 1878; p. 243

TURPIN, William C.; s/o George B. & Elizabeth TURPIN; 24y; sgl; merchant; b. & res. Macon, Georgia; m. 27 Mar 1884 at Christ Church Millwood to NELSON, Evelyn; d/o Wm. W. and Mary A. NELSON; 22y; sgl; b. & res. ClrkVA; (lic) 25 Mar 1884; p. 98

TYMAN, George (col); s/o Alex. & Lucinda TYMAN; 34y; sgl; farm hand; b. Madison Co. Va; res. WrnVA; m. 28 Aug 1886 at ClrkVA to POLES, Julia (col); d/o Randolph & Elizabeth POLES; 23y; sgl; b. RappVA; res. ClrkVA; (lic) 28 Aug 1886; p. 142

TYSON, Jas. E.; s/o Nathan & M. E. TYSON; 49y; wid; merchant; b. & res. Baltimore City; m. 12 Jun 1867 at Berryville to WILLIAMS, Fannie E.; d/o Allen & Helen WILLIAMS; 35y; sgl; b. & res. ClrkVA; (lic) 27 May 1867; p. 35

VANDEVANTER, James H.; s/o Isaac & Mary VANDEVANTER; 42y; sgl; farmer; b. LdnVA; res. ClrkVA; m. 28 Oct 1868 at bride's residence ClrkVA to MORGAN, Emiline M.; d/o Benjamin & Martha MORGAN; 26y; sgl; b. & res. ClrkVA; (lic) 24 Oct 1868; p. 68

VANMELDUS, P. F.; s/o Peter & Rose VANMELDUS; 84y; wid; carpenter; b. Europe; res. Winchester Va; m. 13 Aug 1877 at not given to TAYLOR, Margaret; d/o Griffin & Catharine TAYLOR; 22y; sgl; b. & res. ClrkVA; (lic) 13 Aug 1877; p. 221

VERNON, Chas. H.; s/o Jno. A. & Lucinda VERNON; 38y; sgl; spoke manufacturer; b. New York; res. JeffWVA; m. 30 Apr 1871 at bride's residence to PRITCHARD, Mary; d/o Barney

& Ella PRITCHARD; 21y; sgl; b. & res. ClrkVA; (lic) 29 Apr 1871; p. 111
VOROUS, Benjamin W.; s/o Jacob B. & Margaret VOROUS; 23y; sgl; farmer; b. JeffWVA; res. ClrkVA; m. Thursday 4 Nov 1875 at Berryville to THOMPSON, Ann Eliza; d/o A. Jackson & Turissa THOMPSON; 20y; sgl; b. & res. ClrkVA; (lic) 3 Nov 1875; permission of bride's parents; p. 190
VOROUS, Francis M.; s/o Jacob B. & Margaret VOROUS; 25y; sgl; farmer; b. JeffWVA; res. ClrkVA; m. 4 Sep 1884 at ClrkVA to MYERS, Sarah Jane; d/o Abraham & Catharine MYERS; 18y; sgl; b. FredMD; res. ClrkVA; (lic) 3 Sep 1884; p. 105
VOROUS, Jacob W.; s/o Jacob B. & Margaret VOROUS; 33y; sgl; farmer; b. JeffWVA; res. ClrkVA; m. 23 Apr 1879 at ClrkVA to McCORMICK, Susan E.; d/o Oliver & Sarah Ann McCORMICK; 24y; sgl; b. & res. ClrkVA; (lic) 22 Apr 1879; p. 257
VOROUS, Milton M.; s/o Jacob B. & Margaret A. VOROUS; 25y; sgl; farmer; b. JeffVA; res. ClrkVA; m. 28 Nov 1872 at Millwood to YOWELL, Isabell R.; d/o Simeon & Ann YOWELL; 24y; sgl; b. & res. ClrkVA; (lic) 27 Nov 1872; p. 138
WAGELY, Mann F.; s/o David & Mary WAGELEY; 24y; sgl; miller; b. & res. JeffWVA; m. 19 Oct 1881 at ClrkVA to LIGHT, Florence V.; d/o Peter & ___ LIGHT; 26y; sgl; b. & res. ClrkVA; (lic) 19 Oct 1881; p. 48
WALKER, Bartlett (col); s/o John & Ellen WALKER; 23y; sgl; farm hand; b. & res. ClrkVA; m. 20 Apr 1882 at ClrkVA to WILLIAMS, Lydia (col); d/o George & Nancy WILLIAMS; 20y; sgl; b. & res. ClrkVA; (lic) 20 Apr 1882; father's consent given; p. 58
WALKER, Charles (col); s/o Paul & Judy WALKER; 21y; sgl; farm hand; b. Nelson Co. Va; res. ClrkVA; m. 31 Dec 1879 at ClrkVA to STRANGE, Julia (col); d/o ___ & Lucy HALL; 21y; sgl; b. & res. ClrkVA; (lic) 31 Dec 1879; p. 13
WALKER, George F.; s/o James & Rebecca WALKER; 35y; wid; farmer; b. JeffWVA; res. ClrkVA; m. 12 May 1880 at ClrkVA to HELVESTINE, Judy; d/o Lewis & Elizabeth HELVESTINE; 27y; sgl; b. FredVA; res. ClrkVA; (lic) 11 May 1880; p. 20
WALKER, John (col); s/o John & Ellen WALKER (col); 26y; sgl; farm hand; b. & res. ClrkVA; m. 5 Dec 1872 at ClrkVA to HOLMES, Selie (col); d/o ___ & Maria HOLMES (col); 22y; sgl; b. & res. ClrkVA; (lic) 5 Dec 1872; p. 138

WALKER, John P.; s/o L. D. & E. A. WALKER; 37y; sgl; painter; b. & res. FqrVA; m. 26 Feb 1884 at Millwood to BENN, Fannie E.; d/o John & Annie BENN; 23y; sgl; b. WrnVA; res. ClrkVA; (lic) 25 Feb 1884; p. 95
WALKER, John Wesley; s/o Samuel & Jane WALKER; 22y; sgl; shoemaker; b. PageVA; res. Millwood; m. Tuesday 20 Jun 1876 at Millwood to WHITSELL, Virginia; d/o Betsy & John WHITSELL; 22y; sgl; b. ShenVA; res. Millwood; (lic) 20 Jun 1876; p. 202
WALKER, Joseph (col); s/o Paul & Judy WA[L]KER; 30y; sgl; farm hand; b. Nelson Co. Va; res. ClrkVA; m. 14 Jul 1880 at ClrkVA to CHRISTIAN, Julia (col); d/o Wm. & Jane CARTER; 21y; sgl; b. & res. ClrkVA; (lic) 14 Jul 1880; p. 23
WALKER, Shelton (col); s/o Paul & Judith WALKER (col); 22y; sgl; farm hand; b. Nelson Co. Va; res. ClrkVA; m. 22 Apr 1870 at Berryville to BANKS, Ellen (col); d/o ___ & Polly BANKS (col); 22y; sgl; b. RappVA; res. ClrkVA; (lic) not given; p. 95
WALKER, W. Woodson; s/o Cornelius & Margaret J. WALKER; 26y; sgl; Minister; b. Winchester Va; res. ShenVA; m. 29 Jun 1880 at bride's residence to WILLIAMS, Eliz'th P. G.; d/o Leroy P. & ___ WILLIAMS; 40y; sgl; b. & res. ClrkVA; (lic) 26 Jun 1880; p. 22
WALLACE, Jas. P.; s/o Jas. & Eliza WALLACE; 26y; sgl; tobacconist; b. Baltimore Maryland; res. Georgetown DC; m. 9 Apr 1873 at bride's residence to BRADY, Annie S.; d/o P. and J. M. BRADY; 20y; sgl; b. FredVA; res. ClrkVA; (lic) 8 Apr 1783; brides brother present when issued; p. 144
WALTER, John W.; s/o Henry G. & Hannah WALTER; 28y; sgl; farmer; b. & res. Frederick Co.; m. 27 May 1868 [covered by paper on microfilm] at bride's residence to BRANNON, Hattie; d/o Stewart & Mary BRANNON; 19y; sgl; b. & res. ClrkVA; (lic) 20 May 1869; bride's mother written consent given dated 24 May 1869; p. 82
WARE, John A. W.; s/o John & Eliz'th WARE; 65y; wid; farmer; b. & res. JeffWVA; m. 24 Jun 1886 at Millwood to DORAN, Jane; d/o Jas. & Mary DORAN; 58y; sgl; b. & res. ClrkVA; (lic) 24 Jun 1886; p. 138
WARE, Wm. J. Jefferson (col); s/o Addison & Vilett WARE; 56y; wid; farm hand; b. Nelson Co. Va; res. ClrkVA; m. 2 Dec 1886 at ClrkVA to THOMAS, Vina (col); d/o not known; 30y; sgl; b. & res. ClrkVA; (lic) 2 Dec 1886; p. 148

WARING, Wm.; s/o John & Elizabeth WARING; 22y; sgl; cooper; b. Prince Wm. Co.; res. ClrkVA; m. 2 Sep 1870 at ClrkVA to GRIFFY, Elizabeth; d/o Frank & Maria GRIFFY; 18y; sgl; b. Jefferson Co.; res. ClrkVA; (lic) 31 Aug 1870; Joseph CARPENTER at the request of her mother; p. 99
WARMUX, Jesse; s/o John & Rebecca WARMUX; 22y; sgl; farmer; b. & res. ClrkVA; m. 24 Sep 1884 at ClrkVA to MARPOLE, Asia; d/o Hezekiah & Maria MARPOLE; 24y; sgl; b. & res. ClrkVA; (lic) 20 Sep 1884; p. 106
WASHINGTON, George (col); s/o ___ & Abby WASHINGTON; 31y; sgl; farm hand; b. & res. ClrkVA; m. 11 Oct 1883 at White Post to HELMS, Lizzie (col); d/o Stepney & Mary HELMS; 23y; sgl; b. WrnVA; res. ClrkVA; (lic) 11 Oct 1883; p. 87
WATERS, Henry (col); s/o Thornton & Selva? WATER[S]; 22y; sgl; farm hand; b. PageVA; res. ClrkVA; m. 21 Dec 1875 at ClrkVA to JACKSON, Margaret (col); d/o William & Genetta JACKSON; 18y; sgl; b. & res. ClrkVA; (lic) 21 Dec 1875; p. 194
WATERS, Henry (col); s/o Thornton & Silvy WATERS; 30y; divorced; farm hand; b. PageVA; res. ClrkVA; m. 20 Dec 1883 at Berryville to THOMAS, Annie Maria; d/o Harry & Jane THOMAS; 30y; sgl; b. & res. ClrkVA; (lic) 20 Dec 1883; p. 90
WATERS, James W.; s/o Jefferson & Ellen WATERS; 21y; sgl; civil? engn'r?; b. FredVA; res. ClrkVA; m. 21 Apr 1881 at ClrkVA to CARPENTER, Ann E.; d/o Joseph & Jane CARPENTER; 17y; sgl; b. BerkWVA; res. ClrkVA; (lic) 20 Apr 1881; consent of parents given; p. 38
WATERS, Philip J.; s/o Sandford & Mary E. WATERS; 24y; sgl; carpenter; b. & res. FredVA; m. 21 Jan 1886 at ClrkVA to FELTNER, Peachy V.; d/o Geo. W. & Sidney A. FELTNER; 19y; sgl; b. JeffWVA; res. ClrkVA; (lic) 18 Jan 1885; p. 132
WEAVER, Robert (col); s/o Oliver & Eveline WEAVER; 27y; sgl; farm hand; b. & res. ClrkVA; m. 27 Dec 1882 at Berryville to ALLEN, Minerva (col); d/o both dead, not known; 30y; sgl; b. & res. ClrkVA; (lic) 27 Dec 1882; p. 73
WEBSTER, Daniel H. (col); s/o Daniel & Lucinda WEBSTER; 26y; wid; horse groom; b. FqrVA; res. ClrkVA; m. 3 Jul 1878 at Berryville to BELL, Sidney (col); d/o James & Lettie BELL; 22y; sgl; b. & res. ClrkVA; (lic) 29 Jun 1878; p. 235
WEBSTER, Robert (col); s/o Jacob & Easter WEBSTER; 30y; wid; farm hand; b. & res. ClrkVA; m. 5 Jul 1873 at Rev. Jos.

R. JONES' residence to BYRD, Mary (col); d/o John & Lethia BYRD; 22y; sgl; b. Winchester; res. ClrkVA; (lic) 1 Jul 1873; p. 147

WEDLOCK, Enock (col); s/o Geo. & Charity Beson WEDLOCK; 40y; wid; farm hand; b. WrnVA; res. ClrkVA; m. 15 Jul 1866 at White Post to OLFER, Ann (col); d/o __ and Fannie B. OLFER; 21y; sgl; b. & res. ClrkVA; (lic) 14 Jul 1866; p. 15

WELCH, Franklin E.; s/o Christopher & Patsey WELCH; 22y; sgl; farmer; b. WrnVA; res. JeffWVA; m. 10 Dec 1879 at ClrkVA to SMITH, Mary E.; d/o James W. & Elizabeth SMITH; 25y; sgl; b. JeffWVA; res. ClrkVA; (lic) 10 Dec 1879; p. 9

WELCH, Henry; s/o Timothy & Mary WELCH; 25y; sgl; railroad hand; b. FqrVA; res. ClrkVA; m. 22 Jun 1880 at bride's residence to CREAL, Sarah; d/o Harrison & Eliz'th CREAL; 24y; sgl; b. FqrVA; res. ClrkVA; (lic) 21 Jun 1880; p. 22

WELCH, John Samuel; s/o Christopher & Martha WELCH; 32y; sgl; farm hand; b. WrnVA; res. ClrkVA; m. 3 Oct 1878 at ClrkVA to WASHINGTON [also given as WHITTINGTON], Hannah Ellen; d/o John HODGE, mother not known by applicant; 28y; wid; b. JeffWVA; res. ClrkVA; (lic) 2 Oct 1878; p. 240

WELSTON, James; s/o J. & Sarah WELSTON; 41y; sgl; carpenter; b. Missouri; res. ClrkVA; m. 17 Aug 1876 at ClrkVA to PEYTON, Caroline; d/o Jordan & Mary Ann LAKE; 35y; wid; b. RappVA; res. ClrkVA; (lic) 16 Aug 1876; p. 204

WHITACRE, William T.; s/o Jas. F. & Margaret A. WHITACRE; 30y; sgl; farmer; b. & res. LdnVA; m. 15 Nov 1882 at bride's residence to MOORE, Sallie C.; d/o A. Mason & Susan MOORE; 27y; sgl; b. LdnVA; res. ClrkVA; (lic) 14 Nov 1882; p. 67

WHITE, James Henry (col); s/o Joe and Eliza WHITE; 26y; sgl; farm hand; b. FqrVA; res. ClrkVA; m. 27 Jul 1879 at near White Post to THOMPSON, Carlotta (col); d/o Anna THOMPSON, father's name not known; 21y; sgl; b. BerkVA; res. ClrkVA; (lic) 26 Jul 1879; p. 261

WHITE, Jno. R.; s/o John R. & Mary WHITE; 30y; sgl; bookkeeper; b. LdnVA; res. Sioux City Iowa; m. 12 Jun 1872 at Berryville to McGUIRE, Margaretta H.; d/o Wm. D. & Nancy McGUIRE; 28y; sgl; b. & res. ClrkVA; (lic) 10 Jun 1872; p. 131

WHITE, Simond (col); s/o Mark & Easter WHITE; 22y; sgl; farm hand; b. & res. ClrkVA; m. 27 Nov 1884 at ClrkVA to

CARTER, Jane (col); d/o Nat & Lizzie CARTER; 22y; sgl; b. & res. ClrkVA; (lic) 27 Nov 1884; p. 112
WHITE, Thomas (col); s/o Thos. & Louisa WHITE (col); 24y; sgl; farm hand; b. & res. ClrkVA; m. 19 Jun 1869 at ClrkVA to JONES, Fannie (col); d/o Saml. & Elizabeth JONES (col); 22y; sgl; b. & res. ClrkVA; (lic) 19 Jun 1869; p. 83
WHITING, Francis B.; s/o Francis B. & Mary B. WHITING; 57y; sgl; farmer; b. & res. ClrkVA; m. 27 Dec 1883 at ClrkVA to MEADE, Maria P.; d/o Frank B. & Mary MEADE; 37y; sgl; b. & res. ClrkVA; (lic) 24 Dec 1883; p. 92
WHITMORE, John C. W.; s/o Wm. W. & Julia WHITMORE; 25y; sgl; farmer; b. LdnVA; res. Jefferson Co.; m. 4 Apr 1878 at ClrkVA to JENKINS, Margaret V. [also given as Mary V.]; d/o Thomas & ___ JENKINS; 24y; sgl; b. & res. ClrkVA; (lic) 1 Apr 1878; p. 233
WHITTINGTON, Joseph A.; s/o David & Catharine WHITTINGTON; 23y; sgl; farmer; b. & res. ClrkVA; m. 17 Sep 1867 at ClrkVA to SMITH, Bettie; d/o James & Mary Ann SMITH; 21y; sgl; b. Jefferson Co.; res. ClrkVA; (lic) 16 Sep 1867; p. 41
WILEY, Charles; s/o James & ___ WILEY; 26y; sgl; farm hand; b. not given; res. ClrkVA; m. Wednesday 12 Feb 1879 at ClrkVA to MARSHALL, Mattie; d/o Alexander & Emily MARSHALL; 22y; sgl; b. & res. ClrkVA; (lic) 12 Feb 1879; p. 252
WILEY, Chas. F.; s/o Saml. & Elizabeth WILEY; 19y; sgl; farmer; b. & res. ClrkVA; m. 17 Sep 1868 at Thos. L. HUMPHREY's residence to SHAFFER, Sarah; d/o John Jackson & Miranda SHAFFER; 23y; sgl; b. & res. ClrkVA; (lic) 15 Sep 1868; groom's mother's consent given; letter indicates father Samuel WILEY is dead and he lives with his mother and taken care of her for years. Jesse MERCER who will accompany him can testify that Jackson SHAFFER says she is over 21 years. None of the parties can write their name. Signed Thos. L. HUMPHREY; p. 65
WILEY, Daniel W.; s/o Geo. W. & Mary WILEY; 23y; sgl; farmer; b. & res. ClrkVA; m. 7 Jan 1880 at ClrkVA to HART, Emma F.; d/o Thos. S. & Mary HART; 20y; sgl; b. & res. ClrkVA; (lic) 30 Dec 1879; p. 13
WILEY, George W. Jr.; s/o Hezekiah and Sarah Catherine WILEY; 20y; sgl; farmer; b. & res. ClrkVA; m. 24 Mar 1881 at LdnVA to BAYLES, Sarah F.; d/o Charles H. & Elizabeth

BAYLES; 22y; sgl; b. & res. ClrkVA; (lic) 23 Mar 1881; (oath) Geo. that there is no objection from any source; p. 37
WILEY, James F.; s/o Hezekiah & Susan C. WILEY; 24y; wid; cooper; b. & res. ClrkVA; m. 15 Dec 1868 at John WOLFE's Loudoun to HOUGH, Mary Jane; d/o Bushrod & Jane HOUGH; 21y; sgl; b. LdnVA; res. ClrkVA; (lic) 12 Dec 1868; p. 70
WILEY, Moses B.; s/o James & Nancy WILEY; 28y; sgl; farmer; b. FredVA; res. ClrkVA; m. 20 Sep 1876 at ClrkVA to WILEY, Lavenia E.; d/o Geo. W. & Mary WILEY; 18y; sgl; b. & res. ClrkVA; (lic) 20 Sep 1876; p. 206
WILLIAMS, Adolphus; s/o Branson & Lucy WILLIAMS; 21y; sgl; farmer; b. WrnVA; res. ClrkVA; m. 22 Dec 1869 at bride's residence to GROVES, Julia Ann; d/o James & Mary Jane GROVES; 21y; sgl; b. WrnVA; res. ClrkVA; (lic) 18 Dec 1869; p. 91
WILLIAMS, Albert (col); s/o John & Margaret WILLIAMS (col); 23y; sgl; farm hand; b. CulpVA; res. ClrkVA; m. 13 Jan 1869 at Berryville to CARTER, Margaret (col); d/o Smith & Adelaide CARTER (col); 22y; sgl; b. CulpVA; res. ClrkVA; (lic) 13 Jan 1869; p. 74
WILLIAMS, Anthony (col); s/o Edward & Rose WILLIAMS; 22y; sgl; laborer; b. & res. ClrkVA; m. Thursday 28 Dec 1876 at Berryville to WILLIAMS, Rosa (col); d/o Comfort WILLIAMS (father dead); 20y; sgl; b. & res. ClrkVA; (lic) 28 Dec 1876; mother's consent by her bro. Philip WILLIAMS.; p. 213
WILLIAMS, Bartlett (col); s/o Townshend & Mahala WILLIAMS; 21y; sgl; waiter; b. & res. ClrkVA; m. 7 Dec 1882 at Berryville to WADE, Nancy (col); d/o Thomas & Bettie WADE; 21y; sgl; b. & res. ClrkVA; (lic) 7 Dec 1882; p. 71
WILLIAMS, Charles H. (col); s/o Townsend & Mahala WILLIAMS; 26y; sgl; private waiter; b. ClrkVA; res. Philadelphia; m. 3 Dec 1879 at Berryville to CLARKE, Virginia (col); d/o Edward & Rachel CLARKE; 23y; sgl; b. & res. ClrkVA; (lic) 2 Dec 1879; p. 9
WILLIAMS, Chas. D. (col); s/o Duke & Adaline WILLIAMS; 24y; sgl; work on public works; b. Georgetown DC; res. ClrkVA; m. 28 Oct 1880 at ClrkVA to PRESTON, Emma (col); d/o Geo. & ___ PRESTON; 21y; sgl; b. & res. ClrkVA; (lic) 28 Oct 1880; p. 27
WILLIAMS, Daniel (col); s/o Simon & Rachael WILLIAMS; 24y; sgl; farm hand; b. & res. ClrkVA; m. 31 Dec 1874 at ClrkVA to

FLETCHER, Sophia (col); d/o Mahlon & Clara FLETCHER; 24y; sgl; b. & res. ClrkVA; (lic) 30 Dec 1874; p. 172
WILLIAMS, Geo. (col); s/o Geo. & Polly WILLIAMS (col); 21y; sgl; farm hand; b. Louisa Co. Va; res. ClrkVA; m. 30 May 1869 at White Post to JACKSON, Martha (col); d/o David & Jane JACKSON (col); 21y; sgl; b. & res. ClrkVA; (lic) 29 May 1869; p. 82
WILLIAMS, George (col); s/o William & Mollie WILLIAMS (col); 27y; wid; farm hand; b. & res. ClrkVA; m. __ Jan 1869 at Berryville to LAUCKLY, Betsy (col); d/o ___ & ___ LAUCKLY (col); 25y; wid; b. & res. ClrkVA; (lic) 2 Jan 1869; p. 72
WILLIAMS, George (col); s/o Wm. & Mollie WILLIAMS (col); 33y; wid; farm hand; b. & res. ClrkVA; m. 31 Dec 1872 at Berryville to CARTER, Nancy (col); d/o not given; 37y; wid; b. & res. ClrkVA; (lic) 31 Dec 1872; p. 140
WILLIAMS, George H. (col); s/o Mack & Lucy WILLIAMS; 25y; sgl; farm hand; b. & res. ClrkVA; m. 18 Oct 1882 at ClrkVA to MARSDEN, Clarissa; d/o Nat & Ellen MARSDEN; 18y; sgl; b. & res. ClrkVA; (lic) 17 Oct 1882; p. 65
WILLIAMS, Goodwin H.; s/o Goodwin G. & Mary R. WILLIAMS; 32y; sgl; farmer; b. Baltimore Co. Md; res. ClrkVA; m. 18 Mar 1886 at ClrkVA to McCORMICK, Nannie H.; d/o Edward & Ellen L. McCORMICK; 22y; sgl; b. & res. ClrkVA; (lic) 16 Mar 1886; p. 134
WILLIAMS, Henry (col); s/o Moses & Clary WILLIAMS (col); 25y; sgl; farm hand; b. FqrVA; res. ClrkVA; m. 3 Aug 1871 at Berryville to WILLIAMS, Aisley (col); d/o Edward & Moses WILLIAMS (col); 21y; sgl; b. & res. ClrkVA; (lic) 4 Aug 1871; p. 114
WILLIAMS, Jackson (col); s/o Philip & Lucy WILLIAMS; 28y; wid; farm hand; b. & res. ClrkVA; m. 28 Sep 1882 at Millwood to HOLMES, Fannie (col); d/o Jackson & Fannie HOLMES; 26y; sgl; b. & res. ClrkVA; (lic) 28 Sep 1882; p. 64
WILLIAMS, Jefferson (col); s/o ___ & Evilina WILLIAMS; 40y; wid; farm hand; b. & res. ClrkVA; m. 20 May 1875 at White Post to ROBINSON, Harriet (col); d/o not given; 40y; wid; b. WrnVA; res. ClrkVA; (lic) 15 May 1875; p. 179
WILLIAMS, Jefferson (col); s/o Jefferson & Evilina WILLIAMS; 40y; wid; farm hand; b. & res. ClrkVA; m. 5 Jan 1868 at Winchester, Frederick Co. to RUNNER, Letty (col); d/o James & Henrietta RUNNER; 21y; sgl; b. & res. ClrkVA; (lic) 3 Jan 1868; p. 51

WILLIAMS, John (col); s/o Robert & Violet WILLIAMS; 40y; wid; farm hand; b. & res. ClrkVA; m. Thursday 4 Jan 1877 at ClrkVA to MASON, Alice (col); d/o Lewis MASON, mother not known; 30y; wid; b. AlbmVA; res. ClrkVA; (lic) 2 Jan 1877; p. 213
WILLIAMS, Leroy Eustace; s/o Leroy P. & Ann WILLIAMS; 27y; sgl; farmer; b. Hampshire? [written over] Co. Va; res. ClrkVA; m. 18 Dec 1867 at ClrkVA to McDONALD, Flora; d/o Angus & L. A. McDONALD; 25y; sgl; b. & res. ClrkVA; (lic) 14 Dec 1867; p. 48
WILLIAMS, Levi (col); s/o Levi & Betty WILLIAMS; 24y; sgl; farming; b. & res. ClrkVA; m. 5 Sep 1877 at not given to POTTER, Elizabeth [also give as Ann] (col); d/o George & Ann POTTER; 19y; sgl; b. & res. ClrkVA; (lic) 5 Sep 1877; father of Gent. present giving consent.; p. 221
WILLIAMS, Lewis (col); s/o Kit & Charlotte WILLIAMS; 22y; sgl; laborer; b. & res. ClrkVA; m. Thursday 30 Dec 1875 at Berryville to WEAVER, Louisa (col); d/o Becky WEAVER; 21y; sgl; b. JeffVA; res. ClrkVA; (lic) 30 Dec 1875; p. 194
WILLIAMS, Marshall (col); s/o Lewis and Lydia WILLIAMS; 23y; sgl; farm hand; b. & res. ClrkVA; m. 13 Dec 1883 at ClrkVA to COOPER, Margaret (col); d/o Warner and ___ COOPER; 23y; sgl; b. & res. ClrkVA; (lic) 13 Dec 1883; p. 90
WILLIAMS, Philip (col); s/o Levi & Sarah WILLIAMS; 39y; wid; farm hand; b. & res. ClrkVA; m. Thursday 20 Feb 1879 at Clarke co. to WORMLEY, Mary (col); d/o father's name not known, Fannie JOHNSON; 30y; wid; b. & res. ClrkVA; (lic) 19 Feb 1879; p. 253
WILLIAMS, Richard (col); s/o Ed. & Rose WILLIAMS; 23y; sgl; back?; b. & res. ClrkVA; m. 3 Nov 1881 at Berryville to BELL, Virginia (col); d/o ___ & Lillie BELL; 22y; sgl; b. & res. ClrkVA; (lic) 3 Nov 1881; p. 50
WILLIAMS, Solomon (col); s/o Robert & Violett WILLIAMS (col); 25y; sgl; farm hand; b. & res. ClrkVA; m. 19 Sep 1872 at ClrkVA to KIRBY, Fanny (col); d/o John & Jane STRANGE (col); 30y; wid; b. & res. ClrkVA; (lic) 19 Sep 1872; p. 133
WILLIAMS, Will (col); s/o Townshend & Mahala WILLIAMS (col); 21y; sgl; farm hand; b. & res. ClrkVA; m. 16 Jan 1869 at Berryville to TAYLOR, Bettie (col); d/o ___ & Catharine TAYLOR (col); 22y; sgl; b. & res. ClrkVA; (lic) 15 Jan 1869; p. 74

WILLIAMS, William (col); s/o Townsend & Mahala WILLIAMS; 30y; wid; farm hand; b. & res. ClrkVA; m. 15 Jun 1882 at ClrkVA to COOK, Louisa (col); d/o Henry & Catharine COOK; 26y; sgl; b. & res. ClrkVA; (lic) 13 Jun 1882; p. 60

WILLINGHAM, Charles L.; s/o Wm. & Matilda WILLINGHAM; 26y; sgl; farmer; b. & res. ClrkVA; m. 19 Oct 1869 at ClrkVA to McDANIEL, Fannie; d/o Saml. & Kitty SPICER; 28y; wid; b. & res. ClrkVA; (lic) 16 Oct 1869; p. 86

WILLINGHAM, George F.; s/o William & Matilda WILLINGHAM; 28y; sgl; farmer; b. & res. ClrkVA; m. 23 Oct 1866 at ClrkVA to MADDOX, Hannah E.; d/o Lorenza D. & ___ MADDOX; 32y; sgl; b. Berkeley Co.; res. ClrkVA; (lic) 22 Oct 1866; p. 21

WILLINGHAM, Jacob H.; s/o Wm. & Mati[l]da WILLINGHAM; 26y; sgl; farmer; b. & res. ClrkVA; m. 19 Apr 1866 at ClrkVA to COOPER, Martha J.; d/o Harrison COOPER; 19y; sgl; b. Fredrick Co.; res. ClrkVA; (lic) 16 Apr 1866; in the presence of Mr. COOPER; p. 10

WILLINGHAM, Jas. W.; s/o William & Matilda WILLINGHAM; 30y; sgl; farmer; b. & res. ClrkVA; m. 9 Feb 1869 at bride's residence to MAYHEW, Mary C.; d/o E. E. and Amelia MAYHEW; 19y; sgl; b. Berkeley Co.; res. ClrkVA; (lic) 6 Feb 1869; father was present; p. 76

WILLINGHAM, John W.; s/o George & Mary WILLINGHAM; 22y; sgl; farmer; b. & res. ClrkVA; m. 11 Jan 1882 at ClrkVA to WHITTINGTON, Eliza B.; d/o John & Mary WHITTINGTON; 24y; sgl; b. JeffWVA; res. ClrkVA; (lic) 11 Jan 1882; p. 54

WILLINGHAM, Nelson C.; s/o Wm. & Matilda WILLINGHAM; 26y; sgl; farmer; b. & res. ClrkVA; m. 17 Nov 1879 at ClrkVA to EVERHART, Rebecca J.; d/o Jacob W. & Mary J. EVERHART; 25y; sgl; b. & res. ClrkVA; (lic) 16 Nov 1879; p. 7

WILLINGHAM, William E.; s/o Obediah & Eliza WILLINGHAM; 24y; sgl; farmer; b. & res. ClrkVA; m. 17 Feb 1881 at ClrkVA to OWENS, Mary V.; d/o Alexander & Mary OWENS; 22y; sgl; b. & res. ClrkVA; (lic) 17 Feb 1881; p. 35

WILLINGHAM, William E.; s/o Obid & Eliza WILLINGHAM; 23y; sgl; farmer; b. FredVA; res. ClrkVA; m. 24 Dec 1879 at ClrkVA to LAWYER, Margaret C.; d/o Adam & Frances LAWYER; 18y; sgl; b. & res. ClrkVA; (lic) 23 Dec 1879; p. 11

WILLINGHAM, William J.; s/o John & Margaret WILLINGHAM; 23y; sgl; farmer; b. & res. FqrVA; m. 19 Jun 1884 at ClrkVA to

STICKELS, Sarah E.; d/o Joseph & Harriet STICKELS; 21y; sgl; b. & res. ClrkVA; (lic) 19 Jun 1884; p. 102

WILLIS, George (col); s/o Lewis & Malinda WILLIS; 51y; wid; farm hand; b. & res. ClrkVA; m. 8 Sep 1885 at ClrkVA to WALKER, Mary (col); d/o Jackson & Susan WALKER; 26y; sgl; b. & res. ClrkVA; (lic) 7 Sep 1885; p. 125

WILLIS, Jack (col); s/o Geo. & Patience WILLIS; 38y; sgl; railroading; b. Norfolk Co. Va; res. ClrkVA; m. 29 Dec 1881 at ClrkVA to PRESTON, Jane (col); d/o not known; 38y; sgl; b. & res. ClrkVA; (lic) 29 Dec 1881; p. 53

WILLIS, John Junr.; s/o John & Lucy WILLIS; 26y; wid; farmer; b. & res. Orange Co. Va; m. 26 Oct 1870 at residence of bride's father Berryville to LUPTON, Mary E.; d/o John M. & Ann Eliz'th LUPTON; 23y; sgl; b. JeffVA now W Va; res. ClrkVA; (lic) 25 Oct 1870; p. 102

WILSON, Frank (col); s/o Joseph & Dolly WILSON; 21y; sgl; farm hand; b. & res. ClrkVA; m. 22 Mar 1883 at ClrkVA to RUNNER, Sarah (col); d/o Jeffrey & Susan RUNNER; 21y; sgl; b. & res. ClrkVA; (lic) 21 Mar 1883; p. 79

WILSON, James E.; s/o Benj'n. & Eliz'h WILSON; 38y; sgl; physician; b. & res. JeffVA; m. 17 Nov 1869 at residence of John J. RIELY ClrkVA to RIELY, Mary C.; d/o Edwin A. & Jane RIELY; 21y; sgl; b. JeffVA; res. ClrkVA; (lic) 14 Nov 1869; p. 87

WILSON, John (col); s/o Danl. & Maris WILSON; 22y; sgl; farm hand; b. AugVA; res. ClrkVA; m. 13 Jun 1867 at Berryville to GRAYSON, Charity (col); d/o not given; 21y; sgl; b. & res. ClrkVA; (lic) not given; p. 37

WILSON, John H.; s/o John H. & Mary J. WILSON; 26y; sgl; carpenter; b. Wisconsin; res. ClrkVA; m. 10 Jan 1871 at ClrkVA to STICKLES, Mary M.; d/o Joseph STICKLES; 19y; sgl; b. & res. ClrkVA; (lic) 5 Jan 1871; consent of bride's father in writing; p. 106

WILSON, Joseph (col); s/o Boson & Judy WILSON (col); 50y; wid; farm hand; b. Jefferson Co.; res. ClrkVA; m. 30 May 1868 at ClrkVA to BANKS, Mary (col); d/o ___ & ___ BANKS (col); 23y; sgl; b. AugVA; res. ClrkVA; (lic) 30 May 1868; p. 62

WILSON, Samuel (col); s/o James and Mary WILSON; 27y; sgl; farmer hand; b. & res. ClrkVA; m. 19 May 1866 at Berryville to JACKSON, Mary Jane (col); d/o John and Harriet JACKSON; 18y; sgl; b. & res. ClrkVA; (lic) 18 May 1866; p. 12

WILSON, Thomas E.; s/o Abraham & Mary E. WILSON; 23y; sgl; farm hand; b. Hampshire Co. W Va; res. ClrkVA; m. 7 Nov 1878 at Berryville to LAKE, Anna; d/o Vincent & Fannie LAKE; 22y; sgl; b. & res. ClrkVA; (lic) 6 Nov 1878; p. 244
WILSON, Wm. (col); s/o Joseph WILSON & ___; 21y; sgl; farm Hand; b. & res. ClrkVA; m. 6 Jan 1875 at ClrkVA to SMITH, Rose (col); d/o Thomas & Priscilla SMITH; 18y; sgl; b. & res. ClrkVA; (lic) 6 Jan 1875; p. 173
WINCHESTER, James R.; s/o Jacob & Mary WINCHESTER; 26y; sgl; Minister of the Gospel; b. Maryland; res. Alabama; m. 17 Sep 1878 at Millwood to LEE, Eleza A.; d/o R. H. & E. B. LEE; 21y; sgl; b. & res. ClrkVA; (lic) 16 Sep 1878; p. 239
WOOD, Clarence (col); s/o James & Mary WOOD; 22y; sgl; ware room hand; b. & res. JeffWVA; m. 25 Dec 1873 at bride's residence to FIELDS, Rachiel (col); d/o ___ & ___ FIELDS; 22y; sgl; b. & res. ClrkVA; (lic) 24 Dec 1873; p. 155
WOOD, William T.; s/o Bennett & Mary WOOD; 32y; sgl; farmer; b. & res. ClrkVA; m. 21 Dec 1882 at ClrkVA to SHEPHERD, Nannie M.; d/o Champ & ___ SHEPHERD; 21y; sgl; b. & res. ClrkVA; (lic) 21 Dec 1882; p. 71
WOOD, Wilson (col); s/o Nelson & Cynthia WOOD (col); 23y; sgl; farm hand; b. AlbmVA; res. ClrkVA; m. 28 Nov 1872 at ClrkVA to MOSEE, Sallie (col); d/o Anthony & Judah WASHINGTON (col); 38y; wid; b. RckhmVA; res. ClrkVA; (lic) 26 Nov 1872; p. 137
WOODARD, James W.; s/o not given; not given; wid; farm hand; b. RappVA; res. ClrkVA; m. 22 Jun 1873 at ClrkVA to FRASIER, Lietha; d/o not given; not given; sgl; b. RappVA; res. ClrkVA; (lic) 21 Jun 1873; p. 147
WOOLFOLK, John C.; s/o Wm. G. & Maria B. WOOLFOLK; not given; sgl; merchant; b. & res. Columbus Georgia; m. 18 Dec 1877 at Millwood to NELSON, Eliza A.; d/o W. N. & Mary A. NELSON; not given; sgl; b. & res. ClrkVA; (lic) 17 Dec 1877; p. 228
WORMLEY, Philip (col); s/o York & Silvia WORMLEY; 51y; wid; farm hand; b. & res. ClrkVA; m. 29 Mar 1874 at ClrkVA to JOHNSTON, Mary F. (col); d/o ___ & Frances JOHNSTON; 32y; sgl; b. FredVA; res. ClrkVA; (lic) 27 Mar 1874; p. 160
WRIGHT, George H.; s/o William & Sarah Jane WRIGHT; 29y; sgl; farmer; b. FredVA; res. WrnVA; m. 25 Jan 1872 at ClrkVA to GARDNER, Alberta; d/o George & Parsadess GARDENER; 22y; sgl; b. & res. ClrkVA; (lic) not given; p. 125

WRIGHT, James M.; s/o Martin & Susan WRIGHT; 25y; sgl; farmer; b. FqrVA; res. LdnVA; m. 22 Dec 1880 at ClrkVA to HOFF, Harretta; d/o Humphrey & Malissa HOFF; 21y; sgl; b. & res. ClrkVA; (lic) 20 Dec 1880; p. 30
WRIGHT, Monroe (col); s/o Franklin & Sibry WRIGHT; not given; sgl; farm hand; b. RckhmVA; res. ClrkVA; m. 13 Sep 1877 at Berryville to GARNER, Mary (col); d/o Peter & Maria GARNER; not given; sgl; b. LdnVA; res. ClrkVA; (lic) 13 Sep 1877; p. 222
WRITT, George W.; s/o Thompson & Elizabeth WRITT; 24y; sgl; farmer; b. LdnVA; res. Jefferson Co.; m. 15 Nov 1866 at ClrkVA to BELL, Nancey; d/o James & Rachel BELL; 19y; sgl; b. & res. ClrkVA; (lic) 12 Nov 1866; brides father being present; p. 23
YOST, David F.; s/o Jacob & Rachel YOST; not given; sgl; manufacturer of cigars; b. Ohio; res. Pennsylvania; m. 23 Dec 1886 at ClrkVA to NEWCOME, Fanny; d/o Hiram & Susan NEWCOME; not given; sgl; b. FredVA; res. ClrkVA; (lic) 20 Dec 1886; consent of parents given; p. 149
YOUNG, Albert B. (col); s/o Moses & Sarah C. YOUNG; 26y; sgl; school teacher; b. & res. ClrkVA; m. 30 Apr 1879 at Berryville to BRIGGS, Louisa E. (col); d/o Ezekial & Louisa BRIGGS; 19y; sgl; b. Richmond Va; res. ClrkVA; (lic) 30 Apr 1879; p. 258
YOUNG, Charles Lucius (col); s/o Alfred & Agnes YOUNG; 20y; sgl; labourer; b. & res. ClrkVA; m. 22 Sep 1875 at Berryville to YOUNG, Maria M. (col); d/o Danl. Webster & Fannie YOUNG; 19y; sgl; b. & res. ClrkVA; (lic) 20 Sep 1775; p. 186
YOUNG, Chas. S.; s/o Ezekial D. & Clara YOUNG; 30y; sgl; carriage trimmer; b. JeffWVA; res. ClrkVA; m. 29 Mar 1882 at Berryville to SPENCER, Emma J.; d/o ___ & Willie M. SPENCER; 22y; sgl; b. AlbmVA; res. ClrkVA; (lic) 27 Mar 1882; p. 57
YOUNG, Danl. Webster (col); s/o Moses & Maria YOUNG (col); 34y; sgl; farm hand; b. & res. ClrkVA; m. ___ Jan 1869 at Berryville to BELL, Fannie (col); d/o James & Fannie BELL (col); 31y; sgl; b. & res. ClrkVA; (lic) 9 Jan 1869; p. 73
YOUNG, Isaac (col); s/o Isaac & Louisa YOUNG (col); 37y; sgl; farm hand; b. & res. ClrkVA; m. 29 Dec 1866 at ClrkVA to JOHNSON, Mary (col); d/o Daniel & Lucinda JOHNSON (col); 23y; sgl; b. Jefferson Co.; res. ClrkVA; (lic) 29 Dec 1866; p. 27

YOUNG, Moses (col); s/o Moses & Maria YOUNG; 60y; wid; farm hand; b. & res. ClrkVA; m. 19 Oct 1882 at ClrkVA to WEAVER, Milly Ann (col); d/o Saml. & Winnie WEAVER; 30y; sgl; b. & res. ClrkVA; (lic) 19 Oct 1882; p. 65

ZOMBRO, John L.; s/o John & Lucinda ZOMBRO; 33y in May 1868; wid; farmer; b. & res. JeffWVA; m. 12 Mar 1868 at Berryville to LANHAM, Ann; d/o Enos & Lucy LANHAM; 22y last month; sgl; b. & res. ClrkVA; (lic) 11 Mar 1868; p. 57

ZUMBRO, George W.; s/o John & Lucinda ZUMBRO; 29y; sgl; farmer; b. JeffVA; res. ClrkVA; m. 11 Jul 1871 at ClrkVA to POPP, Margaret; d/o Conrad & Mary M. POPP; 17y; sgl; b. & res. ClrkVA; (lic) not given; p. 113

Index

[does not include groom or parent with the same surname]

ACRES
  Caroline, 25
AFFLICK
  A. G., 129
  Ann E., 129
  Mame, 129
  Nannie V., 158
ALBAN
  Allie M., 138
ALBIN
  Rachel, 46
ALEXANDER
  Adie, 78
  Amanda R., 165
  Annie W., 149
  Eliza, 1
  Elizabeth M., 20
  Hathaway, 1
  Joel, 34
  John, 66
  Laura L., 77
  R. H., 100
  Richard, 14
  Sarah E., 59
ALLEN
  Edgar, 25
  Elizabeth, 72
  Frances T., 25
  Lucy M., 18
  Maggie, 62
  Margaret A., 5
  Mary B., 69
  Minerva, 175
  William, 5, 18
ALVERSON
  Elizabeth, 112
AMBROUSE

  Catharine A., 13
  John B., 13
  Mary A., 18
ANDERSON
  Annie E., 101
  Elizabeth, 147
  G. F., 20
  George F., 21
  Harriet C., 45
  Henrietta K., 2
  J. W., 20
  Jacob, 20, 21
  Jane L., 22
  Joannah G., 41
  John, 23, 46
  John E., 16
  Joseph, 25, 45
  Julia, 39
  Lucretia E., 77
  Maria A., 21
  Maria S., 7
  Mariah A., 20
  Mary A., 55
  Nancy, 17
  Sarah A. V., 16
  Virginia, 107
  Washington, 3
ASHBY
  Araannah, 47
  Harriet, 45
  John, 3, 6, 17
  Martha, 111
  Martin, 2, 17, 30, 45, 47
  Mary, 2
  Nancy, 21
  Nimrod, 31
  Robert, 3, 12, 28

  Robt. G., 35
  Sarah, 30
  Sarah C., 27
  Susan, 134
  Susan A., 147
  Turner W., 22
ATHEY
  Augustina, 14
  Elizabeth, 14
ATKINS
  Annie, 131
  Eliza E., 139
BAKER
  Ann C., 27
  Harriet, 40
  Nannie H., 78
  Sarah E., 58
  William, 4
  Wm., 27
BALCH
  Harriett M., 36
BALDWIN
  Georgia, 78
BALL
  Emily A., 8
  Maria, 143
  William, 48
BALTHAS
  Sarah J., 77
BANISTER
  Louisa, 99
  Rachel, 150
BANKS
  Adeline, 116
  Ellen, 174
  Harriet, 115

Mary, 69, 121, 146, 182
BARBER
 Emily, 166
 Fannie, 54
 Hannah, 75
 Patty, 65
BARNETT
 Mildred N., 9
 Neil, 9
 Sarah H., 98
BARR
 Martha C., 118
 Precious L., 93
BARRETT
 Alice, 130
BARTON
 Mary V., 138
 Tacy C., 168
BATEMAN
 Annie E., 148
 Sallie M., 154
BAXTER
 Henry, 20
 Jane, 20
BAYLES
 Sarah F., 177
 Virginia, 168
BEALE
 Nannie C., 137
BEARD
 Amelia H., 35
BEAVER
 Virginia C., 134
BEAVERS
 Abraham A., 32
 Abraham H., 17, 24, 32
 Abram H., 47
 Ann E., 30
 Richard F., 50
BEEK

James W., 35
BEEMER
 E. Susan, 55
 Rosanna, 110
BEEVERS
 Martha M., 59
BELL
 Caroline V., 144
 Ellen, 139
 Emmeline, 23
 Fannie, 184
 Hatty H., 83
 James, 24, 28, 97, 126
 Lettie, 168
 Lucinda, 42, 97
 Maggie, 99
 Mary F., 29
 Mary M., 83
 Matilda, 28
 Nancey, 184
 Nancy, 97
 Rachel, 126
 Sarah, 126
 Sarah A., 149
 Sarah J., 24
 Sidney, 175
 Strother, 29, 33
 Virginia, 180
BELT
 George A., 26
 Lucy B., 91
BEMERSDAFFER
 John, 1
BENN
 Cecilia F., 23
 Eliza A., 69
 Fannie E., 174
 Robert P., 23
 Sarah F., 118
BERKELEY
 Julia, 22

BERKLEY
 Julia, 22
BERLIN
 Anna M., 97
 Bettie L., 59
 Eliza V. N., 38
 Laura L., 156
 Lucy V., 58
 Mary C., 116
 Mary J., 134
 Philip, 38
 Sarah A., 34
 Wm., 5, 34
BERRY
 Rachel, 82
 William, 12
BILLMIRE
 Andrew J., 6
 Lutie, 129
BILLMYER
 Andrew, 3, 51
 Richard, 51
 Sarah M., 51
BILLMYERS
 Elizabeth, 3
BILLMYRE
 Hannah F., 42
BILMIRE
 Lucy C., 134
 Mary M., 110
BIRD
 Elizabeth, 160
BITTLE
 Margaret, 67
BLACKBURN
 Amanda, 169
 Benj., 125
 Catharine, 125
 Eliza S., 157
 Jane W., 136
 Millie, 125
BLAIR

Frances, 63
BLAKEMORE
  Caroline, 25
  George C., 25
  George P., 31
  John M., 37
  Lucy C., 31
  Thomas L., 39
BLAND
  Charlotte, 123
BLUE
  Sarah E., 126
BOARD
  Geo., 93
  Virginia, 93
BOLTZ
  George J., 38
BONHAM
  Annie, 51
  Danl. S., 44
  Emma V., 143
  Hannah T., 128
  Jno. C., 52
  Kate, 98
  Lucy C., 44
BOSWELL
  Lucy S. H., 66
BOWEN
  Archibald, 44
  Edwin, 7
  Fannie E., 79
  Jane E., 84
  Jennie E., 84
  Jno. A., 7
  Margaret A., 40
  Mary, 163
  Strother H., 5,
    40, 84
BOWLING
  Elizabeth, 39
BOWSER

Catharine V.,
  158
Mary H., 116
BOXWELL
  Edmonia, 95
  Martha V., 135
BOYSTEON
  Emily S., 11
BRABHAM
  Amelia, 135
  Margaret, 1
  Sarah, 114
BRACKETT
  Frances, 153
  Margaret A., 153
  Russell, 39
  Sarah, 94
BRADFIELD
  A. J., 45
BRADLEY
  Sarah S., 13
BRADY
  Annie S., 174
  Rebecca, 15
BRANER
  Sarah A., 28
BRANNON
  Elnora, 69
  Hattie, 174
BRAWNER
  Eliza, 41
  Sarah A., 28
BRIGGS
  Louisa E., 184
  Marion J., 14
  Mollie A. R., 81
BROCK
  Haley A., 104
BROCKENBOROU
  GH
  Mary, 97
BROMLEY

Katie E., 129
Martha E., 88
BROOK
  James R., 22
BROOKE
  Sarah W., 51
BROOKS
  Alice, 80
  Nannie, 128
  Willie A., 128
BROWN
  Betsey, 122
  Bettie, 88
  Eleanor S., 26
  Eliza, 57, 112
  Elizabeth, 106
  Emaline, 13
  Frances, 69
  Henrietta, 57
  Indiana, 171
  Jim, 112
  Jinny, 57
  John, 26
  Lucy P., 100
  Margaretta M.,
    131
  Maria, 20
  Martha, 136
  Minerva, 112
  Mollie E., 74
  Nannie J., 161
  Patsey A., 38
  Sarah, 111
  Sarah E., 153
  Susan, 112
BROWNLEY
  Ann, 26
  Fanny, 48
BROY
  Fannie, 130
BRUMLEY
  Lewis, 50

Clarke County, Virginia Marriages Index

Mary, 40
Nancy, 50
Rebecca, 45
Saml., 40
BRYAN
Minnie, 159
Rebecca C., 154
BRYARLY
Mary L., 76
Mary S., 7, 8
Saml., 8
Thos. F., 7, 8
BUCK
Lillie L., 128
BUCKLEY
Arry M., 80
BUCKLY
Harriet J., 102
BUNT
Christina, 38
BURCH
Delia E., 153
BURCHELL
Lillie F., 100
Marg't., 62
BURNS
America, 81
Kitty, 116
Lucy, 58
Melvina, 74
Villet, 85
BURWELL
Agnes A., 141
Ann C., 12
Dorah, 146
Eliza P., 147
Frances T., 22
Geo. H., 40
Lucy M., 37
Nathaniel, 146
Susie R., 106, 146

BUSH
Martha E., 167
BUSHONG
Susan F., 81
BUTLER
Clara, 65
Florence, 117
Lucy, 94
Sarah A., 41
BYRD
Mary, 176
Mary A., 51
BYRNE
Catharine, 25
Catherine, 25
Sarah A., 25
Thomas W., 21

CAMFORD
Susan, 26
CARLISLE
Lillie D., 96
CARPENTER
Ann E., 175
Harriet, 132
Joseph, 175
Matthew, 132
Minerva C., 132
CARPER
Annie V., 84
Ida B., 151
Julia A., 55
Louisa M., 72
Lucinda, 99
Lucy, 163
Lydia H., 75
Sariot, 55
CARRINGTON
Lucy C., 52
Mary, 26
William G., 26
CARROLL

Caroline M., 15
Eliza, 134
John, 15, 43, 50
Martha E., 43
Mary, 50, 51
CARTER
Arthur W., 48
Catharine E., 126
Edmonia V., 73
Elizabeth R., 23
Fannie F., 147
Francis, 29
Hattie S., 103
James, 33
Jane, 88, 174, 177
Jno. B., 76
Julia, 119, 174
Katie M., 128
Kitty, 172
Louisa, 29, 133
Lucy, 147
Margaret, 178
Maria, 121
Martha A., 60
Mary, 62, 153
Mary E., 22
Mary L., 149
Mattie B., 164
Minnie F., 103
Mollie, 112
Nancy, 179
Rina, 122
Sarah B., 33
Sarah E., 103
Sarah E. V., 94
Watson, 22
Wm., 174
Wm. H., 7
Wm. K., 23
CARVER

Josephine, 161
Lucy E., 65
CASTLEMAN
  Amanda, 14
  Catharine B., 97
  E. Carroll, 74
  Elizabeth U., 37
  Eloisa M., 19
  Emeline F., 31
  James, 14, 26
  John, 8
  Lucinda, 8
  Maggie L., 133
  Margaret V., 11
  Martha M., 66
  Mary F., 142
  Mary J., 37
  Nannie S., 110
  Stephen D., 5
  Virginia C., 80
  Virginia E., 99
  William, 37
  William A., 37
  Wm. A., 1
CATLETT
  Mary, 69
CHAMBERLIN
  John P., 15
CHAMBLIN
  Aaron, 3, 12
  Annie L., 92
  Eveline, 47
  Hemburn T., 47
  Maria, 12
  Mildred, 3
CHAMBLINE
  Martha E., 41
CHAMP
  Mary, 122
CHAPMAN
  Hettie, 165
  John, 21

Lizzie G., 161
Sarah, 80
CHAPPELL
  Amanda M., 156
  George, 142
  Nannie M., 169
  Susan V., 89
  Susie E., 116
CHASE
  Mary, 79
CHATTIN
  Teresa J., 15
CHISM
  Maria, 40
CHRISMAN
  Laura, 84
  Minnie R., 72
  Sue R., 90
CHRISMORE
  Catharine, 154
CHRISTIAN
  Julia, 174
  Lucy, 67
CLAGETT
  Louisa F., 64
CLARK
  Rachel, 65
CLARKE
  Virginia, 178
CLEM
  Sarah A., 164
CLEVENGER
  Sarah, 22
CLINE
  Virginia H., 153
CLINGAN
  Mary E., 109
  Virginia, 93
CLIPP
  Virginia E., 96
COATS
  Amanda E., 32

Sena A., 27
COBB
  Jennett, 158
COLLIER
  Mary L., 60
COLSTON
  Arrena, 147
  Georgie M., 150
  Katie, 109
  Malinda, 79
  Mary N., 93
  Matilda, 74
  Susan R., 78
  Wilhelma B., 93
CONNAR
  MollieV., 102
CONWAY
  Ellen, 159
COOK
  Louisa, 181
  Mima, 143
COOKE
  Alethea C., 133
COOLIE
  Peter, 27
COONTZ
  Emma V., 56
  J. E., 138
COOPER
  Angelina, 46
  Annie V., 151
  Elizabeth M., 61
  Elsey J., 6
  John, 6
  Lettie, 135
  Margaret, 180
  Martha J., 181
  Warner, 116
  William A., 45
COPENHAVER
  Alcinda M., 16
  Jane O., 126

Clarke County, Virginia Marriages
Index

John, 15, 16
Rebecca J., 15
Sarah, 15
Virginia L., 142
CORBIN
  Amanda M., 30
  Elizabeth C., 20
  James N., 20, 30
CORDER
  Melvina, 102
CORNELL
  Thomas, 3
CORNWELL
  Annie, 105
  Malvina, 28
  Rosa A., 48
COTHEN
  Margaret, 6
COUTER
  Margaret, 46
COXEN
  Mary, 74
CRAMER
  Samuel J., 35
CRAMPTON
  Mattie C., 165
CRAWFORD
  Harrison, 41
  Mary, 25
CREAL
  Sarah, 176
CREBS
  Ella G., 133
CRIDER
  Mary E., 83
CRIM
  Jacob, 42
  Juliana, 42
  Maria J., 156
CRIMM
  Catharine L., 31
CRITTENDEN

Charlotte, 97
Emma, 93
CROW
  Catharine E., 98
  Ida G., 137
  M. Ellouisa, 163
  Thomas H., 24, 51
CRUM
  Elizabeth, 38
  Peter, 38
CRUPPER
  Eli, 23
CYRAS
  Eliza, 65

DANKS
  Caroline, 124
DAVIS
  Annie L., 111
  Jaqueline S., 144
  Lucy F., 124
  Margaret, 41
  Mary, 162
  Mary J., 23
  Rebecca, 31
DAVOLT
  Elizabeth, 87
DAWES
  Mary, 21
DEAHL
  Marcella, 53
  William, 22, 50
DEAN
  Jane, 21
  Sarah A., 8
DEARMONT
  Sarah J., 34
DEDFORTH
  Susan, 112
DENNY

Frances L., 101
DEW
  Natilia B., 15
DEWAR
  Sarah C., 89
DIAH
  Betsey, 81
DICKS
  Landora M., 85
DINKLE
  Laura A., 129
DIX
  Mollie F., 103
DOLEMAN
  Mollie, 166
DORAN
  Ann T., 27
  Jane, 174
  Matthew H., 27
DOREN
  Mary E., 113
DOVE
  Martha A., 151
  Susan, 98
DOWNING
  Acinia, 47
  Allie, 113
  Amandy E., 30
  Ann, 12
  Benjamin, 26, 30, 47
  Mary J., 26
DRISH
  Malissa, 24
  Margaret E., 125
  Virginia E., 122
DUBLE
  Aaron, 77
  Mary S., 59
DUKE
  Emily, 36
DUNCAN

Clarke County, Virginia Marriages
Index

Fanny C., 135
Mary L., 85
Susan E., 47
DYER
　Betsy, 115
　Louisa, 111
　Susan, 125, 145

EARLE
　Alex'r. M., 9
　John B., 32
　Mary L., 9
　Nancy, 32
　Sarah J., 15
EATON
　Ellen N. E., 60
　Permellia R., 127
　Sarah O., 92
EDMONDS
　Barbara A., 58
EDWARDS
　Emma, 53
　Maria, 161
　Martha A., 19
　Sarah F., 65
ELEYET
　John, 13, 15
　Mary A., 13
ELGIN
　Rebecca J., 15
ELLIOT
　Catherine E., 46
ELLIOTT
　Elizabeth, 107
　Gertrude, 132
　John M., 7, 8
　Susan M., 16
ELLIOTTS
　Edmonia, 108
ELLIS
　Lucy A., 114

ELSEA
　Annie H., 89
　Bettie E., 89
ERB
　Mary J., 157
EVANS
　Alexander H., 33
　Alice W., 121
　Lulooh B., 98
　Maria, 97
　Mary E., 64
EVERHART
　Ann R., 14
　Ella, 111
　Fannie, 69
　Gertrude J., 66
　Rebecca J., 181
　Rose E., 125
　Susan, 9
　William G., 9
　Wm. G., 18
EVERITT
　Annie R., 70

FAIRFAX
　Lavinia, 166
FARNSWORTH
　Enos, 25
FAUNTLEROY
　Nancy, 67
　Siplin, 67
　Virgin, 67
FELTNER
　Harriet A., 126
　Peachy V., 175
FENTON
　Annie, 171
　Cordelia C., 117
FERGUSON
　Joannah, 146
　John D., 19
　Mary A., 19

Sarah, 100
FESTUS
　Tamson, 150
FIDLER
　Fannie R., 122
　Lettie, 100
　Lucy A., 107
FIELDS
　Malinda, 130
　Maria, 152
　Rachiel, 183
　Rebecca, 81
FINNELL
　Catharine E., 68
　Columbia J., 161
　Henrietta, 108
FISHER
　Catharine A., 39
　Milley, 157
FLAGG
　Sallie B., 105
FLEMING
　Ella, 91
　Joseph, 1, 2, 13, 16, 47
　Louisa, 16
　Margaret A., 102
　Sivannah, 47
　Thos. M., 101
FLETCHER
　Ada, 99
　Emily, 135
FOLK
　Anne E., 99
FORD
　Ella N., 133
　Sarah R., 96
FORSTER
　Jane E., 5
FOWLER
　Catharine V., 144

Ida, 117
Margaret, 33
Martha E., 13
Mary, 3
Mary E., 123
Roxanna, 45
Sarah, 171
Susan, 12
William, 3, 13
FOX
  Lucy A., 167
FRACTIOUS
  Lucy, 104
FRANCIS
  Anna L., 86
FRANKS
  Benjamin, 13
  Malissa, 13
FRASHER
  John H., 37
FRASIER
  Leitha, 183
FRAXTIOUS
  R. P., 109
FRIDLEY
  Abigail, 35
FRYER
  Bettie W., 86
FULLER
  Lula M., 140
  McPharland, 31
  Sarah J., 31
FUNSTEN
  Louisa N., 92
  Margaret, 5
  Mary C., 92
FUNSTON
  Julia A., 48
  Margaret, 5
  Oliver R., 48
FURR
  Ann M., 32

Elizabeth, 5
Emily, 30
Jane, 28
Jane W., 44
John, 28
Maggie, 54
Moses, 44
Olivia, 120

GALLOWAY
  Annie E., 138
  Josey, 139
  Lucy C., 105
GANT
  Harriet N., 43
  John, 12, 43
  Kizzah J., 43
  Martin, 43
  Mary A., 12
GARDINER
  Hannah, 79
GARDNER
  Alberta, 183
  Amelia C., 95
  Levina A., 69
GARNER
  Mary, 184
  Mary E., 21
GARRETT
  Allie W., 132
  Bertie, 124
  Florence, 83
  Ginnie, 100
GARTER
  Ludend, 31
GARVER
  Julia A., 55
GATES
  Jacob, 31
  Lucinda, 31
GATEWOOD
  Sarah C., 9

GAUNT
  Elizabeth L., 145
  S. Jannett, 165
GIBSON
  Catie, 66
  Louisa, 112
  Mary E., 125
  Virginia, 138
GILMORE
  Eve, 116
  Garland, 116
GLASS
  W., 130
GLASSCOCK
  Elvirah, 30
  Emily, 17
  Lewis F., 9
  Nimrod, 30, 47
GOLD
  Isabella A., 13
  Thomas E., 13
GOODRIDGE
  Rachael, 119
GORDON
  Annie B., 61
  Eliza, 24
  John, 45
  John S., 32
  L. V., 57
  Lucy, 163
  Nancy, 45
  Nannie, 157
GOURLEY
  Jonathan, 31
  Joseph B., 26
  Mahala, 37
  Matilda, 7
  Sarah A., 32
  William, 7, 37
  Wm., 32
GRANDERSON
  Ann, 68

GRANT
  Eliza B., 37
  Ellen F., 13
  Ellen J., 13
  Emma F., 164
  John, 37
GRAY
  Hattie, 149
  Mary F., 76
GRAYSON
  Charity, 182
GREEN
  Caroline, 166
  Catharine, 164
  Emily, 106
  Emma A., 108
  Jennie S., 150
  Kate S., 142
  Mary, 143
GREENE
  Eliza T., 86
  Mary, 74
GREENWALDT
  Sarah E., 162
GREENWALT
  Mary A., 95
GREGG
  Sarah N., 141
GRIFFITH
  Mary E., 143
  Susie J., 102
GRIFFY
  Elizabeth, 175
GRIGSBY
  Annie M., 106
  Susan, 169
GRIM
  Abraham, 14, 24
  Jane E., 14
  Mary, 24
GROVE
  Ann R., 37
  Catharine A., 18
GROVES
  Julia A., 178
GRUBB
  Lula R., 119
  Mary A., 41
  Mary B., 119
  Mary L., 77
  Mary V., 132
GRUBBS
  Alberta, 141
  Ann S., 85
  Elizabeth A., 162
  L. Belle, 140
  Minnie L., 54
  Sarah F., 92
  Serepta E., 72
  William, 18
GRUBER
  George, 39
  Orra S., 99
  Rosa B. B., 73
GRYMES
  Lucy, 133
  Rosalie L., 161
GUY
  Eunis, 133

HALL
  Adelaide S., 55
  Lucy, 173
  Sarah M., 159
  Sinah, 110
HAMILTON
  Whiting, 28
HAMMOND
  Florinda J., 169
HAMPSON
  Isabella, 84
HANCOCK
  Ebin T., 43
HANDLE
  Sarah A. V., 33
HANEY
  Elizabeth, 26
  Maheluh, 1
  Robert, 26
HANNUN
  Annie V., 144
  Cora L., 89
HANSUCKER
  Mary E., 78
  Mattie H., 108
HANVY
  Margaret, 145
HARDEN
  Hannah, 36
HARDESTY
  Betty S., 99
  Carrie V., 60
  Catharine E., 11, 126
  Charles W., 11
  Cora H., 61
  Elizabeth R., 97
  Eugenia T., 103
  Julia A., 60
  Mary A., 38
  Mary V., 148
  Richard, 94, 126
  Rose. T., 87
  Sarah, 94
  Sarah E. B., 11
  Sarah E. V., 94
  Virginia S., 56
HARPER
  Jane, 158
HARRAS
  Henrietta, 137
HARRIS
  Arrena, 53
  Caroline, 157
  Kate, 56
  Laura O., 117

Laura R., 169
Octavia L., 83
Wm. B., 22
Wm. G., 129
HARRISON
 Maria H., 70
 Mary C. R., 62
 Sidney E., 135
HART
 Edwin, 44
 Emma, 177
 Jennie F., 102
 Mary, 44
 Sarah C. V., 29
HARTMAN
 Kate, 105
HARVEY
 Mary A., 25
HAUPTMAN
 Annie, 154
HAWS
 Maggie, 162
HAWTHORNE
 Ella V., 160
HAY
 Jno., 46
 John, 44, 49
 Natilia B., 14
 Penelope L., 15
HAYS
 Jno., 1, 13, 18
HAZSLETT
 Laura W., 58
HEATWELL
 Susan A., 36
HEFFLEBOWER
 Elizabeth, 22
 George, 34
 Mary, 33
HEFLIN
 Sarah C., 155
HEIST

William H., 18
HELMS
 Lizzie, 175
HELVESTINE
 Judy, 173
HENDERSON
 Susan, 68
HENING
 Emma V., 78
 Florence L., 84
 James G., 13
HENNING
 Sarah A., 143
HENRY
 Fannie, 106
 Susie R., 146
HERBERT
 Bettie, 153
 Martha, 104
 Sallie, 71
HESKETT
 Wiliner V., 159
HESSOR
 Mary D., 81
HIBBARD
 Mary L., 142
HICKS
 Anna L., 158
 Margaret W., 21
HIETT
 Hannah, 43
 Levi, 18
HIGGINS
 Nannie B., 80
HILE
 Nancy, 168
HIRST
 Albert S., 38
HISKETT
 Louisa J., 45
 William, 45
HITE

Caroline M., 4
James M., 23
HODGE
 Hannah E., 176
 John, 176
HOFF
 Cornelius, 40
 Effa S., 161
 Harretta, 184
 Henrietta, 120
 Martha E., 172
 Mary J., 162
 Mattie, 130
 Nancy, 4
 Permelia, 36
HOLLAND
 Elizabeth G., 89
 Emily H., 151
HOLLINGSWORT
H
 Frances, 65
 H. L., 82
HOLLOWAY
 Teresa, 26
HOLMES
 Fannie, 179
 Lucinda, 54
 Selie, 173
HOLSCLAW
 Jane, 34
 William, 34
HOLTSCLAW
 Fantleroy, 34
 Frances A., 13
HOOE
 Frances A., 27
 James H., 8
 Mary D., 8
HOOK
 Fannie, 126
 Mattie C., 136
HOOVER

Susan, 40
HOPPER
  Almira J., 170
  Elizabeth, 170
HORSEMAN
  Amanda E., 51
HOUGH
  Annie, 113
  Cornelius, 172
  Elizabeth, 114
  G. H., 56
  Malissi J., 40
  Mary J., 178
  Mollie, 87
HOUT
  Joseph, 50
  Mary A., 31
  Rudolph, 31
HOWARD
  Leila, 137
  Martha, 112
HUBBARD
  Betsey, 57
  Matilda, 75
HUFF
  Amelia, 64
HUGHES
  Annie S., 61
  Mary B., 55
HULL
  Alsey, 103
  Josephine, 124
HULVEY
  Susan E., 131
HUMMER
  Elizabeth, 23
  Juli, 36
  Mary A., 11
  William, 11, 36
  Wm., 23
HUMPHREY

Thos. L., 134, 177
HUMPHREYS
  Emily E., 41
HUMSTON
  Annie M., 110
  Mamie, 159
HUNTER
  Millie, 125
  Sarah M., 158
HURT
  Martha A., 12
HUTCHINSON
  Mary T., 55
HUYETT
  Abraham, 26, 50
  Alice, 64
  Henry, 18, 34
  John, 36, 42
  Louisa M., 18
  Mary A., 42
  Mary J., 26
  Rebecca, 50
  Sarah E., 36

IDEN
  Mary C., 46
IRELAND
  James, 88
  Jane, 88
ISLER
  Ann R., 11
  Jacob, 42, 43
  Maria J., 11
  Martha L., 7
  Mattie C., 7, 21
  Rebecca A., 43
  Sarah A., 42

JACKSON
  Amanda, 147, 164

Annie, 71
Caroline, 111, 128
Chas., 106
Ebenezar, 25
Edward, 16
Eliza, 73
Eudora D., 83
Frances C., 28
Francis, 70
Julia A., 107
Lottie, 144
Margaret, 175
Maria F., 113
Martha, 179
Martha E. T., 43
Mary, 104
Mary C., 136
Mary E., 48
Mary J., 182
Matilda, 68, 128
Matilda J., 45
Nannie, 74
Rachel E., 57
Rissa, 132
Sarah, 116
Sarah S., 160
Solomon R., 4, 6, 16, 28
Vena, 129
JAMISON
  Mary, 112
JANNEY
  R. Belle, 48
JEFFERS
  Cilia, 150
  Hamilton, 150
  Tamson, 150
JEFFERSON
  Ann, 97
  Charlotte, 70
JENKINS

Bettie, 121
Harriet, 12
Herod, 31
Jane, 13, 14
Margaret V., 177
Martha E., 131
Nancy, 31
Rachel, 4
Rachel T., 134
Sarah, 39
JOHNSON
Betsy, 154
Catharine, 10
Fannie, 180
Isabell, 24
Leaneh, 109
Margaret, 14
Margaret A., 92
Martha, 152
Mary, 54, 180, 184
Mary F., 10
Sarah, 112
JOHNSTON
Annie C., 99
Catharine, 10
Charles, 104
Ella D., 106
Francis E., 34
James W., 10
Jas. W., 42
Jennie, 104
John S., 24
Mary F., 183
Mary L., 143
Rebecca, 104
Susan, 150
JONES
Christianna, 115
Ella A., 64
Fannie, 177
Hannah, 84

Harriet, 114
Hattie R., 66
Jos. R., 176
Joseph H., 1
Margaret R., 6
Mary, 160
Matthew, 22, 24
Nancy, 122
Phebe, 157
Sarah W., 22
Sidna, 24
W. G. H., 5
William G. H., 5
JORDAN
Louisa, 87
JORDON
Mary V., 111

KEEAN
  Aira, 35
KEELER
  L. C., 149
KEEN
  Margaret A., 153
KEENAN
  Emma S., 126
KEES
  Josiah G., 25
KEIM
  Elizabeth, 8
KELLY
  Cornelia, 10
  Eliza, 36
KENDALL
  Lucy, 86
KENNAN
  Florence, 59
  Jas. C., 41, 45
  Mary, 41
  Mary C., 132
  Virginia B., 161
KENNERLY

Sarah W., 33
Thos., 2
KENNEY
  C. H., 135
KENNON
  James C., 40
  Jas. C., 9, 28
  Sallie B., 62
KENT
  Sarah A., 45
KERBY
  Susan E., 19
KERCHEVAL
  Emma, 109
  Mary M., 58
KERFOOT
  Almira, 170
  Cora L., 63
  Eliza A., 85
  Ellen C., 110
  Emiily S., 10
  Georgie, 121
  Jane A., 7
  John, 10
  L. W., 53
  Lina L., 70
  Lucy J., 7
  Mary L., 85
  Mary S., 44
  Mattie A., 75
  Nellie, 75
  Sarah A., 38
  William C., 8
  Wm. C., 85
KEYES
  William, 4
KEYS
  Florence, 106
KIGER
  Mary E., 134
  Mattie C., 165
KILE

Harriet, 112
KING
  Matilda, 45
  Mildred, 144
KINNAN
  Jas. C., 35
KIRBY
  Fanny, 180
KIRK
  Sally A., 119
KITCHEN
  Lizzie E., 155
KNELLER
  Mary E., 27
  S. G., 34
KNIGHT
  Cornelia, 10
  Diconda, 11
  George, 2, 4, 23, 38
  Kate, 137
  Laura V., 54
  Lucy J., 4
  Maggie, 55
  Margaret R., 38
  Mary E., 157
  Sidney A., 2
KOONTZ
  Elizabeth A., 118
KOUNSLAR
  Elizabeth S., 57
  Lydia, 163
  S. Jane B., 123
KOWNSLAR
  Ellen, 35
KROUSE
  Susan E., 160
KURL
  Martha E., 43

LACEY
  Sallie P., 63
LAKE
  Anna, 183
  Caroline, 176
  Elizabeth, 119
  Elizabeth K., 4
  Jordan, 176
  Mary A., 176
LANCASTER
  Mollie E., 154
  Sally D., 129
LANE
  Elizabeth T., 29
LANGDON
  Lillie E., 56
LANHAM
  Ann, 185
  Annie, 157
  Classy, 94
  Edgar, 32, 47
  Edgar M., 46
  Elizabeth, 47
  Frances, 47
  George, 28
  James A., 157
  Jno. W., 89
  Margaret E., 120
  Priscilla, 105
  Rebecca, 125
  Rebecca C., 101
  Rebecca V., 86
  Virginia, 146
LARKLEY
  Evelina, 136
LARUE
  Annie C., 71
  Frances C., 46
  Maria, 120
LAWS
  Martha, 150
LAWYER
  Margaret C., 181
LEE

Belle, 96
Eleza A., 183
Eliza, 114
Eliza A., 14
Elizabeth, 30
Frances A., 107
Julia A., 127
Lucinda, 67
Maggie, 73
Margaret A., 101
Polly, 158
LESTER
  Adaline, 164
LEVI
  Mary E., 77
  Sarah C., 72
LEWIN
  Maria V., 122
  Millie F., 130
LEWIS
  Alexander, 165
  Amelia, 68
  Eliz'th., 99
  Emily C., 160
  Esther M., 131
  Evelina, 136
  George, 136
  Harriet, 146, 170
  Kitty, 165
  Lucy, 135
  Nancy, 136
  Patty, 165
LIGHT
  Florence, 173
LIGHTFOOT
  Emily, 88
  Kate, 145
LIMERICK
  Mary C., 40
LINDSEY
  J. B., 29
  John T., 7

Clarke County, Virginia Marriages Index

Sarah M., 7, 67
LIPKINS
  Julia, 70
LIPPITT
  Laura A., 141
LITTLE
  Amanda, 76
  Frances, 5
  Laura C., 11
  Robt. H., 50
LITTLETON
  Elizabeth, 59
  John L., 50
  Sarah C., 72
LLOYD
  Adelia D., 108
  Catharine, 92
  Emily J., 105
  Henery, 47
  James, 2
  Laura E., 168
  Lucinda, 120
  Margaret, 157
  Margaret D., 76
  Mary, 90
  Mary E., 143
  Mary F., 42
  Sarah, 143
  Sarah E., 2
LOCK
  Ann R., 49
  Annie V., 56
  Ellen M., 148
  Georgeanna, 72
  Ida L., 69
  John, 20
  Maria J., 20
  Mary, 50
  Rebecca A., 32
  Sallie H., 69
  William, 36
LOCKE

  Lucy G., 151
LONG
  Eliza, 53
  Jane F., 152
  Kate M. F., 153
LONGERBEAM
  Ann, 17
  Anne, 50
  Elizabeth, 59, 88
  Eliz'th., 170
  John, 24, 47
  Mary F., 3
  Rebecca, 50
  Sarah, 4
  Sibby, 50
LOUTHAN
  Amanda, 153
  Georgeanna, 156
  Henriana, 96
  John, 17, 33
  Lizzie L., 78
  Lucy C., 44
  Mary E., 90
LOVETT
  Jane D., 68
  Lucy, 100
  Mary V., 90
  Portia E., 62
  Sarah, 142
LUKE
  Emily W., 19
  Jacob, 19
  John W., 4, 35, 62, 125
  Sarah C., 67
  Susan G., 35
LUPTON
  Mary E., 182
  Rebecca M., 125

MADDOX

  Hannah E., 181
  Letitia D., 98
MANUEL
  Wm., 76
MARKS
  Laura S., 117
MARLOW
  Margaret, 127
  Sarah A., 15
  Tacey, 88
MARPEL
  Jane M., 102
MARPLE
  Hezekiah, 164
  Lela J., 90
MARPOLE
  Asia, 175
MARQUISS
  Mary, 30
MARSDEN
  Clarissa, 179
MARSHALL
  J. Pede, 16
  John, 19, 25, 82
  Mary E., 16, 158
  Mattie, 177
  Nancy, 19
  Sarah, 25
MARSTON
  Maria, 57
MARTIN
  Ellen F., 44
  Mary E., 93
MARTS
  Elizabeth, 50
  John, 35, 50
  Nancy, 35
MARX
  Caroline, 4
MASON
  Alice, 180
  Seth, 15

MASSEY
  Lulu V., 94
  Mary E., 133
MAY
  Jacob, 8
  Virginia, 8
MAYHEW
  Mary C., 181
McCARD
  Joseph, 65
  Mary, 121
  Rachel, 65
  Rebecca, 115
  Rose, 165
  Sarah, 65
McCAULEY
  Amanda, 139
McCLAUGHLY
  Ann E., 25
McCLAUGHRY
  Hannah, 17
McCORD
  Fanny, 141
McCORMICK
  Albert, 18
  Ann B., 8
  Ann E., 49
  Ann J., 41
  Annie R., 9
  Bessie T., 131
  Eliza, 33
  Elvira J., 136
  Frances F., 20
  Hannah T., 108
  Harriet T., 9
  Isaac, 20
  Isabella, 45
  Kate M., 116
  Mary, 18
  Mary E., 5, 29, 132
  Nannie, 125, 131
  Nannie H., 179
  P., 33
  Province, 3, 20, 33, 34, 37
  Rose E., 124
  Samuel, 5
  Susan E., 173
McDANIEL
  Fannie, 181
McDONALD
  Annie L., 60
  Catharine V., 79
  Fannie, 96
  Flora, 180
  Josiah, 109
  Malinda C., 118
  Martha, 152
  Willie L., 169
McENTREE
  Maria J., 92
McGUIRE
  D. H., 28, 30
  Jane M., 32
  Lucy E. H., 44
  Margaretta H., 176
  Mary M., 160
  Wm. D., 156
McKINNEY
  Ellen, 17
McPHILLIN
  Elizabeth A., 24
  John, 24
MEAD
  William, 23
MEADE
  Ann R., 23
  David, 168
  Francis B., 17
  Maria P., 177
  Mary C., 17
  R. K., 23
  Susan, 17
  Susan E., 23
  Susan P., 68
  William, 23
MERCER
  Annie E., 118
  Elizabeth, 36
  Jesse, 1, 36, 177
  Jesse P., 36
  Kissia, 32
  Phebe, 17
  Ruth H., 140
MERCHANT
  Margaret E., 91
MILBURN
  Grace, 73
MILES
  Louisa, 91
  Mary, 78
MILEY
  Moses G., 8
  Sarah M., 171
MILLER
  John S., 15
MILTON
  Elijah, 21
  Maria A., 75
  Selina P., 21
  Wm. T., 51
Minister
  ATKINSON, W. M., 41
  BAKER, Jos., 2, 8, 9, 12, 13, 14, 20, 22, 28, 31, 43, 45
  BELL, Robert S., 26
  BOWENS, H. G., 11
  BROADDUS, W. F., 10

BUCK, Thos., 4, 28, 29
CARLON, Theo. M., 13
DICE, John C., 14, 17
DODGE, H. W., 6, 7, 15, 17, 25, 27, 28, 33, 35, 37, 38, 39, 48, 51
ELGIN, Nimrod T., 16
GRIMSLEY, B., 9, 29
HANSON, W. D., 4
HANSON, Wm. D., 46
HARRIS, Geo. W., 15
HAYNES, J. A., 20
HERNDON, R. N., 23, 35, 40
HERNDON, Thaddeus, 46
HOFF, J. F., 30, 35, 42, 49
HOFF, John F., 23, 25
ISRAEL, F., 7, 10, 36, 46
LEMON, J. H., 8
MONROE, William, 13, 31, 32
PATER, Henderson, 29, 45
PETERKIN, Joshua, 11, 30, 38, 47, 50
PORTER, Jesse, 36
ROBEY, Andrew, 10, 30
SHIRAS, A., 21
SHIRAS, Alexander, 3, 33, 34, 35, 44
SHIRAS, S., 4, 24, 26, 36, 39, 50
SUTER, Henderson, 13
WAUGH, J. Hoffman, 3
WHITE, Chas., 12, 35, 48, 51
WHITTLE, Francis M., 4, 14, 27, 30, 31, 32, 35, 48, 49
WILLIAMS, W. G., 26, 40
WILMER, Richard H., 5, 6, 9, 10, 14, 16, 17, 21, 27, 34, 43, 45, 47, 49
WILMER, Rich'd. H., 2, 6, 9, 12, 14, 19, 22, 24, 31, 41, 42, 46, 49, 50, 52
WYSONG, Thos. J., 33
MITCHELL Agnes, 97
Amanda, 140
Ann, 87
Ann M., 19
Belinda J., 46
Fanny, 141
James, 9
Louisa, 130
Mary, 63, 113
MOORE
Alfred P., 29
Ann, 10
Lucy E., 171
Margaret E., 10
Sallie C., 176
Sarah J., 29
MORELAND
Mary, 47
Mary A., 65
Susan, 144
MORGAN
Benj., 1, 11, 20, 37
Benjamin, 1
Eliza A., 1
Ella C., 155
Emiline M., 172
Fannie S., 97
John, 5
Martha E., 155
Mary C., 48
Saml., 17
Virginia C., 66
William, 43
MORRIS
Mary, 117
MORRISON
Sarah C., 151
MOSBY
Amanda, 54
MOSEE
Sallie, 183
MOSS

Elizabeth D., 49
Evelina T., 37
Gertrude, 44
Nancy B., 34
MUNDY
  Caroline, 146
MURPHY
  Jas. F., 145
MYERS
  Arina, 116
  Mahala, 147
  Mary R., 68
  Sally, 150
  Sarah J., 173
MYRES
  Annie M., 134
  Clara, 90
  Elizabeth, 81

NEILL
  Ann R., 33
  Mary, 4
NELSON
  Eliza A., 183
  Eliza K., 33
  Evelyn, 172
NEVILLE
  Martha S., 42
  Minnie V., 95
NEWCOME
  Fanny, 184
  Fanny C., 57
  Flora A., 84
  Mattie, 101
  Rebecca M., 66
NEWMAN
  Carrie, 167
NORMAN
  Sarah, 118
NORRIS
  Bennett T., 14
  Ginnie, 166

NORRISON
  Fanny, 88
NUCOME
  Mary S., 87
NUNN
  Elizabeth W., 37
  John M., 11

O'CONNER
  Catharine, 18
  Elizabeth, 5
  Martha A., 17
  Mary E., 33
OLFER
  Ann, 176
OREAR
  Mary B., 40
O'REAR
  Maria L., 138
  Susan C., 94
OREM
  Mason, 45
OSBORN
  Sarah A., 160
OSBURN
  Hannah E., 61
  Jane C., 95
  Joel, 120
  Maria, 120
  Massie, 120
OWENS
  Anna E., 89
  Mary V., 181

PAGE
  D. W., 9
  Evelyn B., 28
  Geo. N., 36
  George R., 28
  Jane B., 12, 38
  John, 22, 37
  John E., 9, 32

Lizzie, 111
Lucy A., 156
Lucy R., 75
Margaret H., 28
Maria, 48
Mary, 97
Mary F., 79
R. P., 9
Robert P., 48
Robt. M., 12
Sally, 37
Walker G., 17
William B., 51
PAGET
  Mary, 8
PANGLE
  Mary A., 162
PARKER
  Catharine, 139
  Charlotte F., 33
  Elizabeth, 43
  Fannie, 119
  John H., 35
  Mary, 3
  Mary S., 35
  Rachel, 166
  Susan A., 149
PARSHALL
  Laura V., 59
PATTERSON
  Mollie L., 122
PAYNE
  Margaret V., 122
PEAKE
  Susan D., 5
PEARSON
  Alice S., 89
PEIRCE
  Gertrude N., 118
PEIRSON
  Annie, 121
PENDLETON

Thornton P., 27, 39, 42
Virginia M., 105
PERRY
  Eveline, 149
  Sallie J., 76
PEYTON
  Caroline, 176
  Joseph E., 16, 27
  Susan C., 16
PHILIPS
  Harriet, 139
PIER
  Sarah C., 88
PIERCE
  A. N., 125
  Adalaide V., 96
  Annabel L., 137
  John, 11, 21, 23, 38
  Katie A., 77
  Lucy C., 23
  Mary J., 21, 160
  Nannie, 95
  Paul, 22, 169
PINE
  James M., 51
POAGUE
  Jennie E., 84
POLAND
  Sarah E., 149
POLES
  Julia, 172
POP
  Barbara, 19
  Michael, 19
POPE
  Ann V., 156
  Ella E., 61
POPP
  Lucy, 76

Margaret, 185
Mary, 164
POPPE
  Mary F., 101
POTTER
  Elizabeth, 180
  Fannie, 156
  Milly, 74
  Patsy, 78
  Rachael, 146
PRESCOTT
  Alfred, 4
PRESTON
  Emma, 178
  Jane, 182
PRICHARD
  Mame, 129
PRINCE
  Ann, 113
PRITCHARD
  Mary, 172
PULLER
  Annie E., 153
  Calvin, 20
  Frances V., 20
  Mary C., 2
PULLIAM
  Mary V., 148
  Rhoda E., 156
PURCELL
  Catharine, 103
PURKS
  Catherine, 62
PYLE
  Ann, 133
PYLES
  Maggie, 75, 98

RAMEY
  Daniel J., 23
  Isaac, 1
  Margaret, 1

RAMY
  Isaac, 2
RANDOLPH
  Henrietta E., 38
  Isabella, 145
  Isabelle, 113
  Mary, 130
  Mary C., 39
  Mary H., 76
  Nancy, 67
  Robt C., 15, 38
  Susan W., 39
RAYNOLDS
  Sarah J., 16
  Thomas W., 16
  Thos. W., 13
REDMAN
  Saml. B., 41
REED
  Cornelia, 105
  Eliza, 18
  Ellen, 153
  Frances A., 110
  Henry, 153
  Jane, 68, 70
  Jinnie, 54
  Maggie M., 64
  Martha, 68
  Mary E., 127
  Mary L., 95
  Nancy, 54
  Sarah J., 152
  Sarah K., 6
  Thersa, 48
REYNOLDS
  Sarah J., 16
RIAN
  Jas., 43
RICE
  Susan A. D., 38
RICHARD
  Mary E., 164

RICHARDS
 Martha E., 155
RICHARDSON
 Cornelia A., 60
 Eliza L., 27
 Elizabeth, 26
 John, 27
 Mary C., 39
 Mollie, 63
 Susan O., 42
RICK
 John, 40
RIDGEWAY
 Richard, 40
 Sarah, 40
RIDGWAY
 Eliza A., 40
RIELY
 Edny A., 12
 Elizabeth C., 20
 Harriet C., 7
 Lester, 12
 Mary C., 182
RILEY
 Mary C., 125
 Nancy, 18
 Sarah M., 167
RINNEL
 Debora, 6
RITTER
 Annie S., 71
 Margaret E., 123
 Sarah, 126
ROBERSON
 Mary, 124
 Mary A., 147
ROBERTS
 Julia C., 73
ROBERTSON
 Judah, 71
ROBINSON
 Amanda, 117

Charlotte, 110
Delilah, 163
Eliza, 151
Florence, 170
Harriet, 179
Harriet A., 142
Isabella, 171
Lizzie, 114
Margaret, 114
Milley, 79
Roberta V., 121
Sidney, 111
ROGERS
 Mary J., 148
ROMINE
 Elisha, 13, 18
 Mary A., 107
ROSBROUGH
 Eliza, 155
ROUTZONG
 Jennie F., 137
 Lottie E., 167
ROWLAND
 Fannie A., 71
 Jennie, 145
 Josephine S., 65
 Rebecca J., 81
ROY
 Katie S., 132
ROYER
 Annie E., 56
ROYSTON
 Ann M., 2
 Anna M., 127
 Effa S., 80
 Fannie M., 171
 Hattie, 61
 Lydia E., 101
 Matthew W., 38
 Minerva C., 132
 Nannie E., 140
 Peter, 2, 3, 5

Sarah C., 5
RUDUFF
 Mary A., 142
RUFFINS
 Julia, 111
RUNNELLS
 Patty, 138
RUNNER
 Emily, 83
 Harriet, 73
 Letty, 179
 Sarah, 182
RUSSELL
 Annie V., 144
 Catharine, 51
 Harriet, 144
 James, 144
 James E., 43
 Kate, 105
 Martha E., 83
 Mary J., 144, 170
 Mollie, 163
 Sarah C., 86
 Thomas W., 51
 Virginia, 86
RUST
 Alcinda, 80
 Chas. B., 6
 Harriet, 104
 Virginia W., 92
RYAN
 James, 26
 Joseph F., 41
 Mary A., 43

SANDS
 Almira, 122
SAPPINGTON
 John, 44
SARGENT
 Ferlinda, 58

SAUNDERS
  Barbara W., 94
SCHOPPERT
  Mary B., 88
SCOTT
  Elmina L., 44
SCROGGINS
  Bettie, 140
SCRUGGS
  Susan C., 148
SEEVER
  W. H., 35
SEEVERS
  William R., 23
  Wm. R., 38
SELMAN
  Nannie J., 155
SETTLE
  A. H., 5
  Frances, 5
SETTLES
  Jane, 104
SEWELL
  Julian, 96
SEYMORE
  Catherine, 110
SHACKELFORD
  Hannah V., 139
SHACKLEFORD
  Jane T., 136
  Margaret, 156
  Nannie M., 64
  Rebecca, 159
SHAFER
  Betsy A., 167
  Cartharine, 23
  Catharine, 23
  John, 4, 21, 23
  Margaret A., 154
  Martha A., 125
  Sarah, 4
SHAFFER
  Annie R., 159
  Caroline M., 62
  Jackson, 177
  John, 147
  Mahala, 147
  Sarah, 177
  Winny, 147
SHAVER
  Catharine, 3
  John, 3
  Martha A. M., 6
SHEARER
  Mattie E., 117
  Nettie B., 123
SHELL
  Lucinda, 97
  Nancy A., 72
  Sarah M., 126
SHEPHERD
  Carolina A., 12
  Champ, 11
  Henry, 29
  Jos., 11
  Margaret A., 11
  Mary E., 78
  Nannie M., 183
  P. D., 3, 12
  Sallie C., 157
  Sarah A., 137
SHIMP
  Eliza, 87
SHIP
  John, 48
SHIP
  Lucy L., 48
SHIPE
  Arthealice J., 109
  Elizabeth, 6, 130
  Fannie M., 120
  Harriet C., 89
  Laura, 67
  Mary C., 155
  Melinda, 51
  Sarah, 94
  Virginia, 152
SHIVELY
  Harriett E., 34
  Margaret A., 27
SHOPLAND
  Elizabeth W., 103
SHORES
  Joannah, 34
SHOULKES
  Jennie, 104
SHROUD
  Annie, 71
SHROUT
  Florence M., 115
SHRYOCK
  Asserina C., 140
  Frances V., 140
SHURFSTALL
  Margaret, 6
SICAFOUSE
  Mary E., 130
SIMMERS
  Catharine, 5
SIMMONS
  Fannie, 76
  W. T., 20
SINGHASS
  Alice L., 152
  Kate E., 108
  Mary R., 152
SLUSHER
  Annie M., 128
  Bettie E., 114
  Ida E., 152
SMALLWOOD
  Amanda, 120
  Barnam, 161
  Caroline, 103

Charlotte, 3
Frances, 113
Julia A., 151
Mary, 4
Nannie J., 161
Rebecca A., 172
Sarah, 21
Virginia E., 151
SMIDLEY
  George, 10
SMITH
  Annie M., 139
  Bettie, 177
  Catharine V., 21
  Edmonia J., 49
  Edward J., 10, 21
  Edw'd. J., 8
  Elizabeth B., 9
  Eveline, 62
  Fannie, 128
  Harriet N., 102
  Helen, 162
  Horace P., 5
  J. Rice, 116
  Joseph, 17, 51
  Louisa C., 8
  Lucy E. H., 131
  Lydia K., 18
  Maggie, 136
  Maria, 58
  Mary A., 37, 51
  Mary E., 123, 176
  Mary L., 104
  Rebecca A., 51
  Roberta M., 38
  Rose, 183
  Sarah A., 82
  Sarah J., 82
  Susan C., 17
  Treadwell, 41

Wm. D., 128
SMITHEY
  Martha J., 91
SNYDER
  Ella T., 86
  Georgeanna, 85
  Virginia H., 119
SOMMERVILLE
  Emma L., 64
SOUDER
  Betsy, 154
SOWERS
  Alberta A., 165
  Alice M., 121
  Danl. W., 38
  Elizabeth F., 165
  Emily A., 33
  Fielding L., 22
  Frances M., 137
  Geo. K., 153
  H. L., 82
  John W., 19
  Lucy E., 18
  Lucy V., 42
  Martha A., 9
  Martha L., 29
  Mary E., 22
  Matilda E., 9
  Rose L., 132
  Sallie C., 62
  Sarah C., 39
  William, 9, 12, 39, 42
SPEICER
  Sarah C., 66
SPENCER
  Emma J., 184
SPICER
  Fannie, 181
  Kitty, 181
  Saml., 181
SPILMAN

Edw'd. M., 33
SPOTTS
  Martha E., 34
  Sarah C., 145
SPRINT
  Annie S., 93
  Mary R., 119
STARKEY
  Margaret E., 106
STEEL
  Laura J., 60
  Sarah F., 27
STEELE
  James A., 8, 21
STEPHENS
  Lewis W., 20
  Mary A., 20
STEWART
  Elizabeth J., 11
  Harriet A., 44
  Jinnie, 107
  John, 46
  Mary E., 46
  Minnie F., 141
  Rosa M., 167
  William P., 11
STICKEL
  Barbary A., 120
  Joseph, 120
STICKELS
  Betsey, 114
  Harriet, 114
  Henry, 114
  Sarah E., 182
STICKLE
  Henry, 13
  Martha, 13
STICKLES
  Girtrude, 60
  Henrietta, 165
  Mary, 170
  Mary M., 182

Sarah J., 30
STILLIONS
  Ann M., 2
  Ann Maria, 2
  William, 2
STIPE
  Henry, 18, 24
  Margaret, 24
STOKES
  Sarah E., 150
STOLLE
  William A., 118
STONER
  Judith A., 41
STONESTREET
  Aisley A., 39
  Margaret, 123
  Matilda, 50
STRAIGHT
  Dr., 35
STRANGE
  Bettie, 91
  Charlotte, 85
  Cornelia, 106
  Eliza, 112
  Evelina, 100
  Fanny, 180
  Flora, 138
  Frances, 93
  Jane, 112, 166, 180
  John, 112, 138, 180
  Julia, 173
  Malinda, 96
  Mary, 141
  Mollie, 150
  Nelly, 165
  Susan, 66, 121
STRIBLING
  Alice M., 119

Sigismunda B., 26
STROTHER
  Charlotte, 115
  Eliza, 73
  Emily, 115, 116
  Eveline, 73
  Jaqueline, 73
  Joseph T., 46
  Martha J., 91
  Mary, 111
  Mary A., 22
  Milley A., 62
STUMP
  Alice F., 115
  Annie, 158
  Emma, 75
  Lara J., 145
  Mary C., 148
SUMMERS
  Catharine, 5
SWAINEY
  Clara, 87
SWANN
  C. H., 58
SWARTS
  Mary J., 161
  Susan C., 148
SWARTZ
  Anna K., 123
  Conrad, 1
  Mary F., 49
  Mary M., 38
  Rachael A., 1
  Susan C., 101
SWIFT
  Richard, 50
SYDNOR
  Ann R., 34
  Mary L., 41
SYFRET
  Isabella, 23

SYMONS
  Mary S., 86
TALEY
  Mary A., 129
TALLEY
  Jane E., 16
  John, 16
TANQUARY
  James W., 41
  Sarah M., 22
TAPSCOTT
  Florinda M., 109
  Henry, 145
  Maria, 142
TATE
  Ida M., 117
TAYLOR
  Bettie, 180
  Chas. S., 19
  Edmonia S., 19
  Eliza, 47
  Elizabeth V., 118
  Frances V., 49
  George, 15
  Harriett, 65
  Jesse, 9, 28
  John B., 36
  Judy, 128
  Julia, 167
  Lucy O., 39
  Margaret, 172
  Mary A., 9
  Mary L., 36
  Nancy J., 4
  Sarah C., 33
  Virg'a. E., 32
TETES
  Maria, 110
THARPE
  Virginia L., 90
THOMAS

Annie M., 175
Catharine A., 10
Grace A., 63
Joshua, 63
Laura, 166
Mary, 67
Mary C., 154
Sarah A., 135
Summerville, 61
Vina, 174
THOMLEY
Gertrude, 139
THOMPSON
Alice V., 72
Amanda, 144
Ann E., 173
Benjamin, 35
Carlotta, 176
Charlott E., 30
Charlotte E., 28
Fany, 87
French, 15
Greenberry, 11
Ida J., 146
John, 36
Juliet A., 28
Louisa, 87
Louisa J., 159
Lucy C., 36
M. S., 123
Margaret A., 91
Maria, 46
Martha A., 147
Mary E., 168
Mary F., 83
Mattie, 149
Nancy, 31
Phebe E., 35
Sally, 54
Sarah A., 123
THOMSON
Clara H., 63

Emily, 25
John A., 44
THORNLEY
Annie, 128
THORNTON
Frances H., 48
THROCKMORTON
Fannie, 53
TIMBERLAKE
Addison, 7
David, 7
Eliza S., 170
Fannie G., 59
Isabella, 44
Margaret B., 7
Mary D., 4
Sallie C., 140
Stephen D., 7
TINSMAN
Elizabeth, 24
George, 24
John M., 47
Louisa R., 127
Mary H., 127
Mary J., 11
Mdelle Z., 126
William, 11
TOCAS
Harriet, 112
TODD
T. Alex'r., 37
TOKAS
Matilda, 73
TOLIVER
Florence M., 163
TOMLIN
Catharine, 3
Joanna, 24
TRACEY
Celia, 109
TRAVIS

Maria, 61
Rebecca F., 170
TRENARY
Catharine, 18
Jonas, 1
Lucinda, 20
Sallie, 170
TRIPLIT
Ann E., 15
TRUNNEL
Rebecca, 91
TRUSSELL
Susan I., 142
Tabitha A., 13
TULEY
Joseph, 21
TUMBLIN
Franklin, 3
Louisa, 43
Mary M., 74
Sarah C., 131
William, 21
TUMLIN
Angietta, 56
TURLEY
Catharine K., 159
TURNER
Emily J., 6
Sarah C., 10
Wilson, 6

UNDERWOOD
Mary V., 95
Sarah M., 55

VANCLEAVE
John, 31
Rahamy, 31
VANDEVANTER
Mary N., 81
VINCENT

John, 8
Lucy A., 8
WADE
Nancy, 178
WAINWRIGHT
Eliz'th. M., 70
WALDON
Adelaide, 82
WALKER
Emma, 53
Jane, 102
Mary, 182
Nancy, 93
Nancy V., 84
WALLACE
Annie, 79
WAMAX
Mary J., 148
WARE
Harriet E., 12
James W., 12
Josiah W., 26, 29
Lucy B., 29
WASHINGTON
Anthony, 183
Hannah E., 176
Judah, 183
Laura, 63
Lucinda, 67
Sallie, 183
WATKINS
Mary J., 24
Tacey, 32
Tacy, 32
WATSON
Ephraim, 49
John, 49
Susan, 49
WEAVER
Louisa, 180

Milly A., 185
Sallie, 77
WEBB
Lucinda, 79
Mary, 76
WEDLOCK
Millie, 101
WEITT
Ann J., 23
WHEELER
Bertie, 82
Florinda, 82
Millie A., 168
WHITAKER
Elizabeth, 22
Jonas, 22
WHITE
Annie, 169
Chas., 131, 166
Laura E., 168
Lavinia, 113
Mary A., 73
WHITING
Francis H., 11, 39
Lucy B., 70
Lucy E., 50
Nath'l. B., 39
WHITSELL
Virginia, 174
WHITTINGTON
Alice C., 114
Anne E., 124
Eliza B., 181
Hannah E., 141, 176
WIGGENTON
William P., 14
Wm. P., 45
WIGGINTON
Wm. P., 25
WILEY

Casiah, 117
Catharine, 28
Chas. F., 134
Lavenia E., 178
Mary, 55
Mary J., 47
Rebecca V., 108
Sarah, 1
Sarah A., 32
WILLIAMS
Aisley, 179
Alice, 85, 171
Amanda, 57
Casiah, 112
Catharine, 163
Clora, 162
Comfort, 169
Eliz'th. P. G., 174
Ella, 139
Emily, 100
Fannie E., 172
Frances, 138
Hannah M., 6
Harriet, 86
Judah, 104
Kate, 70
Kitty, 165
Laura, 94
Letitia, 153
Lila, 171
Lillie, 104
Lydia, 173
Margaret, 77
Martha, 146
Millie A., 163
Minerva J., 147
Nannie R., 87
Priscilla, 85
Rachel J., 124
Rebecca, 168
Rosa, 178

Rose, 82
Sarah, 71, 136
WILLINGHAM
  Alice G., 120
  Ann E., 26
  Anne, 126
  Bettie, 80
  Catharine, 1
  Eliza, 53
  Ema A., 94
  Harriet V., 79
  John, 10
  Mary F., 108
  Sarah C., 133
WILLIS
  Catharine, 135
  Lucy, 64
  William, 49
WILMER
  Richard H., 12
WILSON
  Clara, 130
  E. Jane, 135
  Elizabeth, 84
  Mary C., 90
  Mollie, 109
  Rachel, 166
  Sarah J., 51
  Tholemiah R., 51

  Virginia, 166
WINPIEGLER
  Mary A. R., 49
WINSBURROW
  Laura F., 107
WISE
  William, 40
WITHERS
  Missouri, 121
WOLFE
  Hannah E., 129
WOOD
  Alexander, 18
  James T., 46
  Lucinda, 95
  Lucy E., 36
  Lucy F., 46
  Mary E., 63
WOODWARD
  Mary E., 38
  Matilda, 4
  Thos. E., 4
WORMLEY
  Mary, 180
WORMLY
  Sidney, 115
WRIGHT
  G. H., 73
  Margaret E., 127

  Mary E., 98
  Nancy, 71
  Susan, 162
WRITT
  Darcus J., 154
  Edney J., 80
  Mary C., 4
  Susan E., 44
WYNDHAM
  Cornelia F., 90
  Eliz'th., 18
  Jane N., 32
  Mary V., 152
  Sydnor B., 32
WYNKOOP
  Mary F., 141

YATES
  Susan, 144
YOUNG
  Lillie M., 98
  Maria M., 184
  Mary E., 59, 169
YOWELL
  Ann M., 171
  Isabell R., 173
  Mary E., 46
  Simon, 46

Other Heritage Books by Patricia B. Duncan:

1850 Fairfax County and Loudoun County, Virginia Slave Schedule

1850 Fauquier County, Virginia Slave Schedule

1860 Loudoun County, Virginia Slave Schedule

Clarke County, Virginia Death Register, 1853-1896, with Birth Records, 1855-1856, Entered on Death Register

Clarke County, Virginia Marriages, 1836-1886

Clarke County, Virginia Will Book Abstracts: Books A-I (1836-1904) and 1A-3C (1841-1913)

Fauquier County, Virginia, Birth Register, 1853-1880

Fauquier County, Virginia, Birth Register, 1881-1896

Fauquier County, Virginia, Marriage Register, 1854-1882

Fauquier County, Virginia, Marriage Register, 1883-1906

Fauquier County, Virginia Death Register, 1853-1896

Hunterdon County, New Jersey 1895 State Census, Part I: Alexandria-Junction

Hunterdon County, New Jersey 1895 State Census, Part II: Kingwood-West Amwell

Genealogical Abstracts from The Lambertville Press, *Lambertville, New Jersey: 4 November 1858 (Vol. 1, Number 1) to 30 October 1861 (Vol. 3, Number 155)*

Genealogical Abstracts from The Democratic Mirror *and* The Mirror, *1857-1879, Loudoun County, Virginia*

Genealogical Abstracts from The Mirror, *1880-1890, Loudoun County, Virginia*

Genealogical Abstracts from The Mirror, *1891-1899, Loudoun County, Virginia*

Genealogical Abstracts from The Mirror, *1900-1919, Loudoun County, Virginia*

Genealogical Abstracts from The Telephone, *1881-1888, Loudoun County, Virginia*

Genealogical Abstracts from The Telephone, *1889-1896, Loudoun County, Virginia*

Jefferson County, Virginia/West Virginia Death Records, 1853-1880

Jefferson County, West Virginia Death Records, 1881-1903

Jefferson County, Virginia 1802-1813 Personal Property Tax Lists

Jefferson County, Virginia 1814-1824 Personal Property Tax Lists

Jefferson County, Virginia 1825-1841 Personal Property Tax Lists

1810-1840 Loudoun County, Virginia Federal Population Census Index

1860 Loudoun County, Virginia Federal Population Census Index

1870 Loudoun County, Virginia Federal Population Census Index

Abstracts from Loudoun County, Virginia Guardian Accounts: Books A-H, 1759-1904

Abstracts of Loudoun County, Virginia Register of Free Negroes, 1844-1861

Index to Loudoun County, Virginia Land Deed Books A-Z, 1757-1800

Index to Loudoun County, Virginia Land Deed Books 2A-2M, 1800-1810

Index to Loudoun County, Virginia Land Deed Books 2N-2U, 1811-1817

Index to Loudoun County, Virginia Land Deed Books 2V-3D, 1817-1822

Index to Loudoun County, Virginia Land Deed Books 3E-3M, 1822-1826

Index to Loudoun County, Virginia Land Deed Books 3N-3V, 1826-1831

Index to Loudoun County, Virginia Land Deed Books 3W-4D, 1831-1835

Index to Loudoun County, Virginia Land Deed Books 4E-4N, 1835-1840

Index to Loudoun County, Virginia Land Deed Books 4O-4V, 1840-1846

Loudoun County, Virginia Birth Register, 1853-1879

Loudoun County, Virginia Birth Register, 1880-1896

Loudoun County, Virginia Clerks Probate Records Book 1 (1904-1921) and Book 2 (1922-1938)

(With Elizabeth R. Frain) *Loudoun County, Virginia Marriages after 1850, Volume 1, 1851-1880*

Loudoun County, Virginia 1800-1810 Personal Property Taxes

Loudoun County, Virginia 1826-1834 Personal Property Taxes

Loudoun County, Virginia Will Book Abstracts, Books A-Z, Dec. 1757-Jun. 1841

Loudoun County, Virginia Will Book Abstracts, Books 2A-3C, Jun. 1841-Dec. 1879 and Superior Court Books A and B, 1810-1888

Loudoun County, Virginia Will Book Index, 1757-1946

Genealogical Abstracts from The Brunswick Herald, *Brunswick, Maryland: Mar. 6 1891-Dec. 28 1894*

Genealogical Abstracts from The Brunswick Herald, *Brunswick, Maryland: Jan. 4 1895-Dec. 30 1898*

Genealogical Abstracts from The Brunswick Herald, *Brunswick, Maryland: Jan. 6 1899-Dec. 26 1902*

Genealogical Abstracts from The Brunswick Herald, *Brunswick, Maryland: Jan. 2 1903-June 29 1906*

Genealogical Abstracts from The Brunswick Herald, *Brunswick, Maryland: July 6 1906-Feb. 25 1910*

CD: *Loudoun County, Virginia Personal Property Tax List, 1782-1850*

www.ingramcontent.com/pod-product-compliance
Lightning Source LLC
Chambersburg PA
CBHW050144170426
43197CB00011B/1959